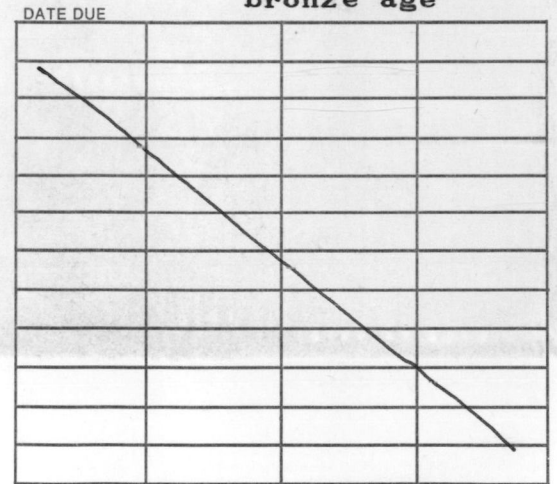

THE CIVILIZATION OF GREECE
IN THE BRONZE AGE

THE CUPBEARER FRESCO : KNOSSOS

(The original is life-size)

THE
CIVILIZATION OF GREECE
IN THE BRONZE AGE
(THE RHIND LECTURES 1923)

H. R. HALL, M.A., D.Litt., F.B.A.

KEEPER OF EGYPTIAN AND ASSYRIAN ANTIQUITIES IN THE BRITISH MUSEUM

AUTHOR OF "THE ANCIENT HISTORY OF THE NEAR EAST"

WITH 370 ILLUSTRATIONS AND TWO MAPS

COOPER SQUARE PUBLISHERS, INC.
NEW YORK
1970

IN MEMORY

OF

R. B. SEAGER

Originally Published 1928 by Methuen and Company, Ltd.
Published 1970 by Cooper Square Publishers, Inc.
59 Fourth Avenue, New York, N. Y. 10003
Standard Book No. 8154-0340-2
Library of Congress Catalog Card No. 78-124270

PREFACE

THIS volume contains the substance of six lectures on the civilization and art of the Greek Bronze Age delivered by me under the terms of the Rhind Bequest before the University of Edinburgh in the autumn of 1923, considerably enlarged and brought up to date. It is illustrated by a large selection of photographs and line drawings covering the whole ground of the lectures and including material both new and old. The lantern-illustrations were the main feature of the original lectures, and on that account it has been considered appropriate that their edition now should also be illustrated profusely. It is, in fact, impossible to present the object-matter satisfactorily without profuse illustration. To give merely a few illustrations of prominent objects of the ancient civilization and art described would be unsatisfactory, as this would mean in the majority of cases merely the reproduction of things already often reproduced. And to illustrate recent finds only would be unsatisfactory and illogical, since the lectures were intended to cover the whole ground and to describe well-known as well as less-known relics of prehistoric Greek culture. In this matter of illustrations I am greatly indebted to the indulgence of my publishers, who have gone beyond any limit of patience that I could have expected in this matter. The delay in the appearance of the book has been largely due to the anxious consideration that I have given to the illustrations, to the weighing of their respective importance, the sifting of them, the rejection of many already decided on in favour of others more recently acquired that seemed more desirable, in view of the necessity of cutting down the pictures to a reasonable number and if possible preventing the book from being overweighted by them. The volume will, I hope, serve not only as a handy account of what is known of the historical development of the Greek civilization of the Bronze Age but also as an album of pictures of its most important achievements, in small things as well as great.

It will also, I hope, help to direct the attention of students and lovers of art to the special treasures of prehistoric Greek art that this country possesses. The British Museum comes next after Candia and Athens as a treasure-house of Greek antiquities of the Bronze Age, owing to its major objects of Mycenæan art from Cyprus and its collection of Late Mycenæan vases from Rhodes and the Islands, in which it is only approached by Constantinople. And next to the British Museum comes the Ashmolean at Oxford, where Minoan Crete is naturally specially represented. Minoan-Mycenæan culture and art should then interest us in England specially.

My thanks are due to all those museum curators, archæologists, and learned societies, who have so willingly given me permission to reproduce their illustrations and discoveries. Their names form a lengthy list which I will not recapitulate here in full, but merely express my general acknowledgments to them and to their publishers, which will be found made individually in the list of illustrations. I ought however to express special indebtedness to Sir Arthur Evans, to the Committee of the British School at Athens, the Council of the Hellenic Society, also to Professor Halbherr and the Academy of the Lincei and to Dr. Xanthoudides, Mrs. Boyd-Hawes, Mrs. Dohan, Dr. Blegen, and Mr. Wace for leave to reproduce antiquities discovered and published by them, and the Keeper of Greek and Roman Antiquities in the British Museum, Mr. H. B. Walters, for permission to use illustrations from Mr. E. J. Forsdyke's *Catalogue of Vases* and the official publication of the discoveries at Enkomi in Cyprus. In the case of photographs where no acknowledgment is made they were (except in the case of objects in museums) taken by myself.

The scheme of the lectures was strictly chronological, the main features of each period of development being described in order, from the end of the Age of Stone to the beginning of that of Iron, covering a period of two millennia, from about 3000 to about 1000 B.C. This was easy to do in the case of the artistic objects described, the pottery and stone carving, etc., and in that of the development of the writing. But I found it more convenient to vary the arrangement in the case of what we know of funerary customs and religion, reference to which in every chapter would have caused too frequent repetition. I preferred to treat these two subjects, as summarily as possible, as a whole, at convenient breaks in the narrative, and have preserved this arrangement in the printed lectures. Also, in order to avoid too lengthy a disquisition on one subject, which would have been disproportionate to the rest, I have relegated much of what I would have said (had time allowed) on the subject of the possible ethnical relations of the Minoans to an appendix.

With these exceptions the plan of each lecture as delivered was to explain the pictures, which followed each other in the order in which they most naturally came up for description and discussion. I have retained this descriptive order of discussion which is not the same in each lecture, but follows the dictates of convenience in each case.

I have to thank my colleague, Mr. E. J. Forsdyke, for having kindly read the proofs of these lectures, and for several suggestions, and to him, to Sir Arthur Evans, Dr. Mackenzie, Dr. Xanthoudides, and Mr. A. J. B. Wace, for information with regard to the results of excavations which I have found most useful. At the same time the responsibility for my treatment of these results is my own, and it must not be supposed that these archæologists necessarily agree in every case with the conclusions I have drawn from them. In case of any considerable divergence I have made the point clear, as in the case of the difficulty I find (in common with others) in using Mr. Wace's term " Helladic " for the " Mycenæan " or imported " Minoan " Cretan culture and art on the mainland, which does not really develop out of that of the older or true Helladic period on the mainland (as exemplified in the pottery) contemporary with the Early and

Middle Minoan periods in Crete. We have then no " Late Helladic " style at all, which would seem illogical if we have a " Middle Helladic." Yet this is merely a question of convenient terminology, and to me it seems convenient, if illogical, to retain the terms " Early " and " Middle " Helladic, while avoiding " Late Helladic " as being an inaccurate name for the ceramic style and general art of the Minoan conquerors of Greece.

Mr. Wace has made the historical certainty of the domination of Minoan culture on the mainland quite clear in his chapters on prehistoric Greece in the *Cambridge Ancient History* (Vol. i., pp. 608–9; ii., p. 451, 1924), which are based on Sir Arthur Evans' epoch-making classification of the nine " Minoan " periods of the parent civilization of Crete. This, revealed by his own magnificent excavations at Knossos and those of the other archæologists who have worked in the great island, shows us that art and culture, human progress, first reached in Crete, of all the Greek lands, a level comparable to those attained by Egypt and Babylonia, and thence spread Crete's civilizing influence over the neighbouring islands and the mainland, to form the unified civilization of Greece in the Later Bronze Age, which fell before the attacks of the iron-bringing barbarians from the North. But before its death it had sowed the seed from which the new Greek culture of the classical period derived the Mediterranean elements of its character, and with these its love of civilized art and beauty.

I would note that I have not discussed geographical conditions at all. The two maps will give a general idea of the position of the chief prehistoric sites, and will enable the reader to appreciate the central position of Crete in the Eastern Mediterranean, which gave her her traditional early thalassocracy (known to us from a tradition that obviously had a secure historical basis), and coupled with her own fertility and natural wealth, made her the focus of civilization in the Aegean world until the Northern invasions destroyed the culture of which she was the mother. For the geographical characteristics of Crete and the Aegean the reader should consult Dr. D. G. Hogarth's *The Nearer East*, p. 122 ff.

x

PREFACE

In conclusion, I have to make my acknowledgments of their kindness to my hosts at Edinburgh, and to ask them to accept this book as an expression of my thanks.

H. R. HALL

MAVROSPELAION
  KNOSSOS
      June, 1927

NOTE

A short bibliography of works on the subject of these lectures up to 1915 will be found in my *Ægean Archaeology*, p. 261 ff. For later works see Mr. Wace's bibliographies in the *Cambridge Ancient History*, i. p. 655, iii. p. 676; and those in the articles *Archaeology* in the *Encyclopædia Britannica*, XIIth and XIIIth editions (new volumes), by Mr. Forsdyke and myself. Also *cf.* footnote-references in this book and in Sir Arthur Evans's *Palace of Minos*.

ABBREVIATIONS

A.H.N.E. = Hall, *Ancient History of the Near East*.

Am. Sch. Ath. = American School at Athens.

'Αρχ, Δέλτ. παράρτ. = 'Αρχαιολογικὸν Δελτίον, παράρτημα.

Ath. Mitth. = Mitteilungen des deutschen archäologischen Instituts, Athen.

B.C.H. = Bulletin de Correspondance Hellénique.

B.S.A. Ann. = Annual of the British School at Athens.

Encycl. Britt. = *Encyclopædia Britannica*.

'Εφημ. 'Αρχ. = 'Εφημερὶς 'Αρχαιολογικὴ.

Jhb. Arch. Inst. = Jahrbuch des deutschen archäologischen Instituts.

J.E.A.; Journ. Eg. Arch. = Journal of Egyptian Archaeology.

J.H.S. = Journal of Hellenic Studies.

Journ. R. Anthrop. Inst. = Journal of the Royal Anthropological Institute.

Liv. A.A.A. = Liverpool Annals of Art and Archaeology.

Mon. Ant. = Monumenti Antichi.

O.C.G. = Hall, *Oldest Civilization of Greece*.

Proc. Soc. Ant. = Proceedings of the Society of Antiquaries.

P.S.B.A.; Proc. Soc. Bibl. Arch. = Proceedings of the Society of Biblical Archaeology.

Y.W. = *The Year's Work in Classical Studies* (Bristol: Arrowsmith).

CONTENTS

PAGE

I Introduction 1

II The Early Bronze Age 40

III From the Early to the Middle Bronze Age 67

IV From the Middle to the Late Bronze Age 109

V The Late Bronze Age (Continued) 179

VI The Transition to the Age of Iron 239

Appendix 287

Additional Notes 292

Chronological Table 294

Index 297

LIST OF ILLUSTRATIONS

(With Acknowledgments)

FIG.   PAGE

THE CUPBEARER FRESCO : KNOSSOS . . . . . *Frontispiece*
("*Monthly Review*," March, 1901, p. 124. *John Murray. Photo by courtesy of Sir Arthur Evans*)

1   THE OLD MUSEUM OF THE SYLLOGOS AT CANDIA 9

2   MYCENAE 9
     (*Photo, G. A. Stübel*)

3   THE LION-GATE, MYCENAE 10

4   THE GRAVE-CIRCLE, MYCENAE 10

5   TIRYNS 11

6   HAGIA TRIADA WITH THE SEASHORE AT DIBAKI AND THE ISLAND OF PAXIMADI . 12

7   PHAISTOS AND MOUNT IDA 12
     (*Hall, Ancient History of the Near East, Pl. ii, 1*)

8   EXCAVATIONS AT KNOSSOS, 1902 13

9   KNOSSOS, 1926 13

10   MOUNT IUKTAS 14
     (*Trevor-Battye, Camping in Crete, p. 183. Witherby & Co.*)

11   THE DOUBLE AXE 15
     (*Evans, Tomb of the Double Axes, Fig. 82. Archaeologia, lxv. Soc. Ant.*)

12   MINOTAUR FIGURES FROM MINOAN GEMS AND A KNOSSIAN COIN OF THE CLASSICAL
     PERIOD 16
     (*Evans, Palace of Minos, i, Fig. 260. Macmillan*)

13   THE STRATA OF KNOSSOS 16
     (*After Evans, B.S.A. Ann. x, Fig. 7 ; Palace of Minos, Fig. 4. Macmillan*)

14   CYPRIAN NEOLITHIC (?) POTTERY 21
     Forsdyke, Brit. Mus. Catalogue of Vases, i, Fig. 23)

15   OBSIDIAN FLAKES AND CORES : MELOS 23
     (*Glotz, Aegean Civilisation, Fig. 15. Kegan Paul*)

16   MELOS AND ANTIMELOS 23

17   PLAN OF CAVE AT MAGASA 24
     (*B.S.A. Ann., xi. p. 262*)

18   BULLS, DOUBLE-AXES, ETC., EGYPTIAN AND MINOAN 26
     (*Partly after Evans, J.H.S. xxi, etc.*)

19   EGYPTIAN AND CRETAN BIRD AND TREE CULTS 27
     (*After P.S.B.A. xxxi, Pl. xvii.*)

20   MINOAN WAIST-CLOUT AND CODPIECE. 27
     (*Evans, Journ. R. Anthrop. Inst. lv, p. 219, Fig. 20*)

21   NEOLITHIC POTTERY FROM KNOSSOS 28
     (*Forsdyke, B.M. Cat. of Vases, i, Fig. 83*)

b

BRONZE AGE GREECE

FIG.		PAGE
22	STEATOPYGOUS FEMALE FIGURES	29
	(*After Evans, Palace, Fig. 13. Macmillan*)	
23	STONE CELTS AND MACEHEADS FROM KNOSSOS	29
	(*Ibid., Fig. 15a. Macmillan*)	
24	GAVDOS, FROM THE S.W.	32
25	A CYPRIAN STAMPED PIG OF COPPER (BRIT. MUS.)	33
26	EARLY AEGEAN MASTLESS OARED BOATS, WITH FISH ENSIGNS. FROM E.M. III POTTERY; SIPHNOS	35
	(*Evans, Journ. R. Anthrop. Inst., lv, p. 205, Fig. 4; after Tsountas, 'Εφημ· 'Αρχ. 1899, p. 90, Fig. 22*)	
27	MODEL OF A HIGH-PROWED MINOAN BOAT WITH CROSS BENCHES AND RUDDER (?)	36
	(*Evans, Ibid., Fig. 3; after Dawkins, B.S.A. Suppl. Palaikastro, 1923, Fig. 4.*)	
28	A PREDYNASTIC EGYPTIAN SQUARE-SAILED SHIP: c. 4000 B.C. (BRIT. MUS.) .	37
29	CRETAN MASTED AND OARED SHIPS	39
	(*Evans, Journ. R. Anthrop. Inst., lv. Fig, 5*)	
30	CRETAN SUB-NEOLITHIC WARE	41
	(*Forsdyke, B.M. Cat. Vases, Fig. 87*)	
31	E.M. I–II POTTERY: HAGIA PHOTIA AND MOCHLOS	42
	(*Evans, Palace, Figs. 27, 41, 42. Macmillan. Seager, Mochlos, Fig. 13. Am. Sch. Ath.*)	
32	IMPORTED EGYPTIAN PREDYNASTIC STONE VESSEL	43
	(*Evans, Journ. R. Anthrop. Inst., lv, Fig. 8*)	
33	IMPORTED EGYPTIAN PROTODYNASTIC STONE VESSEL, WITH CRETAN IMITATION (ASHMOLEAN MUSEUM)	43
	(*Journ. Eg. Arch., i, p. 227*)	
34	THE E.M. OSSUARY-THOLOS AT HAGIA TRIADA, CRETE	44
35	FIGURES FROM KOUMASA, MESARA	45
	(*Journ. Eg. Arch., i, Pl. xvii, 1*)	
36	EGYPTIAN FIGURINES FROM NAQADA	45
	(*Evans, Palace, Fig. 52. Macmillan*)	
37	E.M. II–III HOUSE AT VASILIKI	46
	(*Seager, Vasiliki, Fig. 1 (Univ. Penna); Evans, Palace, Fig. 39*)	
38	E.M. GREY BUCCHERO VASES	47
	(*After Evans, Palace, Fig. 19. Macmillan*)	
39	VASILIKI AND INCISED WARE: E.M. II. (BRIT. MUS.).	48
	(*Journ. Eg. Arch., i, Pl. xvii, 3*)	
40	BIRD VASE: E.M. II	48
	(*Evans, Palace, Fig. 85. Macmillan; after Xanthoudides, Vaulted Tombs of Mesará, Pl. ii, xxviii; Liverpool Univ. Press*)	
41	BEAK-SPOUT, BRIDGE-SPOUT AND STIRRUP VASES. ASHMOLEAN MUSEUM . .	48
	(*Hall, Anc. Hist. Near East, Pl. iii, 2*)	
42	EGYPTIAN METAL AND ALABASTER SPOUTED VASES OF THE OLD KINGDOM. ASHMOLEAN MUSEUM	49
	(*Journ. Eg. Arch., i, Pl. xvii, 5*)	
43	EGYPTIAN IVTH DYNASTY DIORITE BOWL WITH E.M. COPIES IN LIPARITE, AND M.M. I. IMITATION IN SPOTTED BLACK WARE	49
	(*Journ. Eg. Arch., i, Pl. xvii, 4*)	
44	THE ISLAND OF MOCHLOS	50
	(*Photo, G. A. Stübel*)	
45	STONE VASES AND POTTERY VASES: E.M. II; MOCHLOS	50
	(*After Seager, Mochlos, Fig. 18. Am. Sch. Ath.*)	

LIST OF ILLUSTRATIONS

FIG.   PAGE

46   STONE VASES AND LID WITH DOG: MOCHLOS; E.M. II   .   .   .   51
      (*After Hall, Aegean Archaeology, Fig. 3. Medici Society. From Seager, Mochlos, Fig. 46, etc.*)

47   POTTERY DEER: E.M. II   51
      (*After Xanthoudides, Vaulted Tombs of Mesará, Pl. vii. Liverpool Univ. Press*)

48   MINOAN IMITATION OF VITH DYNASTY EGYPTIAN STONE VASE: MOCHLOS   .   52
      (*Seager, Mochlos, Am. Sch. Ath. ; Evans, Palace, Fig. 60. Macmillan*)

49   EGYPTIAN VITH DYNASTY STONE VASES   52
      (*Evans, ibid., Fig. 61. Macmillan*)

50   GOLD JEWELLERY: MOCHLOS: *c.* 2600 B.C.   53
      (*Seager, Mochlos, Fig. 41. Am. Sch. Ath.*)

51   COPPER DAGGERS, TWEEZERS, AND CHISELS: MOCHLOS: .   .   .   54
      (*Evans, ibid., Fig. 44*)

52   SILVER DAGGER: KOUMASA   54
      (*Evans, Palace, Fig. 71. Macmillan*)

53   GOLDEN PIN WITH SPIRAL DECORATION: SECOND CITY, TROY (STAATLICHES
      MUSEUM FÜR VÖLKERKUNDE, BERLIN)   54
      (*Tsountas-Manatt, The Mycenaean Age, Fig. 71. Macmillan*)

54   GOLDEN VASE: SECOND CITY, TROY. (STAATLICHES MUSEUM FÜR VÖLKERKUNDE,
      BERLIN)   55
      (*Cf. Dörpfeld, Troja, i, Fig. 284*)

55   TROY-YORTAN TYPE POTTERY FROM EUBOEA   .   .   .   55
      (*Childe, J.H.S., xxxv, p. 205, Fig. 4*)

56   OWL-VASE: TROY   56
      (*Schuchardt, Schliemann's Excavations, Fig. 67. Macmillan*)

57   E.C. I "SEA-URCHIN" VASE   57
      (*Forsdyke, B.M. Cat. Vases, i, Fig. 57*)

58   E.C. I "DUCK" VASE   57
      (*Forsdyke, ibid., Fig. 68*)

59   THE CYCLADIC PROCHOUS   57
      (*Ibid., Figs. 69, 72, 74*)

60   E.C. VASE WITH EGYPTIAN LILY-PETAL DESIGN (BRIT. MUS.)   .   .   58
      (*J.E.A., i, Pl. xvii, 2*)

61   CYCLADIC LUGGED VASES OF PARIAN MARBLE. (ASHM. MUS.)   .   .   58

62   CYCLADIC MARBLE FIGURINES. (ASHM. MUS.)   .   .   .   59

63   AMORGIAN PYXIS WITH SPIRAL DECORATION .   .   .   59
      (*Tsountas-Manatt, The Mycenaean Age, Fig. 134. Macmillan*)

64   FIRST THESSALIAN NEOLITHIC WARE   62
      (*Forsdyke, B.M. Cat. Vases, i., Fig. 37*)

65   SECOND THESSALIAN (DIMINI) WARE .   .   .   63
      (*Ibid., Fig. 42*)

66   SECOND THESSALIAN (DIMINI) THREE-COLOUR WARE .   .   .   63
      (*Ibid., Fig. 45*)

67   URFIRNIS "SAUCE-BOAT" AND TANKARD .   .   .   65
      (*After Blegen, Korakou, Figs. 6, 10. Am. Sch. Ath.*)

68   URFIRNIS DECORATED WARE   66
      (*Childe, J.H.S. xxxv, p. 198, Fig. 2*)

69   E.M. III POTTERY: MOCHLOS   68
      (*Unpublished. By permission of the late Mr. Seager*)

70   IXTH–XTH DYN. EGYPTIAN SCARABS FROM PLATANOS .   .   69
      (*Xanthoudides, Vaulted Tombs, Pl. xv. Liverpool University Press*)

BRONZE AGE GREECE

FIG. | | PAGE
71 Egyptian XI–XIIth Dyn. Scarabs from Crete (enlarged). . . . 69
(Evans, Palace, Figs. 148, 149. Macmillan)
72 M.M. II Vase with Lily-spiral Design 69
(J.E.A., i, p. 116; after Mon. Ant., xv, Pl. xxxvb)
73 Egyptian Scarabs, Button-seals, etc., VI–IXth Dynasty. (Brit. Mus.) . 70
74 Egyptian Seals: VI–IXth Dynasty. (Brit. Mus.) 70
75 Cretan Seals of Egyptian Type with Figures of Crocodiles and Apes.
E.M. II–M.M. I 71
(After Xanthoudides, Vaulted Tombs, Pls. viii, xiii, xv. Liverpool Univ. Press)
76 M.M. II Polychrome Pottery Fragments 72
(Forsdyke, B.M. Cat. Vases, i, Fig. 113)
77 Egyptian Imitations of M.M. II Pottery 73
(Ibid., Fig. 115)
78 The Abydos Find of XIIth Dyn. and M.M. II Pottery . . . 74
(Hall, Anc. Hist. Near East, Pl. iii, 1)
79 Silver Vase with Pottery Imitations, Gournià: M.M. I . . . 75
(Hall, Aegean Archaeology, Fig. 5. Medici Society: after Boyd-Hawes, Gournià, Pl. C. Phila. Mus.)
80 M.M. II "Egg-shell" Ware 76
(After Evans, Palace, Pl. ii, and Fig. 181. Macmillan)
81 M.M. I Barbotine Ware 76
(Xanthoudides, Vaulted Tombs, Pl. v. Liverpool Univ. Press.)
82 M.M. II Polychrome Vase 77
(Evans, Palace, Fig. 196. Macmillan)
83 M.M. II Polychrome Ware 77
(Dawkins, B.S.A. Ann. Suppl. Palaikastro, 1923, Fig. 9)
84 M.M. II Polychrome Vase 78
(Evans, Palace, Fig. 197. Macmillan)
85 M.M. II Polychrome Vase 78
(Ibid., Fig. 186a. Macmillan)
86 M.M. II Pithos with Imitation of Egyptian Lily-design . . 78
(J.E.A., i, p. 116; after Mon. Ant., xv, Pl. xxivA)
87 E.C. III. Milk-bowls 79
(Forsdyke, B.M. Cat. Vases, i, Figs. 77, 79)
88 E.C. III. Kernoi 79
(Ibid., Fig. 75)
89 Pithos: Mainland Mattmalerei 80
(Blegen, Korakou, Fig. 28. Am. Sch. Ath.)
90 Minyan Kantharoi 81
(After Blegen, ibid., Figs. 18, 19)
91 Minyan Kylix 82
(After Blegen, ibid., Fig. 20)
92 "Yellow Minyan" Ware 83
(After Blegen, ibid., Fig 26)
93 Decorated Ware: Lionokladi III 83
(Childe, Dawn of European Civilization, Fig. 41. Kegan Paul)
94 Model of a Four-wheeled Cart: M.M. I: c. 2200 B.C. . . 85
(Dawkins, B.S.A. Suppl. Palaikastro, Fig. 12, p. 17)
95 Horse and Chariot: L.M. I Gold Ring: Mycenae . . . 86
(Schuchhardt, Schliemann's Excavations, Fig. 220. Macmillan)
96 Horse on Shipboard: L.M. II (sealstone) 86
(Hall, Aegean Archaeology, Fig. 50. Medici Society; after Evans, B.S.A. Ann., xi, p. 13, Fig. 7)

LIST OF ILLUSTRATIONS

FIG.   PAGE

97   INSCRIBED TABLET WITH FIGURES OF CHARIOT AND HORSE, ETC. KNOSSOS, L.M. II   86
(Evans, B.S.A. Ann., vi, p. 58, Fig. 12)

98   COPPER BLADE OF CYPRIAN TYPE (TROY)   87
(Schuchhardt, Schliemann's Excavations, Fig. 63. Macmillan)

99   COPPER BLADE MOUNTED ON A SPEARHEAD: AMORGOS: E.C. III . . .   87
(Childe, Dawn of Europ. Civil'n., Fig. 2. Kegan Paul)

100   MIDDLE MINOAN DAGGER-BLADES AND SOCKETED SPEARHEADS . . .   88
(Seager, Mochlos, Fig. 45. Am. Sch. Ath.)

101   MIDDLE MINOAN DAGGER-BLADE WITH INCISED HUNTING SCENE . . .   89
(Met. Mus., N.Y. Evans, Palace, Fig. 541. Macmillan)

102   MIDDLE MINOAN SWORD. MALLIA   90
(After Charbonneaux, Mon. Piot., 1925–26, Pl. i. Leroux)

103   MIDDLE MINOAN AXEHEAD IN FORM OF A LEOPARD. MALLIA . . .   91
(Ibid., Pl. ii)

104   MIDDLE MINOAN AXES AND CHISELS   91
(Evans, Palace, Fig. 141. Macmillan'; after Xanthoudides, Ἐφημ. Ἀρχ. 1906)

105   MINOAN SEALS WITH HIEROGLYPHS: MOCHLOS   92
(From photo lent by Mr. Seager)

106   A MIDDLE MINOAN SEAL WITH WOLF'S HEAD DEVICE   92
(Hall, Aegean Archaeology, Fig. 86. Medici Society ; after Evans, J.H.S., xvii)

107   EGYPTIAN XII–XIIITH DYN. SCARAB WITH MINOAN SIGNS CUT ON BASE .   93
(Evans, Palace, Fig. 147. Macmillan)

108   MINOAN CURSIVE WRITING INCISED ON BAKED CLAY LABELS AND BARS (M.M. II)   93
(Evans, ibid., Fig. 208. Macmillan)

109   MINOAN AND EGYPTIAN SIGNS COMPARED   94
(Evans, ibid., Fig. 212. Macmillan)

110   THE NORTH GATE, KNOSSOS, FROM THE NORTH   96

111   THE NORTH GATE, KNOSSOS, FROM THE SOUTH   97

112   THE E.M. III HYPOGAEUM: KNOSSOS   98
(Evans, Palace, Fig. 74. Macmillan)

113   THE ORTHOSTATIC WEST FAÇADE: KNOSSOS   99

114   M.M. II PITHOS: PHAISTOS   99

115   PLAN OF DRAINS AND LATRINE: KNOSSOS, c. 2000 B.C.   100
(Evans, Palace, Fig. 171B. Macmillan)

116   MINOAN DRAINPIPES: KNOSSOS ; c. 2000 B.C.   101
(Evans, ibid., Fig. 104. Macmillan)

117   THE "BLUE BOY" FRESCO: KNOSSOS (M.M. II)   102
(Ibid., Pl. iv. Macmillan)

118   THE TIRYNS BULL-FRESCO; L.M. III (LATE MYC.)   103
(Tsountas-Manatt, The Mycenaean Age, Fig. 12. Macmillan)

119   MINOAN HOUSES OF 2000 B.C.: FROM A MOSAIC   104
(Evans, Palace, Fig. 224. Macmillan)

120   WOMAN OF THE E.M. III PERIOD: FROM A SEAL   105
(Evans, Journ. R. Anthrop. Inst., lv, p. 217, Fig. 17D)

121   POTTERY FIGURINE OF A MAN: M.M. I (PETSOFÀ)   105
(Hall, Aegean Archaeology, Fig. 96. Medici Society ; after B.S.A. Ann., ix, Pl. viii)

122   POTTERY FIGURE OF A WOMAN: M.M. I (PETSOFÀ)   105
(Hall, Ibid., Fig. 97. Medici Society ; after B.S.A. Ann. ix, Pl. x, 1)

BRONZE AGE GREECE

FIG.   PAGE

123   MAN AND BOY OF M.M. I : KNOSSIAN SEALING 106
       (Evans, Palace, Figs. 201B, 206. Macmillan)

124   WOMAN'S HEAD : MOCHLOS (M.M. II) 106
       (Hall, loc. cit., Fig. 98. Medici Society ; after Seager, Mochlos, Fig. 21)

125   IMPRESSION OF A BABYLONIAN CYLINDER-SEAL OF ABOUT 2100 B.C. (M.M. I ;
       PLATANOS, CRETE) 107
       (Evans, Palace, Fig. 146. Macmillan)

126   PLAN OF KNOSSOS 110
       (Glotz, Aeg. Civ., Fig. 19. Kegan Paul ; after Evans)

127   GROUND PLAN OF PART OF " DOMESTIC QUARTER," KNOSSOS . . . 111
       (Evans, Palace, Fig. 239. Macmillan)

128   THE " DOMESTIC QUARTER," KNOSSOS, FROM ABOVE 112

129   WINDING STAIRWAY ON THE EAST SLOPE, KNOSSOS 113
       (Photo, W. E. Nicholson)

130   THE GREAT STAIRWAY, KNOSSOS, FROM BELOW 113
       (Hall, Anc. Hist. Near East, Pl. ii, 2)

131   THE GREAT STAIRWAY, KNOSSOS, FROM ABOVE 114

132   A MINOAN PALACE ON A HILL : FROM A M. M. SEAL 114
       (Evans, Palace, Fig. 227A. Macmillan ; after Hogarth, J.H.S., xxii, p. 88)

133   PLAN OF PHAISTOS 115
       (Glotz, Aeg. Civ., Fig. 21. Kegan Paul ; after Mon. Ant., xiv, Pl. xxvii ; and
       B.S.A. Ann., xi, Pl. v)

134   THE GREAT STAIRWAY, PHAISTOS 116

135   THE M.M. I VIADUCT, KNOSSOS (REBUILT IN L.M. I) 117

136   FRESCO OF A PERSONAGE IN A PATCHWORK ROBE, WALKING AMID FLOWERS (PHAIS-
       TOS) 118
       (Bossert, Altkreta, Fig. 69. Wasmuth ; after Mon. Ant., xiii, Pl. xi)

137   THE FRESCO OF THE HUNTING CAT (HAGIA TRIADA ; M.M. III) . . . 118
       (J.E.A., i, Pl. xxxiii, 8 ; after Mon. Ant., xiii, Pl. 8)

138   THE FLYING FISH FRESCO : PHYLAKOPI ; L.M. I 119
       (Phylakopi, Pl. iii, B.S.A.)

139   PROCESSION OF BLACK SOLDIERS ; KNOSSOS 119
       (Encycl. Brit., 13th ed., 1926 ; s.v. Archaeology, Crete ; Fig. 8)

140   FRESCO OF LADIES AT A WINDOW ; KNOSSOS, L.M. I 120
       (Bossert, Altkreta, Fig. 60. Wasmuth; after Encycl. Brit. (11th ed.), Aegean Civilization, Fig. 5)

141   FRESCO SHOWING A CROWD OF MEN AND WOMEN IN A PILLARED SANCTUARY ;
       KNOSSOS : L.M. I 120
       (Evans, J.H.S., xxi, Pl. v)

142   " SHORTHAND " FRESCO OF A CROWD OF MEN : KNOSSOS ; M.M. III . 121
       (Evans, Palace, Fig. 384. Macmillan)

143   VASE WITH PALM DESIGN : KNOSSOS, M.M. II 123
       (Evans, ibid., Fig. 190A. Macmillan)

144   VASE WITH WHITE SHELL INLAY : KNOSSOS ; M.M. III . . . 123
       (Evans, ibid., Fig. 298A. Macmillan)

145   SPHINX, WITH HOLES FOR INLAY. HAGIA TRIADA : L.M. I . . . 124
       (From a cast)

146   THE MAGAZINES AT KNOSSOS : 1926 124

147   PITHOI IN THE MAGAZINE-CORRIDOR, KNOSSOS. MT. IUKTAS BEYOND . . 125
       (Photo, W. E. Nicholson)

LIST OF ILLUSTRATIONS

FIG.   PAGE

148 A MAGAZINE AT KNOSSOS: M.M. III   126
     (*Evans, Palace, Fig. 327. Macmillan*)

149 THE INLAID GAMING-BOARD: KNOSSOS   127
     (*After Evans, ibid., Pl. v. Macmillan*)

150 IVORY CHESSMEN: KNOSSOS   127
     (*Evans, ibid., Fig. 342. Macmillan*)

151 SNAKE-GODDESS OR PRIESTESS, POLYCHROME FAIENCE: M.M. III: KNOSSOS.   127
     (*From a reproduction; J.E.A., i, Pl. xxxiv, 1*)

152 SNAKE-GODDESS OR PRIESTESS, POLYCHROME FAIENCE, M.M. III: KNOSSOS   128
     (*From a reproduction and Evans, Palace, Fig. 359. Macmillan*)

153 COW AND GOAT WITH YOUNG: POLYCHROME FAIENCE: M.M. III: KNOSSOS. 129
     (*Evans, ibid., Figs. 366, 367. Macmillan*)

154 FAIENCE VASES: M.M. III: KNOSSOS   129
     (*Ibid., Fig. 357. Macmillan*)

155 M.M. III VASES: KNOSSOS   130
     (*Ibid., Fig. 416. Macmillan*)

156 BARBOTINE WARE: M.M. III (MOULDED BARLEY-EARS IN RELIEF) .   . 131
     (*Ibid., Fig. 299A. Macmillan*)

157 DOLPHIN-VASE: M.M. III (PACHYAMMOS)   131
     (*Ibid., Fig. 447A. Macmillan; after Seager, Pachyammos, Pl. xiv, Univ. Penna*)

158 GLAZED WARE WITH INK INSCRIPTION ("CLASS A."): KNOSSOS: M.M. III. 132
     (*Ibid., Fig. 450. Macmillan*)

159 CLAY TABLET WITH MINOAN LINEAR INSCRIPTIONS ("CLASS A."): HAGIA TRIADA:
     M.M. III–L.M. I   132
     (*Evans, Scripta Minoa, Fig. 13A; after Halbherr, Lavori eseguiti, p. 28*)

160 ZAKRO SEALINGS: L.M. I   133
     (*From Hall, Aeg. Arch., Fig. 88. Medici Society; after Hogarth, J.H.S., xxii, p. 80 ff.*)

161 THE PHAISTOS DISK   134
     (*From a cast*)

162 MEN AND WOMEN ON THE PHAISTOS DISK   135
     (*Evans, Palace, Fig. 485, Macmillan*)

163 THE MYCENAE SILVER RHYTON-FRAGMENT   135
     (*Tsountas-Manant, Myc. Age, Fig. 95. Macmillan*)

164 DETAIL OF MEN'S HEADDRESS FROM THE MYCENAE RHYTON .   . 135
     (*Evans, Palace, p. 668. Macmillan*)

165 GOLD RING WITH SCENE OF CONTENDING WARRIORS: MYCENAE: L.M. (MYC.) I 136
     (*Evans, ibid., Fig. 513. Macmillan*)

166 GOLD RING-BEZEL WITH INTAGLIO SCENE OF CONTENDING WARRIORS: MYCENAE:
     L.M. (MYC.) I   136
     (*Tsountas-Manatt, Myc. Age, Fig. 75. Macmillan*)

167 IVORY HEAD OF A WARRIOR, SHOWING BOAR'S TUSK (?) HELMET WITH CHEEK-
     PIECES: MYCENAE: L.M. III   136
     (*Tsountas-Manatt, ibid., Fig. 85. Macmillan*)

168 HEAD OF A PHILISTINE (XIITH CENT. B.C.) MEDINET HABU .   . 137
     (*B.S.A. Ann., viii, p. 185, Fig. 9*)

169 ASSYRIANS AND WESTERN ALLIES (?) WEARING THE FEATHERED CROWN AND CREST:
     VIITH CENT. RELIEF   138
     (*Hall, J.H.S. xxxi, p. 123, Fig. 7; after Layard, Mon. Nineveh, ii, 33*)

170 MELIAN VASE WITH BIRD-DESIGN (M.C. III)   .   .   . 138
     (*Hall, Anc. Hist. Near East, Pl. iii, 5*)

BRONZE AGE GREECE

FIG.   PAGE

171 MELIAN VASE-FRIEZE OF EGYPTIAN ORIGIN 139
    (Hall, J.E.A., i, p. 199, Fig. 5)

172 MELIAN IMPS (M.C. III) 139
    (Evans, Palace, Fig. 527, C, D. Macmillan)

173 THE FIRST HUMAN FIGURES IN VASE-PAINTING : M.C. III 140
    (Bossert, Altkreta, Figs. 263, 262 ; after Phylakopi, Fig. 95, Pl. xiii, 17 and 146 ;
    after Mon. Ant., vi, Pl. ix)

174 MIDDLE AND LATE CYCLADIC POTTERY : IMITATION M.M. AND L.M. I WARES 140
    (Forsdyke, B.M. Cat. Vases, i, Fig. 8)

175 SCULPTURED GRAVESTONE : MYCENAE 141
    (Wace, B.S.A. Ann., xxv, Pl. xx)

176 SCULPTURED GRAVESTONE : MYCENAE 141
    (Wace, ibid.)

177 CRETAN (L.M. I) VASE : SIXTH GRAVE ; MYCENAE 142
    (Schuchhardt, Schliemann's Excavations, Fig. 277. Macmillan)

178 NON-CRETAN VASES (CYCLADIC AND HELLADIC) : SIXTH GRAVE, MYCENAE . 142
    (Ibid., Figs. 278, 279. Macmillan)

179 BRONZE DAGGER INLAID WITH GOLD : WARRIORS HUNTING LIONS : FOURTH
    GRAVE, MYCENAE. (RESTORED) 143
    (From a reproduction)

180 BRONZE SWORD-BLADE FROM FIFTH GRAVE, MYCENAE 143
    (Hall, Oldest Civilization of Greece, Fig. 25. D. Nutt ; after Perrot-Chipiez, vi, Pl. xvii)

181 GOLD AND SILVER BULL-RHYTON : FOURTH GRAVE, MYCENAE . . . 144
    (Schuchhardt, Schliemann's Excavations, Fig. 248. Macmillan)

182 GOLDEN MASK OF THE DEAD : FOURTH GRAVE, MYCENAE 145
    (Ibid., Fig. 224. Macmillan)

183 GOLDEN MASK OF THE DEAD, BEARDED : FIFTH GRAVE, MYCENAE . . 146
    (From a reproduction)

184 GOLDEN DIADEM : SECOND GRAVE, MYCENAE 147
    (Schuchhardt, Schliemann's Excavations, Fig. 207. Macmillan)

185 PLAN OF THE ACROPOLIS AND THOLOS-TOMBS OF MYCENAE . . . 147
    (Wace, B.S.A. Ann., xxv, Fig. 49)

186 THE "TREASURY OF MINYAS," ORCHOMENOS 148

187 THE "TREASURY OF ATREUS," MYCENAE 148

188 THE "TREASURY OF KLYTAIMNESTRA," MYCENAE 148

189 M.M. III VASE : TREASURY OF KLYTAIMNESTRA 150
    (Wace, B.S.A. Ann., xxv, Fig. 80)

190 L.M. IB VASE, EPANO PHOURNOS THOLOS, MYCENAE 151
    (Wace, ibid., Fig. 53)

191 PILLARS OF THE FAÇADE : TREASURY OF ATREUS : BRIT. MUS. . . . 152
    (Hall, Aeg. Arch., Pl. v. Medici Society)

192 THE VAPHEIO GOLD CUPS : THE BULL CAPTURED AND TAMED BY MAN.
    L.M. I 155
    (Athens Museum : from a reproduction)

193 THE HARVESTERS' VASE : HAGIA TRIADA 157
    (Hall, Aeg. Arch., Pl. xvii. Medici Society ; from a cast)

194 THE CHIEFTAIN VASE : HAGIA TRIADA 158
    (Ibid., Pl. xv, 2 ; from a cast)

195 THE PRINCE AND THE WARRIOR : CHIEFTAIN VASE, HAGIA TRIADA . . 158

196 THE BOXER OR GLADIATOR VASE : HAGIA TRIADA . . . 159
    (Hall, Anc. Hist. Near East, Pl. iv, 5)

LIST OF ILLUSTRATIONS

FIG.   PAGE

197 FRAGMENT OF STEATITE VASE CARVED IN RELIEF: ASHM. MUS.   160
     (*Hall, Aeg. Arch., Pl. xv, 3. Medici Society*)

198 HAGIA TRIADA .   161
     (*Photo, W. E. Nicholson*)

199 STONE LAMPS, ETC., FROM NIROU KHANI   161
     (*Xanthoudides, Ἀρχ. Ἐφημ, 1922, p. 14, Fig. 11*)

200 THE THEATRAL AREA, KNOSSOS .   162
     (*Photo, W. E. Nicholson*)

201 GOURNIÀ .   162

202 PLAN OF GOURNIÀ .   163
     (*Hall, Aegean Archaeology, Fig. 44. Medici Society ; after Boyd-Hawes, Gournià, Phila. Mus.*)

203 POTTERY PITHOS, IMITATING METAL (L.M. I), PALAIKASTRO .   164
     (*Forsdyke, B.M. Cat. Vases, i, Fig. 164*)

204 THE TOWN OF PSEIRA   165

205 THE ISLE OF PSEIRA, FROM KAVOUSI   165
     (*Photo, R. B. Seager*)

206 L.M. I PLANT-DESIGNS ON POTTERY: NIROU KHANI   166
     (*By permission of Dr. Xanthoudides*)

207 L.M. Ib PLANT-DESIGN: KAKOVATOS (OLD PYLOS)   167
     (*Bossert, Altkreta, Fig. 259. Wasmuth ; after K. Müller, Ath. Mitth., 1909, Pl. xxi*)

208 NATURALISTIC FRESCO OF PLANTS, L.M. I. HAGIA TRIADA .   167
     (*Bossert, ibid., Fig. 68 ; after Mon. Ant., xiii, Pl. x*)

209 OCTOPUS-VASE: L.M. I: GOURNIÀ .   167
     (*Hall, Aeg. Arch., Fig. 25 ; after Boyd-Hawes, Gournià, Pl. H. Phila. Mus.*)

210 ARGONAUT-VASE: L.M. I: BRITISH MUSEUM   168
     (*Hall, J.E.A., i, Pl. xvi, 1*)

211 DUCK-VASE: ARGOS: L.M. I–II   168
     (*Bossert, Altkreta, Fig. 261. Wasmuth ; after B.C.H. 1904, p. 377*)

212 POTTERY FILLER: L.M. I: PALAIKASTRO   169
     (*Hall, Aeg. Arch., Fig. 28. Medici Society ; after B.S.A. Ann., ix, p. 311, Fig. 9*)

213 POTTERY PITHOS: L.M. I: PSEIRA   169
     (*Seager, Vasiliki, Pseira, etc., Fig. 9. Univ. Penna.*)

214 POTTERY PITHOS, WITH DESIGN OF DOUBLE-AXES, BULLS' HEADS, OLIVE-SPRAYS
     AND SPIRALS: L.M. I. PSEIRA   170
     (*After Seager, ibid., Pl. vii*)

215 L.M. I MARINE DESIGN: KAKOVATOS (OLD PYLOS) (IMPORTED CRETAN VASE) 170
     (*Bossert, Altkreta, Fig. 258. Wasmuth ; after K. Müller, Ath. Mitth., 1909, Pl. xvi*)

216 PITHOS WITH SUNFLOWER-DESIGN IN RELIEF: L.M. I–II. ROYAL VILLA, KNOSSOS 170
     (*Evans, B.S.A. Ann., ix, p. 139, Fig. 88*)

217 OCTOPUS-VASE: RELIEF CARVING, MYCENAE: L.M. I.   170
     (*Bossert, Altkreta, Fig. 275. Wasmuth*)

218 CHRYSELEPHANTINE FIGURE OF A SNAKE-GODDESS: BOSTON   171
     (*Boston Museum of Fine Arts ; by permission*)

219 AN IVORY LEAPER: KNOSSOS, L.M. I   172
     (*Evans, B.S.A. Ann., viii, Pl. ii*)

220 BULL: INCISED ON AN IVORY PYXIS-LID: BRITISH MUSEUM   172
     (*Hall, Aeg. Arch., Fig. 83. Medici Society*)

221 BRONZE GROUP OF YOUTH AND BULL: NORTHWICK   173
     (*From a completed cast*)

222 BRONZE GROUP OF YOUTH AND BULL: NORTHWICK: FRONT VIEW .   173
     (*Evans, J.H.S., xli, p. 247*)

FIG.   PAGE

223 BRONZE FIGURE OF A WOMAN : BERLIN 174
(Hall, Aeg. Arch., Pl. xix. Medici Society. From a cast)

224 HEAD AND TORSO OF BRONZE FIGURE OF YOUTH OR YOUNG GIRL . . . 174
(Dawkins, B.S.A. Ann., Suppl., p. 122, Fig. 102)

225 BRONZE FIGURE OF MAN : TYLISSOS : CANDIA MUSEUM . . . 175
(Hall, Aeg. Arch., Fig. 14. Medici Society)

226 BRONZE FIGURE OF A MAN : BRITISH MUSEUM 175
(Pryce, J.H.S., 1921, p. 87, Fig. 1)

227 BRONZE FIGURE OF A MAN : DICTAEAN CAVE 176
(Evans, Palace, Fig. 501. Macmillan)

228 BRONZE FIGURE OF A YOUTH WEARING A PETASOS 177
(Leiden : Museum van Oudheden ; by permission)

229 BRONZE FIGURE OF A YOUTH : TYLISSOS 178
(From a cast)

230 MINOAN INSCRIBED TABLETS, CLAY : "CLASS B," KNOSSOS (BRIT. MUS.) . . 179

231 MINOAN INSCRIBED CLAY TABLET : "CLASS B," KNOSSOS 180
(Glotz, Aeg. Civiln., Fig. 86. Kegan Paul ; after Evans, Scripta Minoa, Fig. 25)

232 L.M. II VASES. (a) CONVENTIONALIZED PLANT-DESIGNS ; (b) CONVENTIONAL SPIRAL
AND OCTOPUS ; (c) IMITATION OF ARCHITECTURAL AND GLYPTIC DESIGNS . 181
(Evans, Preh. Tombs, lix, ci, c, Fig. 144 ; Archaeologia, lix ; Soc. Ant.)

233 THE MARSEILLES VASE : L.M. IB : MARINE DESIGNS 182
(Hall, Anc. Hist. Near East, Pl. iii, 4)

234 BRONZE EMBOSSED BOWL : KNOSSOS : L.M. I 182
(Evans, Preh. Tombs, Fig. 116 ; Archaeologia, lix. ; Soc. Ant.)

235 BRONZE EWER : KNOSSOS : L.M. I 183
(Evans, B.S.A. Ann., x, Fig. 76 c)

236 A MINOAN AMBASSADOR TO EGYPT : WALLPAINTING IN THE TOMB OF REKHMIRE',
c. 1450 B.C. 183
(Hay, 1837 ; Bossert, Altkreta, Fig. 337. Wasmuth)

237 FRAGMENT OF STEATITE VASE WITH PROCESSION OF YOUTHS : KNOSSOS . . 184
(Evans, B.S.A. Ann., ix, p. 129, Fig. 85)

238 FRESCO OF BULL-LEAPING : KNOSSOS 185
(Hall, Anc. Hist. Near East, Pl. iv, 2 ; from a reproduction in the Ashmolean Museum)

239 MEN WEARING βράκαις (?) : SEAL-IMPRESSION, ZAKRO 185
(Hall, Aeg. Arch., Fig. 94. Medici Society ; after Hogarth, J.H.S., xxii, p. 78, Fig. 6)

240 RELIEF FRESCO OF A KING OR GOD : KNOSSOS 185
(Hall, Anc. Hist. Near East, Pl. iv, 1 ; from a reproduction in the Ashmolean Museum)

241 RELIEF-FRESCO OF A WOMAN : PSEIRA : L.M. I 186
(Seager, Vasiliki, Pseira, etc., Pl. v. Univ. Penna.)

242 THE THRONE OF MINOS 186
(Photo, W. E. Nicholson)

243 A BULL TOSSES A MAN OVER THE HURDLES : INTAGLIO (ENLARGED) . 187
(Evans, Palace, Fig. 274. Macmillan)

244 HURDLE-DESIGN : FRESCOED WALL, KNOSSOS. 187
(After Evans, ibid., Fig. 271)

245 PAINTED POTTERY BURIAL-POT : L.M. IA 189
(Seager, Mochlos, Pl. xi. Am. Sch. Ath.)

246 PAINTED POTTERY LARNAX : M.M. I 190
(Evans, Palace, Fig. 110. Macmillan)

247 PAINTED POTTERY LARNAX : L.M. III 190
('Αρχ. Δελτ. Παράρτ, 1920–1, p. 157, Fig. 4 ; by permission of Dr. Xanthoudides)

LIST OF ILLUSTRATIONS

FIG.   PAGE

248   SECTION OF FRONT CHAMBER WITH GABLED RECTANGULAR LARNAKES: L.M. III 191
(Evans, Preh. Tombs, Fig. 25 c. Archaeologia, lix. Soc. Ant.)

249   PLAN OF TOMB CHAMBER WITH FULL-LENGTH AND CONTRACTED BURIALS: L.M. III 192
(Ibid., Fig. 42)

250   THE ROYAL TOMB, ISOPATA: M.M. III–L.M. I. 192

251   PLAN OF THE ROYAL TOMB, ISOPATA 193
(Hall, Aeg. Arch., Fig. 58. Medici Society ; after Evans, Preh. Tombs, Archaeologia, lix, Pl. xciii)

252   INTERIOR OF THE "TREASURY OF ATREUS": MYCENAE 193
(Hall, Anc. Hist. Near East, Pl. ii, 3)

253   SECTION OF THE "TREASURY OF ATREUS" 193
(Tsountas-Manatt, The Mycenaean Age, Fig. 43. Macmillan)

254   PAINTED POTTERY FUNERARY VASE WITH REPRESENTATION OF A HELMET AND SHIELD SUPERIMPOSED ON SPIRALS 194
(Evans, Tomb of the Double Axes, Archaeologia, lxv, Pl. iv ; Soc. Ant.)

255   PIT-CAVE: ZAFER PAPOURA. L.M. III 195
(Hall, Aeg. Arch., Fig. 62. Medici Society ; after Evans, Preh. Tombs ; Fig. 11c)

256   SHAFT-GRAVE: ZAFER PAPOURA: L.M. II 196
(Hall, ibid., Fig. 60. Medici Society ; after Evans, ibid. ; Fig. 8a)

257   RAPIERS: L.M. II 197
(Hall, ibid., Fig. 104 ; after Evans, ibid. ; Figs. 110, 112)

258   SPEARHEADS: L.M. II 197
(Hall, ibid., Fig. 106 ; after Evans, ibid. ; Fig. 57)

259   GLASS PASTE AND STONE BEADS ; EGYPTIAN SCARABS OF THE LATE XVIIIth DYNASTY PERIOD ; SEALSTONES, ETC. 198
(Evans, Preh. Tombs, Figs. 80, 81a, 85, 95, 96, 101)

260   HAY'S DRAWING OF THE WALLPAINTING OF MINOANS IN THE TOMB OF SENNEMUT, THEBES: c. 1500 B.C. 199
(Hall, J.E.A., i, Pl. xxxiii, 1)

261   MARBLE (?) VASE WITH NAME OF QUEEN HATSHEPSUT: c. 1480 B.C. (CAIRO MUSEUM) 200

262   (a) ASIATICS AND A MINOAN : TOMB OF MENKHEPERRE'SENB ; (b) MINOANS IN THE TOMB OF MENKHEPERRE'SENB 201
(From facsimile copies by Mrs. N. de G. Davies : by permission of Dr. A. H. Gardiner. Cf. W. M. Müller, Egyptological Researches, ii, Pls. 8, 11, 12)

263   MINOANS IN THE TOMB OF MENKHEPERRE'SENB, BEARING A MINOAN FILLER, a MINOAN "VAPHEIO" CUP, AND A MINOAN BULL-FIGURE . . . 202
(Ibid. Cf. W. M. Müller, ibid., ii, Pl. 9)

264   MINOANS IN THE TOMB OF USER-AMON WITH MINOAN BULL-RHYTON, STANDING BULL, ETC. 203
(N. de G. Davies, Bull. Met. Mus. N.Y., 1926, ii, p. 42, Fig. 1 ; by permission)

265   MINOAN GIFTS FROM THE TOMBS OF USER-AMON AND REKHMIRE' . . . 203
(Ibid., Figs. 3, 6)

266   "THE GREAT MEN OF KEFTIU AND THE ISLES" : TOMB OF REKHMIRE': c. 1440 B.C. 204
(From copy by Mrs. N. de G. Davies, by permission of Dr. A. H. Gardiner)

267   MINOAN IN THE TOMB OF REKHMIRE'. 205
(Hall, B.S.A. Ann., viii, p. 171, Fig. 2)

268   DETAIL OF MINOAN DRESS : TOMB OF SENNEMUT 205
(Hall, B.S.A. Ann., x, p. 156, Fig. 2)

BRONZE AGE GREECE

FIG.   PAGE

269   CASTS FROM THE LIVING : PORTRAIT HEADS OF EUROPEANS (?), AMARNA : *c.* 1370
        B.C. (BERLIN MUSEUM) 208
        (*By permission*)

270   PROFILE AND FULL-FACE VIEWS OF A PORTRAIT-CAST FROM THE LIVING OF A
        EUROPEAN (?) WOMAN : AMARNA : *c.* 1370 B.C. (BERLIN MUSEUM). . 209
        (*Ibid.*)

271   EGYPTIAN AND MYCENAEAN GOLD JEWELLERY : ENKOMI, CYPRUS, *c.* 1400 B.C.
        (BRIT. MUS.) 210

272   EGYPTIAN AND LOCAL IMITATION OF EGYPTIAN FAIENCE : ENKOMI, CYPRUS, *c.*
        1400 B.C. 210
        (*Hall, J.E.A., i, Pl. xxxiv, 3*)

273   EGYPTIAN VASE WITH NAME OF AMENHETEP III : MYCENAE, *c.* 1400 B.C. (ATHENS
        MUSEUM) 211
        (*By permission*)

274   FAIENCE MONKEY WITH PRENOMEN OF AMENHETEP II : MYCENAE, *c.* 1430 B.C. 211
        (*Hall, B.S.A. Ann., viii, p. 188, Fig. 13*)

275   NATIVE CYPRIAN BRONZE AGE POTTERY. (BRIT. MUS.) 212

276   L.M. III (MYCENAEAN III) NATIVE CYPRIAN, AND IMPORTED SYRIAN POTTERY :
        ENKOMI, CYPRUS, *c.* 1400 B.C. (BRIT. MUS.) 213
        (*Murray, Smith and Walters, Excavations in Cyprus, Fig. 74*)

277   SECTION OF THE LATE-MYCENAEAN BUILDINGS ; PALACE OF MYCENAE . . 214
        (*Wace, B.S.A. Ann., xxv, Fig. 38*)

278   L.M. I–II (MYC. I–II) FRESCO : PALACE OF MYCENAE . . . 215
        (*Wace, ibid., Pl. xxvii*)

279   THE FORTRESS OF GHA 216

280   FRESCO : BOEOTIAN THEBES 216
        (*Bossert, Altkreta, Fig. 214 ; after Keramopoullos, Ἐφημ.Ἀρχ. v, 1909*)

281   L.M. I–II (MYC. I–II) FRESCO FROM THE OLDER PALACE : TIRYNS . . 217
        (*Hall, Aeg. Arch., Fig. 70. Medici Society ; after Rodenwaldt, Tiryns, ii, Pl. i :
        Eleutheroudakis and Barth*)

282   MYC. II (" EPHYRAEAN ") WARE 218
        (*Blegen, Korakou ; Am. Sch. Ath.*)

283   MYCENAEAN (L.M. III) KYLIKES : IALYSOS 218
        (*Forsdyke, B.M. Cat. Vases, i, Figs. 206, 207*)

284   LATE MYCENAEAN (L.M. III) BIRD-VASE 220
        (*Bossert, Altkreta, Fig. 172. Wasmuth ; after Mon. Ant., xiv, Pl. xxxvii*)

285   LATE MYCENAEAN (L.M. III) BIRD-VASE : PALAIKASTRO . . . 220
        (*Dawkins, B.S.A. Ann., ix, p. 318, Fig. 17*)

286   LATE MYCENAEAN VASE : ENKOMI 220
        (*Hall, Aeg. Arch., Fig. 32. Medici Society*)

287   L.M. III STIRRUP-VASE : GUROB 221
        (*Forsdyke, B.M. Cat. Vases, i, Fig. 256*)

288   EGYPTIAN IMITATIONS OF STIRRUP-VASES IN FAIENCE AND ALABASTER (BRIT. MUS.) 221

289   ALABASTER STIRRUP-VASE : XVIIITH DYN. (REA COLLECTION) . . 221

290   FAIENCE STIRRUP-VASE : LOCAL IMITATION OF EGYPTIAN WARE : ENKOMI, CYPRUS,
        c. 1400 B.C. (BRIT. MUS.) 221

291   EGYPTIAN IMITATION OF MINOAN " FILLER " IN FAIENCE : THEBES : EARLY
        XVIIITH DYN. (BRIT. MUS.) 222
        (*Cf. Hall, Oldest Civilization of Greece, Fig. 53*)

292   FILLER OF EGYPTIAN ALABASTER : POSSIBLY MINOAN WORKMANSHIP. (BRIT MUS.) 222
        (*Forsdyke, J.H.S., xxxi, p. 117, Fig. 5*)

LIST OF ILLUSTRATIONS

FIG.   PAGE

293   SIDE OF THE PAINTED POTTERY LARNAX FROM HAGIA TRIADA: L. M. III . 223
      (*Mon. Ant. xix, pls. 1–3*)

294   CYPRIAN KRATER: ENKOMI   224
      (*Hall, Aeg. Arch., Fig. 34, Medici Society*)

295   HORSE-HEAD CUP: MINOAN FAIENCE, ENKOMI (BRIT. MUS.)   .   . 224

296   RAM-HEAD CUP AND JANUS-CUP: MINOAN FAIENCE, ENKOMI (BRIT. MUS.) . 225

297   WOMAN'S HEAD CUPS: MINOAN FAIENCE, ENKOMI (BRIT. MUS.) .   . 225

298   VASES OF MINOAN FAIENCE: ENKOMI (BRIT. MUS.)   225

299   UPPER PART OF A VASE OF MINOAN FAIENCE, ḲALA'AT SHERḲAT (ASHUR), ASSYRIA (BRIT. MUS.) 226

300   WOMAN'S HEAD CUP OF MINOAN FAIENCE: ḲALA'AT SHERḲAT (ASHUR), ASSYRIA (BRIT. MUS.) 226

301   BRONZE EWER AND VASE AND SILVER CUP: ENKOMI. (BRIT. MUS.)   .   . 227

302   THE IVORY DRAUGHT-BOX AND TWO IVORY MIRROR-HANDLES: ENKOMI. (BRIT. MUS.)   228

303   CYPRIAN MYCENAEAN INSCRIPTION: ENKOMI   230
      (*Hall, Oldest Civilization of Greece, Fig. 64. D. Nutt*)

304   FRESCO OF WOMAN HOLDING PYXIS. TIRYNS   230
      (*Hall, Aeg. Arch., Fig. 76. Medici Society; after Rodenwaldt, Tiryns, ii, Pl. viii. Eleutheroudakis and Barth*)

305   CHARIOT-FRESCO: TIRYNS   231
      (*Hall, ibid., Fig. 74. Medici Society; after Rodenwaldt, ibid., Pl. xii*)

306   HUNTSMAN-FRESCO: TIRYNS   232
      (*Hall, ibid., Fig. 73; after Rodenwaldt, ibid., Fig. 47*)

307   STAG-FRESCO: TIRYNS   232
      (*Hall, ibid., Fig. 112; after Rodenwaldt, Fig. 62*)

308   FRESCO OF BOAR-HUNT: TIRYNS   233
      (*Hall, ibid., Fig. 75; after Rodenwaldt, Pl. xiii*)

309   PLAN OF TIRYNS   234
      (*Hall, ibid., Fig. 47; after Rodenwaldt, Fig. 1*)

310   A TIRYNTHIAN CASEMATE   235

311   MYC. IIIB. (L.M. IIIb) CLOSE STYLE OF DECORATION   .   . 235
      (*Forsdyke, B.M. Cat. Vases, i. Fig. 289*)

312   MYC. IIIB. PANELLED STYLE   236
      (*Forsdyke, ibid., Fig. 286*)

313   MYC. IIIB. SKYPHOS (BRIT. MUS.): KALYMNOS   .   . 236
      (*Forsdyke, ibid., Fig. 270*)

314   LATE MYCENAEAN SKYPHOS   236
      (*Blegen, Korakou, Fig. 86. Am. Sch. Ath.*)

315   VASE OF THE CLOSE STYLE, MYCENAE   237
      (*Wace, B.S.A. Ann., xxv, Pl. ixB*)

316   MYCENAEAN GOLD STIRRUP-VASES, FROM A WALLPAINTING IN THE TOMB OF RAMESES III, *c.* 1180 B.C.   238
      (*Hall, Oldest Civilization of Greece, Fig. 26. D. Nutt*)

317   SHARDINA MERCENARIES: 13TH CENT. B.C. TEMPLE OF RAMESES II, ABYDOS . 240

318   SHARDINA BOARDING A PHILISTINE SHIP; TEMP. RAMESES III (12TH CENT. B.C.): MEDINET HABU   241
      (*Hall, B.S.A. Ann., viii, p. 186, Fig. 11*)

FIG.		PAGE
319	A Philistine Chief seized by the Falcon symbolizing the Royal Name: Medinet Habu	241
	(Hall, P.S.B.A., 1909, Pl. xxxi)	
320	Heads of Philistines: Medinet Habu	241
	(From a cast by Sir F. Petrie, Brit. Mus.)	
321	Caricature Doll of faience, representing a Philistine. Found in Malta	242
	(Hall, J.H.S., xxxi, p. 122, Fig. 6)	
322	Zakaray (Cretans ?) of the 12th cent. b.c.: Thebes	242
	(Hall, Oldest Civilization of Greece, Fig. 51. D. Nutt)	
323	Shardina (Sardians) of the 12th cent. b.c.: Thebes	242
	(Hall, ibid., Fig. 50. D. Nutt)	
324	Heads of Shardina.	243
	(From a cast by Sir F. Petrie ; Brit. Mus.)	
325	Stag's-horn Head of Bearded Man in Feather Headdress (British Museum)	243
	(Forsdyke and Pryce, J.H.S., xl, Pl. vi)	
326	Philistine Pottery: Gezer	245
	(Pal. Expl. Fund)	
327	Philistine Vase of L.M. IIIb Style: Gezer	245
	(Pal. Expl. Fund)	
328	Philistine Kraters and other Vases	246
	(Macalister, The Excavation of Gezer, Pl. clxiii. Pal. Expl. Fund)	
329	Shardina Bronze Broadsword, found at Gaza. (Brit. Mus.) . . .	254
	(Hall and Burchardt, Proc. Soc. Ant., 1914–15, p. 137)	
330	Shardina Guards, with Broadswords	254
	(Rosellini, Mon. Storici, Pl. CI.)	
331	Greek Bronze Swords with Cross-Hilts: XIVth–XIIth cent. (Brit. Mus.)	255
332	Cretan Bronze Broad and Leaf-shaped Swords, Fibulae, etc. Earlier Burials ; Tombs A and B.: Mouliana	256
	(Xanthoudides, Ἐφημ.,Ἀρχ. 1904, p. 30, Fig. 7 ; p. 46, Fig. 11)	
333	Bronze Spearhead and Fibulae: Crete	257
	(E. H. Hall, Sphoungaràs and Vrokastro, Fig. 100. Univ. Penn.)	
334	Bronze Fibula.	258
	(Tsountas-Manatt, The Mycenaean Age, Fig. 58. Macmillan)	
335	Sub-Mycenaean Vases found with Iron Weapons. Later Burial ; Mouliana, Crete	259
	(Xanthoudides, Ἐφημ.' Αρχ. 1904, Pl. 3)	
336	Myc. IIIb. and Sub-Mycenaean Stirrup-vases ; Ialysos and Assarlik. (Brit. Mus.)	261
	(Forsdyke, B.M. Cat. Vases, Figs. 231, 295)	
337	Greek Vase-design showing Minoan Survivals : Crete . . .	261
	(Evans, Tomb of the Double Axes, Fig. 24. Soc. Ant.)	
338	Procession on Warrior-vase, Mycenae	262
	(Schuchhardt, Schliemann's Excavations, Fig. 284. Macmillan)	
339	Achaian Vase Fragment : Mycenae	262
	(Bossert, Altkreta, Fig. 267. Wasmuth ; after Schliemann, Tiryns.)	
340	Frieze of Running Deer : Achaian Vase (Brit. Mus.) . . .	263
	(Forsdyke, B.M. Cat. Vases, i, Fig. 280, Pl. xvi)	
341	Transitional Ware, Vrokastro : Crete	263
	(E. H. Hall, Vrokastro, Fig. 61. Univ. Penn.)	
342	Egyptian Scarabs, Vrokastro	264
	(ibid., Fig. 81)	

LIST OF ILLUSTRATIONS

FIG.   PAGE

343   TRANSITIONAL WARE, PRAISOS, CRETE   264
        (*Droop, B.S.A. Ann., xii, Fig. 9*)

344   CRETAN EARLY GEOMETRIC VASE OF TYPE FOUND AT VROKASTRO   .   .   . 264
        (*Forsdyke, B.M. Cat. Vases, i., Fig. 307*)

345   BRONZE GREAVES: ENKOMI. (BRIT. MUS.) 265
        (*Hall, Aeg. Arch., Fig. 102. Medici Soc.*)

346   SURVIVAL OR REVIVAL OF MINOAN STYLE ON A GREEK SEAL OF THE FOURTH
        CENTURY 271
        (*Evans, J.H.S., xxxii, p. 295, Fig. 7A*)

347   MAN WRESTLING WITH A SEA-MONSTER; FROM A CRETAN BLACK-FIGURED PINAX   271
        (*Hopkinson, B.S.A. Ann., x, Pl. iii*)

348   MINOAN GEMS (*galopetras*)   273
        (*Evans, J.H.S., xxi, p. 154, Figs. 30–32*)

349   LATE MYCENAEAN PAINTED STONE HEAD 273
        (*Bossert, Altkreta, Fig. 249. Wasmuth; after 'Εφημ.' Αρχ, 1902*)

350   THE HUNTRESS-GODDESS WITH HER LION 274
        (*Hogarth, B.S.A. Ann., xvii, p. 265, Fig. 2*)

351   THE MOTHER-GODDESS, ATTENDED BY PRIESTESSES—GOLD RING: MYCENAE   . 276
        (*Schuchhardt, Schliemann's Excavations, Fig. 281. Macmillan*)

352   POTTERY LARNAX WITH REPRESENTATION OF THE YOUNG GOD DESCENDING UPON
        THE SEA 276
        (*Hall, Aeg. Arch., Fig. 52. Medici Society; after Evans, Preh. Tombs, Fig. 107*)

353   THE CLASHING OF THE DOUBLE-AXES: FROM A SEAL-IMPRESSION   .   . 276
        (*Evans, B.S.A. Ann., viii, p. 103, Fig. 61*)

354   GODDESS HOLDING THE DOUBLE AXE AND RITUAL GARMENT. SEAL-
        IMPRESSION 277
        (*Evans, B.S.A. Ann., viii, p. 102, Fig. 59*)

355   GOLDEN REPRESENTATION OF A SHRINE WITH PILLARS BETWEEN THE HORNS OF
        CONSECRATION, AND DOVES: MYCENAE 277
        (*Tsountas-Manatt, The Myc. Age, Fig. 40. Macmillan*)

356   THE GODDESS IN A BOAT, BENEATH A TREE. GOLD RING .   .   . 277
        (*Seager, Mochlos, Fig. 52, Am. Sch. Ath.*)

357   THE GORGE OF KAVOUSI 278

358   BOATMAN ATTACKED BY A SEA-DEMON. (SEAL-IMPRESSION) .   .   . 278
        (*Evans, B.S.A. Ann., ix, p. 58, Fig. 36; Palace, Fig. 520. Macmillan*)

359   WATER-DEMONS WITH TREE AND ALTAR (SEAL-IMPRESSION) .   .   . 278
        (*Evans, J.H.S., xxi, p. 101, Fig. 1*)

360   PILLAR GUARDED BY GRYPHON. (SEAL-IMPRESSION) .   .   . 279
        (*Evans, ibid., p. 158, Fig. 36*)

361   GRYPHON AT THE FLYING GALLOP. GOLD: MYCENAE   .   .   . 279
        (*Schuchhardt, Schliemann's Excavations, Fig. 186. Macmillan*)

362   THE BEZEL OF THE GOLD "RING OF NESTOR" 279
        (*Evans, J.H.S., xlv, p. 65, Fig. 55*)

363   THE "SACRAL KNOT": FAIENCE: MYCENAE   280
        (*Schuchhardt, Schliemann's Excavations, Fig. 253. Macmillan*)

364   POTTERY RITUAL TRUMPET (?) 280
        (*Boyd-Hawes, Gournià, Pl. xi. Phila. Mus.*)

365   PRIESTESS BLOWING A CONCH BEFORE THE ALTAR, WITH SACRED PINE-TREES AND
        HORNS OF CONSECRATION. (SEAL-IMPRESSION) .   .   . 280
        (*Evans, J.H.S., xxi, p. 142, Fig. 25*)

FIG.   PAGE

366   BULL-RHYTON : LITTLE PALACE, KNOSSOS 282
        (*Evans, Tomb of the Double Axes, p. 80, Fig. 87B. Soc. Ant.*)

367   LUSTRAL AREA : KNOSSOS 283
        (*Evans, Palace, Fig. 292. Macmillan*)

368   CRUDE HOUSEHOLD IMAGE OF A GODDESS : L.M. III. : KNOSSOS . . . 283
        (*Glotz, Aeg. Civiln., Fig. 42. Kegan Paul ; after Evans, B.S.A. Ann., viii, Fig. 56*)

369   THE MYCENAEAN SPHINX 286
        (*Schuchhardt, Schliemann's Excavations, Fig. 187. Macmillan*)

MAPS

                                      To face page

THE NEAR EAST IN THE XVTH CENTURY B.C. 179
    (*Hall, Ancient History of the Near East*)

GREECE WITH INSETS OF CENTRAL GREECE AND CRETE 296
    (*Hall, Aegean Archaeology. Medici Society*)

THE CIVILIZATION OF GREECE IN THE BRONZE AGE

LECTURE I

INTRODUCTION

THE lectures which are here printed in an expanded form deal with the prehistoric civilization of Greece in the Bronze Age. I have avoided using the term Aegean Civilization, though it is commonly used. Still more have I avoided using the term Minoan Civilization. The latter term can be used only of the civilization of Crete, to which I have in these lectures confined it, and in dealing with the contemporary cultures of the Cyclades and Greece we have in general use the terms Cycladic and Helladic. Probably to the non-specialist the term Minoan or even the older " Mycenaean " may cover these two latter fields as well as that of Cretan prehistoric archaeology. But such an extension of Sir Arthur Evans's well-known term is erroneous. I prefer to speak of " Mycenaean " rather than of " Helladic " for the later phase of the Bronze Age culture of Greece proper, of " Helladic " for the earlier phase. " Mycenaean " can be used to cover the whole prehistoric culture of Greece only in the later Bronze Age, which in Crete and in the lands directly affected by Crete we call " Third Late Minoan." The word " Aegean " may be used, as I and others have used it, to cover the whole of the peculiar culture which dominated the Aegean and part of continental Greece during the Bronze Age, a culture of which the Minoan, Cycladic, and Helladic-Mycenaean are the chief divisions. But there were non-Aegean elements in the prehistoric culture of Greece, elements such as the so-called Minyan, possibly related to the west Anatolian civilization of Troy which appeared in continental Greece during the period under discussion ; and the Thessalian, even more distinct from the Aegean and forming a solid *bloc* in northern Greece which was but superficially effected by Aegean culture. Further there is the ancient Trojan culture and its congeners, in Anatolia, of which that of Yortan in Lydia is a type ; there is the known culture of Lycia and Caria of which the Phaistos Disk is our only relic, though we can see that the later Philistine invaders of Palestine must have sprung from this source. And there is the civilization of Cyprus before the Aegeans came to the island. All these must be considered, at any rate subsidiarily, besides the Aegean culture, in a general survey of Greek prehistoric civilization, and the Aegean culture cannot be treated adequately without some consideration of its neighbours. I have not therefore entitled these lectures simply " The Aegean Civilization of Greece." I might have spoken of the " Prehellenic Civilization of Greece " ; but while it is practically certain that the Aegean culture was non-Hellenic and prehellenic, so that as regards the greater part of the Greek area such a description would be correct of the Bronze Age culture, yet the Thessalian culture may well have been protohellenic and have belonged, at least in part, to the ancestors of the Indo-European Greeks of history. I might have spoken of " Heroic Greece," but the civilization of heroic Greece would mean to most that of the Homeric age ; the term somewhat begs the question, though we shall see that it can be justified. The term " Prehistoric Greece," though still correct, since we cannot read the Minoan inscriptions or the Phaistos Disk, is yet open to the objection that to most the word " prehistoric " connotes barbarism very different from the great, ordered, and artistic culture of Bronze Age Greece, which was further, though still prehistoric to us, as it lies beyond the ken of Greek historical knowledge, contemporary with the great civilizations in Egypt and Babylon which were by no means prehistoric. It does not belong to the prehistoric world, and it may not long remain prehistoric : we hope that it will not. The term " Preclassical " would bring me too far down in time, and would include the Early Iron Age. I am therefore disposed to prefer the term " Civiliza-

INTRODUCTION

tion of Greece in the Bronze Age," though this must not be understood to debar me from a brief sketch of the beginnings of Greek culture in the Later Age of Stone. The close of the Bronze and the beginning of the Iron Age however marks the transition from Greek prehistory to history and the definite close of my subject.

It is impossible in the course of six lectures to give more than a brief conspectus of the development of civilization in Greece during this period. The subject is now so complex, our knowledge of the culture and art of Greece during this period of high civilization is now so great, that I cannot do much more than trace the history of this remarkable ancient culture in outline, and give you an idea of the salient characteristics of the civilization of each successive period of its development, with the aid of pictures. The selection of these has been a work of difficulty. We have so much material. I should so like to shew you everything, that you must bear with me if I seem to shew you too much. My own work has, of course, lain specially in the direction of tracing the connexion between the Minoan culture and Egypt, a research in which Sir Arthur Evans himself is also specially interested. I shall therefore in these lectures lay stress on this side of our enquiry. It is the Eastern rather than the Western connexion of Early Greek culture that will absorb our attention so far as its foreign relations are concerned. The question of relations with the West in detail I must leave to the consideration of specialists in the lore of the West European Bronze Age.

The Bronze Age culture of Greece has a special interest for British readers, since, although its first discoverer was a German, and Germans have since taken a notable part in the study of one phase of it, the chief discoveries since the time of Schliemann have been made by Englishmen, Scots, Americans and Italians, and it is in the museums of Britain that the chief collections of " Minoan " and " Mycenaean " antiquities exist outside Greece (including Cyprus). The Museum of Candia is of course first with the treasures of Crete ; Athens second, with those of Mycenae, Vapheio, and elsewhere. Third is London. We omit Nikosia, as concerned only with Cyprian things. The British Museum contains the third most important Minoan collection in the world, owing to its possession of the capital objects from Enkomi in Cyprus (pp. 224 ff.) which rank with those from Knossos at Candia and from Mycenae at Athens. And in its stores of pottery from Ialysos in Rhodes and from Kalymnos it shows an unrivalled collection of typical " L.M. III" pottery (see p. 220 ff.) of the best periods and also of the decadence, which have lately been catalogued by Mr. E. J. Forsdyke.[1] Fourth comes Oxford, where the Ashmolean Museum worthily exhibits Crete as London does Cyprus and the Isles. But the Ashmolean, despite the care of Sir Arthur Evans, cannot compete with London in the possession of capital objects, and so must yield place. Constantinople has " L.M. III " vases from Rhodes and Kalymnos, like London, and may be placed fifth in the list. The Fitzwilliam at Cambridge has the new stone goddess, if she be genuine (see p. 171). The ivory and gold snake-goddess at Boston, Massachusetts, is the chief representative of Bronze Age Greece in America, where there are other objects at Philadelphia and the non-Minoan Cesnola collection of Cyprian pottery at New York. Berlin has vases, also Brussels, Copenhagen, and Rome ; vases from the Islands represent Cycladic and Mycenaean culture in the Louvre ; and Sicily has colonial Minoan pottery. We may indeed congratulate ourselves on the foremost place which British Archaeology has taken in the discovery and study of the oldest remains of Greece, and on their first-rate representation in our museums.

Quite recently attention has been drawn to the civilization and art of Bronze Age Greece by the work at Mycenae of Mr. Wace and the British School at Athens and by the renewed discoveries made by Sir Arthur Evans at Knossos, the private house of about 1600 B.C., with its frescoes of plants and flowers, of African apes amid Egyptian papyrus-plants, and of black Sudanese soldiers led by a Minoan (Fig. 139) ; its wall-inscriptions, the first of their kind discovered ; also the great road across Crete from the south coast to Knossos. The palace of Minos and its surroundings seem inexhaustible mines of archaeological treasures. For over twenty years (if we leave out the four years of the war) Sir

[1] *British Museum Catalogue of Vases,* Vol. i, Pt. i (1925).

INTRODUCTION

Arthur Evans has laboured at Knossos, and every year his spade has recovered to us something new and unexpected, adding to our knowledge of the wonderful Knossian culture of the Bronze Age. It is indeed a new world of ancient civilization that has been revealed, of which our fathers never dreamed, and which they would have deemed impossible. And it is one that means much more to us than the world of Egypt or of Assyria which the nineteenth century reconstituted for us, much more than the tomb of Tutankhamon or the sculptured palaces of Ashur-banipal. For the Minoan civilization was in part the ancestor of Greek culture, which is our own today : it is the firstfruits of the Greek genius that are here revealed to us : these Minoans were our own culture-ancestors.

It is this fact that has caused us to greet each new revelation of the Bronze Age culture in Crete and the neighbouring lands of Greece with expectancy and enthusiasm. The discovery of Greek Bronze Age inscriptions is undoubtedly the greatest archaeological triumph of the last half-century. It lacks only one thing to complete the triumph ; the decipherment of these inscriptions. As yet they are silent for us. We know the actual history of Egypt and Assyria, we do not yet know that of Bronze Age Greece their contemporary. The omens as yet are unfavourable. Attempts have been made to interpret the famous Phaistos Disk, discovered by the Italians in Crete, but with no success. They are merely guesses, often of the fantastic character which at once stamps them as improbable. All that can be done as yet has been done by Sir Arthur Evans. As yet in the matter of the true Cretan inscriptions (the Phaistos Disk is a foreign importation), he has identified the numerals and we can count in Minoan although we do not know the names by which the Minoans knew their numerals. Beyond this we can guess that some picture signs mean the objects which they depict. But this guess may often be wrong. Egyptian picture-signs do not always by any means mean the things they represent. Thus for instance in Egyptian the picture of an eye need not necessarily or always mean an eye, or even " to see " or " to weep." It may mean " to make," because the word " *iri*," to make, was the same as another word " *iri* " which

5

probably existed meaning the eye; ἶϱις, the *iris*, in fact. Knowledge of the complexity and peculiarity of Egyptian writing bids us to pause before we assume that Cretan inscriptions may soon be read. But when they are read we shall hear the true account of the events of which we distinguish confused echoes in the legends of the demi-gods, of the deeds of great men before Agamemnon and his compeers themselves, of the siege of Troy, of the Perseids and of the Atridae, of Minyans and Cadmeians, of Minos the lawgiver himself and his thalassocracy, of his relations with the Carians; we shall know the reasons for the migrations of the Philistines and the Sardinians and the Etruscans; what part the Phoenicians really played in the civilization of the Mediterranean; and many another prehistoric event or question will be made clear to us that at present we see only dimly apparent through the mist of Greek tradition, illumined rarely by the knowledge of historic happenings, derived from the records of Egypt and Mesopotamia. Till that day comes we must possess our souls in patience; but not in resigned and impotent patience. We do indeed wait for something to turn up, namely a bilingual Egyptian-Cretan or cuneiform-Cretan inscription which shall solve the problem at a blow; but we wait for it eager and alert to follow any clue which may bring us any nearer the goal even without the aid of a bilingual. And if it should be by Sir Arthur Evans himself that the solution is found well might he write " Finis coronat opus."

When I say that the reading of the inscriptions should give us an Ariadne-thread to lead us through the labyrinth of Greek legend to light, I should remind you that it is to the Minoans and their contemporaries in the Aegean and in continental Greece that the forgotten history enshrined in Greek tradition is to be assigned. They were the tribes of which the Greeks recounted the legends; it is in the legendary seats of the heroes at Troy, at Boeotian Thebes, and Orchomenos, at Mycenae, Argos and Tiryns, at Pylos and at Knossos, that the most important remains of the Minoan and its related cultures of the Bronze Age have been found, and at Mycenae the mighty Lion Gate and the tombs of the princes still remained above ground to be described

INTRODUCTION

faithfully to us by Pausanias as relics of the legendary days of the heroes.

It would seem therefore that I should, after all, have been justified in entitling this book "the Civilization of Heroic Greece." But heroic Greece to us is not the real heroic Greece of the excavations, but the poetical heroic Greece of Homer, the days of the Heroes described to a large extent in terms of Homeric days, as the days of Arthur and Uther Pendragon are described to us by Malory in mediaeval guise. And until the historical originals of Agamemnon and his predecessors and peers are disclosed to us as those of Osymandyas and Sesostris, of Sardanapalus and Semiramis, have been disclosed to us by the decipherment of the Egyptian and Assyrian inscriptions, to speak of the Bronze Age culture as the Heroic is (though our belief that it was that of the originals of the Heroes is hardly open to reasonable objection), to some extent begging the question or at any rate assuming what is at present not proven. We must wait for the proofs though they be long in coming.

To the fact that we cannot yet read the inscriptions is due our ignorance of much in relation to the Minoans that is connoted by the word " civilization." I cannot tell you anything of that subject beloved of the moderns, " economics," in relation to them, of the relation of " labour " and " capital," of the existence or non-existence of a Minoan " middle-class " between priest-kings and slaves, and so forth. I can only tell you that they certainly kept accounts and that commerce overseas flourished ; that their polity at the end of the second millennium B.C. was seemingly in many ways as highly-developed as that of Egypt or Babylon. I can tell you something of their religion and their dwellings, much of their burial-customs and writing, and more of their costume and arms. Whether they were great warriors or not we do not know : evidently they thought they were, but they fell before warriors stronger and more energetic than they. What I can tell you of them at far greater length than anything else is that they were great architects and artists : in some ways theirs was the most artistic, certainly the most aesthetic, civilization of the ancient world. We must therefore infer their general state of civilization chiefly from the remains of their art [1] discovered in the excavations. It is probable enough that the artists were organized in gilds.

I have spoken of the epoch-making work of Sir Arthur Evans, assisted by Dr. Duncan Mackenzie, at Knossos. Mycenae like Troy was the scene of the labours of the bearer of that other great name in the story of the discovery of heroic Greece, Schliemann. And the discovery by Schliemann of that circle of graves at Mycenae, described by Pausanias, with their marvellous treasures of gold in 1876, was the event that drew the attention of the learned world to the revelation of a new world of Greek antiquity. It was a discovery that at first provoked the incredulity of the sceptics and even the ridicule of the prejudiced and ignorant. But I should like to place on record here that a name honoured in Edinburgh, that of Professor Sayce, was associated from the first with Schliemann as that of a whole-hearted appreciator of the importance of the discoveries at Mycenae. That he may see the crowning of the work of Schliemann and Evans by the decipherment of the Minoan inscriptions is indeed to be hoped.

Naturally the best known of the excavations are those of Troy, Mycenae and Knossos. Many of my readers have probably in the comfortable days before the war, or since, visited Troy, Mycenae and the neighbouring Tiryns, and have landed at Candia to make the four-mile excursion to Knossos, or perhaps ridden a day's journey across Crete to the village of Hagii Deka, the modern representative of Gortyna, and have thence visited Phaistos and Hagia Triada. Some of us will well remember the old museum of the Syllogos at Candia, an ex-Turkish barrack, which with its dangerous wooden floors for many years safely housed the treasures of Knossos and Phaistos (Fig. 1). It is now replaced by a modern, if unbeautiful, building, which though safer in case of fire, is by no means earthquake-proof, as the event of June 1926 proved. Many will recall the round grey-green Acropolis-hill of Mycenae nestling at the foot of bare Mount St. Elias (Fig. 2), and the gorge between them which leads round past the great domed Tholos-tombs, the " Treasuries "

[1] For me, unlike Mr. Hogarth (*The Twilight of History*, p. 4 ff.) apparently, ancient civilization without art was not civilization.

INTRODUCTION

FIG. I.—THE OLD MUSEUM OF THE SYLLOGOS AT CANDIA

of Atreus and Klytaimnestra, as they are called, into the nook of Argos, ἐν μυχῷ Ἄργεος, where Mycenae stood. They will recall the

FIG. 2.—MYCENAE

FIG. 3.—THE LION-GATE, MYCENAE

Lion-gate (Fig. 3), and with it the stone circle surrounding the famous graves described by Pausanias (Fig. 4); of these five were found by Schliemann and the sixth was found after he had closed his excavations. Recently much important work has been done at Mycenae by the British School at Athens under the leadership of Mr. Wace, which has directed renewed attention to the famous site. Mr. Wace has come to some conclusions with regard to the great Tholos-tombs which are at variance with those usually held hitherto.[1] Instead

FIG. 4.—THE GRAVE-CIRCLE : MYCENAE

[1] See p. 147 ff., below.

INTRODUCTION

of regarding the most important of them as relics of the First Late Minoan period like the rest and the Acropolis-tombs, he would place them later in date, at the beginning of the Third Late Minoan Age (the "Late Mycenaean" properly so-called), when Knossos and Crete had ceased to be the centre of the Aegean world and power and dominion had migrated to the mainland. However this may be, (and we shall return to this matter later), we may be certain that the Acropolis burials are of the earlier time and probably are those of the immediate descendants of the Cretan colonists whom both archaeology and tradition tell us were the founders of the great civilization on the mainland.

Tiryns also was founded by these colonists. Its casemates, as they are called, of huge stone blocks, so huge that the place was fabled to have been built for King Proitos by the Kyklôpes, are so cyclopean that this low mass of rocks, piled up by human hands, seems one of the wonders of the world (Fig. 5). Here also recent work by the Germans has added much to our knowledge and has confirmed the Cretan origin of its builders, though the date of the casemates, which look so ancient, is probably as late as the fourteenth century B.C. All will remember the unforgettable view from Tiryns of the Gulf of Nauplia, framed between the heights of Palamidi and the opposite coast, with the little islet of Bourtzo in the midst.

FIG. 5.—TIRYNS

It reminds me of another view, in Crete this time, of the bay of Mylopotamos from Hagia Triada, with Kedros and Ida to the right and the lower ridge of Kophinos to the left, and the island of Paximadi, "The Cake," swimming between them (Fig. 6). Hagia Triada and Phaistos (Fig. 7) are indeed set in the midst of splendid surroundings, though we do not know if this had anything to do with their being

11

where they are. Still, rulers with such an eye for natural beauty as those who decorated their palace with the Cretan frescoes of plants and flowers, rocks and greenery, may perhaps be acquitted of the charge

FIG. 6.—HAGIA TRIADA WITH THE SEASHORE AT DIBAKI AND THE ISLAND OF PAXIMADI

that we habitually bring against the ancients of being insensible to the charms of nature.

FIG. 7.—PHAISTOS AND MOUNT IDA

Knossos (Fig. 8) can boast of no such surroundings. The low howe of Kephala on which it stands (Fig. 9) is uninteresting and the hill on the other side of the Kairatos beck is even less interesting, being but a

FIG. 8.—EXCAVATIONS AT KNOSSOS, 1902

dull stony fell. Only the view of Candia and the Island of Dia out at
sea, looking like a long swimming dragon pursuing its " calf," a smaller

FIG. 9.—KNOSSOS, 1926

13

island, have any interest, unless we except that remarkable fell Iuktas, on which Zeus (so the Cretans said) died, an idea that was peculiar to Crete and must have puzzled other Greeks. Iuktas is just an isolated cone, but from one point of view (not seen from Knossos) is like the head of a reclining man with features clearly marked (Fig. 10).[1] This may have something to do with its early sanctity. To the ancient Knossians we know it was a holy mount.

It was on the low Kephala hill that the chief centre of the Bronze Age art and culture of Greece was raised. We here see the maze of corridors and halls and stairways paved with shining gypsum, that Sir Arthur Evans has brought to light,—the lair of the Minotaur, the Labyrinth itself. Knossos, despite the tameness of its surroundings, arouses an interest that not even Troy with the memory of its great siege, or even golden Mycenae itself, with its memory of the tragedy of the Atridae, can rival. This is not due to the greater

FIG. 10.—MOUNT IUKTAS

splendour of its remains. It is due to the incomparable glamour that surrounds the place, the halo of weird, almost faery, legend with which it is invested. For it is the Labyrinth of Theseus and the Minotaur. Its mazy courts and passages are those through which, said Greek legend, Theseus found his way by the aid of Ariadne's thread and slew the Minotaur. To it, Plutarch says, went the ship with the black sail from Athens with the tribute of youths and maidens for the grisly Minoan bull, and thence Theseus sailed, forgetting, to Athens, where the aged Aigeus, not seeing the sign he awaited, cast himself headlong from the rock into the sea.[2] Knossos was the seat of the worship of that Zeus whose

[1] See illustration in Trevor-Battye, *Camping in Crete*, p. 183, reproduced above (Fig. 10).
[2] Prof. Bury (*Cambridge Ancient History*, ii, p. 476) would object to this referring of the

14

emblem was the double axe, the *Labrys* (Fig. 11), which really gave its name to the Labyrinth, the place of the double axe. And here took place the sports of the Minoan arena where young men and maidens dared (probably were compelled to dare for religious reasons) the dangerous and often sanguinary game of bull leaping, the *Taurokathapsia*, leaping in the face of the bull's charge and seizing his horns in the leap and turning a back somersault over him as he rushed, either to safety or to a gory death amid the trampling hooves. Over Knossos broods the spectre of the bull, the wraith of the Minotaur (Fig. 12). While we admire the beauty of Knossian civilization, we cannot forget that background of terror, that persisted in legend, and are

Minotaur story to the pre-Achaian days of Knossos and would put it in the thirteenth century B.C., because he believes that Minos was a pure Achaian (see pp. 18, 267 *n.* 2). But the Labyrinth and its bulls were not Achaian and belong to the fifteenth century and earlier.

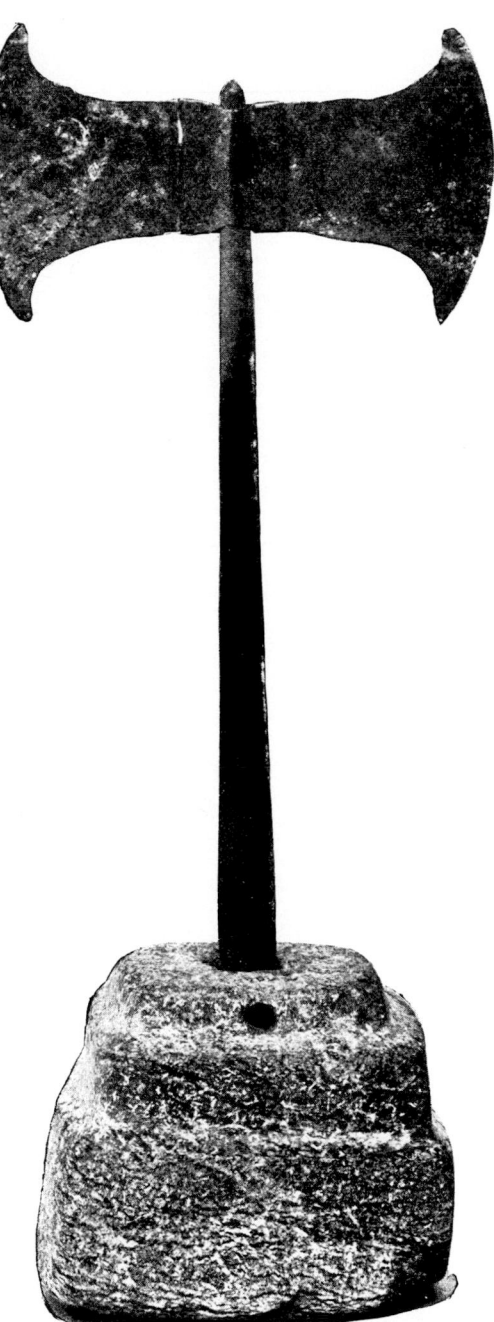

FIG. 11.—THE DOUBLE AXE

15

reminded unwillingly of Watts's terrible picture of the Minotaur brooding over the ramparts of Knossos, for the black sail from Athens across the sea spying.

FIG. 12.—MINOTAUR FIGURES FROM MINOAN GEMS AND A KNOSSIAN COIN OF THE CLASSICAL PERIOD
(*Enlarged*)

The hill of Kephala had been inhabited from the earliest days. Sir Arthur Evans has found beneath the buildings of the Bronze Age deep neolithic deposits, that take the place back as a human settlement far into the mists of antiquity, the beginnings of human activity in the Greek lands. Other sites such as Phaistos have neolithic strata beneath them no doubt, but none have been investigated as at Knossos, and it is the careful examination of the stratification of Knossos (Fig. 13) from the earliest days to the catastrophe of its final destruction (at the hands perhaps of avengers from Greece, who are personified in legend as Theseus the Athenian), that has led towards the construction of the chronological scheme on which our reconstruction of the development of Greek Bronze Age Civilization is based. This scheme is founded on

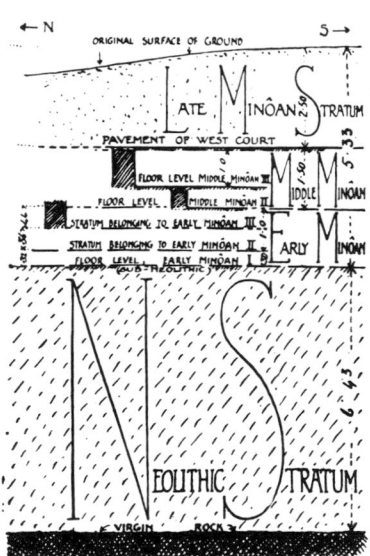

FIG. 13.—THE STRATA OF KNOSSOS

the experience of Knossos; but other excavations in Crete have shewn that with slight variations it is applicable in all its entirety to all their results also. And similar schemes for the Cyclades and continental Greece,

16

INTRODUCTION

based upon it, fit into it without difficulty. An enormous service has been done to the study of early Greek archaeology by Sir Arthur Evans; for the first time we have a reliable chronology of the development of the Bronze Age culture in Greece. Before this nothing was certain. We spoke of Mycenaean and pre-Mycenaean periods, the one earlier than the other. We knew the place of the latter period in time, because with its remains were found (as at Mycenae, at Ialysos in Rhodes and at Enkomi in Cyprus), Egyptian objects which invariably dated from the time of the Egyptian XVIIIth and XIXth Dynasties, and often bore the names of Pharaohs of these dynasties on objects which we knew were contemporary with them. No remains of later Egyptian date were found with them, so that we know that the Mycenaean age went back to at least as early as 1400 B.C. And the discovery of Mycenaean potsherds at 'Amarna, the seat of the XVIIIth Dynasty heretic king Akhenaton, confirmed this date. Then came Prof. Petrie's acute diagnosis of certain potsherds of the XIIth Dynasty (c. 2000 B.C.), found at Lahun or " Kahun " in Egypt, as Aegean and evidently pre-Mycenaean.

Crete now came upon the scene; Prof. J. L. Myres and Prof. Mariani published polychrome pottery, of the same kind as that from " Kahun," which had been found in the Kamarais cave on the south slope of Mt. Ida.[1] This Kamarais pottery then was contemporary with the XIIth Dynasty and so was at least as old as 2000 B.C. At Knossos Sir Arthur Evans found the same pottery in strata older than those which yielded the pottery that we had previously called Mycenaean, and knew dated to about 1400 B.C. or later. This relative position of these two strongly differentiated types of pottery has never been contradicted by other excavations, but has always been confirmed. The fact gave Sir Arthur Evans the basis of his scheme and to it he fitted all the other evidence he had amassed at Knossos.[2] It is now accepted by all who have excavated in Crete, or who have studied the excavations at first hand, and by those who know the Egyptian evidence upon which it is based and are entitled to express an opinion on it.

[1] See p. 74. " Kahun " appears to be a misunderstanding of *Il-lahun*, wrongly taken to be "il-*ahun*" (Cairene for "il-qahun," which does not exist).

[2] *Essai de Classification des Époques de la Civilisation Minoenne*, London, 1906.

" Using the Egyptian evidence as his guide,[1] and checking the results of excavation with its aid, Sir Arthur Evans finds that the Bronze Age pottery and with it the general culture of Crete divides itself into three main chronological periods : Early, Middle, and Late, each of which is divided into three sub-periods. To these periods of the Early, Middle and Late Bronze Age he has given the name ' Minoan,' after the great Cretan lawgiver and thalassocrat of tradition."

Prof. Sir Wm. Ridgeway objected to the name [2] because in legend the two Minoses (he was convinced that two kings of the name were carefully distinguished from each other) are connected with the later Achaian ruling houses, who belong to the very end of the period only (if indeed they do not come after it), and not with the Pelasgi, to whom the greater part of the Bronze Age culture is to be assigned. For him Minos was the destroyer rather than the creator of the " Minoan " culture. Prof. Bury[3] and Mr. Hogarth[4] seem to make much the same objection, and so, while they accept only one Minos, put the Minoan sea-power, the one in the XIIIth, the other in the XIVth century B.C., thus dissociating it entirely from the older Cretan sea-power which archaeological discovery proves to have existed in the XVth and before. We however know of no such Achaian sea-power in the thirteenth century from archaeological discovery, except such as may be deduced from Egyptian mention of raiding Achaian pirates, themselves hunted probably from their islands and seeking new lands to live in, or from doubtful references in Hittite cuneiform tablets (see p. 249). The certain Egyptian mention gives no hint of an ordered power such as was that of Minos in tradition ; and it is probable that the older Cretan thalassocracy has in later legend been brought down at least two centuries and assigned to the Achaians, who were not only seagoers but also Greeks. We cannot ignore archaeology, and depend only on literary sources, in attempting to reconstitute the early history of Greece. Those for whom archaeology provides hard sayings because it seems sometimes to invalidate literary traditions may prefer to believe that " Minos " represents an Achaian power, and so refuse to use the term " Minoan " of the pre-Achaian sea-dominion of

[1] I take the following sentences from my *Aegean Archaeology*, pp. 3, 4 (Medici Society).
[2] " Minos the Destroyer," *Proc. Brit. Acad.*, iv (1910).
[3] *Cambridge Ancient History*, ii, p. 475. [4] *The Twilight of History* (Oxford, 1926), p. 7.

INTRODUCTION

Knossos ; but it must be remembered that the actual question is one of names only, and as the positions of Professors Ridgeway and Bury and Mr. Hogarth's view that the Cretans of L.M. III were Achaians and so the only true "Minoans" are disputable, there can be no objection to the retention of a name which, though it may be considered by some fanciful, is convenient, and has undoubtedly come to stay.

"We cannot properly speak of 'Knossian' periods, because many of the Minoan periods, though represented at Knossos, are far more fully represented elsewhere in Crete. And we cannot speak of 'Early Cretan,' 'Middle Cretan' and so forth, without the addition of 'Bronze Age,' when the term at once becomes clumsy. So we continue to use the term 'Minoan,' which has universally been adopted, with the chronological scheme which it denotes. For the sub-periods numbers are used, and we speak of 'Early Minoan I,' 'II,' 'III,' 'Middle Minoan I,' and so on, abbreviating them for convenience to the phrases 'E.M. I, II, III,' 'M.M. I, II, III,' and 'L.M. I, II, III.'"[1]

Sir Arthur Evans and Dr. Duncan Mackenzie go further in subdividing even these periods into "a" and "b," as "L.M. Ia," "L.M. IIIb," and so on ; but these archaeological nuances are at present more in place in purely archaeological publications than in lectures intended for a public, learned indeed, but not purely archaeological, and so I have eschewed them as much as possible in what follows.

"For the Cyclades a corresponding scheme of successive periods of development has been worked out, which we know as 'Early Cycladic I' (E.C. I) and so on, till in the Late Minoan period the Cycladic culture was absorbed in that of Crete."[2]

Mr. Wace and Dr. Blegen have recently put forward[3] a similar scheme for the Bronze Age culture of the Greek mainland, based largely upon the recent American excavation at Koràkou near Corinth, directed by Dr. Blegen, which has for the first time given us a connected view of the development of the Aegean culture in Greece, and some idea of its relation to the indigenous native culture. Excavation has not, however, yet proceeded far enough in Greece for us to obtain the same certainty that we have in the case of Crete. To the Neolithic age, which in the south is well represented in Corinthia only, succeeded an Early "Helladic" or Premycenaean age which corresponds to the Early Minoan and Cycladic, then a Middle Helladic age

[1] Hall, *Aegean Archaeology*, p. 4.   [2] *Ibid.*   [3] *Korakou*, p. 121.

corresponding to Middle Minoan and Cycladic, and then the so-called
" Late Helladic periods I, II, III," of Wace and Blegen corresponding
to the Late Minoan periods I, II, III of Crete, " Late Helladic III "
corresponding with Late Minoan III and being the true Mycenaean
period of Greece generally. Cretan influence, first apparent in the Early
and revived in the Later Middle Helladic period, dominates in the " Late
Helladic " I and II. In the Mycenaean period the cultures are fused.
The exact contemporaneity of Early Helladic III and Middle Helladic
I with Early Minoan III and Middle Minoan I are at present uncertain
and the whole scheme is evidently provisional. Sir Arthur Evans
rightly objects to the use of the term " Late Helladic " to signify
the Mycenaean age, because he considers that there was a definite
break between the old " Helladic " inhabitants of Greece and the
Minoan conquerors, so that the later Mycenaeans were not properly
speaking " Helladic " at all. And he regrets the abandonment of
the existing and intelligible term " Mycenaean." The German scholar
Fimmen [1] proposed to retain the term " Mycenaean " and use " Early,"
" Middle," and " Late Mycenaean " for three periods corresponding
in time to M.M. III, L.M. I, II, and L.M. III respectively. But
here " early " does not correspond in time to " early " in Crete and
the Cyclades, and it would seem best to refer to these periods as the
First, Second and Third Mycenaean (Myc. I, II, III). The first
two are so strongly influenced by the invading contemporary
Cretan culture that their products are practically identical in style
with those of L.M. I–II,[2] and on this account it is quite usual to
extend the term " Minoan " to the mainland, and to speak of " Myc.
I " pottery as " L.M. I," though it may have been made as well as
found in Greece proper. It would then seem advisable while using
the term " Helladic " for the earlier *periods* (not styles, see Preface)
before the coming of the Cretans, to abandon it for the later age and
speak of this as " Mycenaean."

The remains of the Neolithic period in Greece are usually sparse
and disconnected. While in Crete and in Northern Greece we have

[1] *Zeit u. Dauer der kret.-myk. Kultur*, p. 27 ff.   [2] See p. 216.

INTRODUCTION

evidence of a long period of neolithic occupation and development, and there is distinct evidence of neolithic inhabitance of the Peloponnese, in Cyprus there is hardly any trace of neolithic culture[1] (Fig. 14), and in the Cyclades absolutely none. In fact whatever we may think of Cyprus there is little doubt that in purely neolithic days the southern Aegean islands were not inhabited at all. The Copper Age begins in the

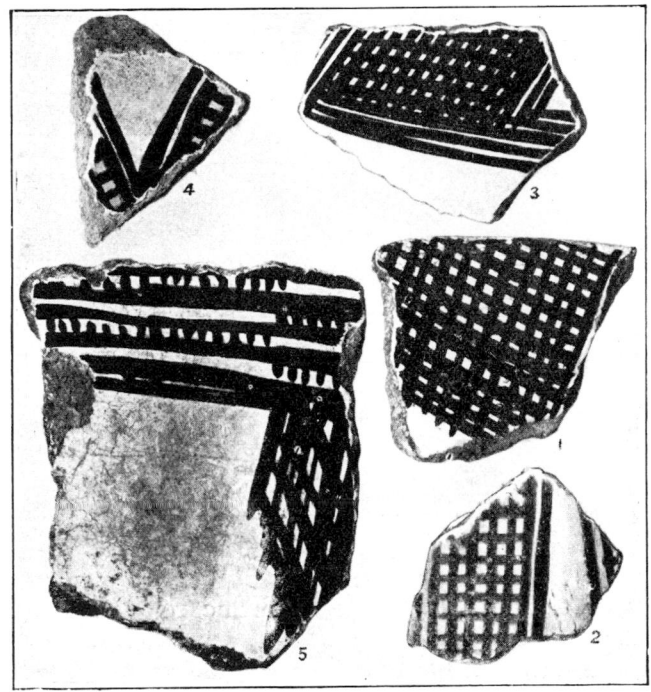

FIG. 14.—CYPRIAN NEOLITHIC (?) POTTERY (BRIT. MUS. CATALOGUE)

islands without preface, and we can have little doubt that its inception in them marks the beginning of their occupation by colonists from Anatolia

[1] Mr. Einar Gjerstad has recently discovered a Neolithic deposit in Cyprus, which is published in the *Antiquaries' Journal*, Jan., 1926. The pottery from Kalavasò (Fig. 14, above) in the British Museum (Hall, *P.S.B.A.* 1909, p. 311 ; Forsdyke, *Brit. Mus. Cat. Vases*, I, p. 15) is considered by Gjerstad to be possibly Neolithic. It is a very thick coarse ware, compared by Forsdyke with "some red or white Thessalian neolithic pottery," and also resembling Cappadocian neolithic. The red-painted (on white slip) lattice decoration is of a type common to neolithic and chalcolithic pottery from Thessaly to Babylonia (see Hall, *loc cit.* and *al 'Ubaid*, pp. 9, 10), quite different from anything Aegean.

and Crete, hardly earlier than 3000 B.C. On the mainland the Peloponnese had neolithic occupants, who have left traces of their presence in their pottery, some of which is identical with that of neolithic Thessaly, in Argolis and Corinthia, thus proving an extension south of the Isthmus of Corinth not only of the characteristic neolithic culture, quite distinct from that of Crete or Asia Minor, of Northern Greece, but also, a little later, of the invading (chalcolithic) culture of the Dimini-people (see p. 62) from the north.[1] Its remains are found in Boeotia, Phokis, and Thessaly, chiefly in Thessaly (see p. 61). Its pottery and the little else that we have discovered of its remains are entirely unlike the Cretan. Black ware of the Danubian type has also been identified in central Greece, as well as the native ware, and may point to some early incursion from the North.[2] In Boeotia and Phokis it was overlaid or dispossessed by the coming of a new cultural (and evidently racial) element which, we may if we wish, call the Helladic, certainly akin to the Cretan-Cycladic. In Thessaly the local culture passed from the neolithic to the metal-using stage, apparently without experiencing conquest from the south, about the same time. We shall refer later to this peculiar Thessalian culture.

Reverting to Crete, the *locus classicus* of the neolithic age in that island is of course Knossos, where deep neolithic strata underly the buildings of the later palace. Neolithic remains are found elsewhere in the island as at Magasà near Palaikastro on the east coast, including a very simple house of undressed stone blocks.[3] It is of the simplest " but-and-ben " type with a small square entrance-chamber and a larger room within. At Magasà were found stone axes and knives of obsidian, which shew that although Melos may have been as yet uninhabited, neolithic sailors went there to get the precious obsidian. The obsidian flakes from Knossos were found with so great a number of cores that it is evident the Melian obsidian (Fig. 15) was imported

---

[1] Blegen, *Korakou*, p. 123. Three-colour Dimini pottery (see p. 62, Fig. 66) is common in Corinthia (Gonia and Corinth). In Boeotia copper occurs in very early deposits.

[2] Frankfort, *Studies of Early Pottery*, ii, p. 42 ff.

[3] Dawkins, *B.S.A.*, xi, p. 260 ff.

to be worked in Crete, which is what we should expect if the Cyclades were still uninhabited. Probably it was the obsidian that first drew

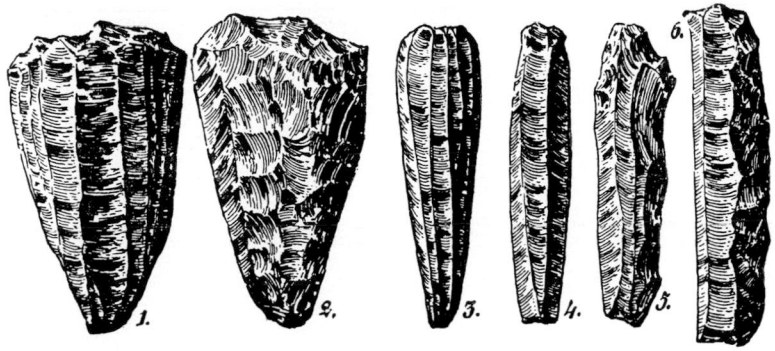

FIG. 15.—OBSIDIAN FLAKES AND CORES: MELOS
(*Actual size*)

Cretan and Anatolian colonists thither, and then to the rest of the Cyclades (Fig. 16). After a time some of the seekers of obsidian would settle on the island with their women, and then the general desirability of the uninhabited islands on other grounds would attract other colonists. But the colonization did not take place till after the beginning of the Copper Age ; and obsidian was in demand for sharp knives and razors and arrowheads until comparatively late in the Bronze Age[1].

Caves and rock shelters were also used as habitations by the neolithic Cretans.

FIG. 16.—MELOS AND ANTIMELOS

There is one at Magasà (Fig. 17), and a cave which had had neolithic inhabitants was found by Professor R. C. Bosanquet near Praisos,[2]

[1] On obsidian see Wainwright *in Anc. Egypt*, 1927, p. 77 ff.   [2] *B.S.A.*, viii, p. 235.

also at the eastern end of the island. At Phaistos, as at Knossos, there are neolithic deposits beneath the palace,[1] but they have not yet been examined properly.

It is only at Knossos that this examination has been carefully carried out (Fig. 13). The hill of Kephala, as Sir Arthur Evans has said,[2] is a

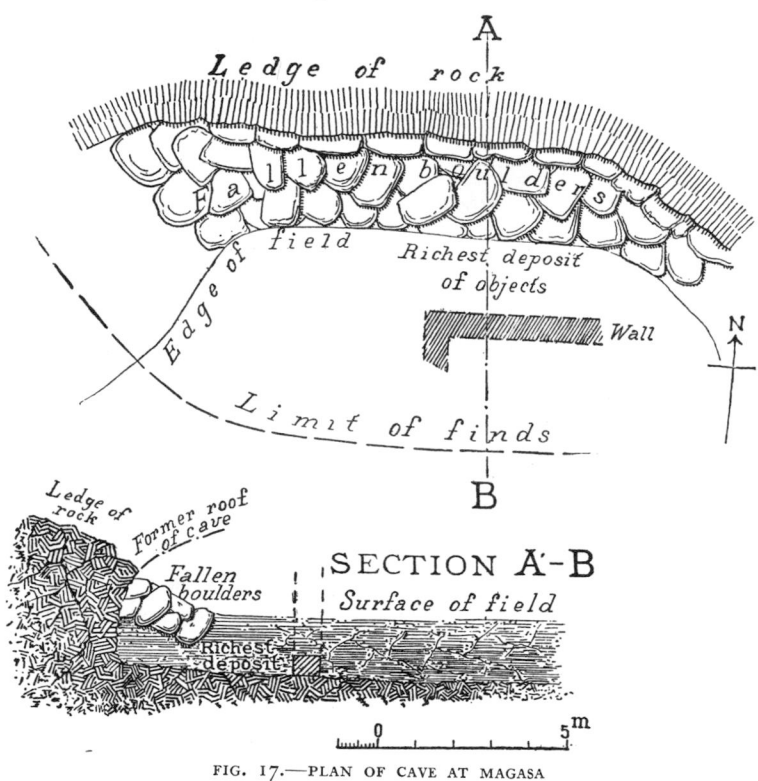

FIG. 17.—PLAN OF CAVE AT MAGASA

regular "Tell" (as the town mounds, piled up by the successive deposits of the ages in Egypt, Syria and Mesopotamia, are called in Arabic). Above the virgin rock of Kephala are no less than 6·43 metres (24⅓ feet) of neolithic strata before the earliest Bronze Age deposits are met with, and the whole of these strata, covering Knossian civilization during the Bronze Age, from about 3000 to 1300 B.C., and the slighter traces from that day to this, when Knossos was uninhabited, together measure

[1] Pernier, *Mon. Ant.*, xii; *Rend.*, 1897, p. 268 ff.; Mosso, *Mon. Ant.*, xix.
[2] *Palace of Minos*, i, p. 34.

only 5·33 metres (about 19 feet).   Calculations of time derived from these figures are of course liable to error and highly untrustworthy. At some periods deposits accumulated more quickly than at others, and there are all sorts of other *imponderabilia* which must be taken into account.   But Sir Arthur Evans does not see how the neolithic period can be taken to represent less than 4,500 years at the very least, so that human habitations at Knossos must go back at least to about 8000 B.C. at the most modest computation.   Some moderate probability may be claimed for this date because these strata at Knossos do not seem to have suffered ever from much disturbance, and the development of neolithic culture from its most primitive beginnings can be studied by the aid of the pottery fragments found at different levels, up to the beginning of the Bronze Age, whose culture develops in Crete directly out of that of the preceding period, just as the whole of later Cretan culture of the Bronze Age develops, each successive period out of the other, without a single break, till the end.   The population remained the same from the Neolithic period till the end of the Age of Bronze.

Very ancient relations between Crete and Egypt[1] are suggested not only by resemblances in the material culture of both countries in the early period, which the recent excavations of M. Xanthoudides in the Mesarà have brought to light,[2] but by a study of Egyptian and Minoan religion, chiefly in respect to cults of the Delta, where among other things the double axe appears as a religious emblem,[3] and the characteristic Cretan figure-of-eight shield is the same as the shield of the goddess Neith of Sais (Fig. 18), which probably goes back to early neolithic days and the possible origin of at any rate one element of the Cretan race in

[1] See Evans, Huxley Lecture, 1925 (*The Early Nilotic, Libyan, and Egyptian Relations with Minoan Crete*), R. Anthrop. Inst.   The comparison of the trefoil or star-like representation of the spots on a cow's or bull's hide, which is seen on the sacred cow of Hathor in Egypt and on Mycenaean representations of bulls on Cyprian vases, made by me in *P.S.B.A.*, *loc. cit.*, in 1909, is also paralleled in Sumerian representations of bulls.   The idea must have had a common source, but as this is not necessarily to be sought in Egypt, the argument drawn from its occurrence obviously loses force.

[2] Xanthoudides, *Vaulted Tombs of Mesarà*, *passim*.

[3] Schäfer, *Grabdenkmal des Königs Ne-user-Rě'*, p. 120.   I owe this reference to Prof. Newberry.

northern Africa.[1] The lower Egyptian representation (in connexion
with the worship of Ptaḥ) of the hawk painted on the *Ded* symbol
(originally a conifer[2]), is paralleled in the Hagia Triada Sarcophagus (see
p. 224) of the bird (possibly a magpie) perched on a pollarded tree-

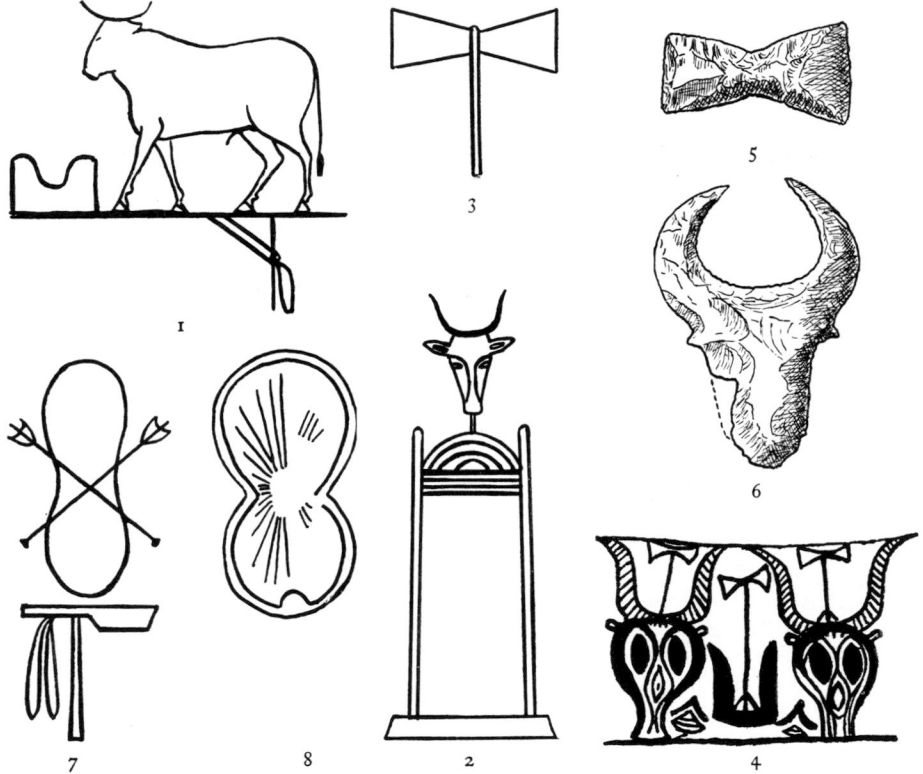

FIG. 18.—BULLS, DOUBLE-AXES, BUCRANIA, AND HORNS OF CONSECRATION

1–3, Egyptian ; 4, Minoan ; 5, 6, predynastic Egyptian flint double axe and bucranium (Brit. Mus.) ;
7, shield of Neith ; 8, Minoan shield

trunk (Fig. 19).[3] The relation of the Ægeans and the other Mediterranean races, on the one hand to the peoples of north Africa, and

[1] Newberry, *Liverpool Annals of Archaeology*, i. The double-axe appears as an amulet
in Upper Egypt in predynastic times (Hall, in *Essays presented to Sir A. Evans*, p. 42).

[2] Newberry, *Egypt as a Field for Anthropological Research*, Brit. Assoc. 1923 ; Sect. H.
Presidential Address, p. 14.

[3] Hall, *Proc. Soc. Bibl. Arch.*, 1909, p. 144 ; pl. xvii. The Egyptian representations are
from scarabs of the XIXth Dynasty (13th cent. B.C.), the Minoan from the Hagia Triada
sarcophagus (14th cent.) (Fig. 19.)

on the other to those of Anatolia, is not improbable. The national costume of the Cretans, the simple waist-clout and its developments (Fig. 20), the kilt and the baggy breeches, is not a natural European

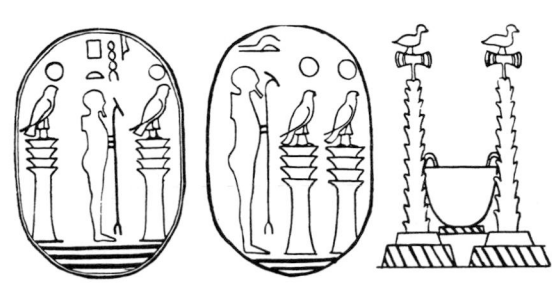

form of clothing, and its actual resemblance to the similar basic costume of the Egyptians and still more to that of the Libyan tribes, with its characteristic penis-sheath or codpiece (also Cretan), is so marked as to argue intimate relationship.[1] The

FIG. 19.—EGYPTIAN AND CRETAN BIRD AND TREE CULTS : ROUGHLY CONTEMPORARY REPRESENTATIONS (XIXTH DYNASTY ; L.M. III)

physical resemblance of the Minoan Cretans to one of the dominant Egyptian types is evident from the Egyptian representations of them (see p. 201). In feature, expression and figure they resembled each other more than either resembled either the Semites or the Anatolians. That the brunet Mediterranean race sprang from the southern shore

of that sea is probable, and that, while the predominant aspect of Minoan religion seems Anatolian, there were common elements in the cults of Crete and Egypt, is undeniable. While the majority of the original neolithic inhabitants of Crete probably came from Anatolia (as a study of Cretan religion and place-names indicates), another element may well have come in oared boats from the opposite African coast, bringing with them to the southern plain of the

FIG. 20.—MINOAN WAISTCLOUT AND CODPIECE

Messarà the seeds of civilization that, transplanted to the different conditions of Crete, developed, when touched by the magic wand of copper that was stretched out to them first from Asia, and possibly later also from Egypt, into the great Minoan culture, a younger, more brilliant, and less long-lived sister of that of Egypt.

[1] Mackenzie, *B.S.A. Ann.*, xii, p. 233 ff. Cf. Evans, Huxley Lecture, 1925.

Until the psychological moment arrived the Cretan culture was almost static, as we have seen, for more than 4,000 years. But still there was a slow but sure development through the neolithic strata of Knossos. We can trace the gradual improvement of the pottery for example. The neolithic culture of Crete does not go back to the beginnings of the period. The earliest inhabitants did not arrive until what we may call the proto-neolithic age elsewhere was over. Three stages

FIG. 21.—NEOLITHIC POTTERY FROM KNOSSOS (BRIT. MUS. CATALOGUE)
(*Scale* ½)

of the later neolithic can be distinguished at Knossos by the criterion of the pottery, which improves with time.[1] In the earliest strata it is of rough burned clay, in the second it is much blacker and is often chased ; the raised geometric decoration of simple design being later filled in with white and, rarely, red pigment (Fig. 21). A rippled surface is also found, probably effected with a bone spatula. There is no resemblance whatever to the Egyptian predynastic pottery of Upper Egypt

[1] Evans, *Palace of Minos*, p. 32 ff.

at any rate. The ware is European in appearance. Forms so far as they can be reconstituted are limited to rude cups, small handled vases and trays. Then in the upper neolithic strata the decoration dies out and the pottery improves, and it is possible that the pottery-baker's oven first made its appearance. Pottery whorls, and rude figures of birds, oxen, and human beings covered with incised decoration occur

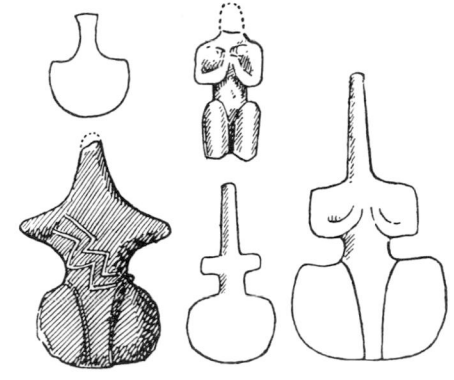

FIG. 22.—STEATOPYGOUS FEMALE FIGURES

in the Middle Neolithic age : the women being steatopygous like other female figures from all over the Mediterranean and south-east Europe at this period (Fig. 22). Bone implements such as needles and shuttles are common and prove the existence of the textile industry. The stone implements of serpentine, jadite, diorite, and obsidian are of the usual types, such as celts of the common European and Asiatic style (rarely found in Egypt, except in the Fayyūm region, but common in Mesopotamia) and the round or ovoid maceheads which are found from Italy [1] to Mesopotamia [2] and are common in Egypt (Fig. 23).[3] The fact that the celt

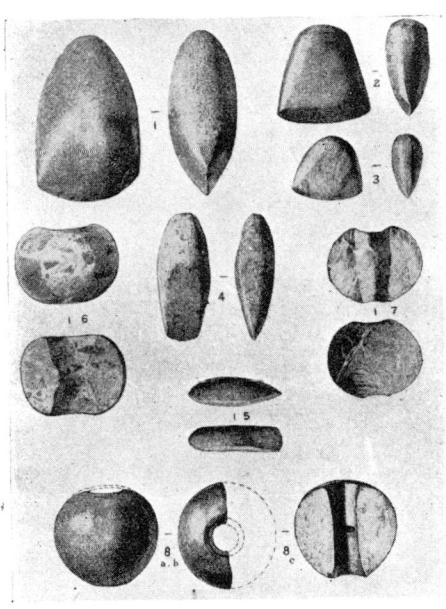

FIG. 23.—STONE CELTS AND MACEHEADS FROM KNOSSOS (⅕ c.)

[1] Peet, *Stone and Bronze Age in Italy*, p. 250.

[2] Hall, *J.E.A.*, 1922, p. 253.

[3] In Egypt they appear to have come from outside, probably from Syria, about midway in the predynastic age. The original Nilotic form is the inverted conical or " plate " macehead, which seems unknown elsewhere (see Wolf, *Bewaffnung des altäg. Heeres*, p. 4 ff.).

is so uncommon in Egypt is perhaps a hint that this form of stone implement came to Crete and Egypt from Anatolia. Did the ovoid macehead come to Crete from the northern Egyptians or from Asia ? The whole series of the Upper Egyptian stone implements of the pre-dynastic period is with exception of this macehead, which is in Egypt late predynastic, very different from the Greek or Asiatic. The neo-lithic and chalcolithic pottery of Upper Egypt was equally distinct from that of Greece and Asia. We know next to nothing of the Lower Egyptian culture of the predynastic age except the few hints that may be obtained from finds in the Fayyūm, so cannot yet say whether its pottery and its flints were entirely different from those of the south, and akin to the Mediterranean types, though the celts of the Fayyūm argue an approximation to Cretan and Anatolian types in the north and a peculiar black pottery found at Gizeh and Turrah has been considered to belong to the prehistoric Delta.[1] Yet very early Cretan connexions with Libya and the Delta are evident, as has been said. With the prehistoric culture of Upper Egypt, however, no genuine resemblance can be seen except in the matter of the macehead, which again, like the celt, may really have come to the Aegean through Anatolia from Meso-potamia.

The resemblance between certain early Minoan figurines and some of the predynastic age found in Upper Egypt will be discussed on p. 44. The resemblance is striking, but there are difficulties in the way of its acceptance as proof of connexion on account of the later date of the Cretan figurines : this difficulty however may be explained away (see p. 45). If so, we have a connexion with Upper Egypt which may mean that a Libyan or Lower Egyptian type of figurine had been adopted in Upper Egypt. Another type of figurine, the steatopygous woman, common in early Crete as elsewhere, existed in early pre-dynastic days in Upper Egypt, but, as has been said above, is so uni-versal that little can be deduced from the fact. But late-predynastic Upper Egyptian stone vases were imported into Crete in the Early Minoan period, and locally imitated there. Now these Egyptian

---

[1] Scharff, *Grundzüge der äg. Vorgeschichte*, p. 45 ; Junker, *Turah*, p. 2, Fig. 1.

stone vessels of the predynastic age must have been fashioned with aid of emery, which, so far as we know, can only have come from the Aegean and from West Anatolia. The island of Naxos was and is its chief source. Enough emery for the manufacture of the older predynastic (neolithic) Egyptian stone vessels could no doubt be imported in very small boats. The finer stone vessels of the late predynastic age date to the period when copper was already used, but emery must have come to Egypt long before then, for the ruder stone vessels of early predynastic times must also have been made with the aid of emery. And if the obsidian found in Egypt in pre-dynastic days [1] was really Melian and not (as may be possible) Armenian or Abyssinian[2], the neolithic connexion is again attested in very early days. It was probably maintained in oared boats, until the invention of masted ships made it possible to transport copper ore to Crete in bulk and the age of regular commercial connexion began, with the resulting swift development of Cretan civilization.

As we have said, the introduction of the use of metal was marked by no violent revolution, no conquest by copper-using invaders, and destruction or displacement of a distinct stone-using population. The neolithic Knossians passed gradually from the use of stone to that of metal. They developed their usage of metal themselves, though they probably got their first knowledge of it from outside. There is little copper in Crete except, it is said, on the west coast, in the eparchies of Kydonia and Selinos, and on the island of Gavdos to the south-west (Fig. 24).[3] The scoriae of copper-smelting operations in the isthmus of Hierapetra do not prove that copper was found there, though Hatzidakis is of opinion

---

[1] Petrie, *Prehistoric Egypt*, p. 43.   [2] *Cf.* Wainwright, *Anc. Egypt*, 1927.

[3] Hatzidakis, *Ann. Brit. Sch. Athens* (*B.S.A.*, xix, p. 47, quoting the observations of M. Bambakas : cf. Xanthoudides, *Vaulted Tombs of the Mesará*, p. 27. M. Bambakas has personally inspected and analysed copper from deposits in Gavdos, Kydonia, and Selinos. M. Xanthoudides, to whom I have referred this matter, kindly writes to me as follows :—that M. Kalikeris, a Cretan chemist, informs him that as well as in Gavdos there are deposits of copper ore at Prase and Phourne in Kydonia, and also in Selinos, but these are poor except at Phourne, where there is a good deal of native copper, as well as remains of ancient mining.

that the copper was actually dug on the spot.[1] No doubt, however, native copper was both mined and smelted in Gavdos and on the west coast, and used for the manufacture of weapons at least as early as the Third Early Minoan period ; [2] but we can hardly doubt, in view of the chronological conditions for the beginnings of the use of metal in Crete and further east, that copper originally came to Crete from the East, and possibly also from Egypt, and that it was not until the knowledge of it had reached the island that its own copper was discovered and made use of.[3]

FIG. 24.—GAVDOS, FROM THE S.W.

Copper was already in use and the chalcolithic age had begun in Egypt before the middle of the predynastic age, probably before 4000 B.C. Most weapon-forms are of the simplest " flat-based triangle " type ; imi-

[1] Communicated by M. Xanthoudides.   There seems to be however no real proof of the Minoan date of these scoriae, or that the copper was found nearby.   All that can be said is that in view of the importance of the Hierapetra district in Minoan times it is quite possible that the smelting operations were Minoan.

[2] M. Bambakas is of opinion (*B.S.A.*, xix, p. 47) that the metal of the E.M. III dagger-blades found by Hatzidakis at Arkalokhori was Cretan ; he says : " I drew this conclusion from the fact that all the specimens analysed contained silicic acid.   I have examined copper ores from many parts of Crete, Gavdos, Kydonia, Selinos, etc., and all contained this acid in large quantities."   M. Xanthoudides concludes that the Minoans certainly used their own native copper, mined in Crete.   He agrees however (*Vaulted Tombs*, p. 27) that they obtained their first knowledge of metal from elsewhere ; only " this does not exclude the supposition that, once they had learned how, the Cretans made use of native copper."

[3] Even then we cannot be sure that the native copper in use was not merely that of Gavdos, for we have no traces of Bronze Age inhabitants of Western Crete, which may well have been covered with dense and impenetrable forest till late Minoan days, though of course small settlements along the coast may have existed.

32

tated from a flint dagger,[1] like the most primitive forms of Cyprus and Crete. We do not know yet whether Egypt first communicated the knowledge of working copper to Cyprus, whether this knowledge came to both from Syria, or whether Cyprus is the original home of metal working (Fig. 25). It has been argued that the comparative absence of neolithic remains in Cyprus is in favour of the latter conclusion. Chronological conditions however are in favour of Egyptian or Asiatic priority. We do not know yet that we can trace back the archaeological history of Cyprian culture to a period sufficiently early to make it possible for her to have communicated the knowledge of copper to Egypt, still less to Asia. The probabilities are against the Cyprian claim.[2]

FIG. 25.—A CYPRIAN STAMPED PIG OF COPPER (BRIT. MUS.)

The first Cretan copper weapons are of the simplest type like those of Cyprus and Egypt. But as those of Cyprus may be much later in date,[3] it would seem that Egypt has the better claim to have been their originator, unless the Cretan, Cyprian, and Egyptian types all originated in a common source. Copper, it may be supposed, was first brought to Crete by the copper-users and not fetched by the stone-users. We

[1] Petrie, *Prehistoric Egypt*, pp. 25, 50.

[2] Mr. Einar Gjerstad tells me that he is strongly of opinion that the working of copper was not a Cyprian invention at all, but came to Cyprus with the first invaders from Anatolia, who brought the making of red pottery akin to that of Yortan. They were copper-users when they arrived, and naturally exploited the Cyprian stores of the metal to good advantage. There is much to be said for this view. (On Cyprian copper see Dussaud, *Civ. Préhell.*, p. 249.)

[3] We do not know that the Cyprians were not still in the neolithic stage much later than 3000 B.C. If, however, it is argued that the resemblance between some early Egyptian and Cyprian dagger-blades argues that there was a connexion in early days, it seems to me more probable that it means influence on both countries from a common source.

3

need not, it is true, suppose that the neolithic Cretans were unable to build boats with their stone tools that would be capable of navigating the Mediterranean, at any rate without getting out of sight of land. How else did they fetch obsidian from Melos ? They no doubt made big mastless oared boats such as we see in Fig. 26, represented on pots from the Cycladic isle of Siphnos, which with their abrupt prows and fish-banners are closely paralleled in predynastic Egypt.[1] But still bigger boats, able to transport great copper ingots or masses of ore, can only, one could think, have been built satisfactorily with the aid of copper tools and may naturally be supposed to have been the invention of the original copper-users of the East.

The question of a possible original derivation of the Cretan knowledge of copper and silver from Spain I need not discuss in view of its much more probable origin nearer home in Cyprus (?), Egypt (Sinai), or Anatolia, and in this connexion we must remember the great body of archaeological evidence that closely connects Crete, not only with Anatolia, but also with predynastic Egypt : evidence that conclusively points to the connexion across the sea. In view of the fact that Crete had not much copper and no place nearer than Cyprus, or the Anatolian-Syrian coast, whence she could get it, while Egypt had at any rate some quantity of copper close at hand in the Sinaitic peninsula,[2] we might conclude that Crete perhaps got her first knowledge of copper from Egypt. As a matter of fact we know that the Egyptians built big boats not only for the Nile but also for the sea [3] in predynastic days, and that under the Old Kingdom their ships went to Phoenicia to

---

[1] The fish-banners on the high prow are notable, as a fish-banner of the same kind is seen on a predynastic boat from Naqada shewn in Fig. 26. Also *cf.* the prow with Fig. 28.

[2] It must be pointed out that the Egyptian copper-sources in Sinai can never have been very great. The observations of mining engineers go to shew that not very much copper was actually mined there at all, the Egyptian miners having chiefly sought for turquoise (communicated by Mr. J. A. Rickard). Since there is practically no copper in the Eastern Desert, most of the Egyptian copper then probably came through Syria from the North. (But *cf.* Lucas, *J.E.A.*, 1927, p. 165 ff.)

[3] On the remarkable gold-handled knife of predynastic date found at Gebel al-'Araq, we see, apparently, predynastic Egyptian boats of the Red Sea coast (Bénédite, *Le Couteau de Gebel el-'Arak*, Mém. Fondation Piot, 1916 ; *cf.* Hall, in *Cambridge Anc. Hist.* i, 581).

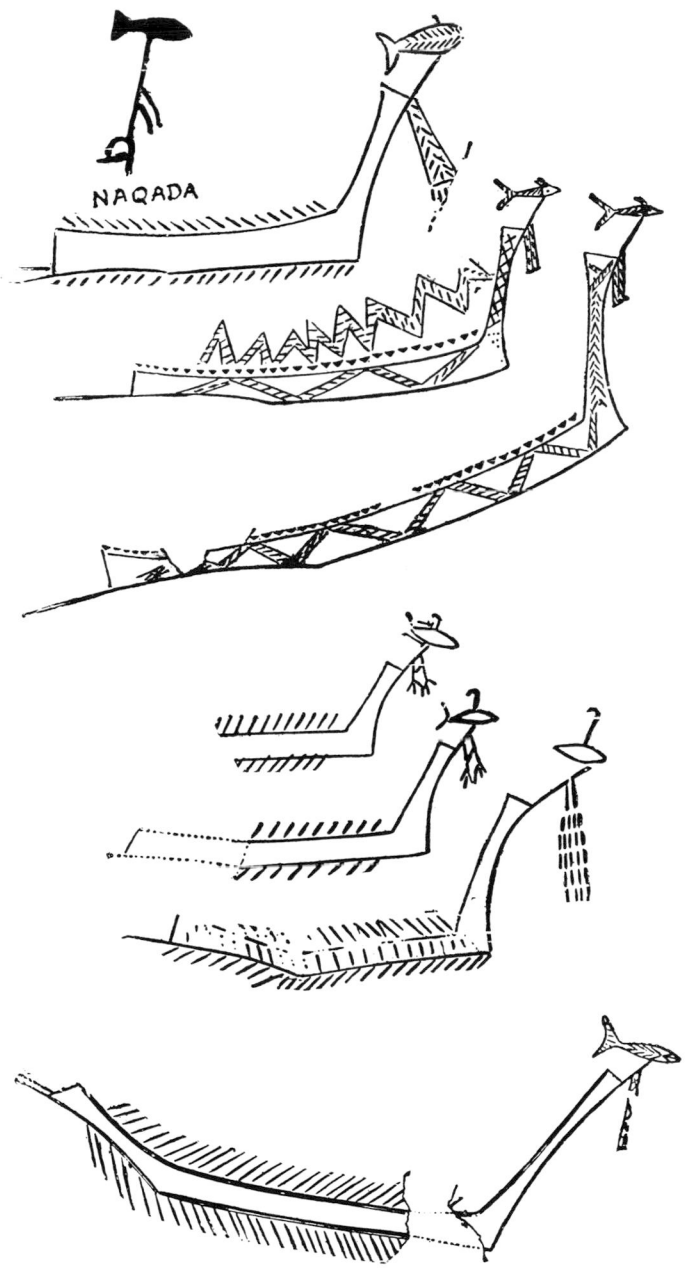

FIG. 26.—EARLY AEGEAN MASTLESS OARED BOATS, WITH FISH-ENSIGNS

35

fetch the great trunks of the cedars of Lebanon, that were so valuable in woodless Egypt. We know too that the Egyptians had already navigated the Red Sea in predynastic times; and that Byblos was already held from the sea by the Egyptians as early as the time of the IIIrd Dynasty, we see from the recent excavations of M. Montet. It would therefore be by no means an impossible supposition that Egyptian sailors were the first to carry copper to Crete, which then would owe her first knowledge of it to Egypt, as all the eastern world did, according to Prof. Reisner, in spite of the comparatively small extent of the Sinaitic mines. But Prof. Newberry has recently pointed out [1] that Egypt can provide no tree long enough, straight enough, or strong enough to make a ship's mast. The great

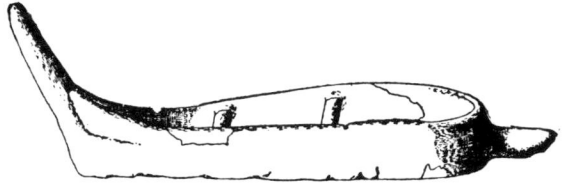

FIG. 27.—CLAY MODEL OF A HIGH-PROWED MINOAN BOAT WITH CROSS BENCHES AND RUDDER (?) ($\frac{1}{3}$)

Nile boats of predynastic days were generally mastless; we have only one representation of a prehistoric Egyptian boat with a mast (Fig. 28). Egypt in fact could not mast her boats until she became acquainted with the cypresses, cedars and pines of Lebanon and Cyprus, or equally of Crete. The Egyptians were then not the first to fetch the cedar trunks of Lebanon or the cypresses of Crete : the sailors of the Isles and the Syrian coast must have brought them to Egypt. I pass over the theory that the Egyptians may have fetched them from Syria by land. We can hardly think of them dragging the tree-trunks all the way from Lebanon over the rough ways of primitive Palestine with ass or ox transport, when sea transport in boats of the Syrian coast dwellers would be so much more direct and profitable. But then the

[1] *Egypt as a Field for Anthropological Research*, p. 18.

INTRODUCTION

Syrians and Cretans or other northerners must have built the ships and they probably used copper tools to do so. Since there is so little native copper in Crete, are we not justified in the conclusion that the knowledge of copper and of the building of big ships came to both Crete and Egypt from Syria, and to Cyprus later, either thence or from Anatolia ? To Syria the knowledge of copper must have come from the Asiatic *hinterland*, where we do not know, or when. The Babylonians used weapons

FIG. 28.—A PREDYNASTIC EGYPTIAN SQUARE-SAILED SHIP ; *c.* 4000 B.C. (BRIT. MUS.)

of copper as early as the Egyptians, probably earlier,[1] and of far more highly developed type. It came to them by land no doubt from the same source. Personally I consider the Asiatic theory the most

[1] Copper daggers of highly developed type, analogous to those of the Twelfth Dynasty (*c.* 2000 B.C.) in Egypt, date in Babylonia at least as far back as 3000 B.C. One of that date, of the time of the First Dynasty of Ur, was found by Woolley at Tell al-'Ubaid, near Ur, in 1924 (*Antiq. Journ.*, iv, pl. xlviib). And since then he has in 1927 made most remarkable discoveries in a cemetery of the First Dynasty and earlier of a gold dagger with a golden sheath, and of electrum and silver socketed axe-heads, which put anything of the kind and time known in Egypt into the shade. The evidence seems to me now to incline decidedly in favour of the greater antiquity of the Sumerian weaponsmiths.

probable, and that copper first reached both Egypt and Crete from Asia *via* Syria. Then in Egypt as in Crete and elsewhere the native stores of copper would be utilized : Egypt had them in Sinai.

And these Syrian sailors : how else can we describe them but as Phoenicians ? Who dares to speak of Phoenicians in the fourth millennium B.C. ? Yet there must have been seafarers in Phoenicia then. And whether they were already Semitized or not, the people of the Syrian coast were as much Phoenicians in the fourth as in the first millennium B.C.[1] So that while holding that the Phoenicians were but common carriers of culture then as later, carriers of the knowledge of copper, not its inventors, yet I think we must credit them, as probably as the Cretans, with at least a part in the one great invention that made distant seamanship possible, that of the mast, for they had to their hands the great straight trees of Lebanon, as the Cretans had, Sir Arthur Evans points out, their cypresses.[2] Such is the conclusion to which Prof. Newberry's acute observation of the absence of mast-making wood in Egypt has led me. If it seems a digression from my theme, I must point out that it is a conclusion of moment to the origin of the Greek knowledge of metal. That the prehistoric Greeks owed it at least partly to the Phoenicians,[3] whom of late we have been accustomed to despise, is a curious conclusion, and one that would rejoice old-fashioned archaeologists. But I do not see what we can call Syrian mariners at this time except Phoenicians.

Yet direct connexion between Egypt and Crete in the early days before the invention of the masted ship is distinct enough. Whether Cretan or Syrian sailors introduced the masted ship into Egypt, the Egyptian ships could and did go to Syria, and if they could go to Syria they could also go to Crete, and that the Cretans came uninterruptedly to Libya and Egypt is possible enough. Fig. 29 shews later Cretan

---

[1] Personally I think that the inhabitants of the Syrian coast were already semitized and true Phoenicians long before the end of the fourth millennium B.C., and so differ from Köster, *Schifffahrt, etc., des östl. Mittelmeers*, pp. 3, 4.

[2] Evans, Huxley Lecture, 1925 ; *The Early Nilotic, Libyan, and Egyptian Relations with Minoan Crete*, p. 10.

[3] Some knowledge of copper may have come directly through Anatolia by land.

representations of ships on seals. The suns and moons shewn behind the vessels undoubtedly refer to length of voyages. An exactly similar convention is seen in European medieval representations of ships; *cf.* on the seal of the town of Dunwich.[1]

In the second lecture we shall begin to trace the story of the development of the Greek civilization of the Bronze Age.

[1] Lacroix, *Science and Literature in the Middle Ages*, Fig. 197.

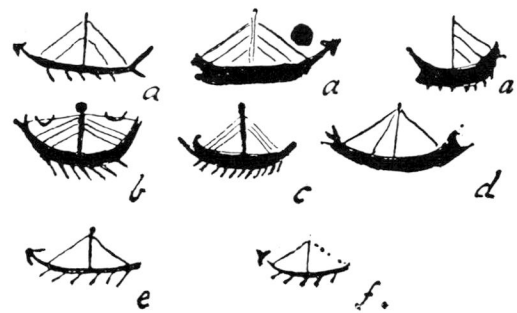

FIG. 29.—CRETAN MASTED AND OARED SHIPS

butterfly arrangement, in black or red on buff (Fig. 31). Forms while remaining more primitive develop, and the beaked jug or prochous appears with usually a round not flat base as if modelled after a gourd.[1]

Important evidence of the date of the First Early Minoan period is afforded by the presence at Knossos of the imported Egyptian vases

FIG. 31.—E.M. I–II POTTERY : DARK OR LIGHT DECORATION (HAGIA PHOTIA AND MOCHLOS)
($\frac{1}{3}$; $\frac{1}{2}$)

of late predynastic (Fig. 32) and early dynastic types already mentioned, and of local Cretan imitations of them (Fig. 33). The original vases would not be imported at any other date than their own ; the early

[1] Frankfort, *Studies in Early Pottery*, ii, sees in these shapes a dependence of the early Minoan potter on Anatolia (Yortan types, etc.). Anatolian influence in Cretan forms is possible and probable enough.

42

FIG. 32.—IMPORTED EGYPTIAN PREDYNASTIC STONE VESSEL

nations did not collect ancient foreign curios. They are not likely to have been often imported before the beginning of the Bronze Age, when commerce on a large scale and in bigger ships became possible,[1] but fragments of them occur in a late-neo-lithic house at Knossos (*J.H.S.*, 1924, p. 261). They do not belong to the second Early Minoan period, which was contemporary with the third to sixth Egyptian dynasties, as Egyptian and imitated Egyptian objects of that period shew.[2] They can therefore

FIG. 33.—IMPORTED EGYPTIAN PROTODYNASTIC STONE VESSEL WITH CRETAN IMITATION (ASHMOLEAN MUSEUM) ($\frac{1}{5}$)

[1] And when of course the emery necessary for their production could have been imported into Egypt, if it came from the Aegean, in bulk. The older types of predynastic vessels are not found in Crete, only those of the chalcolithic (late predynastic and early dynastic) period.

[2] For a conspectus of the evidence, see Xanthoudides, *Vaulted Tombs of Mesarà*, p. 128 ff.

43

small round Laputa-like island, off the north coast of Crete, from which it is separated by only a few yards of water (Fig. 44). In

FIG. 44.—THE ISLAND OF MOCHLOS

early Minoan days it was a peninsula, being the isthmus between two harbours ; the whole has sunk since Minoan days and the two harbours

FIG. 45.—STONE AND POTTERY VASES : E.M. II ; MOCHLOS ; SHEWING BEGINNING OF SPIRAL DECORATION $\left(\frac{1}{6}\right)$

have become a sound. On the island thus formed Mr. Seager [1] found houses and tombs of the period we are describing. Chief among the

[1] *Mochlos, op. cit.*

50

triumphs of this work are firstly a series of small vases and vase-lids in steatite and coloured stones (Fig. 45), some purely Minoan (among which should be specially noted the lid on which is a hound lying, in high relief (Fig. 46), a splendid piece of naturalism,[1] and the oldest Minoan sculpture), some of them imitated from Egyptian originals, one (Fig. 48) being a very close copy in Cretan marble of a type common in the VIth Dynasty in calcite or aragonite (Fig. 49) ;[2] and secondly a number of gold chains, necklaces, bracelets, diadems, and pins with their heads in the form of flowers and leaves, which

FIG. 46.—STONE VASES AND LID WITH DOG : MOCHLOS ; E.M. II ($\frac{1}{2}$ TO $\frac{2}{3}$)

FIG. 47.—POTTERY DEER : E.M. II ($\frac{1}{4}$)

are among the most unexpected revelations of Cretan art (Fig. 50).

We are now of course in the full tide of the age of metal. Copper is still used in Crete, bronze, as in Egypt, not having

[1] Fig. 45. Cf. Fig. 47, a deer in pottery, found by Xanthoudides in the Mesarà.

[2] Seager, *Mochlos*, pl. ii, M.3, p. 80 ; Hall, *J.E.A.*, i, p. 114 ; Evans, *op. cit.*, p. 92. Fig. 48 shews a characteristic marble cup of this period side by side with similar Egyptian forms of the VIth Dynasty (Fig. 49).

made its appearance (though at Troy and the Cyclades it seems to

FIG. 48.—MINOAN IMITATION OF VITH DYNASTY EGYPTIAN STONE VASE : MOCHLOS ($\frac{4}{5}$)

have appeared from Anatolia before 2000 B.C.)[1]; weapons are still somewhat primitive in type, consisting chiefly of short triangular daggers (Fig. 51); but luxury tools too, in the shape of tweezers, have made their appearance, as they had long before in Babylonia.[2] A silver dagger that may belong to the previous age was found at Koumasa by Prof. Xanthoudides (Fig. 52).[3] Silver also occurs at Mochlos, as elsewhere at this time, but the main treasure is of gold. One makes the comparison at once with the golden treasure that Schliemann found in the second city of Troy, and with reason, as the two are more or less contemporary. Schliemann believed that his second city of Troy was the Homeric city,

FIG. 49.—EGYPTIAN VITH DYNASTY STONE VASES ($\frac{4}{5}$)

[1] Frankfort, *Studies*, ii, p. 151. [2] At Ur, *c.* 3000 B.C. or earlier.
[3] Evans, *op. cit.*, Fig. 71.

52

but even the sixth goes back as far as the Middle Minoan period, as the occurrence in it of "Minyan" pottery shews.[1] The third to fifth settlements were ephemeral, and we know little or nothing of their culture. The second city we know was contemporary with the Early Cycladic period and with the second Early Minoan period in Crete

FIG. 50.—GOLD JEWELLERY : MOCHLOS : c. 2600 B.C. ($\frac{1}{3}$)

and lasted into Middle Minoan times, and so dates to c. 2800–1900 B.C.[2] On its cultural importance see Frankfort, *Studies*, ii.[3]

Above the rude neolithic settlement at Hissarlik comes the village of the chalcolithic period, that is the First City : then the copper, bronze and gold-using Second City with its imposing walls of crude brick on a

[1] Forsdyke, *Brit. Mus. Cat. Vases*, i, p. xiv.
[2] Frankfort, *loc. cit.*, p. 152, n. 2. [3] Also Childe, *Dawn of Eur. Civ.*, p. 62.

53

FIG. 51.—COPPER DAGGERS, TWEEZERS, AND
CHISELS : MOCHLOS ($\frac{1}{4}$)

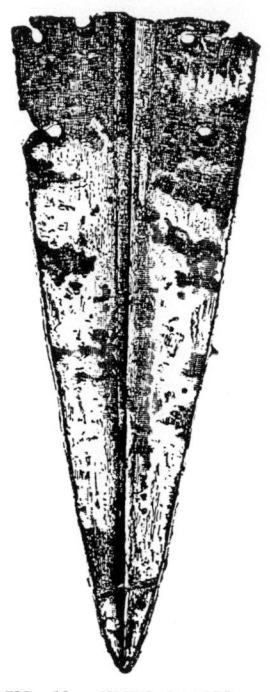

FIG. 52.—SILVER DAGGER :
KOUMASA ($\frac{1}{2}$)

stone foundation,[1] a characteristic that connects Troy (as might naturally be expected from its position on the Asiatic mainland) rather with the great Babylonian culture to the east and its ramifications than with Crete that had developed no such great walls, and in its insular position did not need them. The Trojan gold, "The Treasure of Priam" as Schliemann, thinking that this was the Priamid city, called it, with its pins (Fig. 53) and chains and gold and silver vases (Fig. 54), is curiously parallel to the treasure of Mochlos, and so alike are they that their contemporaneity could be indicated for this reason as well as on general grounds of chronological probability. Evidently the Trojans were already great metal workers,

[1] Dörpfeld, *Troja und Ilios* (1902).

FIG. 53. — GOLDEN
PIN WITH SPIRAL
DECORATION :
SECOND CITY,
TROY ($\frac{7}{8}$) (BERLIN.)

54

and it was natural that this should be so since they had at their back the metal resources of Anatolia, especially its silver and its gold. The silver of the ancient east nearly all came from Anatolia, except in later days when it also came from Spain, and the silver-working of the Hellespontine region and the gold of Pactolus are traditional. Though some may have come from Egypt, probably most of the Mochlos gold came from Anatolia, as did also the silver for the dagger (Fig. 52), and many other silver objects of this period. We

FIG. 54.—GOLDEN VASE : SECOND CITY, TROY : (BERLIN : MUSEUM FÜR VÖLKERKUNDE) $(\frac{1}{4})$

may then regard Cretan work in the precious metals as largely of Anatolian (and so perhaps ultimately of Babylonian) origin. But the

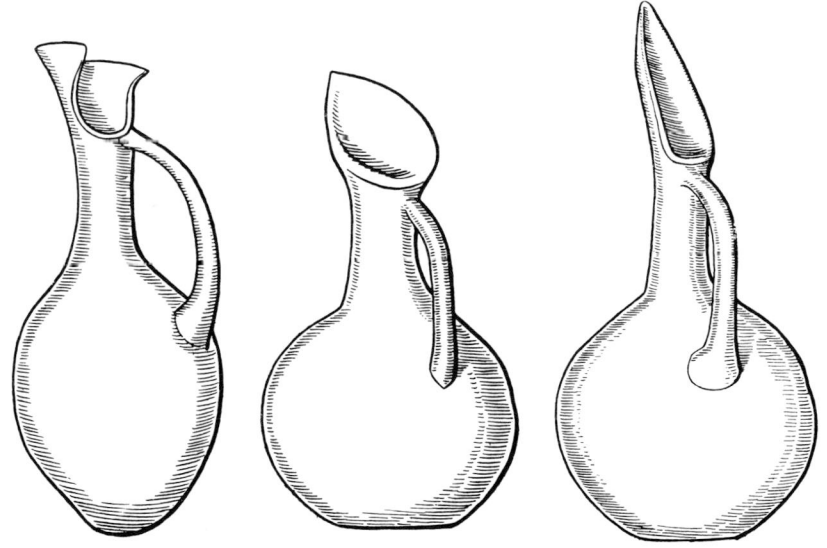

FIG. 55.—TROY-YORTAN TYPE POTTERY FROM EUBOEA

pottery of Anatolia, whether the painted geometric style of the northern inland region or the cruder black to brown wares of Troy and their red and black relations further south along the coast, as at

55

Yortan,[1] akin ultimately to the red and black wares of Syria, in no way affected the native development of the Aegean ceramic, though at one moment the island of Euboea was occupied by an Anatolian invading tribe that brought there its pottery of the Troy-Yortan type (Fig. 55).[2]

Between the pottery of Troy and that of Crete at this time there

exists no connexion whatever. The Trojans used their own style of black (later brown) ware with its peculiar "owl-headed" vases (Fig. 56), high kantharos-like handles, and incised decoration. The influence of metal on pottery is already visible, especially on the cups which are paralleled in gold and silver.

We find in the gold work at Troy a motive of decoration that also now occurs for the first time in Crete and the Cyclades on stone; the spiral, which obviously originated,

FIG. 56.—"OWL"-VASE: TROY II.

partly at any rate, in wire-work (Fig. 53). We are now to find the spiral adapted to pottery and to stone vases and platters in the Aegean, and this not at first in Crete, but farther north in the Cyclades, as is natural.[3]

We have seen that the Cyclades were probably colonized from Crete, as also probably from Anatolia in the early chalcolithic period. As in Crete the first early Cycladic pottery shews the imitation of the old burnished black neolithic ware, by the use of a black wash on which patterns were incised and often painted white. But the Cycladic pottery soon shows characteristic divergence from that of Crete.[4] Vases

---

[1] Forsdyke, *Brit. Mus. Cat. Vases*, i, p. 1 ff.   [2] Childe, *J.H.S.* xxxv, p. 205, Fig. 4.

[3] An E.M. III bucchero kylix from Arkalokhori in Crete (see above, p. 47) is figured by Hatzidakis, *R.S.A. Ann.*, xix, p. 38, and described as ornamented with an irregular spiral design, faintly impressed on the inside of the lip, which "is possibly the earliest example of the spiral yet found on Greek soil" (p. 40). Sir A. Evans considers it merely an imitation of wood-graining, not a spiral at all (*Palace*, p. 58). The oldest Cretan spiral is on a small vase from the Mesarà (Xanthoudides, *l.c.*), which is of stone. Then comes an E.M. III vase from Mochlos (Seager, *op. cit.*, pl. Va.), of pottery.

[4] Frankfort, *Studies*, ii, p. 49, finds strong Danubian traces in the oldest Cycladic ware, which do not exist in Crete.

56

at first are lacking in form and look as if they were intended to imitate the sea-urchin (Fig. 57); then the characteristic " duck-vases " (Fig. 58) develop, which are related to the Cretan beak-spout pots, but already shew divergence, and resemblance to the characteristic leather jug (" black jack ") types of Asia,

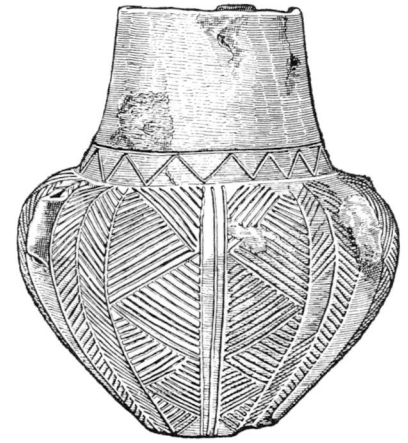 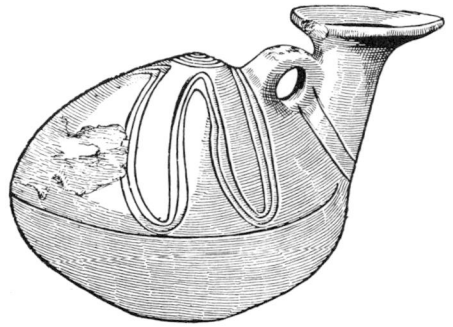

FIG. 57.—E.C. I " SEA-URCHIN " VASE ($\frac{1}{3}$)   FIG. 58.—E.C. I " DUCK " VASE ($\frac{1}{5}$)
(BRIT. MUS. CATALOGUE)

which are common in Cyprus and Syria to a much later time. This divergence is fully marked in the second Early Cycladic period (Fig. 59).

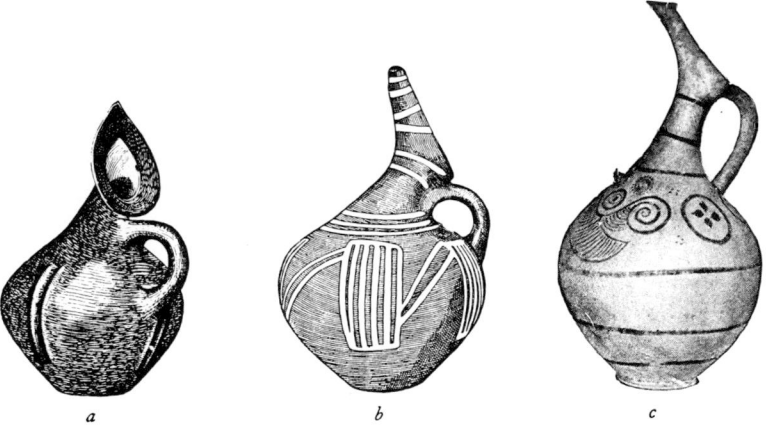

a   b   c

FIG. 59.—THE CYCLADIC PROCHOUS: (a) E.C. II, (b) AND (c) M.C. (a and b, $\frac{1}{6}$; c, $\frac{1}{8}$)
(BRIT. MUS. CATALOGUE)

We can already see the Egyptian influence on Crete carried on to the Cyclades in a vase with the Egyptian lily-petal design (Fig. 60).[1]

[1] Hall, *Aegean Arch.*, pl. xiii, 5.

The red or black varnished ware (*Urfirnis*) which is so characteristic of the Greek mainland is also found in the Cyclades, where

FIG. 60.—E.C. VASE WITH EGYPTIAN LILY-PETAL DESIGN (BRIT. MUS.) ($\frac{1}{2}$)

it may have originated (see below): early Cycladic pottery " is essentially the same as the Helladic ware."[1] Our knowledge of the development of the Cycladic pottery is derived chiefly from the excavations of the successive settlements at Phylakopi in Melos, conducted by Sir Cecil Harcourt-Smith and the British School at Athens, twenty-five years ago.[2] The stone cist-graves of the Cyclades (E.C. II–III) had been known long before and had been described by Bent and Dümmler, with their characteristic lugged vases and pyxides of white marble (Fig. 61), and their small flat stone idols of the same material (Fig. 62).[3] These idols were in E.M. III imported into Crete where they appear to have been valued.[4] On two of the pyxides of Siphnian stone from Amorgos, one made in the shape of a granary, the other in the shape of a coni-cal lidded basket (Fig. 63), we

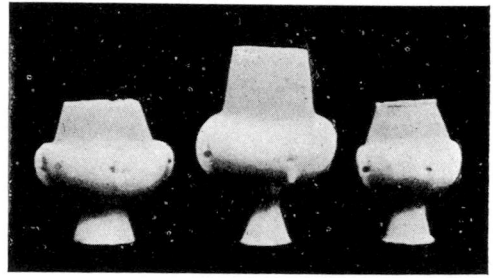

FIG. 61.—CYCLADIC LUGGED VASES OF PARIAN MARBLE (ASHMOLEAN) ($\frac{1}{8}$)

find the important appearance of the spiral coil decoration transferred

---

[1] Forsdyke, *Catalogue*, i, p. xxviii.   [2] *Excavations at Phylakopi in Melos*, 1904.

[3] I am unable to find any reason to suppose, with Childe, *Dawn of European Civilization*, p. 48, that the " finer type " of Cycladic idol may be of Sumerian origin. The Sumerian made figures of nude women (goddesses), but why should not the Cycladic people have done the same independently ? They are merely non-steatopygous figurines, and they and the steatopygous figures are closely connected.

[4] Xanthoudides, *Vaulted Tombs of the Mesará*, pl. vii.

to the ornamentation of the stone surface from that of gold wire-work or pottery-ornament to which it properly belongs.[1]

It was not long before this beautiful motive passed on from the Cyclades to Crete, where in the Second Early Minoan period it first appears on stone and in the Third on pottery. Thence it passed to Egypt, where again somewhat later, at the beginning of the XIIth Dynasty (*c.* 2200–2000 B.C.), it makes its first

FIG. 62.—CYCLADIC MARBLE FIGURINES (ASHMOLEAN) (¼)

appearance in the incised decoration of the bases of scarab seals, soon to be combined with the lily in a typically Egyptian motive, which then came back to Crete and was used, as we shall see, by the Minoan artists with effect in its Egyptian form. There is now no doubt that the spiral was thus brought into Egypt from the Aegean.[2] Where the wire spiral originated is an important question. Personally, I look to Anatolia and ultimately to Babylon, to the metal-workers of the Caucasian region and their Elamite or Sumerian developers for its origin. And in this connexion it is significant that it appears on the golden *étui* found by

FIG. 63.—AMORGIAN PYXIS WITH SPIRAL DECORATION

Woolley at Ur in 1927, which dates to at latest 3000 B.C.[3] This is the oldest true spiral known, and it is of *appliqué* wirework. Curiously

[1] See Tsountas-Manatt, *Mycenaean Age*, Figs. 133, 134 ; Bent, *J.H.S.*, V, 47 ; Dümmler, *Ath. Mitth.*, xi (1886). [2] Hall, " The Relations of Aegean with Egyptian Art," *J.E.A.*, i, p. 115. The true spiral motive was unknown in Egypt till now. The disconnected whorls on some predynastic pots are mere imitations of stone markings, and never developed into a spiral design. [3] *Brit. Mus. Quarterly*, 1927, pl. XXa.

enough, the gold dagger-sheath of the same date (*c.* 3200–3000 B.C.), also found by Woolley this year at Ur, and mentioned above (p. 37, n. 1) has the triangular fret decoration which we also see in the Amorgian pyxis !

Some would derive the spiral decoration on pottery from " the Continental North," the " Black Earth " and Danubian centres of neolithic culture, where spirals appear early.[1] If so, we find two independent foci of origin for the spiral : in metal wire-work from Troy, Anatolia, and eventually Babylonia (see p. 59), and in ceramic ornament from Central Europe.

The early Cycladic culture extended to the Asiatic mainland, at its south-east corner, where remains of this period have been found on the Myndos peninsula, near Assarlik.[2] It would seem probable enough that the native Carian or Lelegian population of this region was thus early influenced by the Cretan-Cycladic culture. We may notice in this connexion the famous archaeological report of Thucydides (i, 8) that in his own time Carian graves had been discovered on Delos. There can be little doubt that these were graves of early Cycladic type like those described above in Amorgos and Pelos, and that a traditional connexion between Caria and the Cyclades caused them to be identified as Carian. The Carians were supposed to have ruled the Aegean before their expulsion by Minos, and it may well be that their early civilization, of which we know practically nothing, was akin to that of the Cyclades. From Tchangli, near the site of the Panionion on Mount Mykalè, " have come other vases of the later Cycladic types of which Phylakopi in Melos yielded an abundant harvest "[3] (see p. 79). Their subjugation by

[1] This view is favoured by Childe, *Dawn of European Civilization*, p. 27, and Frankfort, *Studies*, ii, p. 116. I do not consider it to be proved, though of course it is not impossible. Is it not likely that ideas of this sort came originally from the East and South to Central Europe rather than the reverse way ? The Babylonian wire-spirals date from 3000 B.C. at latest, and are probably older. Cucuteni II must date about 2000 B.C., because it contains Minyan ware : it may be later. Is Cucuteni I as old as 3000 B.C., as it should be if the spiral came thence to the Aegean, where it appears well before 2500. Cucuteni I is contemporary with Erösd in Hungary, where copper is already found in the lowest levels (Childe, *Dawn of European Civilization*, pp. 156–7). Had copper already reached Hungary from Anatolia as early as 3000–2700 B.C. ? On Mediterranean connexions with the Danubian region *cf.* Childe, *ibid.*, p. 176, and *Essays presented to Sir A. Evans*, p. 1 ff.

[2] Hogarth, *Cambr. Anc. Hist.*, ii, p. 554.   [3] Hogarth, *loc. cit.*

"Minos" may well date to the Middle Minoan period, when Cretan influence appears so strong in the Cyclades as to argue political domination of the islands (p. 138). But Lycia, further south, seems from the evidence of the Phaistos Disk to have had a separate culture, more distinct from that of Crete, and arguing political independence (p. 135).

From the Cyclades the Cycladic-Cretan or (as we may now call it) Aegean culture passed on to the mainland of Greece, probably somewhere about 2800 B.C. The early inhabitants of the Peloponnese and of central Greece (see p. 22) were probably conquered by the newcomers[1], who brought them the "glaze" or rather varnish-paint technique in pottery. This varnish-paint, as in the Cyclades, often covers the whole body of the vase. It is usually (so far as continental Greece is concerned) known by the German name of *Urfirnis*, "primaeval glaze". But it should be remembered that this Greek lustrous paint was not really a glaze, like that of Egyptian faience. Though it was fused, there was no glass in it, and lustrous or varnish-paint is a more correct term for it.

In central Greece the newcomers overthrew and overlaid, besides elements possibly of Danubian origin (p. 22), a native neolithic to chalcolithic culture of distinct character and promise of development, exemplified in Corinthia, at Chaironeia and Orchomenos in Boeotia, Drachmani in Phokis, and Lianokladhi in the Spercheios Valley, and at Sesklo, Zerelia, Tsangli, and Tsani in Thessaly, which in Thessaly lasted for centuries without changing its character or making much use of metal.[2] The Othrys range seems to have formed a barrier which the Aegean conquerors did not pass. This native neolithic culture is characterized by its hand-made but fine pottery, often with painted cross-hatched and "comb" designs, very different from the burnished black of Crete with its incised white-filled patterns (Fig. 64). At first (neolithic) the colour was the simple red of the ware itself, and then we find

---

[1] This hypothetical earlier invasion is not to be confused with the later invasion of Cretans from Crete in the Middle Minoan period, which started the "Mycenaean," or mainland form of the Cretan culture (see p. 140).

[2] Wace and Thompson, *Prehistoric Thessaly*, 1912 ; Frankfort, *l.c.*, ii, p. 11 ff.

white paint on the red surface and then red on a white slip, both in Boeotia and in Thessaly. Then at Dimini in the second (chalcolithic) Thessalian period (corresponding in time to E.M. II–III), appears an

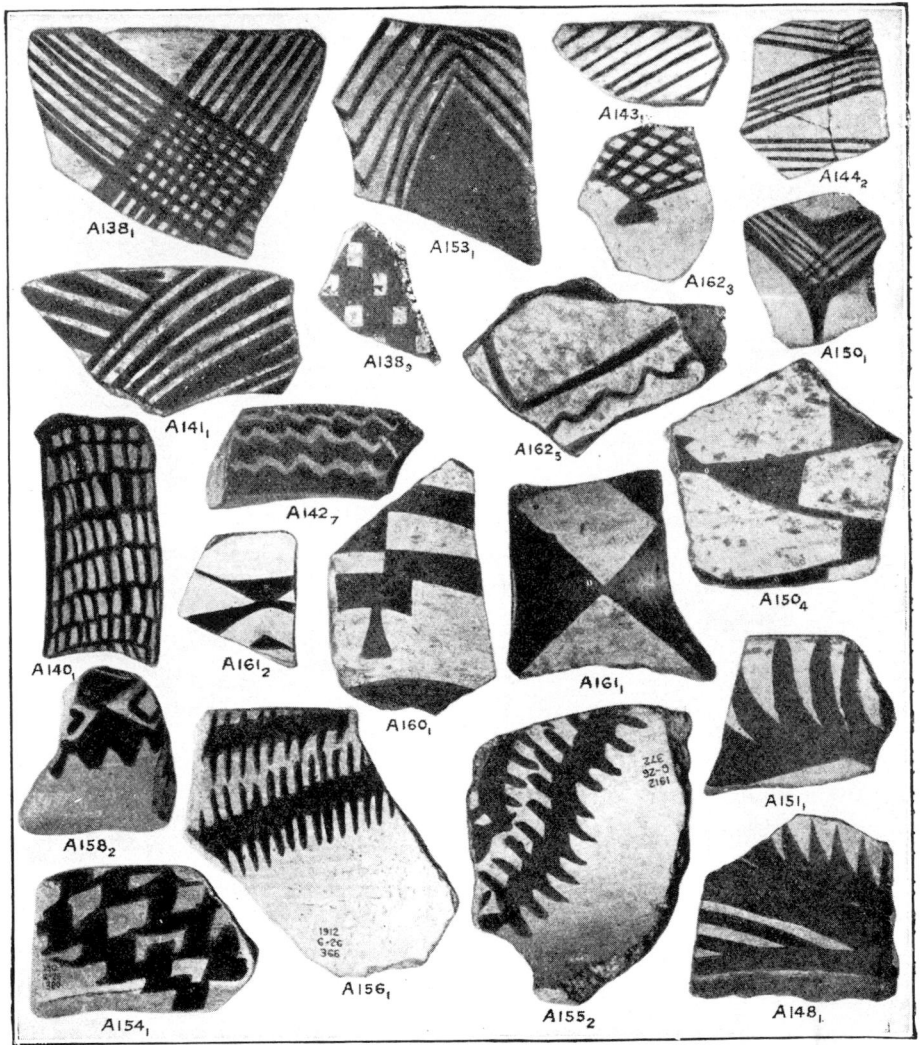

FIG. 64.—FIRST THESSALIAN NEOLITHIC WARE (BRIT. MUS. CATALOGUE)

invading style, apparently from the north, strikingly original with its geometric designs in black or brown on a red or buff ground (Fig. 65), and even a three-colour scheme in brown-black, orange-red, and white

(Fig. 66). And now rude spirals appear, a motive derived possibly from

FIG. 65.—SECOND THESSALIAN (DIMINI) WARE (BRIT. MUS. CATALOGUE)

the northern Aegean and passed on through Thessaly northwards and westwards, by way of the Vardar valley into Europe, where we find it e.g., at " Danubian " Butmir in Bosnia,[1] and at Tripolje and Cucuteni,

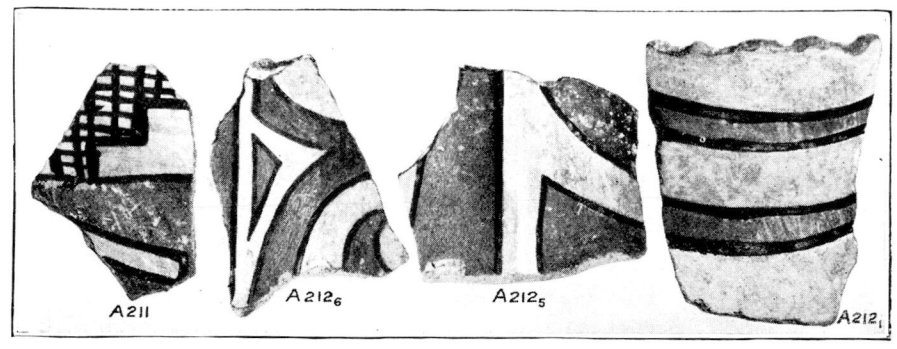

FIG. 66.—SECOND THESSALIAN (DIMINI) THREE-COLOUR WARE (BRIT. MUS. CATALOGUE)

[1] Illustrated by Childe, *The Aryans*, Fig. 23 (p. 140).

in the " Black Earth " region of S. Russia, Galicia and Roumania ; unless, as we have said (p. 60), the movement was in the reverse direction, and the Dimini-spiral on pottery, at any rate, came from Central Europe. In Macedonia we find Dimini ware in the Vardar and Struma valleys. The native Macedonian black ware was of a simpler description, with rough ornament, painted in white, incised or rippled. The Dimini ware of Macedonia may of course not have come from Thessaly, but may mark an *étape* of the style on its way south to Thessaly where it is intrusive, and not connected with the older styles.[1]

The neolithic northern Greeks lived in houses, rectangular in shape, built of crude brick on a low stone foundation (an idea that possibly came from the Trojan centre of culture-diffusion), of a type in which we already see the prototype of the later Achaian house, which, characteristic of continental Greece, is sharply differentiated from the Cretan type. There are the usual axes, celts and hammers of stone, and knife-flakes of obsidian, imported, whether Melian or not.

The fortunes of the Thessalians, who were not conquered by the newcomers from the Cyclades like the tribes south of the Othrys, now become obscure. They gradually adopted the use of metal but their own culture degenerated, their pottery, once polychrome and geometric, for a time becomes crude, poor and uninteresting, losing its ancient characteristic style of decoration. A new ethnic element, possibly coming from the Trojan region, entered Northern Greece and considerably affected the " Helladic " culture of the conquering Aegeans further south, bringing with it its peculiar fine pottery which we know as Minyan, which will be described in the next lecture. But the race remained, possibly to form a most important factor in late-Mycenaean days, when the break-up of Aegean civilization took place. For, while we know nothing of the ethnic affinities of the earliest non-Aegean northern Greeks, the intrusive element represented by the Dimini culture was possibly that of the ancestors of the Achaians, and if so the

---

[1] Cf. Forsdyke, *Cat. Vases*, i, p. xvii ff. The Dimini ware is closely connected with the neolithic pottery of the " Black Earth " region, Transylvania, Galicia and the Ukraine. See Childe, *J.H.S.*, xliii, p. 254 : " The East European relations of the Dimini Culture."

Dimini people were Greek-speaking Indo-European Greeks. Whether this view is capable of any kind of proof remains to be seen.

The pottery of the first period of Aegean culture on the mainland, succeeding the neolithic, is well represented from the Greek excavations at Hagia Marina near Drachmani in Phokis [1] and from the American excavations at Korakou, near Corinth,[2] and from those of the Swedes at Asiné in Argolis.[3] Messrs. Blegen and Wace call this period "Early Helladic." There is first of all a coarse burnished ware of red or black, of sub-neolithic type, then a ware with a smooth polished slip imitating the older burnished ware, and the varnish or "Urfirnis" ware with its sauce-boat and tankard (Fig. 67) shapes. A big water-jar and fragments of pithoi shew that larger pots were made. Even the slow wheel was still unknown. Side by side with the plain "Urfirnis" a "patterned

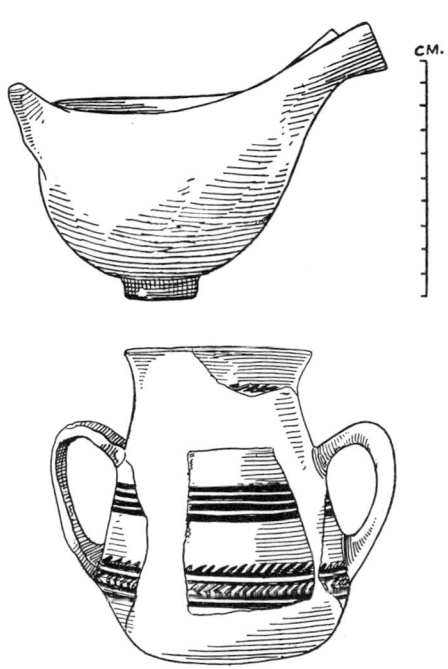

FIG. 67.—URFIRNIS "SAUCE-BOAT" AND TANKARD: KORAKOU

ware" with simple linear decoration in the glaze-paint, dark or light, was also used. The designs are not very Aegean in type and point to influence from the native neolithic geometric style of ornament. A light on dark style, more directly imitating Cretan E.M. III, also prevailed. A white painted Urfirnis was found at Hagia Marina (Fig. 68). The characteristic "Urfirnis" is found from the Argolid to Thessaly, and in the Cyclades.[4]

[1] Soteriadis, *Rév. Et. Grecques*, 1912, p. 260 ff. Childe, *J.H.S.*, xxiv (1915), p. 196 ff.
[2] C. W. Blegen, *Korakou*, Boston, 1921.
[3] Persson, *K. Hum. Vet. Lund, Årsberättelse*, 1924–5, p. 59 ff.
[4] For a list of sites see *Korakou*, pp. 110-11, and Forsdyke, *Cat.*, i, pp. xxiii, xxix.

A very important relic of the metal-work of the early Aegeans on the mainland is a golden " sauce-boat " in the Louvre, recently published by Mr. V. G. Childe.[1] I am however not able to deduce from it the far-reaching conclusions as to a cultural parity of the mainlanders

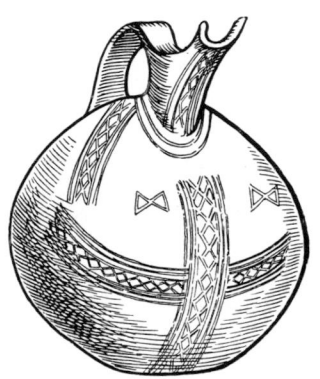

with the Cretans and the equal participation of the Mainland " with Crete and the Cyclades in a great maritime confederacy " at this time, which commend themselves to him. After all the form is crude, like the pottery which it imitates, as a gold object it is poor compared with Trojan work, and the existence of this unique object cannot prove great wealth or power.

FIG. 68.—URFIRNIS DECORATED WARE
HAGIA MARINA : WHITE-PAINTED

We have now reached the lower limit of the Early Bronze Age in Greece. The next lecture will deal with the great development of civilization that took place during the Middle Bronze Age, approximately between 2400 and 1800 B.C., beginning with the Third Early Minoan and concluding with the end of the Second Middle Minoan Age in Crete, marked by the building of the great palaces of Knossos and Phaistos in Crete and the establishment of the full Minoan culture in continental Greece.

[1] *J.H.S.*, xliv (1924), p. 163 ff.

LECTURE III

FROM THE EARLY TO THE MIDDLE BRONZE AGE

(EARLY MINOAN III TO MIDDLE MINOAN II, *c.* 2400–1800 B.C.)

IT is somewhat difficult to disentangle, so to speak, the last phase of the Early Minoan period in Crete from the first phase of the Middle Minoan period. The two overlapped, and when Knossos had already developed the typical Middle Minoan ceramic the technique of the Third Early Minoan period was still in use at the eastern end of Crete. Also certain characteristics of the Middle period already appear in E.M. III, which differentiate it considerably from E.M. II and make it more convenient to deal with it in the lecture devoted to the Middle period. Similarly there are differences between M.M. II and M.M. III, and relations between M.M. III and L.M. I which make it convenient to conclude this lecture with the catastrophe and destruction of the early Knossian palace at the end of M.M. II, and to reserve the consideration of M.M. III and L.M. I, the first phase of the Late Bronze Age, for the next.

Characteristic of the beginning of the Middle Bronze Age in Crete about 2500 B.C. is the reverse action on Crete of the artistic impulses characteristic of the Cyclades and even further north, and the intensification of the influences of Egypt already noted as existing in the First and Second Early Minoan periods as well as the first appearance in Egypt of Aegean influences.[1] First among these phenomena we may note the spiral design which now first appears on Cretan pottery vases, painted in

[1] See p. 43 ff., Hall, *J.E.A.*, i, p. 113 ff.

light on dark technique, characteristic of E.M. III (Fig. 69), and incised on vases of steatite, an idea obviously derived direct from the Cyclades. Later on it appears in Egypt on scarabs, on royal scarabs suddenly in the reign of king Senusret I (*c.* 2150 or 1950 B.C.),[1] about the middle of the Second Middle Minoan period, but on private scarabs probably earlier. It was not long before, owing to the intensified relations between Egypt and Crete, which developed owing to the contemp-

FIG. 69.—E.M. III POTTERY : MOCHLOS

orary existence in both countries of powerful governing dynasties, which could carry out great public works in peace and ensure peace in their respective lands, that the scarab with the spiral engraved upon it reached Crete from Egypt [2] (Figs. 70, 71), and was imitated by the Cretan lapidaries, with the lily that the Egyptians had added to the spiral

[1] Hall, *Brit. Mus. Catalogue of Scarabs*, p. xiii, 7.

[2] Imitated scarabs are already found at the end of E.M. III or beginning of M.M. I at Gournais (see p. 74), and an imported Egyptian scarab from Platanos with spiral design (Fig. 71) can hardly be earlier than the XIth Dynasty.

design.[1] The new combined Aegaeo-Egyptian design was soon transferred to pottery (Fig. 72). An older importation from Egypt going back to the VIth Dynasty and E.M. II, found already on the mainland in Early Helladic days,[2] was the plain ivory seal, the predecessor of the scarab seal, with the maeander designs and the crude figures of men and beasts, characteristic of the period of the VIth–XIth Dynasties [3] (Figs. 73, 74). It may be the form of this stamp or button-seal, as it is called in Egypt, (usually a round disk or rectangular plaque of ivory or glazed steatite with a hole or ring for suspension at the back,) was of foreign, perhaps Syrian, origin ; certainly many of the designs on the Egyptian button-seals are not Egyptian. On some of the Cretan seals of this type however we notice for the first time the so-called antithetical group of two animals, such as crocodiles, squatting apes or couchant lions or jackals placed feet to feet or back to back, ("tête-bêche"), which was of Egyptian origin : the crocodile and the

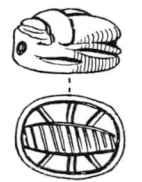

FIG. 70.—IXTH–XTH DYN. EGYPTIAN
SCARABS FROM PLATANOS
(*Actual size*)

FIG. 71.—EGYPTIAN XITH–XIITH DYN.
SCARABS FROM PLATANOS
(*Enlarged*)

FIG. 72.—M.M. II VASE WITH
LILY-SPIRAL DESIGN : PHAISTOS
($\frac{1}{8}$ c.)

[1] At Platanos in M.M. I*a* was found an imported Egyptian scarab (Fig. 71) with a figure of the goddess Thoueris and a monkey on it (Evans, *Palace*, Fig. 148). This and the other scarab in the same figure are not Cretan imitations.

[2] Persson, *Årsberättelse, loc. cit.*, 1923–4, p. 162 ff. ; 1924–5, p. 65.

[3] Evans, *l. c.*, pp. 122 ff.

FIG. 73.—EGYPTIAN SCARABS, BUTTON-SEALS, ETC., VITH–IXTH DYNASTY (BRIT. MUS.) (½)

FIG. 74.—EGYPTIAN SEALS : VITH–IXTH DYNASTY (BRIT. MUS.) (*Actual size*)

ape are decisive as to its origin (Fig. 75). Later on it becomes a characteristic feature of Minoan designs. The ivory of these seals in Crete (which are mostly not imported Egyptian but of local make, many with adaptations of designs found in Egypt)[1] of course came from Egypt. Whether the common use of steatite in both countries was of independent origin we do not know ; probably it was.

The Egyptians had already made their great invention of true glaze, in blue, which they had used for faience and to glaze steatite and quartzite, as early as the predynastic period. This now in the Early Minoan period was communicated to Crete, where it appears usually as a glaze paste for beads,[2] in the

[1] In Fig. 75 (from Xanthoudides, *loc. cit.*) we see a copy of the Egyptian design of two crocodiles side by side, which is often found on Egyptian button-seals (Fig. 74), and two apes back to back, which is equally Egyptian (*ibid.*).

[2] Seager, *Mochlos*, p. 55.

70

pale blue colour characteristic of Old Kingdom faience. The Egyptians now themselves developed a deep blue glaze, often with designs in manganese black, which is characteristic of the Twelfth Dynasty. But when the Cretans began to make their local faience at about the same time (M.M. II), they retained the old Egyptian pale blue colour, while adding to it a brown that imitated the Egyptian black. The ordinary pottery of Egypt, though now made with the slow wheel, was unglazed, and the Egyptians never adopted the Cretan lustrous paint, preferring to confine themselves to the elaboration of their wonderful faience, a sandy paste not worked on the wheel but held together by a light gum or mucilage in a mass out of which the vase was cut, and then coated with the magnificent glass-glaze. The

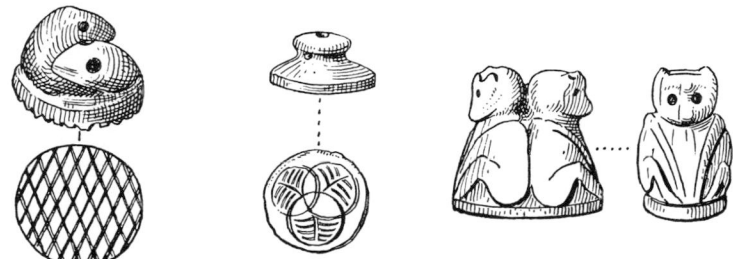

FIG. 75.—CRETAN SEALS OF EGYPTIAN TYPE, WITH FIGURES OF CROCODILES AND APES.
(MESARÀ) E.M. II–M.M. I
($\frac{1}{2}$ to actual size)

Cretan having his own fine and beautifully decorated pottery did not use his faience much to make pots, but rather figures and other objects that could not be turned on the wheel. The Egyptian development of fine glass about this time does not seem to have been taken up in Greece, where however a characteristic vitreous paste was used for making beads until late Mycenaean times. Glass seems to have come from Egypt to Babylonia very early, as I found at Abu Shahrain a piece of blue glass (definitely so identified by Mr. H. C. Beck) in a deposit older than the Third Dynasty of Ur (c. B.C. 2300).

At the beginning of the First Middle Minoan period the tournette, or slow wheel (see p. 47) came (whether from Egypt or from the East we do not know), and by the end of the period had established itself for

the making of the finer and the smaller vases. Very probably the tournette was not an Egyptian invention but itself came to Egypt towards the
close of the Old Kingdom from further east, from Babylonia. Its invention may plausibly be assigned to the Elamites, as pottery made with

FIG. 76.—M.M. II POLYCHROME POTTERY FRAGMENTS FROM XIITH DYNASTY DEPOSITS, EGYPT.
(BRIT. MUS. CATALOGUE)

it is found in Elam, at Susa at least as early as the beginning of the fourth
millennium B.C. At Troy it appears in the later period of the Second City.

Very soon the further step was made to the invention of the fully
developed or " quick " wheel (see p. 47) which we find already in use

in the Second Middle Minoan period. This invention was quite possibly Cretan, made in Crete at this time.

Cretan pottery fragments of the Middle Minoan period and even some Middle Helladic fragments of the same kind have been found in Egypt,[1] and always in deposits of XIIth Dynasty date (Fig. 76). The synchronism is absolutely certain (*c.* 2000 B.C.). Its most striking characteristic, its remarkable polychrome decoration, was probably

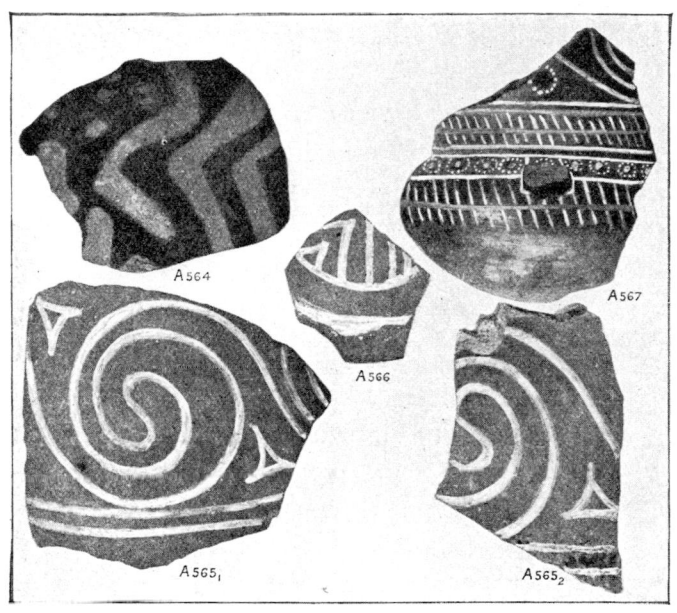

FIG. 77.—EGYPTIAN IMITATIONS OF M.M. II POTTERY: XIITH DYNASTY (BRIT. MUS. CATALOGUE)

admired though the Egyptian could not imitate it. He tried to, or perhaps Cretan potters settled in Egypt tried to, with Egyptian clay burnt in the Egyptian fashion, but failed (Fig. 77). This we know[2] from some of the specimens found by Professor Sir Flinders Petrie at Lahun (long miscalled 'Kahun') in 1890, now in the British Museum, in the house ruins of a XIIth Dynasty settlement of foreign workmen near the pyramid of king Senusret II (*c.* 2100 or 1900 B.C.). These were then,

[1] For the M.H. polychrome fragments see Forsdyke, *Catalogue*, pp. 50, 51 ; Fig. 52.
[2] Forsdyke, *B.M. Cat. Vases*, I, i, p. 93.

73

before anything was known in Crete itself of this ware, very remarkably diagnosed by the discoverer as Aegean.[1] Confirmation of this diagnosis was obtained by Mr. J. L. Myres's publication in 1895, followed by that of Prof. Mariani, of the same ware found in the Kamarais cave on Mt. Ida.[2] We now know it to be of M.M. II date. It was in the M.M. II period, to which the Lahun deposit belongs, that the polychrome ware reached its highest development.

FIG. 78.—THE ABYDOS FIND OF XIITH DYNASTY AND M.M. II POTTERY

And a remarkable specimen of its highest type was later found by Prof. J. E. Garstang at Abydos in a tomb associated with Egyptian deposits dated by inscriptions to the reign of Senusret II, first published, by Prof. Garstang's permission, in my *Ancient History of the Near East* (1913) (Fig. 78).[3]

This splendid polychrome pottery is probably the most typical and characteristic product of the Cretan Middle Bronze Age, and belongs only to this period.

The first appearance of polychromy as applied to pottery is found in Crete in the Third Early Minoan period, and is one of the phenomena that link this period with the succeeding rather than the preceding one. Now in addition to the decoration of the white bands, or stripes, or spirals, on the dark ground which is characteristic of E.M. III, we find at Gournais [4] for the first time red, soon to develop the fine deep red of

[1] Petrie, *Illahun, Kahun, and Gurob*, p. 9 ff.

[2] Myres, *Proc. Soc. Ant.*, 1895 (2nd ser. xv.), p. 351 ff. ; Mariani, *Mar. Ant.*, vi. (1895), p. 333 ff. ; pl. ix–xi. The later work of Mr. Dawkins in the cave (1913) yielded more of this ware ; *B.S.A. Ann.*, xix (1913), p. 1 ff., pll. i–xii.

[3] Hall, *Anc. Hist. N.E.*, pl. iii, 1 ; Garstang, *Liv. A.A.A.* 1913, p. 107.

[4] Hatzidakis, 'Αρχ. Δελτ. 1915, p. 59 ff.; also 1918. Gournais should not be confused with Gournià (p. 75). The finds at Gournais are apparently transitional from E.M. III to M.M. Ia.

the Middle Minoan period. There is no doubt that the inspiration to use this red, and the developed polychromy that follows in the next period, was derived from the variegated stone vases, that we have seen were so popular in the Second Early Minoan period as at Mochlos : the particoloured serpentine marbles and variegated breccias which were used for stone vase making (especially the latter and their red markings which are almost exactly of the same hue as that of the red of the pottery) inspired the potters to successful imitation in their glaze-paint. And the combination of the new colours with the spiral and other designs produced the result which we see in the Second Middle Minoan period.

In the M.M. I period we also find imitations in pottery of the white spotted black liparite carinated bowls which were still made after an Old Kingdom Egyptian type imported in E.M. III (see p. 49). A shell of liparite has been found at Hagia Triada.[1] But besides stone, metal was now imitated by the Cretan potters.

We have seen that the end of the E.M. period marks a great advance in metal working, derived probably from Troy and eventually N.E. Asia Minor. In M.M. I have been found at Gournià pottery vases of various shapes, obviously derived from metal originals,

FIG. 79.—SILVER VASE WITH POTTERY IMITATIONS : GOURNIÀ (M.M. I) ($\frac{1}{4}$ c.)

nals, side by side with one of these metal originals, a silver vase with fluted sides[2] (Fig. 79). And now begins the fine egg-shell pottery (with of course polychrome designs), which is a typical product of the time, and in the thinness of its wall obviously imitates metal (Fig. 80). Another typical product of the M.M. I potters is the black " barbotine

[1] Mosso, *Dawn of Medit. Civilization*, Fig. 199.   [2] Boyd, *Gournià*, pl. C.

75

FIG. 80.—M.M. II "EGG-SHELL" WARE ($\frac{1}{3}$ c.)

ware," as it is called, with its fantastic relief decoration of knobs, horns, and twists (Fig. 81), associated also in the next period, M.M. II, with

FIG. 81.—M.M. I BARBOTINE WARE: KOUMÁSA ($\frac{1}{2}$ TO $\frac{3}{8}$)

polychromy. In M.M. II the riot of colour and weirdness of design on the pottery increases to its zenith, and then suddenly dies down. This strange pottery is as characteristic in its bizarrerie of the fantastic side of the Cretan genius as is the egg-shell ware of its lightsomeness and lighthandedness, or the polychromy of its love of startling effects, but neither the barbotine nor the polychromy found favour in the next age. The Later Bronze Age reverted to the plain technique of dark on light, which had never died, and preferred more sober and refined effects. The riotous character of the Middle Minoan pottery was a youthful excess.

Within the bounds of this lecture it is impossible to say more of the poly-chrome Middle Minoan pottery, or to enlarge further on its interest and beauty, its fine and striking designs of spirals, lily-spirals, plant-motives, quirks, stripes, bands, etc., in black, deep red, and white, and sometimes in pink, rarely with the addition of blue, covering the whole vase (Figs. 82–85). Though it photographs well owing to its strong contrasts in colour it can

FIG. 82.—M.M. II POLYCHROME VASE ($\frac{1}{2}$)

only be adequately represented in colour, and it is so represented with splendid success in Sir Arthur Evans's *Palace of Minos*, in the coloured

FIG. 83.—M.M. II POLYCHROME VASE: PALAI-KASTRO ($\frac{1}{2}$)

plates of the first volume. Besides the lily-spiral, it sometimes imitated other Egyptian designs, such as the bunches of lilies hanging downwards from an imitated string round the neck of the vase (Fig. 86).[1] One thing we notice is the comparative absence of marine objects which we rightly consider so characteristic of the Minoan pottery. They do not make their general appearance till the First Late Minoan period, when naturalism takes the place of elaborate Middle Minoan patterns as the simple light and dark technique supplants the polychromy.

[1] Hall, *J.E.A.*, i, p. 116.

FIG. 84.—M.M. II POLYCHROME VASE $(\frac{1}{2})$

In the Cyclades at this time (E.C. III–M.C. II) we find spirals, as was to be expected, common on pottery. The *Urfirnis* style, general in the earlier period in the Cyclades, and the old incised ware are dis-

FIG. 85.—M.M. II POLYCHROME VASE

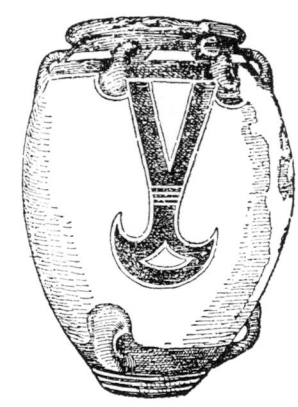

FIG. 86.—M.M. II PITHOS WITH IMITATION OF EGYPTIAN LILY-DESIGN

placed by imitations of Cretan dark on light technique, which did not succeed owing to the greater poverty of the Cycladic clay, that prevented the varnish-paint from ever acquiring the brilliant lustre of the Cretan

78

originals. So the Cycladic potters abandoned the attempt, and confined themselves to producing a white slip ware with dull black (matt) painting, at first in rectilinear, later in curvilinear designs. Characteristic are flat milk-bowls (Fig. 87) and elaborate clusters of vases on a common stem (*Kernoi*) of which the British Museum possesses fine examples (Fig. 88).[1] A " stand " in the form of a flower (Ashmolean Museum) is shown in *Aegean Archaeology*, Pl. XX, 4. But in spite of these imitations, the Cycladic artists preserved considerable individuality, and we see in their pottery of M.C. III that they represented the human figure, which the Cretans only did under

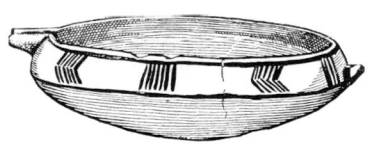

FIG. 87.—M.C. MILK-BOWLS (BRIT. MUS. CATALOGUE) (*c.* $\frac{1}{3}$)

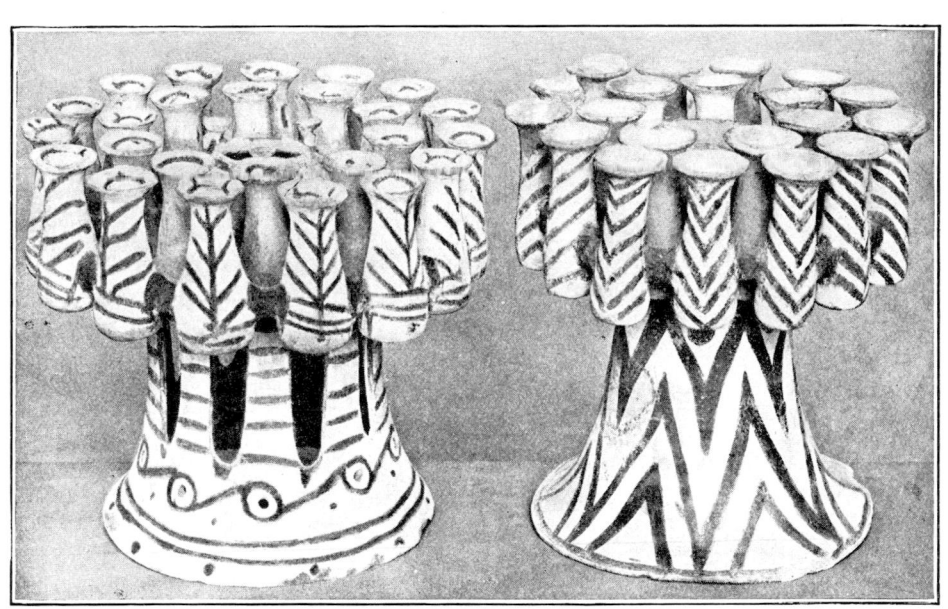

FIG. 88.—M.C. KERNOI (BRIT. MUS. CATALOGUE) ($\frac{1}{6}$ *c.*)

the strong Cycladic influence characteristic of E.M. III–M.M. I ;[2] a

[1] First Vase Room, A. 343, 344. (Forsdyke, *l. c.*, p. 63.) [2] See p. 139, n. 2.

79

notable peculiarity which the Cyclades transferred to the Mycenaean style (p. 139). Cretan polychrome ware was however imported into the Cyclades, in M.M. (M.C.) II, and also the important foreign " Minyan " ware from the mainland. The Cretan polychrome painting was not imitated till later, in M.C. III, and then with very poor results. On the mainland of Greece we find the same matt-painted pottery (*Mattmalerei*), for the mainland clays were as porous as those of the islands, and took the Cretan varnish-paint as badly, so that it could only be imitated in dull colour. This succeeds the *Urfirnis* at Korakou after a gap in culture, represented by a burnt stratum which means destruction.

FIG. 89.—PITHOS : MAINLAND *MATTMALEREI* : KORAKOU. (MIDDLE HELLADIC)

This, a new settlement, contains totally new pottery ; there is no *Urfirnis* (plain varnish ware), only *Mattmalerei* (dull-painted ware with geometric designs) (Fig. 89) and " Minyan " ware. This last is a very important appearance both here and in the Cyclades, where it is found with Cretan polychrome pottery. It does not occur in Crete. It is a much finer pottery than anything else outside Crete, and is completely distinct from any true Aegean ware. It is apparently wheel-made,[1] whereas the wheel seems to have been as yet unknown on the mainland, and possibly in the Cyclades, though known in Crete. Its forms are distinctly imitated from metal originals with carinated bodies, projecting lips, and high stems. Characteristic types are a two-handled cup of the later *kantharos* shape (Fig. 90), and a tall-stemmed wide-bowled *kylix* (Fig. 91), both new to the Aegean. Its clay is equally peculiar, being curiously greasy to the feel, and with a natural lustre, firing to a light grey colour. It appears suddenly in Greece. Its

[1] This has been disputed, and its fabric described as made in a mould, by Persson, *l.c.*, 1924–5, p. 68. This however seems very improbable.

relationships are definitely with the pottery of Troy, where it is found in the Sixth City, and the Hellespontine region. That is to say, it is of North-west Anatolian origin. The delicate grey colour, as well as the metallic shapes, as Mr. Forsdyke well says, " doubtless

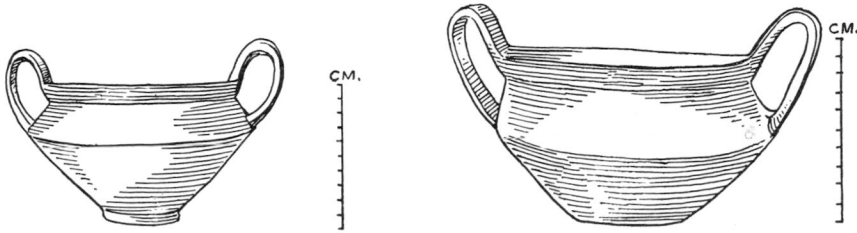

FIG. 90.—MINYAN *KANTHAROI*: KORAKOU (MIDDLE HELLADIC)

reflect the traditional Hellespontine silver industry."[1] It should then be of foreign origin, and perhaps represent an ethnic invasion from the Trojan region, which will have taken place at the end of the early Helladic period, well before 2000 B.C. There had been an earlier Anatolian invasion of Greece than this, when, in the Early Helladic period, at a time that can be synchronized with the Second Early Cycladic Age (about 2500 B.C.), a tribe from Asia settled in Euboea, and buried with its dead pottery of the Anatolian type known as that of Yortan, from the place where it was first discovered (see p. 55). But the " Minyan " invasion, if it was one, was of much greater importance. The widespread use of its ceramic means in all

FIG. 91.—MINYAN *KYLIX*: KORAKOU

probability a real conquest by the foreigners from the Hellespont. It might be objected : why should even so widespread an use of foreign pottery as this necessarily mean foreign invasion and conquest ? Why should it not signify merely highly developed commercial relations with

[1] Forsdyke, *loc. cit.*, p. xxv.

the Hellespontine region, whose pottery being so much superior to the native product, became universally popular in Greece ? It could be pointed out that there is a case similar in the Egyptian use of the Mycenaean stirrup-vase, and of much Syrian pottery, in the times of the XVIIIth and XIXth Dynasties (see p. 222). There was certainly no Minoan or Syrian conquest of Egypt then. But the cases are really not parallel. The foreign pottery in Egypt is by no means so universal as the Minyan in Greece. From Greece the stirrup-vase was imported evidently because it contained olive oil or some other Greek unguent which the Egyptians liked to have in the original bottles. The Egyptians were a highly civilized people who would adopt foreign objects of this kind brought to them in commerce. The Middle Helladic Greeks were a semi-barbarous people who would naturally cling to their own pottery, and not willingly adopt a foreign style. Since it is associated with a peculiar form of cist-burial in houses, it is more probable that the general use of the Minyan ware means a foreign occupation.[1] If there was such an invasion, was it that which brought into the Aegean from Anatolia the influx of broad-skulled people mentioned later, p. 111 ? And is it represented by the legends of the Pelopids ? That the name " Minyan " is a misnomer is evident. This pottery has nothing to do with the Minyae of Orchomenos, after whom it was called on its first discovery at Orchomenos by Schliemann. But the name has probably come to stay. The foreign ware was imitated in the so-called Argive Minyan, in which the surface of the vase received a pigment imitating the peculiar Minyan grey, and the " yellow Minyan," which imitated the foreign forms in unsophisticated native pottery (Fig. 92). It came to Thessaly and Macedonia also, where it is found with the native wares, and was often imitated. At Lianokladi (III) in the Spercheios Valley it occurs with a peculiar type of geometric ware (Fig. 93), apparently of Macedonian origin, and no way related to the old neolithic bichrome pottery found at the same place. It is almost omnipresent from the

[1] Persson, *loc. cit.*, p. 67, assumes a foreign invasion now, at the beginning of the Middle Helladic period, and notes a temporary cessation of connexion with Crete and Egypt, resumed later (see p. 83, below).

Argolid to Macedonia,[1] and is found as far north as the " Black Earth "
region, at Cucuteni in
Rumania. It should be
noted that the theory of
its foreign (Hellespontine)
origin, maintained by Mr.
Forsdyke, is partly accepted
by Prof. Childe,[2] but Mr.

FIG. 92.—" YELLOW MINYAN " WARE : KORAKOU

Frankfort regards it with, I think, less probability, as purely a local
Greek manufacture that arose in Phokis and Boeotia.[3] Whence then
the distinct relationship to Trojan ware ? And why the un-Helladic
use of the wheel ?

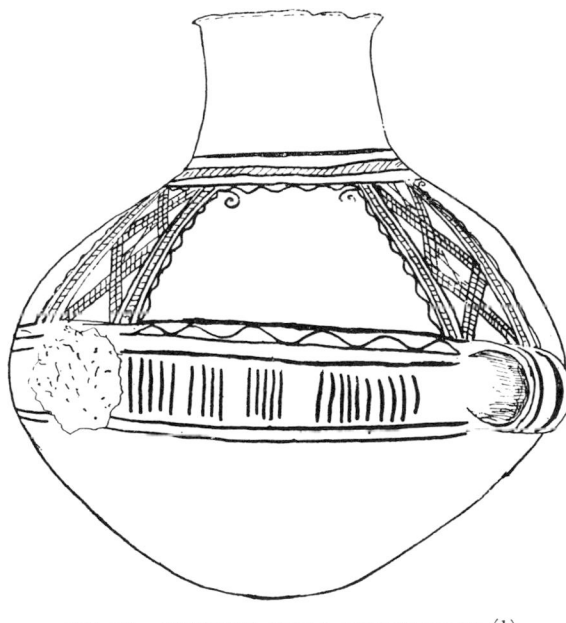

FIG. 93.—DECORATED WARE : LIANOKLADI III ($\frac{1}{4}$)

Thus we see that the
Cyclades and Greece pro-
per were, so far as their
ceramic art was con-
cerned, placed between
two much more highly
developed ceramic " pro-
vinces," the Cretan
"Middle Minoan" and the
" Minyan," which would
be sure to impinge upon
and influence the native
styles to a very great
extent. We shall see that
in the sequel they did so,
to the destruction of the

local styles. And then the intrusive " Minyan " ware gave way to the
native highly developed Aegean ceramic of Crete, which was only one

[1] On Minyan pottery, see Forsdyke, *loc. cit.*, p. xxv ; and *J.H.S.*, xxxiv, p. 126 ff. ;
Childe, *J.H.S.*, xxxv, p. 196 ff. Miss J. R. Bacon, *The Voyage of the Argonauts*, brings it
into connexion with the legend of Jason and the Argonauts. But in so far as her arguments
rest on any supposed connexion of the pottery with Minyans, they are of doubtful force.
[2] Childe, *Dawn of Europ. Civ.*, p. 79. [3] Frankfort, *Studies*, ii, pp. 140 ff.

of the weapons employed by a culture already enormously superior to its neighbours. In the Middle Cycladic period the " local style," however, still was predominant in other matters besides ceramic. The Cycladic culture was still " no mere copy of that of Crete," and " indeed in E.M. III the influx of numerous idols and vase-forms of Cycladic type and the introduction of the spiral motive shews that the little islands of the north were influencing the big one in the south,"[1] which the mainland was not sufficiently advanced to be able to do. The Cycladic culture had eventually to give way to the higher culture of Crete, but it could make a better fight than the mainland, which, " in alliance," so to speak, with Crete, it had civilized.

The consideration of Middle Minoan pottery shews us what a great advance in art was effected in this period in Crete, an advance paralleled in other branches of handicraft and culture. About the same time as the horizontal potter's wheel came the other kind of wheel, the vertical cart-wheel, to Crete, but by a different route. Egypt was not responsible for the introduction of the cart-wheel to the Aegean. She herself did not use it, and never adopted it till the chariots of the lordly Hyksos proved to her that it had its uses even in Egypt, with its network of canals and absence of roads. The Egyptian still remained faithful to the ox-drawn sled, but the Babylonians had long used the wheel. Already in the fourth millennium B.C. the chiefs of the Sumerians went to battle in ass-drawn chariots,[2] the horse being as yet unknown west of Iran. It was in Babylonia (in spite of its being a country almost as much cut up by waterways as the Egyptian Delta) or more probably in the hills of Elam that the wheeled cart was invented, and to the Aegean this invention probably came through Asia Minor, as eastward it passed to India, where we find horse and chariot in the Vedic

[1] Childe, *Dawn of European Civilization*, p. 49.

[2] The well-known instance of the Chief of Lagash, Entemena, in the " Tale of the Vultures " in the Louvre (*c.* 2800 B.C.) is now deposed from its pride of date, since Mr. Woolley at Ur has this year (1927) found a much older representation of a kingly chariot, dating not later than 3200 B.C. and probably earlier. Its wheels are spokeless, built up of three pieces, the centre elliptical, between two demilunar, held together by cross-battens. This is the most ancient record of the wheel (*Brit. Mus. Quarterly*, ii, Fig. XXI*b*). But *cf. The Times*, Jan. 4, 1928, where prehistoric India claims seniority !

age (*c.* 1200 B.C.).[1]   In M.M. I we get the first Greek representation of it, a model four-wheeled cart in pottery (Fig. 94) from Palaikastro.[2] What animal drew it (the horse being presumably still unknown) we do

FIG 94.—FOUR-WHEELED CART (PALAIKASTRO) : M.M. I. : *c.* 2200 B.C. ($\frac{1}{2}$)

not know : possibly asses were imported from Egypt.   The horse and with it the war-chariot do not appear till M.M. III (Figs. 95–97), practically contemporaneously with their introduction into Egypt.[3]   We know

[1] For the date see Berriedale Keith, in *Cambr. Hist. India* (1925), i, p. 113   This date agrees very well with the facts that Aryan Indian gods, Indra, Varuna, Mitra, and the Nāsatya-twins are mentioned in the Boghaz Kyöi tablets as worshipped by the Mitannians in North Mesopotamia, and that Aryan names of Indian form were prevalent in Western Asia about 1400 B.C., when we may suppose the ancestors of the Aryan Indians and Iranians were on the move eastward from Europe and had left behind some of their race as rulers of Mitanni. Prof. Keith's caution in accepting the identification of these Aryan gods in Mitanni (*ibid.*, p. 110) is, by the way, excessive : there can be no doubt whatever on the subject in the minds of those directly engaged in elucidating the ancient history of the Near East ; (cf. P. Giles, *ibid.*, p. 72 ; for references, *ibid.*, p. 320, and my *Ancient History of the Near East*, 6th ed. (1924), pp. 201, 230, 331, 410).   On the relation of this date and the newly discovered fact that the Hittites spoke an Aryan tongue to the question of the date of the coming of the Aryan Greeks to Greece, see p. 290.

[2] Dawkins, *B.S.A. Suppl. Paper*, I (1923), Fig. 12.

[3] Evans, *J.H.S.*, 1925, p. 34.   Sir Arthur Evans distinguishes two forms of Minoan chariot, one earlier, with axle immediately beneath the centre of a square box-like car, which we see in the M.M. III gravestones of the shaft-graves at Mycenae and on various rings (Figs. 95, 175–6), gems, etc., and the other later in which the axle is well back of the centre and the car has a projecting standing-board at the back with a curved rail, which we see on the list-tablets from Knossos (Fig. 97), the Hagia Triada sarcophagus (Fig. 293) and on Cypriote vases (Fig. 294).   The first may be of Oriental, the second is pretty certainly of

Egypt, as also by the land-route through Syria, whence came the Hyksos. It is possible that the military success of the Hyksos (who were no wandering Beduins, but highly civilized Syrians) was not only due to their possession of the horse and chariot, but also to superior weapons. Still the fine weapons of great men were now made of bronze in Egypt and the same was the case in Crete. Forms of daggers from E.M. III on are simple and analogous to the Egyptian in the same stage of development. They are longer than in E.M. II and are approaching the sword (Fig. 100). This form spread west, probably from Crete, even as far as Ireland. A good example (broad-bladed) on which are engraved on one side a scene of a man sticking a pig (Fig. 101), and on the other one of two bulls fighting, foreshadows

FIG. 100.—MIDDLE MINOAN DAGGER-BLADES AND SOCKETED SPEARHEADS : MOCHLOS ($\frac{1}{5}$ c.)

the "illustrated" daggers of Mycenae (p. 143). The sword proper had already appeared in M.M. I at Mallia, where the French excavators have recently discovered a magnificent broad-bladed sword 97 cm. long, with a hilt of fine grey limestone covered with thin gold, from which springs a pommel of rock-crystal of very Sumerian appearance. (Fig.

88

102).[1] The more developed types which were evidently invented in Syria, such as the *khepesh* or scimitar and the war-pickaxe, are not represented,

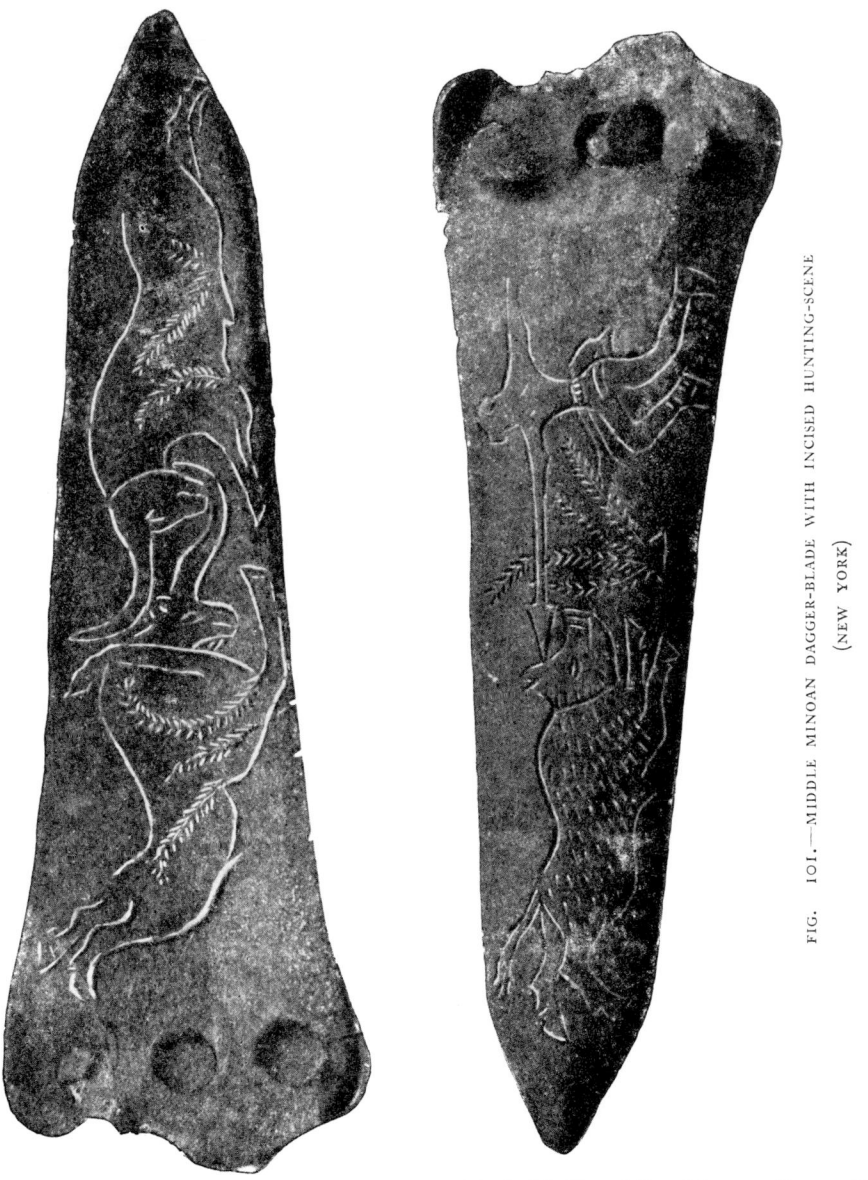

FIG. 101.—MIDDLE MINOAN DAGGER-BLADE WITH INCISED HUNTING-SCENE (NEW YORK)

[1] Charbonneaux, *Trois Armes d'apparat du palais de Mallia* ; *Mém. Piot.*, xxviii, p. 1 ff. ; pl. I. It is not said whether the blades of the sword and of a dagger found with it are bronze or copper. With the sword-pommel *cf.* recent finds at Ur, of 3000 B.C.

FIG. 102.—BROAD-
SWORD WITH
STONE HANDLE:
M.M. I. MALLIA
($\frac{1}{7}$)
(*Mon. Piot.*,
1925–6)

nor was the scimitar ever adopted by the Aegeans as it was by the Egyptians. The axe, except in the ancient sacred double form, and in that of an axe-adze (Fig. 104), was rare. The last was of a type certainly of Sumerian origin, with a hole or socket for the haft, not like the Egyptian axe, which was always stuck in the haft.[1] Magnificent examples of the socketed axe and adze-axe or war-pick have been found by Mr. Woolley at Ur, in gold and electrum as well as copper, of a date certainly no later than 3000 B.C., which conclusively prove the enormous superiority of the Sumerian over the Egyptian weaponsmithy. And this explains why the Sumerian, and not the Egyptian, weapon-forms were adopted in the Aegean. At Mallia has been found a remarkable bronze (?) axe-head, illustrated in Fig. 103, covered with engraved spirals and zigzags, rather like the decoration of the gold *étui* from Ur (p. 59), and with its pick in the shape of the forepart of a leopard.[2] The socketed spearhead appeared early in M.M. III.

Further, in this age the Cretan artist began to engrave hard stones. Hitherto he had cut his seals out of ivory or the soft steatite. Now in the Second Middle Minoan period he uses hard crystalline stones such as crystal, agate, or cornelian, for his seals and beads. The lapidary has entered the field of art, and contemporary with this event comes the art of writing, which in Crete was closely connected with the art of seal-making. The Egyptian had evolved a primitive form of writing by means of simple ideographs as early as the latter part of the predynastic period (4000 B.C.) and by

---

[1] Childe, *Dawn of European Civilization*, p. 34. For its further European developments, see Childe, *The Aryans*, Fig. 27 (p. 190). Prof. Childe notes the fact that the Greek word for axe, πελέκυς, was the same as the Assyrian *pilakku*, which was apparently of Sumerian origin.

[2] Charbonneaux, *loc. cit.*, pp. 6, 7, pl. ii.

the end of the Ist Dynasty, 500 or more years later, this had developed into a complicated system of hieroglyphic writing, which

FIG. 103.—AXEHEAD IN THE FORM OF A LEOPARD, WITH SPIRAL DESIGN: M.M. I. MALLIA
(*Mon. Piot.*, 1925–6) (¾)

by 3000 B.C. had reached its complete form, and not long after had developed a cursive form which we know as hieratic, to be written

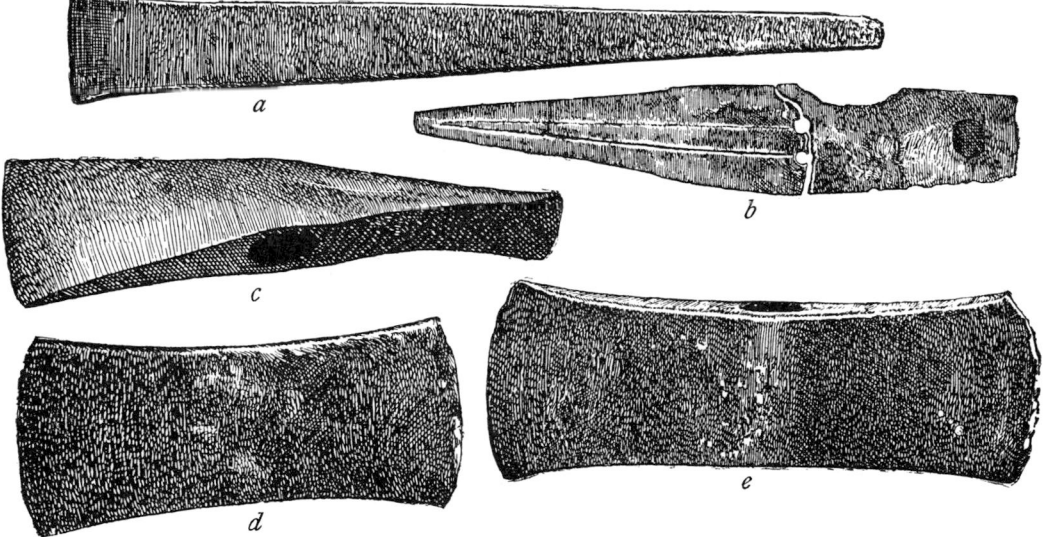

FIG. 104.—MIDDLE MINOAN AXES AND CHISELS: KHAMAËZI (³⁄₇ c.)

on papyrus with ink. The Babylonian had as early as 3200 B.C. or earlier reduced his pictographic signary to a shortened system which

91

when incised on clay tablets became what we call cuneiform. In

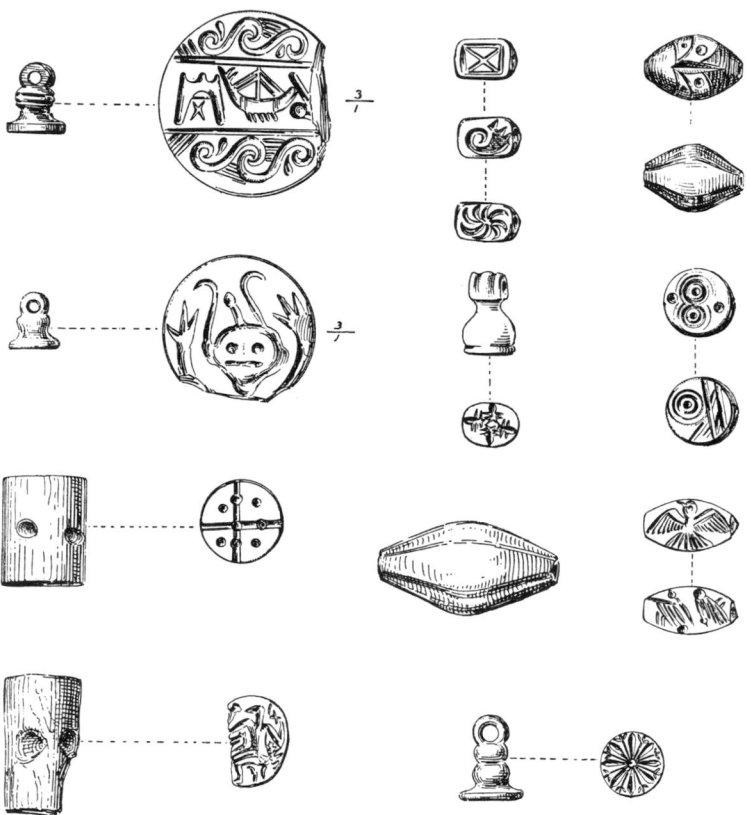

FIG. 105.—MINOAN SEALS WITH PICTOGRAPHS
(*Partly enlarged*)

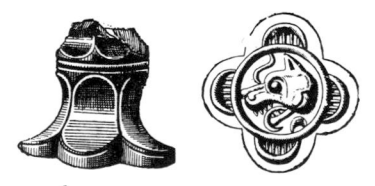

FIG. 106.—A MIDDLE MINOAN SEAL WITH
WOLF'S HEAD DEVICE
(*Enlarged*)

Crete we find no writing till the end of the Early Minoan period, when, some time before 2500 B.C., native pictographic signs begin to be employed on seals (Figs. 105, 106). In M.M. I we find Minoan signs cut on an imported Egyptian XIIth Dynasty scarab (Fig. 107).[1] Then we find that by *circâ* 2200 B.C. this had evolved into a regular system of writing, of which a

[1] Evans, *Palace of Minos*, Fig. 147.

linear or cursive form had come into use, as early as M.M. I*a*,[1] on baked clay labels, bars, and tablets (Fig. 108), an idea derived ultimately from Babylonia through the Semitic population which had colonized eastern Anatolia in the beginning of the third millennium.[2] We do not see that any of the signs of the Minoan ideographic system were derived from Babylonia, however. The Minoan system was also independent of that of Egypt, but it borrowed from Egypt a limited number of signs, some intact, others in altered forms (Fig. 109). This would seem to give us at first sight some foundation on which to essay the interpretation of the

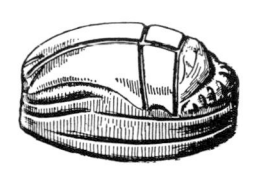

FIG. 107.—EGYPTIAN XIITH– XIIITH DYN. SCARAB WITH MINOAN SIGNS CUT ON BASE

(Enlarged)

Minoan script, but of course we do not know that the borrowed

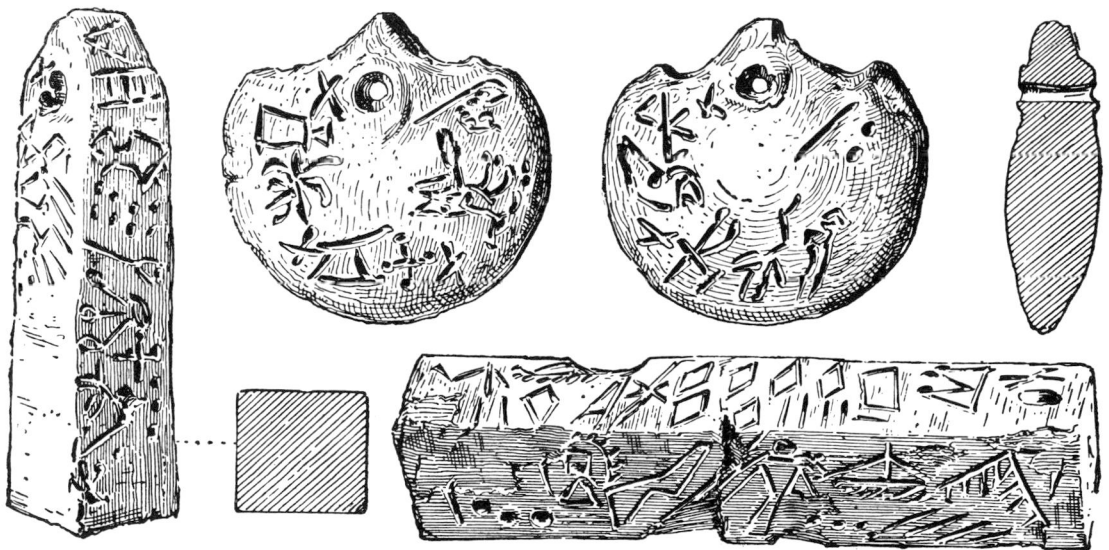

FIG. 108.—MINOAN CURSIVE WRITING INCISED ON BAKED CLAY LABELS AND BARS (M.M. II)
(Actual size)

Egyptian signs retained their original phonetic values or approximations

[1] This is known from a discovery of the French excavators at Mallia, kindly communicated to me by Sir A. Evans. [2] Hall, in *Anatolian Studies pres. to Sir W. Ramsay*, pp. 171–2.

93

most astonishing discovery at the south end of the palace : [1] the foundations of a stepped portico of this early period, with a rising line of supporting pillars ascending the slope, in fact " a prolonged state entrance to the palace on the south side." This was approached by a stone viaduct which was discovered beneath an alluvial deposit that had become indurated by infiltrating gypsum, its piers being thus

preserved beneath a stalagmitic deposit. At its further end, beyond a bridge over a small stream, a bridgehead connected with the line of an ancient roadway, the traces of which Sir Arthur has followed across the island to Komò on the southern sea.[2] The portico served in a remodelled shape till the end of the Third Middle Minoan period, and then was swept away, with the south-west porch to which it led, in the alterations at the end of that period (see p. 116). But fragments of it remain. The viaduct was rebuilt at that time (Fig. 135), but the bases of its piers go back to " M.M. I," like the portico.[3]

FIG. 110.—THE NORTH GATE, KNOSSOS, FROM THE NORTH

These were not absolutely the oldest buildings at Knossos. To the Third Early Minoan period belongs an extraordinary vaulted hypogaeum, circular and of beehive shape with a descending staircase on one side of it from which windows look out into the chambers (Fig. 112).[4] Its circumference at the base was about 100 metres and its original height at least

[1] *The Times*, June 11, 1924. [2] *Ibid*. Oct. 16, 1924.
[3] *Ibid*. June 11, 1924. [4] *Palace of Minos*, p. 104.

16 metres. What its purpose was cannot be said. It may have been a dungeon or a storehouse : probably not a tomb though the *tholos* had been used and was still being used for the ossuary tombs characteristic of the period. The rounded corners of the keep may be compared with the oval house discovered at Khamaézi in Crete, which is of the same date, M.M. I.[1] Most houses of the time were rectangular. The vault of the E.M. III hypogaeum had been cut off in the First Middle Minoan period when the hilltop was cut down and levelled for the building of the

FIG. 111.—THE NORTH GATE, KNOSSOS, FROM THE SOUTH

palace. It was at the end of this age or the beginning of M.M. II that the orthostatic west façade of Knossos (looking on to an open court), with its walls of gypsum on limestone foundation blocks (Fig. 113), was built in its present form, replacing an older M.M. I line ; also the North Gate, later remodelled. The later palace was certainly open and unfortified : Crete, rendered secure by the thalassocracy of " Minos," needed no towers upon the steep, but in the older building with which we are now concerned there is a note of fortification or at any rate a

[1] Xanthoudides, ’Εφημ. ’Αρχ., 1906, p. 117 ff.

7

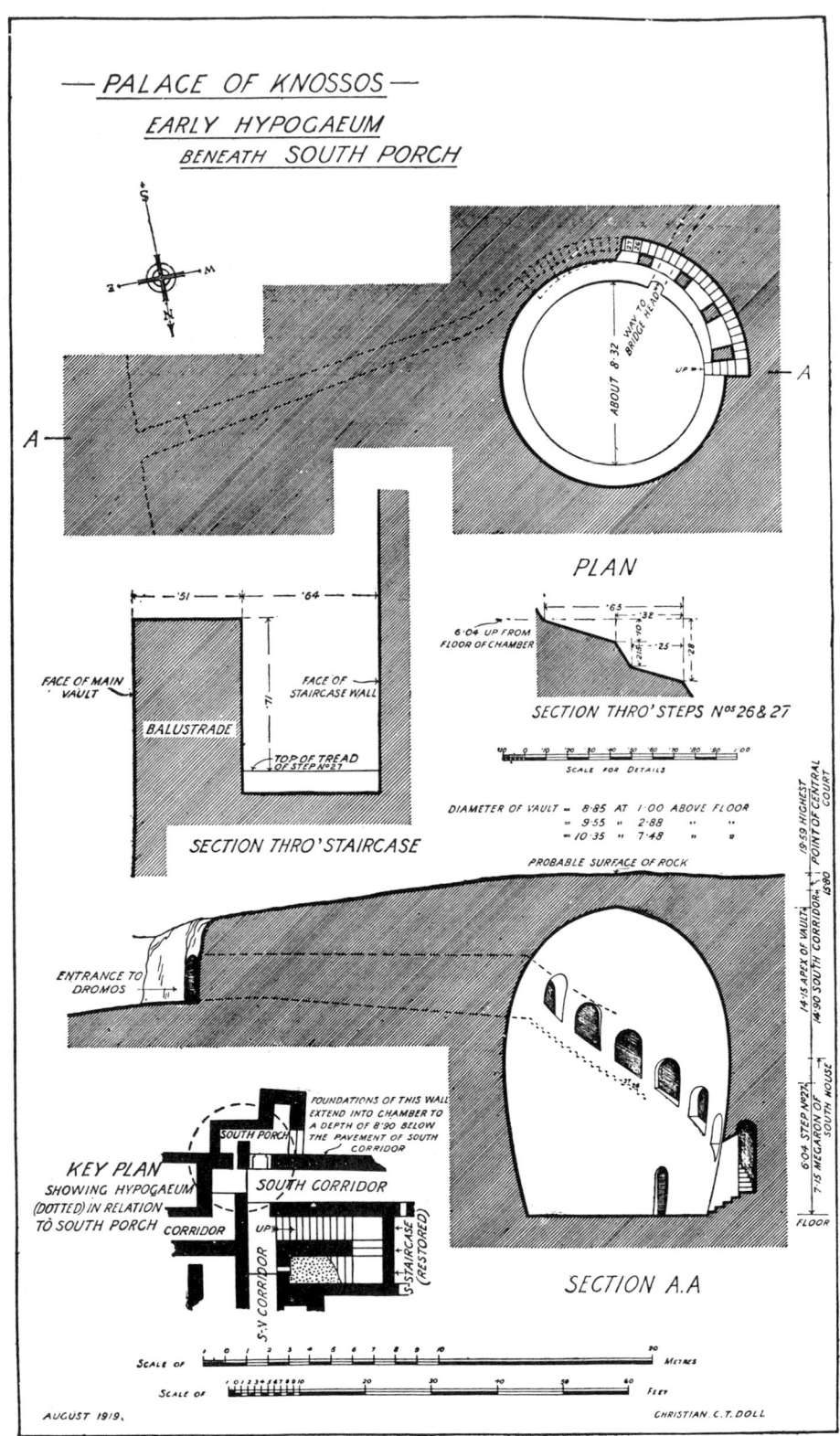

FIG. 112.—THE E.M. III HYPOGAEUM : KNOSSOS

survival of it in architecture, though nothing comparable to the great
walls of Asiatic towns
seems to be indicated.
The older Knossos
bears the same rela-
tion to the later that,
let us say, Hampton
Court does to Knole.

Of the details of
the earlier Knossos we
do not know much.
At Phaistos there are
the lower part of the
great stairway (pp.
109, 112) covered, and
the magazines filled

FIG. 113.—THE ORTHOSTATIC WEST FAÇADE, KNOSSOS

up, with concrete to provide a floor for the M.M. III palace ; one

FIG. 114.—M.M. II PITHOS : PHAISTOS

of the great knobbed Phaestian **M.M. II** *pithoi* from there is shewn in

Fig. 114. The palace of Knossos as it was reconstructed we shall describe later (p. 112 ff.).

The plan and mode of construction of the palace is but a development of the houses we have seen at Mochlos, and is the same as that of the contemporary houses of a Minoan town like Gournià, which we shall mention presently. The same methods of construction are employed in both, the same rubble and gypsum walls faced with plaster, the

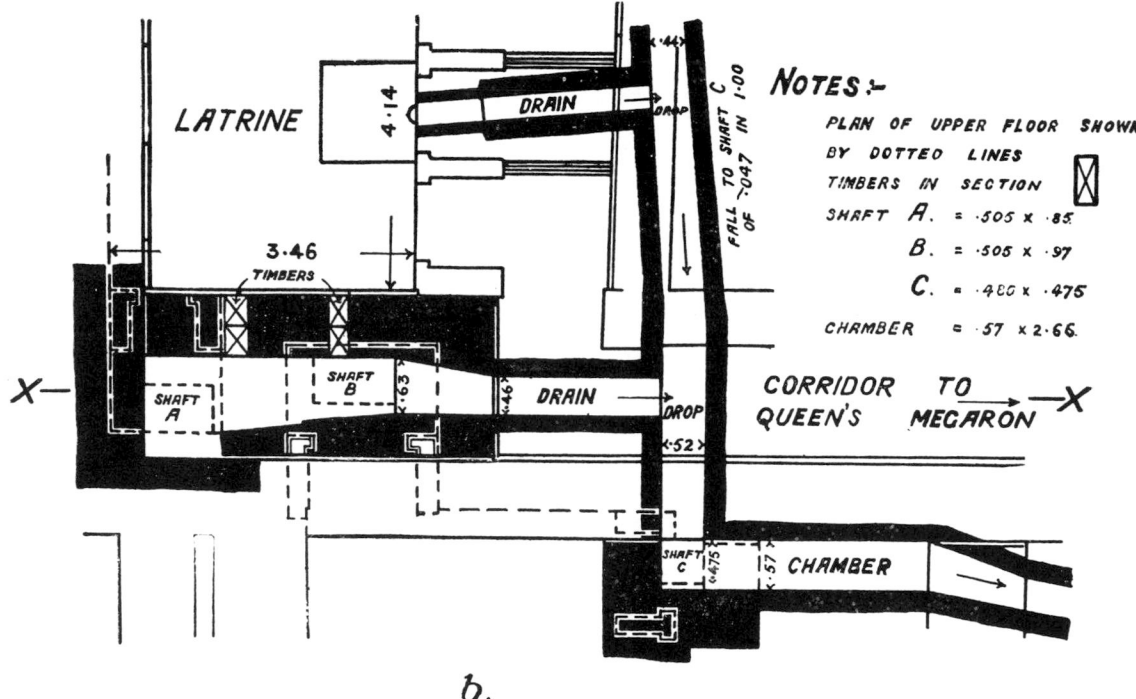

FIG. 115.—PLAN OF DRAINS AND LATRINE: KNOSSOS: *c.* 2000 B.C.

same use of wooden beams to strengthen the construction and bear the weight of the roof. But the occasional use of ashlar to fix a corner firmly has become of regular use for the facing of walls, and the occasional small pillars placed in the centre of lower rooms have become, as at Mallia, great crypt-pillars often ranked in colonnades. The bases of these pillars, whether the latter were of wood or stone, were always of stone, usually of plain limestone or gypsum in later days, and sometimes, as at Mallia, circular. In the earlier days however there was a much greater use of coloured stones, such as variegated breccia, and conglomerate, veined marble, and limestone, serpentine or porphyry, the materials employed often resembling those of the early stone vases. These polychrome bases of the early palace at Knossos were decidedly higher than the later class. The circular base is identical in form with the usual Egyptian type, and may well be of Egyptian origin. But the columns themselves were doubtless always of the familiar Minoan type, tapering to the base and with heavy moulded capitals. The system of " light-wells "

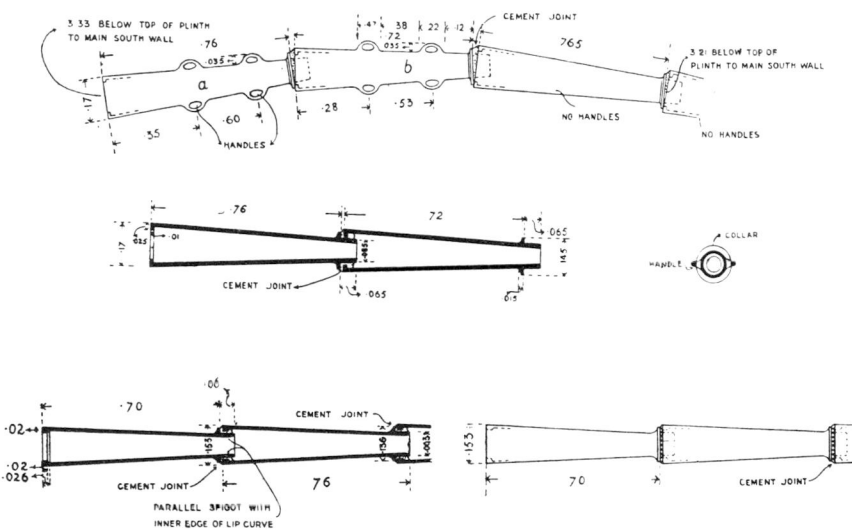

FIG. 116.—MINOAN DRAINPIPES : KNOSSOS, c. 2000 B.C.

or roofless spaces by which the lighting of the rooms in the palace complex was effected was doubtless already in existence. And one of the remarkable phenomena in the Cretan palaces is clearly observable in the older building in Knossos, its most extraordinary drainage system with its up-to-date latrines (Fig. 115) and conical pottery pipes (Fig. 116), which, as Sir Arthur Evans has remarked, are more scientific in design than those we use today. And they first appeared in M.M. I. Nothing like this scientific system of sanitation is known to us in ancient times until Roman days, or anywhere after that till the

England of the nineteenth century.[1] A delightful rebuke to our modern self-sufficiency! One idea however we must give up, and that is that the square depressions with steps leading down to them (Fig. 367), which are a characteristic feature of Cretan palaces, are baths. They can hardly be regular baths, as they are often built of gypsum, which water would gradually dissolve, and there is no outlet in them for the water; Sir Arthur Evans now supposes that they were used for some ceremonial religious purpose, probably lustral.[2]

The walls of the palaces were already in the Second Middle Minoan period adorned with frescoes. The crude painting on the

FIG. 117.—THE " BLUE BOY " FRESCO : KNOSSOS
(M.M. II). (c. $\frac{1}{6}$)

stucco walls of the Early Minoan houses at Mochlos had thus developed *pari passu* with the other arts. The first early example from Knossos, and early examples are rare, is the fresco of the saffron-gatherer or "blue boy" (Fig. 117), reproduced in colour in *The Palace of Minos* (pl. IV), as completed by Mr. Gilliéron. This shews what the Middle Minoan fresco-painter could do. He painted in true fresco, not as the Egyptians did in distemper; that is to say he could not obliterate anything he had once painted, his original line had to stand. To this is no doubt due the sketchiness and at the same time the freedom and command of line that the Cretan painter possessed. The nature of his swift-drying material compelled him to dash off his picture as quickly as he could, and the greater the power of summary execution and decided drawing he possessed the better painter he was. And often the effect is masterly. The well-known fresco of the leaper and the bull from Tiryns, (later in date), quaintly illustrates the difficulties of the

[1] *Palace of Minos*, i, p. 225 ff. [2] *Ibid.* pp. 5, 405.

fresco-painter's work (Fig. 118), since the bull has two tails, the painter having been unable to erase the first wrongly-drawn tail.[1] We shall see that in the hands of inferior artists the effect can be crude and childish, whereas in Egypt except in times of manifest degeneration of the arts, there is always the same high level of accomplishment, always high but never inspired; the craftsman had created a medium which he could handle easily, and the artist had become a craftsman.

In the Middle Minoan strata of the palace have been found a number of small coloured faience tablets forming a mosaic representing a group

FIG. 118.—THE TIRYNS BULL-FRESCO (L.M. III)
(Illustrated here in order to shew limitations of fresco-work) (⅕)

of houses which are extraordinarily modern in appearance, with their two stories, square windows and flat roof (Fig. 119). They are very like Greek houses of to-day. No doubt they faithfully represent the appearance of the houses of the city of Knossos, of which little has yet been excavated, though its great extent can be traced, and a large population (for that day) deduced from its extent. As now in Crete the roofs were flat, no doubt made of mud laid on wooden beams and rafters, and kept flat by the stone roller (usually a bit of an old column) which lies for this purpose on the roof. The fronts were stuccoed and painted in stripes, the windows must have been open. We have no

[1] Schuchhardt, *Schliemann's Excavations*, Fig. 111.

proof that talc was used for window glazing at this time, and no glass fit for the purpose was produced anywhere till Roman times. Glass, an invention derived from their glaze by the Egyptians,[1] had not yet reached Crete. Under the contemporary XIIth Dynasty (*c.* 2200–2000 B.C.), it was still only used, even in Egypt, to make blue beads, apparently. The polychrome opaque glass of the XVIIIth

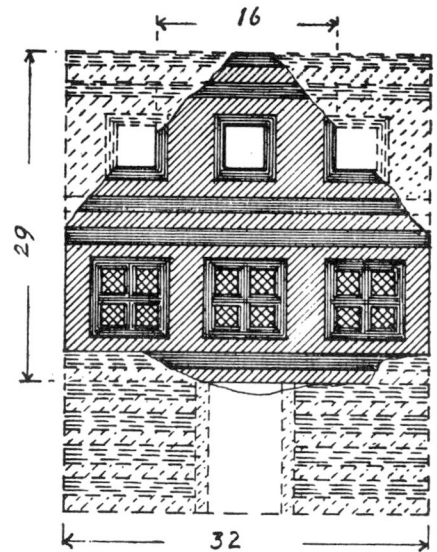
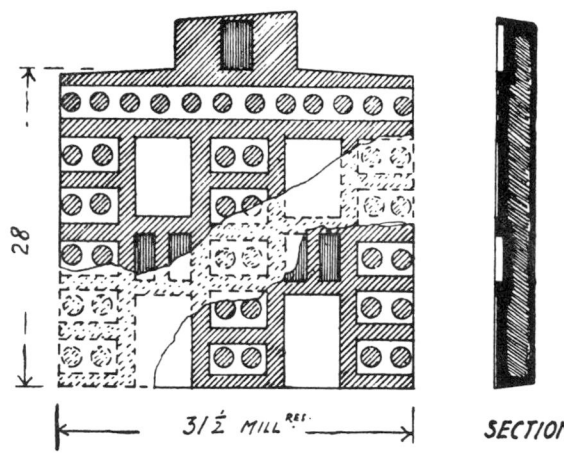

MEASUREMENTS IN MILLIMETRES

DARK GREY GROUND, WITH
CRIMSON STRIPES & WINDOW FRAMES
UPPER WINDOWS OPEN RIGHT THROUGH
LOWER WINDOWS, SUNK, WITH SCARLET FILLING

ALL GREY & WHITE.
WINDOWS, SUNK, WITH SCARLET FILLING

SECTION

FIG. 119.—MINOAN HOUSES OF 2000 B.C. : FROM A MOSAIC, KNOSSOS

Dynasty, which was used to make vases, bottles and other small objects, had not yet been invented, and transparent window-panes were still in the future.

[1] Prof. Newberry points out that the Egyptian word for glass, *tehen*, means " Libyan," " the Libyan thing " ; so that it ought to have been invented on the Libyan side of the Delta. If invented in Egypt as seems probable, it must have reached the East very early, as I found a lump of blue glass in an ancient house at Abu Shahrain (Eridu) in Southern Babylonia, that dated before the time of Bursin, a king of the Third Dynasty of Ur (*c.* 2300 B.C.). See p. 71.

We now know something of what the people who lived in these houses looked like. A seal of E.M. III shews a woman with a chignon and a long high-collared garment (Fig. 120). In a M.M. I votive deposit, found by Prof. Myres at Petsofà near Palaikastro on the east coast of Crete (*B.S.A. Ann.*, ix, p. 356 ff.), were a number of small painted pottery figures of men, women, and animals : from them we can see the costume was much the same as in the next age, when we have so much more information on the subject. The men were nude except for a waistcloth and a necklace ; a short dagger hung across the front of the waistcloth, high white boots were worn as now (Figs.

FIG. 120. — WOMAN OF THE E.M. III PERIOD : FROM A SEAL

(Enlarged)

120, 121). The figures are so crude that the men's hair is represented only by a sort of " pat " on the top of the head, which evidently represents the topknot in which their long hair was sometimes coiled (see p. 122). The women wore the great petticoat which we see later, with a short jacket, or " zouave,"

FIG. 121. — POTTERY FIGURINE OF A MAN : M.M. I (PETSOFÀ) ($\frac{1}{4}$)

FIG. 122.—POTTERY FIGURE OF A WOMAN : M.M. I (PETSOFÀ) ($\frac{1}{2}$)

(Reconstructed type)

open in front and with a sort of high " Medici " collar behind which we have already seen a little earlier (see above). On the head is a great horned turban pointed to the front (Fig. 122 ; reconstruction drawn from several figures by Prof. Dawkins). The hair is put up beneath the turban, not hanging : in this respect the Middle Minoan I. ladies differ from those of the great period, and it shews that they had already claimed their right to be more inconstant in their

105

or a century later, and scarabs that can hardly be older than the XIth Dynasty, *c.* 2350 (earliest) to 2000 (latest).[1] The M.M. II vase from Abydos and the sherds from Kahun date at earliest from about 2050 B.C. The Egyptian seals of E.M. II–III date about 2600–2200 B.C. The Third Early Minoan period began the time of the Sixth Dynasty, *i.e. c.* 2500–2400 B.C.[2] So that the period described in this lecture may be given roughly as dating from about 2400 to 1800 or 1700 B.C.

[1] See above, p. 69 ; and cf. Gournais (*p.* 68 *n.*)

[2] In company with other students of Egyptian antiquity, I do not feel convinced that the date assigned to the Twelfth Dynasty by certain astronomical calculators (viz. 2000–1788 B.C.) is beyond criticism (see *Cambridge Anc. Hist.*, i, p. 173). The Cretan evidence seems to me also to point to a rather longer period between the end of the XIIth Dynasty (M.M. II.) and the beginning of the Eighteenth (1580 B.C., L.M. I) than is allowed by the astronomical calculation. We can hardly allow only two centuries for this period. On the other hand, the Cretan evidence is dead against Petrie's view that a whole Sothic period of 1,460 years (*plus* two centuries) intervened between the end of the XIIth Dynasty and 1580 B.C. Such an immense period of time as 1,700 years is impossible between M.M. II and L.M. I. If Petrie were right, we should have to put the Babylonian seal from Platanos (Fig. 125), which = M.M. I = XIth–XIIth Dynasty, back to *c.* 3600 B.C., whereas on Babylonian evidence it cannot be earlier than about 2000 B.C., a very possible date for the XIth–XIIth Dynasty on Egyptian evidence. As Frankfort points out (*Studies*, ii, p. 101, n.), the chronological evidence from Egypt, Crete, and Babylonia is now so interwoven that there is no room for an independent scheme for Egypt such as Petrie's. And if we do not accept a hypothetical date for the XIIth Dynasty two hundred years earlier (*c.* 2212–2000 B.C.) than the astronomical date, the only alternative is the astronomical date (B.C. 2000–1788). I have noted this possibility by dating King Senusret I to *c.* 2150 or 1950 B.C. (p. 68, above), and Senusret II to 2100 or 1900 (p. 73). I think it quite probable that the VIth Dynasty was as late as 2500–2400, and Meyer's new date for the First Dynasty, 3200 B.C. instead of 3315, seems to me very probable (see dates on pp. 40, 44).

LECTURE IV

FROM THE MIDDLE TO THE LATE
BRONZE AGE

(First Period 1800–1500 b.c., M.M. III and L.M. I)

WE have now come to the greatest and most flourishing period of the Greek Bronze Age culture, as exemplified in Crete and at Mycenae—the period covered by the Third Middle Minoan and First and Second Late Minoan epochs.

The Second Middle Minoan period closed both at Knossos and Phaistos with a catastrophe, which involved the burning and partial destruction of the older palaces, and their rebuilding, after a short period of desolation, by the men of the Third Middle Minoan period in a more elaborate and magnificent, if possibly less beautiful form, which, at Knossos, is practically that which we see to-day, exposed to view by the labours of Sir Arthur Evans (Fig. 126).[1] A disaster overtook it towards the end of the Third Middle Minoan period, attended again by partial conflagration, but the buildings were not destroyed as they had been two hundred years or so before : and were soon repaired. There is good reason to attribute this second destruction to a natural agency, a volcanic disturbance, no doubt attended by widespread earthquake, which has doubtfully (since the dates do not quite fit) been identified with the great catastrophe that blew the original island of Thera into two parts as it is to-day. " At the south-east angle of the palace several

---

[1] *Palace of Minos*, i, p. 315 ff. However the upper and only visible part (see p. 99) of the great stepway at Phaistos, which is M.M. III, is perhaps more imposing than anything similar at Knossos. The wonderfully preserved M.M. III stairway there is of a different type. For the Italian excavations, see Halbherr and Pernier, *Mon. Ant.*, xii (1902) ff.

huge blocks of masonry were found 20 ft. out of place, having been hurled to that distance by an earthquake shock, and having demolished a house in their fall. The pottery and other objects abandoned in the house give an accurate date for the catastrophe at the end of the Middle Minoan period (1600 B.C.)." [1]   The earlier and more complete destruction may be attributed to human agency : to a political convulsion.

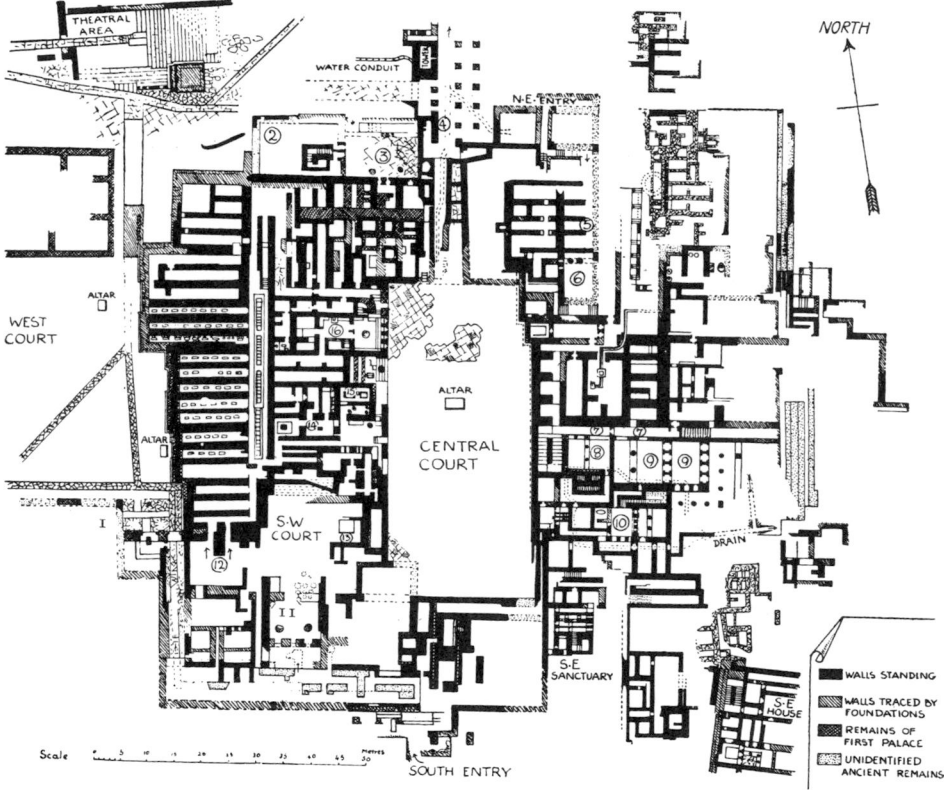

FIG. 126.—PLAN OF KNOSSOS

Presumably this was internal, as we have no warrant to postulate any foreign invasion at this time. It is true that we notice a gradual

[1] Forsdyke, *Encycl. Britt.*, 13th ed., new vol. i, *s.v.* Archaeology, Crete, p. 176 : " Some parts of the palace structure were not rebuilt after their collapse, and this house and another that shared its ruin were methodically filled in after a religious sacrifice had been performed to propitiate the earthshaking power. Relics of the rite were found in two skulls of long-horned bulls and fragments of portable tripod altars."

110

influx of broad-skulled people into Crete, no doubt from Anatolia, during the earlier period of the Bronze Age, which sensibly modi-

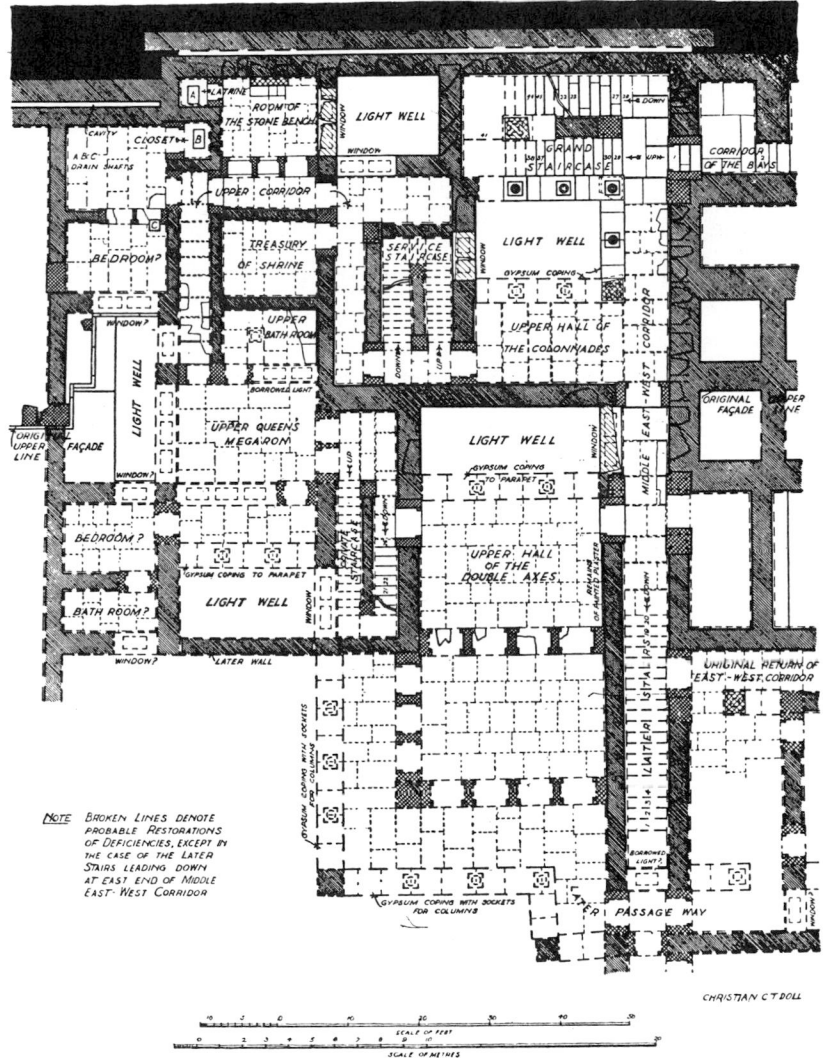

FIG. 127.—GROUND PLAN OF PART OF THE "DOMESTIC QUARTER," KNOSSOS

fied the cranial type of the Cretans, originally long-skulled Mediterraneans;[1] but we have no warrant to suppose that any marked

[1] Xanthoudides, *Vaulted Tombs*, pp. 126–7, sums up the evidence ; *cf*. S. Dudley Buxton, in *Biometrika*, xiii (1920), pt. i, on inhabitants of the E. Mediterranean.

invasion of the kind took place now. The people, their costume, and their art remain the same : the culture of the Third Middle Minoan period continues that of the Second, after a short interval such as would follow a local revolution, and with a difference that marks the opening of a new age. It is to the new age that the storied complex of buildings on the slope above the Kairatos which

FIG. 128.—THE " DOMESTIC QUARTER," KNOSSOS, FROM ABOVE

Evans calls " the Domestic Quarter " (Fig. 127) belongs, in its final form, with its light-wells, halls, corridors, living-rooms (Fig. 128), and stairways (Fig. 129),[1] above all, its magnificent grand stairway, the perservation of which on its old lines is Sir Arthur Evans's greatest

[1] Alongside the steps of this stairway, illustrated in Fig. 129, is a runnel or gutter for carrying off water from the roofs, of a most scientific as well as artistic design, consisting of a series of short convex-curved lengths, which in heavy rain would carry the water swiftly down to the river in a series of miniature waterfalls. This is comparable with the drainage-system (pp. 100–101) as an instance of Minoan skill in water-leading.

112

FIG. 129.—WINDING STAIRWAY ON THE EAST SLOPE, KNOSSOS

triumph. It is indeed rarely that natural conditions allow an ancient building of three or four stories to be dug out, its charred beams carefully replaced by iron girders, and its calcined pillars replaced by new on the old lines, so that we can mount, as at Knossos, an ancient grand stairway of three flights on its original steps, and with the original steps above us as we mount, in their proper place as they were built (Figs.

FIG. 130.—THE GREAT STAIRWAY, KNOSSOS, FROM BELOW

130, 131). This stairway, with its pillared parapet and steps of low tread, perhaps more than anything else at Knossos impresses us with

8   113

the magnificence of conception and capacity of execution that now distinguished the Cretan architects and placed them on a level with, if

not indeed above, those of contemporary Egypt, and only to be surpassed by the architects of Rome and of the Renaissance. We can imagine what the terraced palace of Knossos must have looked like, with its superimposed tiers of flat roofs, from the hill on the other side of the Kairatos-stream : some-

FIG. 131.—THE GREAT STAIRWAY, KNOSSOS, FROM ABOVE

thing like the Vatican or the Potala of Lhasa to-day, or what the Palatine must have looked like in Roman imperial times (*cf.* Fig. 132),

towering above the town[1] which still remains largely unexcavated. We are equally impressed by the grandeur of the great and broad steps leading up from the Phaestian " theatral area " to the M.M. III propylaeum of the palace of Phaistos (Figs. 133-4 ; pp. 99, 109 n.).[2] The Aegean civilization had now come to its own. For a short time it was probably the most beautiful and most aesthetic, though possibly not the most luxurious culture of the world.[3]

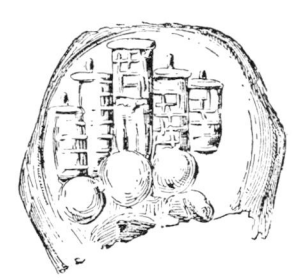

FIG. 132.—A MINOAN PALACE ON A HILL : FROM A M.M. SEAL (*Enlarged*)

For a short time, that is, in comparison with the longer-lived and more static civilizations of Egypt or Babylonia. This dynamic culture of Crete

[1] At Hagia Triada we have a street of the town at the foot of the palace, called by the Italians the agora.

[2] Evans, *Palace of Minos*, Suppl. pl. II.

[3] The civilization of Egypt under the XVIIIth Dynasty was no doubt the most luxurious of the time, but not by any means the most tasteful in all respects. At the end of the dynasty the art is realistic and bizarre, but taste is becoming rococo.

reached its apogee about 1800 B.C. and ceased to exist as a peculiarly Cretan culture about 1400 B.C. Its Mycenaean development perished in chaos and barbarism after 1200 B.C. This period of about 600 years' duration can be conveniently divided for purposes of discussion, parallel with Sir Arthur Evans's period-division, into four periods : (1) M.M.

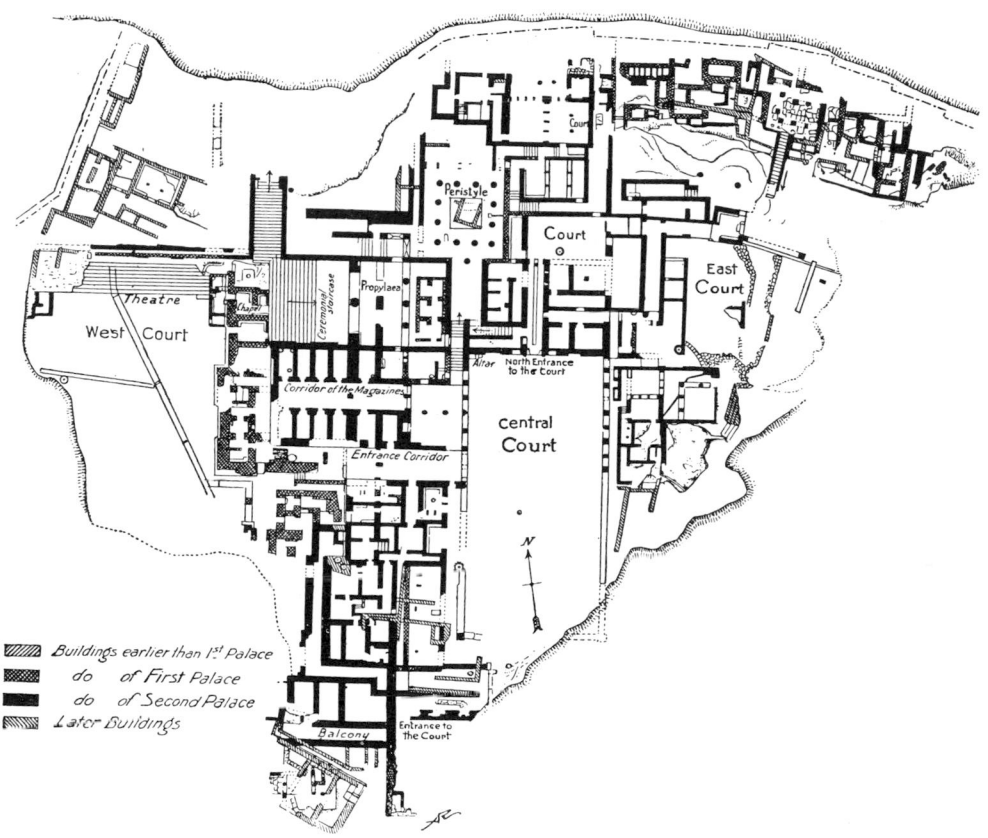

FIG. 133.—PLAN OF PHAISTOS

III–L.M. Ia ; 1800–1500 B.C. (2) L.M. Ib–L.M. II ; 1500–1400 B.C. (3) L.M. IIIa ; 1400–1300 B.C. (4) L.M. IIIb ; 1300–1150 B.C.

It is extraordinarily interesting to trace the swift development, splendid triumph, and speedy fall of this fascinating civilization, especially as exemplified in the progress and changes in the buildings at Knossos. The Knossian dynasts planned, re-planned, re-cast, and altered as much as Italian potentates of the Cinquecento. For aught we know Knossos in the Third Middle Minoan period may have had, too, its Louis XIV, its Mansard, and its Le Nôtre : some great Minos who had that great stairway built, for instance, for his Versailles. And did he build a Grand Trianon, the " Royal Villa " not far off ; or is it really a Petit Trianon of the First Late Minoan time, Louis Quinze rather than Louis Quatorze ?

We have an example of rebuilding in the recently discovered remains by the bridgehead of the ancient M.M. I viaduct leading to the equally

FIG. 134.—THE GREAT STAIRWAY, PHAISTOS

ancient stepped portico that led up to the south-west porch of the palace (p. 96). The porch and portico were removed in M.M. III, and, probably, as a result of the great earthquake (p. 109), and the viaduct rebuilt in L.M. I in solid masonry : " the stepped intervals between the piers, through which the flood-waters were released, are precisely like the spillways of a modern dam " [1] (Fig. 135). The removal of the gypsum deposit that had covered it has revealed what seems to be a

[1] Forsdyke, *Encycl. Britt.*, 13th ed., new vol. i, *s.v.* Archaeology, Crete ; p. 176.

116

rest-house or inn of transitional M.M. III–L.M. I age, with an " elegant little pavilion " adorned with frescoes of partridges and plants,[1] and a bath, " preserved intact in its petrified shell," and with a fountain, with stone benches and basin, ledges for stone lamps, and a niche,[2] which continued in use till L.M. III, and in latest Minoan days and the proto-geometric period " became a place of cult." With its stone shelves and its little basin filled with clear water, this holy well has

FIG. 135.—THE M.M. I VIADUCT, KNOSSOS (REBUILT IN L.M. I)

an oddly Roman appearance. What the Minos intended to effect in altering the viaduct and portico after the earthquake is not clear ; but that he did not stop the way into the palace is evident by the fact that the viaduct was repaired and continued in use till L.M. II and by the apparent purpose of the new buildings, which also continued to be used till then.

The frescoes of the " Caravansarai," as Sir Arthur Evans calls it, call us to consider the remarkable wall-paintings that now become

[1] Illustrated *J.H.S.* 1924, p. 265.   [2] *Ibid.*, p. 263.

characteristic decorations of the palace corridors. Of these the restored fragment of the fresco of " the ladies in blue " gives a good idea.[1] This is of the M.M. III period, and so are the Dolphin fresco of Knossos, and a curious fragment shewing the hand of a man touching a gold bead necklace with pendant beads of negroid type with double earrings, probably of Egyptian origin.[2] Of the same period are the figure wearing a curiously dagged robe from Phaistos (Fig. 136), the cat stalking a pheasant from Hagia Triada

FIG 136.—FRESCO OF A PERSONAGE IN A PATCHWORK ROBE, WALKING AMID FLOWERS (PHAISTOS). ($\frac{1}{18}$)

Fig. 137),[3] and the flying fish from Phylakopi in Melos (Fig. 138),[4] a fresco that was certainly by a Cretan artist, and possibly executed in Crete and exported as it stood to Melos. Of the transition to L.M. I are the newly discovered fresco of monkeys amid Egyptian papyrus-plants at Knossos (1923) and possibly

FIG. 137.—THE FRESCO OF THE HUNTING CAT (HAGIA TRIADA ; M.M. III) ($\frac{1}{10}$)

[1] The faces in this fresco have been restored by M. Gilliéron (*Palace of Minos*, Fig. 397), and they are perhaps " Parisian " rather than Minoan, reminding us forcibly of the feminine types immortalized by the French artist " Mars " ; but we feel that the Minoan artist would quite have approved of them ! I do not, however, illustrate the fresco here as it is so much restored, and might give a wrong impression to the general reader.

[2] Evans, *Palace*, i, Fig. 383.

[3] Halbherr, *Mon. Ant.*, xiii, pl. VIII.   [4] *Phylakopi*, pl. 3.

the famous " Cupbearer Fresco " (Frontispiece ; p.182).   The naturalism

FIG. 138.—THE FLYING FISH FRESCO : PHYLAKOPI, L.M. I $(\frac{1}{3})$

of these animal frescoes, and the extraordinary "style" of that of "the ladies in blue" is characteristic of the period. Of the L.M. I period are the procession of black soldiers from Egypt, led by a Cretan (Fig. 139), found in the house of a local magnate of this time (as was also the fresco of the monkeys, but at a lower level), and the "Miniature-frescoes" of Knossos and Tylissos,[1] in which we see groups of men and women sketched in slight, but masterly fashion : at Knossos ladies at a window (Fig. 140) and a crowd of men

YELLOW
BLUE
RED

FIG. 139.—PROCESSION OF BLACK SOLDIERS : KNOSSOS

and women near a temple or great altar (Fig. 141) ; at Tylissos, men

[1] *B.S.A. Ann.*, vi, p. 47 ; *J.H.S.*, xxi, pl. V ; Ἐφημ. Ἀρχ. 1912, pls. 18, 19.

119

and women sitting or standing, alone and in groups. We are reminded of the frescoes of the Ajanta caves or of those of Duke Borso in the Schifanoia palace at Ferrara, so far as the idea is concerned ; but of

course the scale is smaller and the execution quite summary. Here the speediness of the work (necessary in true fresco painting) has developed a sort of " shorthand " representation : a crowd is shewn by a mass of faces, heads in outline with no bodies ; and to indicate the difference between the sexes the men's heads are drawn in black outline on a red

FIG. 140.—FRESCO OF LADIES AT A WINDOW : KNOSSOS, L.M. I ($\frac{1}{3}$)

ground, and the women's on white ; both have white specks for eyes.

Another fragment of a similar subject, with much the same convention, from Knossos of rather earlier date (M.M. III) is shewn in Fig. 142.

FIG. 141.—FRESCO SHEWING A CROWD OF MEN AND WOMEN IN A PILLARED SANCTUARY
KNOSSOS, L.M. I ($\frac{1}{3}$)

Here the white specks for the eyes are used, but the picture is not quite so summary as the other, since the men are shown in the usual manner, according to the convention borrowed from Egypt, with red faces and black hair : women having white or yellow faces. The men are distinguished from the women only by their colour and by slight differences in their hairdressing; for the Minoan men were

FIG. 142.—" SHORTHAND " FRESCO OF A CROWD OF MEN : KNOSSOS, M.M. III ($\frac{2}{3}$)

clean-shaven and now wore their hair as long as the women, and as elaborately dressed.[1]

[1] It is now usually represented as worn at its full natural length, falling normally to the waist. The man of the bronze figure illustrated by Fig. 227 has a mass of hair on his back in two locks tied or knotted together at the level of the shoulders; below this they reach the small of the back. A metal figure from Gournià (*Gournià*, p. 55 ; pl. XI) and another at Vienna (Bossert, *Altkreta*, Fig. 149a) have it in spiral curls. On the top of the head fantastic knots, horns, and curls (Gladiator Vase (Fig. 196) and Figs. 139, 142, above) were so often worn that they were noted by the Egyptian artists of the XVIIIth Dynasty as a feature equally characteristic with the long locks down the back, which were usually unconfined though the back hair is seen tied at the neck on the Vaphio cups (Fig. 192) and the British Museum figure (Fig. 226). The prince on the "Chieftain Vase" (Fig. 195) wears it confined by slides or clasps on the top of his head and at the sides. A similar slide is seen on the top of the head in Fig. 224. On the fragment of the steatite vase, Fig. 237, the hair is partly done up on the top of the head, partly twisted in a hanging pigtail; the Tylissos figure (Fig. 229) has it also partly piled up on the head, partly hanging in tails down the back. The hair was sometimes worn simply knotted on the top of the head, as we see in the case of the warrior on the "Chieftain Vase" and on the signet-ring with the fighting

The effect of this summary method of representing a crowd is very curious : these floating heads give an eerie impression, as if we were looking at the ghosts of these Minoan men and women, dead three thousand years ago and more.

We can see Egyptian inspiration in these frescoes in the picture of the monkeys and the papyrus-plants, and that of the cat stalking the pheasant, but the Minoan painter depicts the animals, and more especially the cat, in his own free way, in a spirit quite different from that of an Egyptian artist. Egyptian pictures of animals, admirable as they are, are like accurate coloured illustrations for a work on natural history; the Minoan are impressions, inspired however by Egyptian art. We sometimes in Minoan art see plants depicted as stiffly and formally as in Egypt (until the age of Akhenaten), and so no doubt under Egyptian influence; at other times more freely than in Egypt (Fig. 208), a foretaste of the naturalistic vase-designs of L.M. I. In the fresco of the black soldiers we see the first Minoan representation of Nubians or negroes, who must have come from Egypt (the restored separate head in Fig. 131 is certainly that of a negro, and has been so restored : it has curly black hair).[1] If the man on the " Harvesters

warriors from Mycenae (Fig. 165). No doubt it was often so worn in war or the chase. The " pats " on the heads of the Petsofà figurines of men (Fig. 121) are more probably topknots than caps. The round caps of the young men on the Harvesters' Vase (Fig. 193) probably conceal topknots. There are however two heads, one of a boy, the other of a man, in M.M. II (Fig. 123) on sealings that seem to represent short hair, at any rate in the case of the boy. In L.M. III we see short-haired men on the Hagia Triada sarcophagus (Fig. 293), but this is unusual and may be merely a sign of grief (see p. 281). Possibly unshorn hair became the usual fashion in the Middle Minoan period (see p. 106).

The fashionable coiffures of the L.M. I ladies, with the hair knotted loosely on the crown and hanging in shoulder curls at the sides as we see it in the Knossian frescoes, much resembled those in vogue at the court of Charles II and sometimes have a look of the Paris fashions of the Second Empire (Fig. 140). In older days fashions were simpler, as in the case of the men. In M.M. III we have the hair hanging loosely down the back, but shorter than that of the men ; and great turbans or " poloi " on the head, as in the case of the " snake-goddesses " (Fig. 128). Or it is concealed by a sort of turban, as in the case of a M.M. II head from Mochlos (Fig. 124), which has often been taken to be that of a man, but from the traces of white paint on it should, according to Mr. Seager, be regarded as a woman. In M.M. II at Petsofà we have seen a high horn on the head (Fig. 122).

[1] It has been supposed that the Egyptians did not come into contact with the true

Vase" from Hagia Triada, carrying an Egyptian sistrum and with a bigger waist than his Minoan companions (see below, p. 156), is, as has been thought, an Egyptian, we have the earliest Minoan representation of an actual Egyptian (M.M. III), somewhat earlier than the negroes-fresco, and perhaps two centuries earlier than the first Egyptian representation of Minoans (pp. 182, 199 ff). In architectural details we see Egypt in the columnar lamp of purple gypsum with its palm-leaf capital,[1] in ceramic decoration on the M.M. II vase with the palms, from Knossos (Fig. 143).

FIG. 143.—VASE WITH PALM DESIGN : KNOSSOS, M.M. II

In the famous Egyptian vase-lid with the name of the Hyksos king Khayan, written , found at Knossos,[2] we see evidence of the continued connexion with Egypt : his date is about 1650 B.C. It is of course no proof of a Hyksos conquest of Crete at this time or of anything but commercial and diplomatic connexion : nor in the succeeding age, contemporary with the conquering Egypt of the Eighteenth Dynasty, is there any record or archaeological proof of political subjection to Egypt, even in the "spacious days" of king Thutmosis III (see p. 205). Babylonian influence is distinctly seen in the stone vases with white shell inlay, a characteristic and ancient Babylonian technique (Fig. 144).[3] And we

FIG. 144.—VASE WITH WHITE SHELL INLAY : KNOSSOS, M.M. III $(\frac{1}{3})$

negroes till the time of the XVIIIth Dynasty (Junker, *Das erste Auftreten der Neger*, Vortr. Wiener Akad., 1920). But it is unwise to press this view, which may be upset at any moment by some such discovery as this Minoan fresco, which certainly seems to depict negroes rather than Nubians, and is certainly anterior to the XVIIIth Dynasty. *Cf.* also the M.M. III fresco of the hand with the necklace of beads in the form of earringed negroid heads (Evans, *Palace*, Fig. 383). Blacks are more likely to have come to Crete through civilized Egypt than through Libya.

[1] Evans, *Palace*, i, p. 345, Fig. 249. [2] *Ibid.*, p. 419 ; Fig. 304b.
[3] They were imitated in pottery.

123

shall see it again in the stone vases with reliefs (p. 156 ff.) from Hagia Triada (L.M. I) which owe their inspiration ultimately to Sumerian, not to

Egyptian art. Babylon was further away from Egypt, yet her influence, evident in the clay tablet, and documented by such objects as the cylinder-seal from Platanos (Fig. 125), was, if not by any means equally potent, yet definite.

FIG. 145.—SPHINX, WITH HOLES FOR INLAY : HAGIA TRIADA, L.M. I. (½)

The curious little stone sphinx from Hagia Triada (Fig. 145) shews holes for shell or other inlay, but is otherwise not in the least Babylonian. It is, we must suppose, Minoan, though the head is curiously like those of the sphinxes at Euyuk, and we must not ignore the possibility of such Hittite influences on Minoan art.

To the M.M. III period at Knossos belong the series of long magazines (Fig. 146) with

FIG. 146.—THE MAGAZINES AT KNOSSOS : 1926

their great oil-jars or *pithoi* (Fig. 147) and their stone receptacles for valuables in the pavements, called now *kasellais* (Fig. 148). Besides there have been found much larger stone "repositories"

124

in which were found one of the most famous of Sir Arthur Evans's discoveries, the polychrome faience group of the " Snake Goddesses " and its accessories. The royal gaming-board (Fig. 149), found elsewhere in the palace, with its elaborate intarsia work in ivory and crystal backed by blue *kyanos*,[1] its men of ivory (Fig. 150), and the snake-goddesses [2] (Figs. 151, 152) with their delicately coloured faience which shews how the Cretans had modified the Egyptian invention, are indeed amazing products of this strange art of the Greek Bronze Age. The

FIG. 147.—PITHOI IN THE MAGAZINE-CORRIDOR, KNOSSOS. MT. IUKTAS BEYOND

figures of the goddesses (partly restored) are interesting. The high tiaras and turbans of the goddesses (if they are goddesses), differing from the headdresses of the somewhat later L.M. I frescoes, show that as ever the ladies were more fickle in their attachment to fashions than the men, whose long hair and waistcloth-kilt were from M.M. II on as immutable, apparently, as modern male evening dress ! However, the voluminous skirts now affected by the ladies, with their aprons and their flounces like those of the skirts of the 1870's and early 1880's, remained

[1] Evans, *Palace of Minos*, pl. V.
[2] *Ibid.*, p. 495 ff.

FIG. 148.—A MAGAZINE SHOWING *KASELLAIS* : KNOSSOS : M.M. III

the same in Late Minoan days, though coiffures might alter. The cow and the goat with their young (Fig. 153) are characteristically Minoan in their style : the constant tendency to an exaggerated length of body being very noticeable. And the faience shells and flying-fish strike a marine note suitable to Crete.

The faience vases found with these figures are very graceful in shape, and decorated with naturalistic plant-sprays or spiral coils in relief ; the

FIG. 149.—THE INLAID GAMING-BOARD :
KNOSSOS (M.M. III) ($\frac{1}{12}$ c.)

FIG. 151.—SNAKE-GODDESS OR PRIESTESS,
POLYCHROME FAIENCE : M.M. III : KNOSSOS
(c. $\frac{1}{3}$)
(Restored)

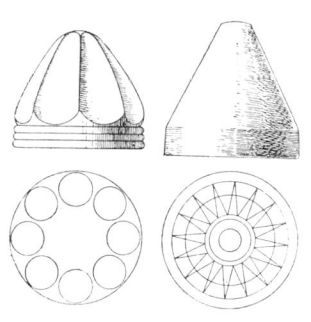

FIG. 150.—IVORY GAMING-PIECES :
KNOSSOS (Enlarged)

plant-sprays stray over the lip of the vase in very modern wise (Fig. 154).

Perhaps, as in Egypt, owing to his attention being attracted to faience at this time, the Cretan potter did not take so much trouble with his painted pottery as in the preceding age. There was a sharp revulsion in taste from the brilliant polychrome black and red and white of the

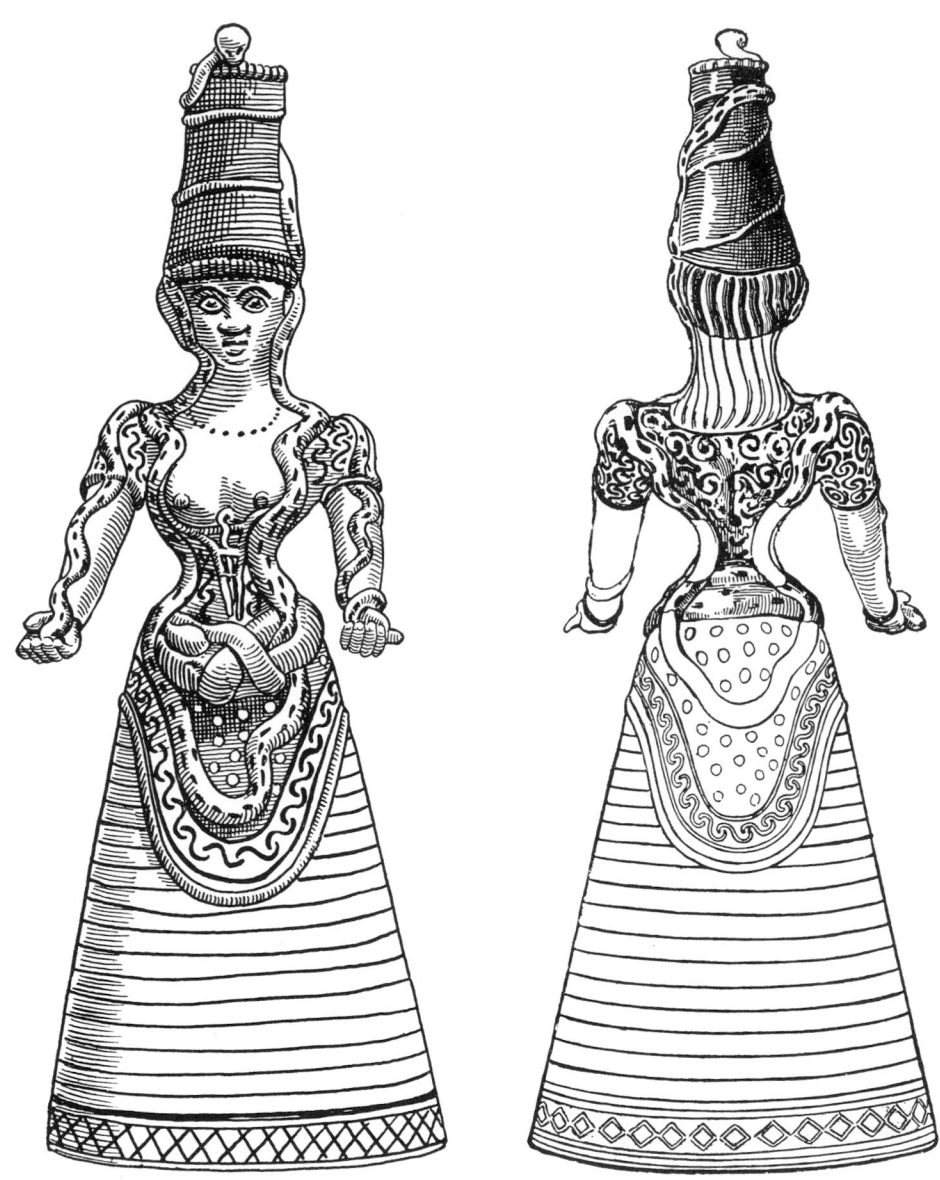

FIG. 152.—SNAKE-GODDESS OR PRIESTESS, POLYCHROME FAIENCE : M.M. III : KNOSSOS $(c. \frac{3}{7})$

(Restored)

Kamárais style, and simpler, rougher pots were in vogue, sometimes with a decoration imitating the " trickle " of oil down the outside of the vase (Fig. 155). We see the same idea carried out in glaze on some

128

Japanese vases. The barbotine style produces vases like Fig. 156, with barley-ears moulded in relief on the surface. On some pots we see

FIG. 153.—COW AND GOAT WITH YOUNG : POLYCHROME FAIENCE : M.M. III : KNOSSOS (⅟₄)

FIG. 154.—FAIENCE VASES : M.M. III : KNOSSOS (⅟₃)

fine spiral designs still in a large and bold style ; on others we find the naturalism of the L.M. I period beginning with fine plant-

9

forms, such as lilies [1] and with the greater beasts of the sea such as dolphins (Fig. 157), like those in the frescoes. There is little doubt

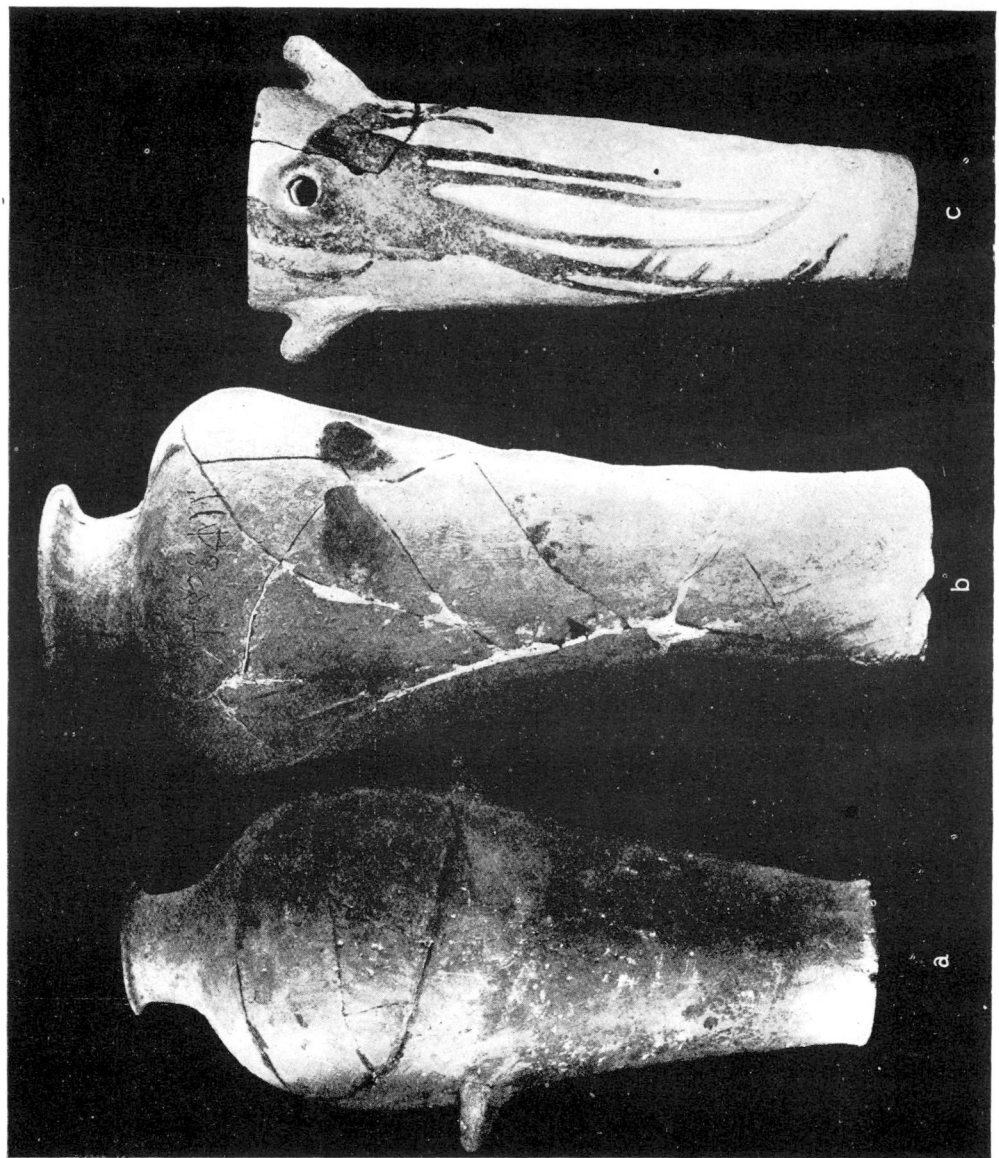

FIG. 155.—M.M. III VASES : KNOSSOS (C. ⅓)

that the fresco-paintings were the source of the new bent towards

[1] Evans, *Palace of Minos*, Fig. 443.

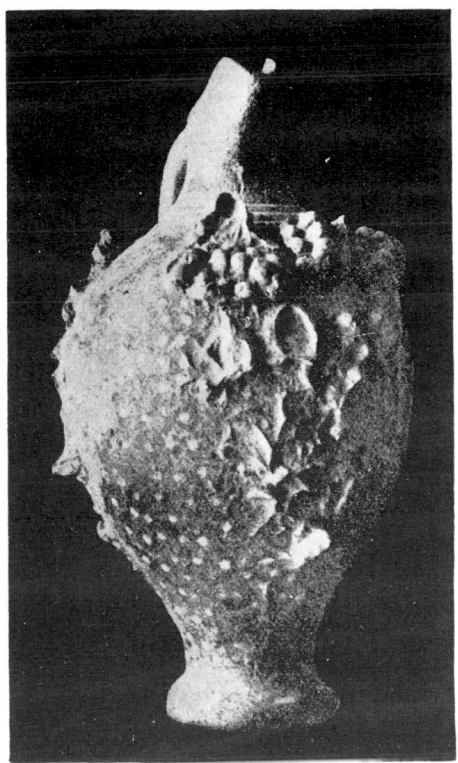

FIG. 156.—BARBOTINE WARE : M.M. III. ($\frac{3}{5}$)

naturalism. The potters copied the wall-painters.

Generally speaking the taste of this period was more restrained than that of the preceding and succeeding ages : of all the Minoan pottery that of M.M III would most please a Japanese connoisseur.

We find at this period (M.M. III–L.M. I) for the first time, besides incised graffiti, inscriptions formally painted on walls (house

FIG. 157.—DOLPHIN-VASE : M.M. III

of the frescoes, Knossos), and inscribed on pots in ink (Fig. 158), another Egyptian invention that now reached Crete. These inscriptions are in the linear form (Class A) of the hieroglyphs that had now evolved (see p. 93) from the older seal-hieroglyphs, for use in cursive writing. This is found incised on tablets (Fig. 159), as before, and on large stone objects of importance, such as

FIG. 158.—GLAZED WARE WITH INK INSCRIPTION : CLASS A, KNOSSOS : M.M. III
(*Slightly reduced*)

the famous offering-table from the "Dictaean" Cave in Lasíthi, found by Sir Arthur Evans,[1] while on seals hieroglyphs are mostly displaced in favour of representations of deities, of religious dances, fights with bulls, lions, and sea-monsters, scenes of the chase and of war, and also, somewhat later, by purely fantastic designs such as those seen

FIG. 159.—CLAY TABLET WITH MINOAN LINEAR INSCRIPTIONS (CLASS A) : HAGIA TRIADA : M.M. III–L.M. I ($\frac{1}{2}$)

[1] Evans, *Palace of Minos*, Figs. 465–7; p. 625 ff.

132

on the L.M. I clay impressions of seals found at Zakro by Dr. Hogarth, with their weird fantasies of stags with women's heads and butterfly-wings, stag-headed men like Herne the Hunter, bull-headed men like the Minotaur, winged bucrania and cherub-heads, and so forth, which are among the most strange and fantastic in all art, ancient or modern [1] (Fig. 160). If the Cretan potter of this time was restrained in his art, the seal-cutter was not! An unique signet of gold in the form of a

FIG. 160.—ZAKRO SEALINGS : L.M. I
(*Enlarged*)

miniature ring with linear signs incised on the bezel in a helical path, like that of the Phaistos Disk, dates to this time (M.M. III). It was found by Mr. Forsdyke in his tomb-excavations at Knossos in 1927.

Among the written clay documents of the Third Middle Minoan period

[1] *J.H.S.*, xxii (1902), pl. VI–X. It may be wondered whether in these fantasques an influence is not present from the Cyclades, where queer imps were popular motives in design (see p. 139). They are worthy of Hieronymus Bosch!

is that unparalleled object, the Phaistos Disk (Fig. 161), with its helical inscription impressed by wooden (?) moveable types.[1] There is reason to suppose that at this time wooden stamps (like our butter stamps) were employed to effect the relief decoration of some of the larger Cretan vases or *pithoi*, but the Cretans never used this device for stamping inscriptions. And though their snail-wise path may be Cretan (to

FIG. 161.—THE PHAISTOS DISK $(\frac{1}{2})$

judge by Mr. Forsdyke's ring), the signs of the Phaistos Disk are not Cretan : they do not belong to any system otherwise known in Crete. Various indications point to this being a foreign object, most probably from the coast of Lycia ; a solitary relic of the non-Minoan (yet possibly

[1] *Palace of Minos*, p. 657 ff. ; *Scripta Minoa*, p. 22 ff. ; original publication by Pernier, *Ausonia*, 1909, p. 255 ff.

134

related) culture of the south-west coast of Asia Minor, probably distinct from that of the Carians and Leleges (which was perhaps akin to the Cycladic (see p. 60)), and specifically Lycian. One thing too is notice-

FIG. 162.—MEN AND WOMEN ON THE PHAISTOS DISK

able, that though the women's dress shewn in these Lycian hieroglyphs resembles that of the Cretan women, the men's heads are apparently clean-shaven, or wear a close-fitting skull-cap surmounted by a high brush-like feather-crest (Fig. 162), quite a different coiffure from that of the Cretan

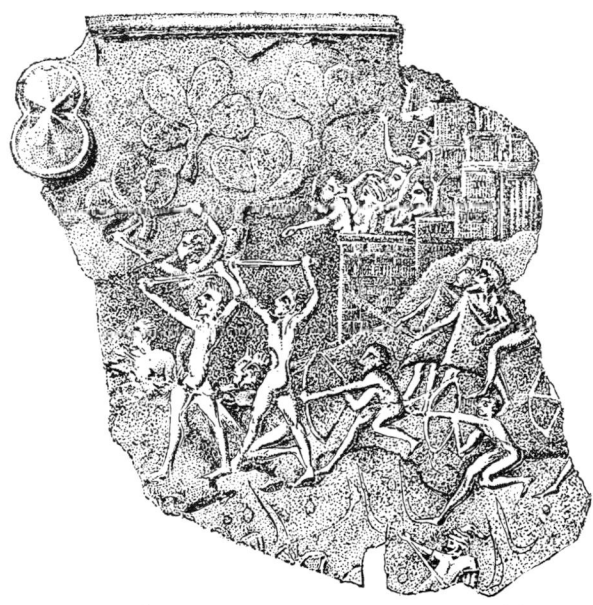

FIG. 164.—DETAIL OF MEN'S HEAD-DRESS FROM THE MYCENAE RHYTON

men. This feather-crest is also seen on the well-known fragment of a silver rhyton (now com-

FIG. 163.—THE MYCENAE RHYTON-FRAGMENT ($\frac{4}{5}$)

pleted) from the Fourth Shaft Grave at Mycenae (Fig. 163), in which short-crested slingers (Fig. 164) are shewn defending a town against an attack from the sea (?) of warriors wearing helmets with

135

long horse-tail crests.[1]   The crest was a national characteristic of the Lycians and Carians down to classical times, and the λόφος or helmet-crest was said to have been invented by the Carians, who communicated it on the one hand to the Greeks and on the other to the Hittites[2] and Assyrians.   The Cretan warriors sometimes wear a long horse-tail nodding above

FIG. 165.—GOLD RING WITH SCENE OF CONTENDING WARRIORS: MYCENAE: L.M. (MYC.) I
(*Enlarged*)

their helmets when they donned them : but they often fought bareheaded, with the hair knotted on the top or at the back of the head as we see on the "Chieftain Vase" (Figs. 194–5) and the ring and gem shewing warriors fighting (Figs. 165, 166), some with tailed helms, others bareheaded.   In Greece, a peculiar form of helmet, without crest, and ornamented with boar's tusks (?), was often used later on (Fig. 167), and the crestless helm both there (Fig. 278) and in Crete, as on the "Gladiators' Vase" (Fig. 196) and on the remarkable vase

FIG. 166.—GOLD RING-BEZEL WITH INTAGLIO SCENE OF CONTENDING WARRIORS: MYCENAE: L.M. (MYC.) I
(*Actual size*)

FIG. 167.—IVORY HEAD OF A WARRIOR, SHOWING BOAR'S-TUSK (?) HELMET WITH CHEEK-PIECES: MYCENAE: L.M. III
(*Actual size*)

[1] Hall, *J.H.S.*, xxxi (1911), p. 119 ff ; Evans, *Palace of Minos*, i, p. 668.
[2] Hogarth, *Carchemish*, I, pll. B2, B3.

136

from a Knossian tomb, with representations (Fig. 254) of a laminated helm with knob on the top, cheekpieces, and neck-guard, like that of Fig. 278. A similar laminated helm is seen on a Minoan faience fragment from the Third Grave, Mycenae.[1] The helm of the "Gladiators" appears to be all metal, however; and the metal helmet may have been a Cretan invention which later passed eastward to the Assyrians and later descended to the classical Greeks, unless of course it came to Crete originally from Babylonia; the Sumerians used it. Not from Egypt: it was never used there.

But the appearance of Minoan warriors with helmets, tailed or not, above their long hair is quite different from that of the foreigners on the Phaistos Disk, with their brush-like crests above apparently bare skulls. They wore no helmet with tails, which may have been a Cretan invention to which the brush-like Carian crest was added: we see both in the case of the later Hittites. This crest of feathers is represented in a modified form as a crown in the later Egyptian representations of the Philistines (Fig. 168), who with other Aegean tribes attacked

FIG. 168.—HEAD OF A PHILISTINE (XIIITH CENT. B.C.) MEDINET HABU

Egypt in the days of decadence, about 1200 B.C., before they settled in Palestine (p. 241): and in Assyrian representations of much later date (VIIth cent.) we see western warriors wearing both the crown of feathers and the cock's comb crest (without the tail) (Fig. 169). The Lycians are mentioned by name as early as 1400 B.C., as an important "people of the sea," and there is little doubt that the Philistines were of the same race, and came from Caria and Lycia.

[1] Schuchhardt, *Schliemann's Excavations*, Fig. 198. On the top of the helm is an ornament which seems much to resemble the crescent and ball of the Shardina warriors (Fig. 317). This is however uncertain. I have not reproduced Schuchhardt's illustration, which seems to me rather sophisticated. A new photograph of the object is desirable.

137

We then find evidence on the Phaistos Disk of peaceful connexion with Anatolia at this time, and on the silver rhyton from Mycenae of warlike connexion : this may well represent a Cretan or Mycenaean

FIG. 169.—ASSYRIANS AND WESTERN ALLIES (?) WEARING THE FEATHERED CROWN AND CREST : VIITH CENT. RELIEF

attack on a Lycian stronghold. To the same period in all probability is to be assigned the destruction of the thalassocracy of the Carians by " Minos," recorded by Herodotos (i, 171) and Thucydides (i, 4). We

FIG. 170.—MELIAN VASE WITH BIRD-DESIGN (M.C. III) (ASHMOLEAN) (c. $\frac{1}{2}$)

have seen that there is some reason to suppose that the tradition of Carian dominion in the Aegean may be connected with a probable relation of the early Carians with the Cycladic culture (p. 60) : which seems to have extended to the Carian coast now as earlier. And it is now that the peculiarities of Cycladic art near their end in absorption by Crete. Imported Minoan ceramic and fresco-painting (e.g. the Flying Fish fresco, Fig. 138) are evidently the most prized artistic possessions of the Melians of this period : they dominate the native art, though a peculiar native style of vase-painting still continued, with matt designs (M.C. III) sometimes of

138

strange splodgy birds in brownish black and red (Fig. 170), sometimes imitated from Egyptian animals[1] or adapted from an Egyptian frieze of *rekhyut*-birds 🐦 🐦 🐦 (Fig. 171), sometimes shewing imp-like figures (Fig. 172) reminding us of the Zakro seals (Fig. 160), while

FIG. 171.—MELIAN VASE-FRIEZE OF EGYPTIAN ORIGIN

here (though rarely in Crete)[2] the human figure appears on pottery, crudely enough, however (Fig. 173).[3] A crude polychromy tries in M.C. II–III to imitate the achievements of the Kamárais potters,

FIG. 172.—MELIAN IMPS (M.C. III)

and then in " L.C. I " the characteristics of L.M. I design are imitated equally crudely (Fig. 174).

[1] Hall, *J.E.A.*, 1914, p. 200 (Fig. 6).

[2] A rude human figure occurs on a M.M. I cup from Palaikastro (*B.S.A. Ath. Suppl.* i : pl. v), probably owing to Cycladic influence.

[3] Dugas, *Céramique des Cyclades* (1925), p. 43, thinks that the queer Cycladic representations of men on pots were influenced by the marble idols. But the idols (E.C. III) were far more ancient than M.C. III, though a tradition of such rude picturing may have survived. M. Dugas is often difficult to follow because he does not adopt the usual classification of the Cycladic periods, which he oddly attributes to Mr. Wace and Mr. Blegen (p. 12).

139

On the mainland Cretan colonists have established their dominion, and we see its first-fruits in the contents of the six shaft-graves in the

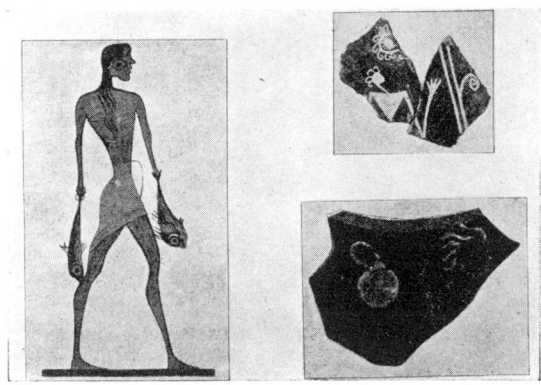

FIG. 173.—HUMAN FIGURES IN VASE-PAINTING: M.C. III

necropolis of Mycenae, with their crudely executed gravestones (Figs. 175, 176, see p. 153), and their unparalleled treasures of gold, inlaid metals

FIG. 174.—MIDDLE AND LATE CYCLADIC POTTERY: PHYLAKOPI: IMITATING M.M. AND L.M. I WARES (BRIT. MUS. CATALOGUE)

and crystal, interspersed with imported Cretan M.M. IIIb and L.M. I (Fig. 177) and Cycladic and local Helladic (matt-painted and often

140

FIG. 176.—SCULPTURED GRAVESTONE: MYCENAE ($\frac{1}{10}$)

FIG. 175.—SCULPTURED GRAVESTONE: MYCENAE ($\frac{1}{10}$)

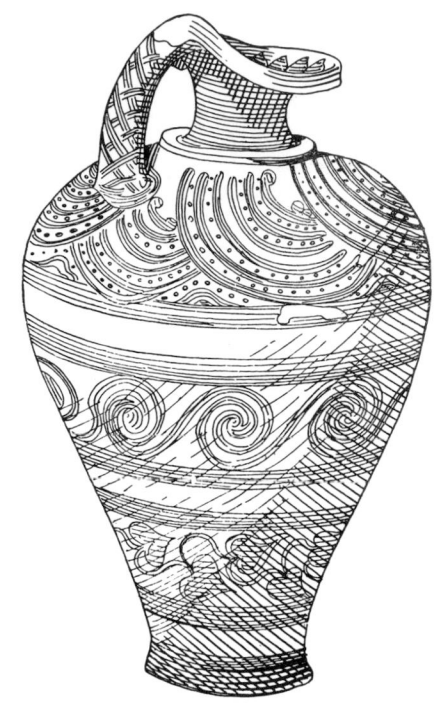

FIG. 177.—CRETAN VASE; M.M. III–L.M. I: SIXTH GRAVE, MYCENAE $(\frac{1}{4})$

FIG. 178.—NON-CRETAN VASES; CYCLADIC AND HELLADIC (M.H.): SIXTH GRAVE, MYCENAE $(\frac{1}{4}, \frac{1}{6})$

hand-made) pottery (Fig. 178). This last pottery is of course extremely crude compared with the imported Cretan ware, and cannot possibly be considered to be related to it directly. " It is," Mr. E. J. Forsdyke goes so far as to write,[1] " as if native American pottery were found in graves of New England settlers : the makers of these coarse, ill-decorated

FIG. 179.—BRONZE DAGGER INLAID WITH GOLD : WARRIORS HUNTING LIONS : FOURTH GRAVE, MYCENAE (RESTORED). ($\frac{1}{3}$). (*From a reproduction*)

Helladic fabrics were no more capable of throwing, painting, or firing fine Minoan vases than Indian potters could reproduce Delft glazed ware." The marvellous inlaid daggers with their pictures in metal and in differently tinted gold[2] and in silver or bronze, of kilted and bare-headed Cretan

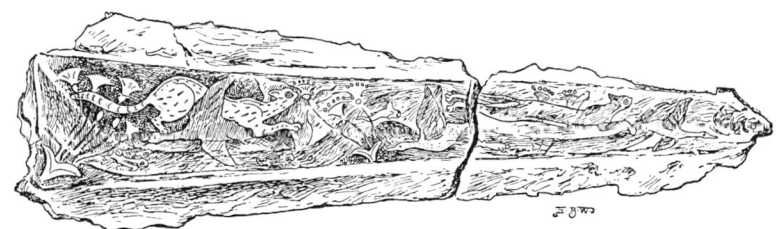

FIG. 180.—BRONZE SWORD-BLADE FROM FIFTH GRAVE, MYCENAE, WITH INLAID EGYPTIAN DESIGN OF CATS HUNTING WILDFOWL ($\frac{1}{3}$)

warriors with their great figure-of-eight shields, fighting with lions (Fig. 179), and other scenes of the chase, Egyptian cats hunting wild-fowl (Fig. 180), etc. ; the gold signet-ring with the chariot (Fig. 95) and with the two helmetless warriors overthrown by one who wears

---

[1] *Catalogue of Greek vases in the British Museum*, i, pl. 1, p. xxxix.

[2] On the neck of one of the ducks that are hunted is a spot of red gold, probably shewing the iron-oxide technique that is found on (later) Egyptian objects from the tomb of Tutankhamen (Lucas, in Carter, *Tutankhamen*, ii, p. 174). Dr. Alexander Scott, F.R.S., has proved this Egyptian technique by experiment. Whether this method of tinting gold was of Egyptian or Cretan origin we do not yet know.

FIG. 181.—GOLD AND SILVER BULL-RHYTON: FOURTH GRAVE, MYCENAE ($\frac{1}{2}$)

the helmet with flying horse-tail (Fig. 165) ; the golden vases ; the gold and silver bull's head (Fig. 181) ; the golden masks (Figs. 182, 183) that shew the mainlanders sometimes wore the beard and moustache (a significant difference from the Cretan custom) ; [1] the

FIG. 182.—GOLDEN MASK OF THE DEAD : FOURTH GRAVE, MYCENAE ($c. \frac{1}{3}$)

golden diadems (Fig. 184) ; the plaques of gold in the form of sphinxes (Fig. 369), gryphons, and octopods, and all the other wonderful things that Schliemann found, are of this age, the end of the Middle and the beginning of the Late Minoan (Mycenaean) period, and, like the Phaistos

[1] I know of only one instance of a Cretan beard before L.M. III. the old man on the Harvesters Vase (p. 156). Here we have probably a mainland fashion.

Disk, date to about 1600 B.C. The sixth grave is apparently the oldest, and its contents can be regarded as definitely imported Cretan " M.M. III." Graves ii, iv, and v are M.M. III–L.M. I. The rest are L.M. I. To this time used to be considered to belong the famous Lion-Gate (Fig. 3), with its simple relief decoration of the antithetical group of two lions rampant against a typical Cretan pillar, a group often paralleled

FIG. 183.—GOLDEN MASK OF THE DEAD, BEARDED ; FIFTH GRAVE, MYCENAE $(\frac{1}{3})$
(*From a reproduction*)

on Minoan seals. But Mr. Wace [1] considers it to be much later, as late as L.M. (Myc.) III, with the whole fortification-system of Mycenae. The casemates of Tiryns (p. 153) too, which one would naturally regard at first sight as early, are assigned by the German excavators to the later period, probably correctly.[2] The *tholos*-tombs of Mycenae

[1] *B.S.A. Ann.* xxv, p. 12. [2] *Ibid.*, p. 13.

(Fig. 185), and that of Orchomenos (the "treasury of Minyas," Fig. 186), must belong to the period succeeding the shaft-graves, and Mr. Wace would put some of them, including the famous "treasuries" of Atreus (Fig. 187) and Klytaimnestra (Fig. 188), very late, dating them to early L.M. (Myc.) III (*c.* 1400

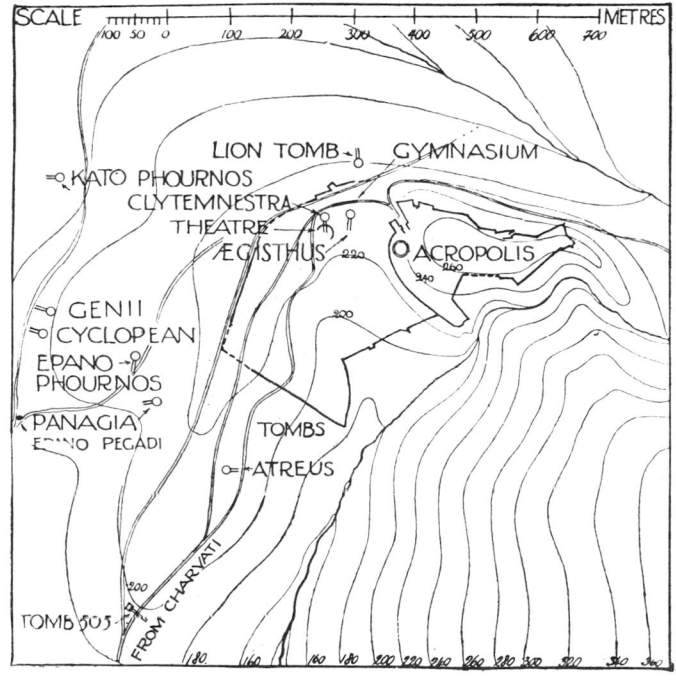

FIG. 184.—GOLDEN DIADEM; SECOND GRAVE, MYCENAE

FIG. 185.—THE ACROPOLIS AND THOLOS-TOMBS OF MYCENAE

B.C.)[1] The arguments *pro* and *con* are too detailed and depend too much on disputed archaeological data to be recapitulated profitably here. There is, for instance, the matter of a fragment of pottery found beneath the threshold of the Treasury of Atreus, which would appear to be of the very latest L.M. III*b* type: it is of a type generally considered

---

[1] *Ibid.*, p. 391.

FIG. 186.—THE "TREASURY OF MINYAS," ORCHOMENOS

FIG. 187.—THE "TREASURY OF ATREUS," MYCENAE

to be almost "sub-Mycenaean," of the kind associated with the Philistines in Palestine, and dated not earlier than 1200 B.C., but which Mr. Wace attributes to the beginning of the older L.M. III*a* period, about 1400 B.C. Bowls of

FIG. 188.—THE "TREASURY OF KLYTAIM-NESTRA," MYCENAE

this kind are according to him at Mycenae quite early, and the "panelled" decoration of L.M. III*b* is derived from the older Helladic vase-decoration. This is a hard saying, and confirmation of his view will be looked for with interest. He considers that the portion of the threshold from beneath which it came was undisturbed, while Sir Arthur Evans considers that the threshold has so evidently been re-made that the piece proves nothing.

There is no doubt whatever that the tholoi discovered by the Germans at Kakovatos (Pylos) in Triphylia and at the Messenian Pylos, and that of Vapheio (Amyklai) in Lakonia, are of L.M. I date (c. 1550 B.C.), judging by the pottery found in them,[1] and on the same criterion so also must be the tholos called " The Tomb of Aigisthos " at Mycenae [2] in which, among other things, was found a typical imported Egyptian alabaster jug of the mid-XVIIIth Dynasty.[3] The fragments of a L.M. I*b* amphora (Fig. 181), resembling vases from Kakovatos, found by Mr. Wace in the *dromos* of the " Epano-Phournos tholos at Mycenae [4] (Fig. 190), are accepted by him as proof of the L.M. I date of that tholos, as such a vase must have belonged to the original tomb-furniture as did those of similar period at Kakovatos. Sir Arthur Evans strongly maintains a similar date for all the Mycenae *tholoi*, and would even place the " treasury of Klytaimnestra " as early as M.M. III. A stone vase found in it in fragments (Fig. 189) would in Crete be dated M.M. III, but Mr. Wace is not inclined to regard this as any proof that the tholos itself is not considerably later, in view of his theory of the development of the tholoi.

Mr. Wace adopts an *a priori* theory of a regular development of the Mycenaean *tholoi* based upon their style, Atreus being earlier than Klytaimnestra, which needs examination in the light of all the other evidence from Crete as well as from the mainland. Certainly the tomb of Klytaimnestra looks weaker and inferior in style to that of Atreus. Contrary to Mr. Wace, Sir Arthur Evans makes Klytaimnestra the earlier, and would presumably date it about 1600 B.C. Its weaker style will then be due to its greater age. It will have been one of the first transplanted examples of the ashlar buildings

---

[1] At Kakovatos including fine imported Knossian painted pithoi of L.M. I *a* and *b* styles. Bosanquet, *J.H.S.*, xxiv (1904), p. 317 ff. ; Evans, *J.H.S.* (1925), p. 45 ; Hall, *Aeg. Arch.* p. 100. Original publication : Müller, *Ath. Mitth.*, xxxiv, pl. xvi. ff.

[2] Bosanquet, *loc. cit.* ; Wace, *B.S.A. Ann.*, xxv, pl. 50.

[3] Bosanquet, *loc. cit.*, pl. xiv, *e*.

[4] Wace, *B.S.A. Ann.*, xxv, p. 295, Fig. 53.

that had been so common in Crete since M.M. II (as I had myself supposed in 1915)[1] ; and Atreus developed out of it. *Tholoi* are in any case more likely to be of Cretan than of mainland origin. We find them first in Crete in the Early Minoan period (p. 44), and we may

FIG. 189.—M.M. III VASE : TREASURY OF KLYTAIMNESTRA. ($\frac{1}{8}$)

yet find earlier editions of the Mycenae *tholoi* there in the Middle Minoan period, as we have lately found unexpected chamber-tombs there (p. 188)[2]

[1] *Aegean Archaeology*, p. 167.
[2] Although no M.M. III tomb of the type of Atreus and Klytaimnestra has been found in Crete, the style of building was known there in L.M. I*a*, as we see from a circular well-

150

FROM THE MIDDLE TO THE LATE BRONZE AGE

Sir Arthur Evans writes :

" The details of the magnificent façade of the ' Atreus ' tomb (exhibited in the British Museum Archaic Room) themselves find their nearest parallels in the ornamental fragments,

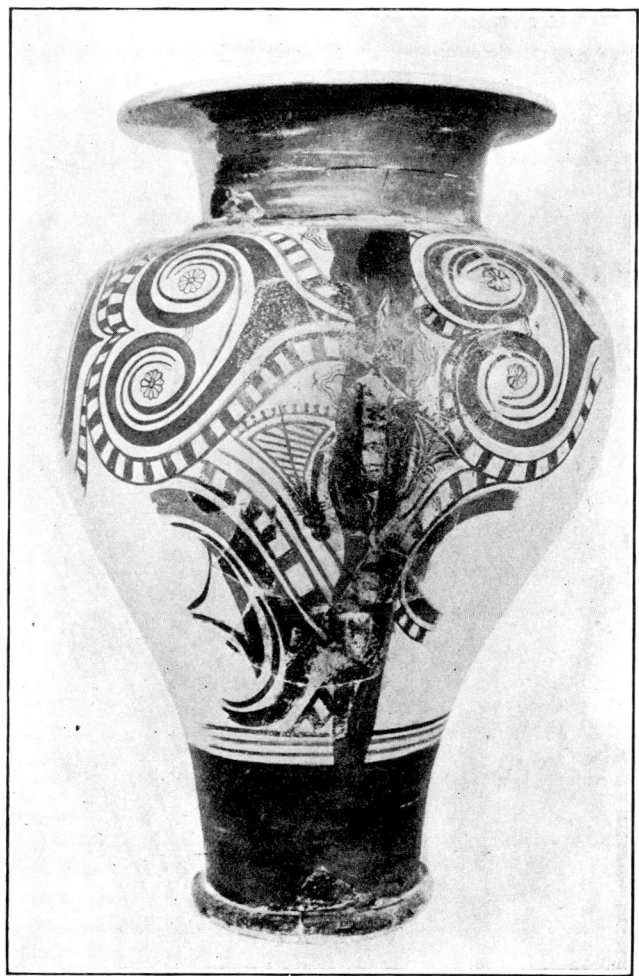

FIG. 190.—L.M. 1*b* VASE, EPANO-PHOURNOS THOLOS, MYCENAE. $(\frac{1}{6})$

the spiral reliefs and undercut rosettes from the South Propylaeum of the restored Palace

house found by Evans at Arkhanais in 1922. Crete was the original home of the tholos, and the Isopata tomb marks a different style of development of it. There are no early *tholoi* on the mainland.

151

at Knossos. They bespeak the crowning technical achievement of that great transitional epoch which links the latest Middle to the Earliest Late Minoan."[1]

There are of course resemblances to similar sculpture at Tiryns which is presumably L.M. III, but not of so fine a style. The Atreus sculp-

FIG. 191.—PILLARS OF THE FAÇADE : TREASURY OF ATREUS : BRITISH MUSEUM

tures seem to take a middle place between those of Knossos (M.M. III) and Tiryns (L.M. III), thus arguing a date midway between them.

Practically the only point in dispute is the date of "Atreus" and "Klytaimnestra". Mr. Wace implicitly accepts Sir Arthur Evans's

[1] *J.H.S.*, xlv (1925), p. 45.

contentions with regard to the other Mycenaean tholoi except that of " the Genii," which he thinks is L.M. III.[1] In fact most of the Mycenaean tholoi, like those of Kakovatos and Vapheio, belong to the first Late Minoan Age and seem the successors of the shaft-graves. Sir Arthur Evans has however recently (Brit. Assoc. address, 1926) revived Prof. Percy Gardner's theory (*New Chapters in Greek History*, p. 77 ; March *Quarterly Rev.*, 1877) that the shaft-graves are really later receptacles dug in the acropolis for the reception of the bodies of the princes originally buried in the great tholoi. If this could be proved it would of course entirely support Sir Arthur's view of the date of the tholoi. We obtain no hint of the true date of the shaft-graves from their type, as Minoan burial-customs seem chaotic (see p. 188) and various kinds of burial were often in use at the same period. On this view the gravestones (Figs. 175, 176), which are so curiously barbaric in style, will be, as I suggested in 1915 (*Aegean Archaeology*, p. 199), of comparatively late date, "well on in the L.M. III period," and very probably sub-Mycenaean. They might well, in fact, belong to the Achaian period, as I personally have always thought. They are really almost too crude for even colonial M.M.III–L.M. I work and seem to me to have been all made at the same time by the same barbarous sculptors.

Though the casemates and outer wall of Tiryns may be L.M. (Myc.) III (and there seems to be now good reason to suppose so), the older palace there, with its fragmentary frescoes of warriors (paralleled by some from the palace at Mycenae) should, as Mr. Wace says, be L.M. III at latest (see p. 215, Figs. 278, 281), if the later frescoes at Tiryns (Figs. 304–308) are, with those of Boeotian Thebes (p. 215, Fig. 280), L.M. III*a* (fourteenth century)[2].

The older Tirynthian and Mycenaean frescoes are painted in a distinctly cruder style than those of Crete. Generally one obtains the idea of a culture cruder and less tasteful than that of Crete : a colonial version of the great Cretan civilization of the time mingled

---

[1] The L.M. (Myc.) III tholoi at Menidi, Spata, Delphi, and Volo are definitely inferior to those at Mycenae, and obviously later.

[2] Rodenwaldt, *Tiryns*, II (Arch. Inst., 1912).

(at first only) with a very few comparatively barbaric native elements. But masterpieces of Cretan art were prized in Greece. We have many objects of the finest Cretan workmanship from the shaft-graves at Mycenae, and the Vapheio cups and the vases from Vapheio, Kakovatos and the Aigisthos tholos, some of which may have been local creations, but the majority certainly importations from Crete. The entirely sudden and unprepared appearance of these things on the mainland bears out, to my mind, entirely the thesis of Sir Arthur Evans,[1] " that the earlier phase at Mycenae represents the result . . . of actual conquest and the abrupt and wholesale displacement of a lower by an incomparably higher form of culture," not the result " of a gradual ' Minoization ' of the native Helladic community." It is hardly possible to speak of any " minoization " of mainland art at all. We know of no mainland art except in pottery and occasional gold-work such as the Helladic " sauce-boat " (p. 66), before the sudden irruption and triumph of the Minoan art, in all its varied branches, in M.M. III and L.M. I. There was little to be minoized.

And the pottery of the Mycenaean age which succeeded the Cretan conquest of the mainland is not " minoized " mainland pottery. It is Cretan, made in Greece ; and we shall see that the older ceramics of the mainland, which disappeared swiftly before it, exercised some, but little, influence upon its form and decoration.

The superiority of Cretan art was indeed overwhelming, and we can well imagine that the people who imported and used such things as the Vapheio cups would have very little use for the crude productions of the native craftsmen.

The famous Vapheio cups (Fig. 192) of embossed gold, with their scenes of bulls controlled by and escaping from man's hobble and nets, are, although found in the Peloponnese, undoubtedly *chefs-d'œuvre* of a Cretan studio of the Third Middle Minoan or the First Late Minoan period, and so of the same date as the other examples of Cretan gold-work found in the shaft-graves at Mycenae. One wonders what Benvenuto Cellini would have said of them. He would have noted their

[1] *J.H.S.*, xlv (1925), p. 45, n. 1.

FIG. 192.—THE VAPHEIO GOLD CUPS: THE BULL CAPTURED AND TAMED BY MAN, L.M. I. ($\frac{4}{5}$)

difference from the classical style of antiquity that he knew so well. But nevertheless he would not have refused his admiration to that wonderful figure of the bull escaping from man's nets and gins, and tossing his would-be captors this way and that while he makes his escape, while the other struggles furiously in the stout rope meshes that hold him. Also, would he have disdained the naïf art with which is expressed the complacency of the other bulls that peaceably allow themselves to be hobbled by the lanky cattle-man?—though it might have amused him.

Gold vases cf this kind were probably not seldom made in Crete at this time, though none have come down to us in Crete itself. We possibly have contemporary imitations of such work in the vases of black steatite with relief carving that have survived whole at Hagia Triada and in fragments at Knossos. The Hagia Triada vases are the three known as the "Gladiator," "Harvesters," and "Chieftain" vases, discovered and first published by the Italians,[1] and the finest objects found by them. They date from the transition-period between M.M. III and L.M. I. The largest is that of the Gladiators, the finest (in some ways) that of the Chieftain, the most remarkable as a work of art that of the Harvesters. On this last (Fig. 193) we see a procession of kilted youths, wearing kilts and with, apparently, close caps on their heads, stamping and tramping along in a wild procession, singing and shouting as they go, to the music of an Egyptian sistrum shaken by one of their number, and led by an elderly bearded man with shaggy hair, in a great capote.[2] They carry over their shoulders what look like flails. This is of all the most outstanding work of Minoan art. Its freedom is absolutely unrestrained by any convention. The technique of the relief is superior to that of any Egyptian relief at that period. It was probably originally gilt, and

[1] Often republished since, see my *Aegean Archaeology*, pl. xv, xvi, xvii. For the original publication see *Rendiconti*, xxiii ; *Mon. Ant.*, xiii, etc.

[2] This capote, which also appears worn by a man on a seal-impression from Hagia Triada (*Mon. Ant.* xiii, p. 41, Fig. 35), and is on a Knossian gem (Fig. 354, below) carried by a woman who shoulders a double-axe (*B.S.A.*, viii, p. 102, Fig. 59), is claimed by Nilsson, *The Minoan-Mycenaean Religion*, i. p. 137, as a sacral garment. It is, cf course, as Evans pointed out, *J.H.S.*, 1912, p. 290, n. 14, not a military cuirass.

reproduces faithfully the appearance of an embossed gold vase. But the possibilities of the soft steatite were greater than that of the metal.

The " Chieftain " Vase (Fig. 194) shews in small space a farewell from

FIG. 193.—THE HARVESTERS' VASE : HAGIA TRIADA. ($\frac{3}{4}$)

or reception of an officer with his soldiers by a prince, extraordinarily reticent and restrained in conception and execution, and having all the feeling of a classical Greek tomb-relief or funerary lekythos-design. Its note is solemnity, as that of the Harvesters is riotous jollity.

157

In both we have here something we do not often find in Egyptian art : untampered truth and humane feeling : it is the first note of the true Greek spirit in art.

The warrior stands upright in his tight-fitting kilt, high-booted, and with his hair knotted on his head (as on the gold ring from Mycenae : no doubt it was often so worn by warriors) : he holds in one hand a long sword resting on one shoulder, in the other a long curved *falx*-like weapon (?). Before him stands the prince, with his hair streaming to his exaggeratedly narrow waist, and confined at the top of his head and back of his

FIG. 194.—THE CHIEFTAIN VASE : HAGIA TRIADA. $(\frac{1}{3})$

neck by bands or " slides," probably of gold. He wears a tight kilt, a necklace, armlets and bracelets, and high boots or puttied sandals, and in his right hand holds a long staff or sceptre. Neither wears any head-covering (Fig. 195).

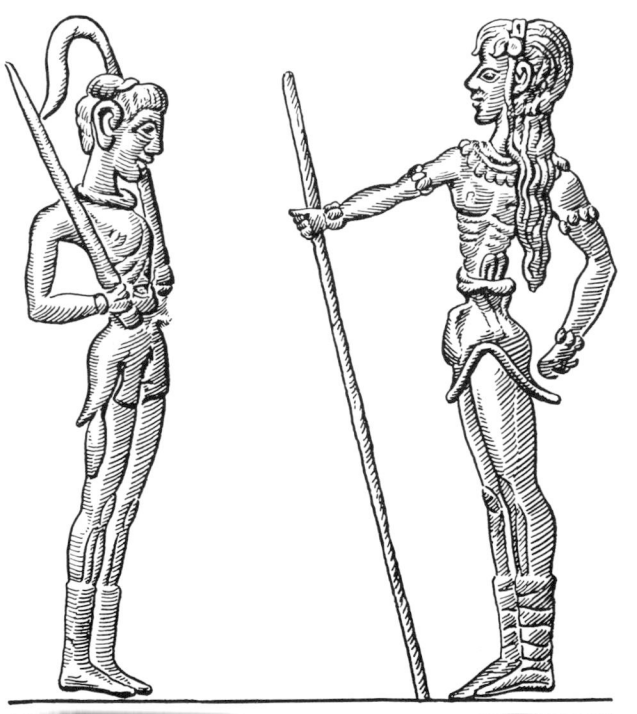

FIG. 195.—THE PRINCE AND THE WARRIOR : CHIEFTAIN VASE, HAGIA TRIADA
(*Enlarged ; top of Prince's staff restored*)
(For the warrior *cf.* also Bossert, *Altkreta*, Fig. 87).

Behind the officer are three of his men bareheaded, with flowing

158

hair, carrying huge round-topped oxhide (?) shields " like towers," that completely hide their figures from their necks down. In strength, simplicity, and feeling, the scene is unequalled, though perhaps the workmanship is not so good as on the " Harvesters " vase.

This is certainly the case with the "Gladiators" or "Boxers" vase (Fig. 196), on which we see scenes in several registers of warriors contending in some sort of *pankration*, kilted, with cestus on hands, and with the heads both helmeted and bare. There is also a scene of bull-leaping. In the lowest register apparently it is the youths who are boxing ; the figures are ephebic, and the emphasized thickness and shagginess of their unbound hair points to this conclusion. Above are mature men wearing a metal helmet with cheekpieces, of Roman rather than of Greek form, sometimes with the horsetail, from beneath which streams their hair. A pillar like a *meta* is represented. The fighting was evidently to the death or at any rate to the complete " knock-out " of the defeated. The attitudes of the beaten are contorted and the figures are all awkward : the bull and his leaper are poor in design and execution. So this is an inferior work compared to the other

FIG. 196.—THE BOXER OR GLADIATOR VASE : HAGIA TRIADA. ($\frac{1}{5}$)

two. The style of the Vapheio cups themselves is inferior to that of the two great Hagia Triada vases.

On a fragment of a similar vase, of greenish steatite, in the Ashmolean Museum (Fig. 197) we see two men in attitudes that are not easily interpretable, one running with his hands behind his back, the other seated on the ground : behind them is a wall of polygonal stones with an olive-tree beyond it and in front of it a

159

pedestal of isodomic masonry, on which is a horned altar. On another fragment from Knossos are two youths marching in procession, with behind them an ascending series of similar altars or pedestals (Fig. 237).

We have here remarkable examples of what the Cretan artists of about 1600–1500 B.C. could do. It is probable that, though the actual imitation from gold embossing is evident, the technique of the low relief in stone was derived ultimately from Babylonia, where even so far back as the Akkadian period (2700–2600 B.C.) vases with similar low relief decoration were made in steatite and alabaster. They were unknown in Egypt. A similar technique was in vogue in the Gudea period (2500 B.C.). There is sometimes an odd resemblance, too, in style between Sumerian statuettes of goddesses and Minoan figures.

FIG. 197. — FRAGMENT OF STEATITE VASE CARVED IN RELIEF: OXFORD. ($\frac{1}{2}$)

The Hagia Triada vases belong to the earlier phase of the First Late Minoan period, to which we have now come, or to the transition from M.M. III. The two fragments mentioned are rather later. It is difficult to draw an exact line of demarcation between M.M. III and L.M. I; the two styles overlap and there was a short period of transition between them to which many of the objects which we have described above as L.M. I may more properly be said to belong. But the palace of Hagia Triada [1] in which they were found is almost entirely of definitely L.M. I date, and with it we pass finally into the Late Minoan Age.

The palace of Hagia Triada is a typical building of the First Late Minoan period (Fig. 198). It was no doubt built by the princes of the neighbouring Phaistos, a few miles away to the east, which also was remodelled and added to in this age. The style of architecture is the same as that of Knossos. Another building of the same period is the

---

[1] *Rendiconti*, xiv ff.; *Mem. R. Ist. Lombardo*, xxi.

FIG. 198.—HAGIA TRIADA

FIG. 199.—STONE LAMPS, ETC., FROM NIROU KHANI

FIG. 200.—THE THEATRAL AREA, KNOSSOS

" megaron " of Nirou Khani, near Knossos, the hall, probably, of a
Minoan magnate, a building of fine rooms, magazines, and open courts.[1]

FIG. 201.—GOURNIÀ

[1] Xanthoudides, *Ἀρχ. Ἐφημ.* 1922, p. 1 ff.

162

Fig. 199 shews some stone lamps of good shape, and a three-legged stone cooking-bowl, excellent examples of the household furniture of the time (see p. 164), from Nirou Khani.

Knossos itself was largely rebuilt at this time, as the result perhaps

FIG. 202.—PLAN OF GOURNIA

(but not certainly; see p. 109) of overthrow and fire caused by the great Theraean earthquake of about 1600 B.C., that blew the island of Thera in two, and no doubt was felt widely all over the south-Aegean area. Very probably the "theatral area" (Fig. 200) dates to this period of rebuilding. Another Cretan palace that was built chiefly in the L.M. I period is that of Tylissos, where the Cretan archaeologist M. Hatzidakis has made interesting discoveries, including frescoes which I have already mentioned (p. 119).[1] We have important remains of this age in the two towns of Gournià and Pseira, excavated respectively by Miss Boyd (Mrs. Boyd-Hawes)[2] and by the late Mr. Seager.[3] Gournià lies on the Aegean coast of the Hierapetra isthmus, the narrowest part of Crete ; Pseira is a small island off the coast, a few miles to the eastward. Gournià, as excavated by the American archaeologists, is

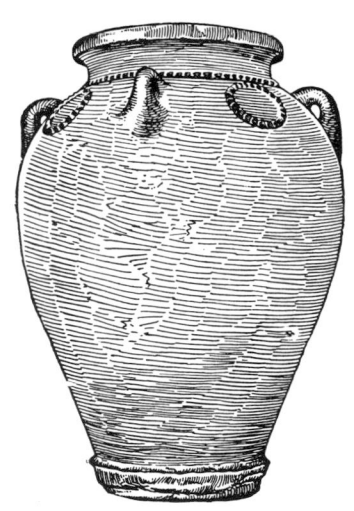

FIG 203.—POTTERY PITHOS, IMITATING METAL FORM (L.M. I), PALAI-KASTRO. ($\frac{1}{10}$)

a small Minoan Pompeii, with its narrow streets (very like those of a modern Cretan village, but narrower) and houses built of rough stone walls, leading up to the tiny palace of the local chief, built on an ashlar foundation of fine stone blocks (Figs. 201, 202). The town dates back at least to the Middle Minoan period, of which important relics have been found. Apart from its painted pottery of M.M. and L.M. I date, it is also noticeable for its great stores of the ordinary household utensils of pottery and metal, which do not ordinarily, in view of our wealth of fine objects of art of this age, attract so much interest in Crete as they would elsewhere. We have already noted at Nirou Khani some objects of this kind, which seem more highly developed in the Aegean than, e.g., in Egypt. At Gournià we have kitchen as well as living-room utensils : whole batteries de cuisine of copper as well as of stone. At Tylissos have been found some enormous copper cauldrons apparently for seething animals whole. Fig. 203 shews a

[1] Hatzidakis, ᾽Εφημ. ᾽Αρχ. 1912. The French edition of this article (Tylisos à l'époque minoenne, 1921) has been spoilt by the translator, M. Franchet, who has introduced into it comments on the work of others, for which, of course, M. Hatzidakis is not responsible.

[2] Gournià, Philadelphia, 1908.

[3] Excavations in the Island of Pseira (Univ. Penna. Mus. Anthrop. Publ. III, i, 1910).

FIG. 204.—THE TOWN OF PSEIRA

FIG. 205.—THE ISLE OF PSEIRA, FROM KAVOUSI

piece of common L.M. I household pottery, a *pithos* from Palaikastro, of a type that again looks imitated from metal, like the vases we noted from Gournià in the M.M. period (Fig. 79).

The small town of Pseira (Fig. 204), with its narrow alleys and

FIG. 206.—L.M. I PLANT-DESIGNS : NIROU KHANI. $(c. \frac{1}{4})$

small houses running down into the sea (the coast has sunk since Minoan days), can never have been much more than a fishing-settlement, on so small an island (Fig. 205). Nowadays it has no water, but then wells must have existed. The fishermen of Pseira must have been the most artistic fishermen that ever lived, for in their

166

houses have been found some of the finest known examples of the painted pottery of the First Late Minoan period. The settlement of Palaikastro on the east coast has also yielded fine specimens.

This pottery strikes an entirely new note, that of complete natural-

FIG. 207.—L.M. 1*b* PLANT-DESIGN : KAKOVATOS (IMPORTED CRETAN VASE). $(c. \frac{1}{25})$

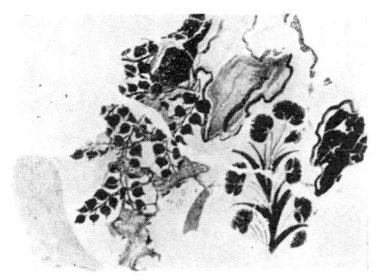

FIG. 208.—NATURALISTIC FRESCO OF PLANTS, M.M. III, L.M. I, HAGIA TRIADA. $(c. \frac{1}{12})$

ism, in its painting. Also its motives are chiefly derived from the sea and its denizens. Instead of the polychrome patterns of **M.M. II** or the severely simple motives of **M.M. III**, the naturalism we have remarked as beginning in the latter period now comes to fruition, and

the naturalistic marine and plant-motives of **M.M. III** on pottery are now greatly developed. The plant-motives of L.M. I are often very beautiful (Figs. 206–7). They were of course inspired by the frescoes (Fig. 208), the lesser art by the greater. Naturalism began with the fresco-painters of **M.M. III**. The flying-fish and dolphins of the **M.M. III** frescoes had already been transferred to the surfaces of pots, and now with

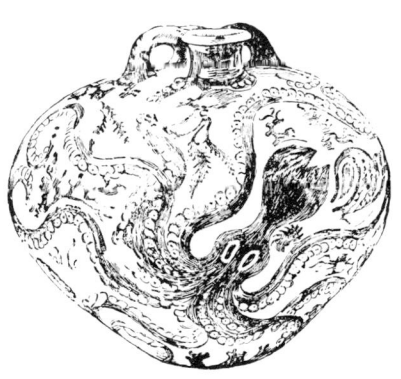

FIG. 209.—OCTOPUS-VASE : L.M. I : GOURNIA. $(c. \frac{1}{5})$

them we find the octopus (already known in **M.M. III**), the argonaut, and sea-shells, specially the triton-whelk, while the worn and fretted limestone rocks of the Cretan coast in all their fantastic forms, with the bunches of seaweed that stream out from them, frame the vase-painter's

167

FIG. 210.—ARGONAUT-VASE FROM ERMENT: L.M. I, BRITISH MUSEUM. ($\frac{1}{2}$)

picture. The greatest triumph of this L.M. I painting is the wonderful octopus on a vase from Gournià that seems to be swimming at us

FIG. 211. — DUCK-VASE : ARGOS: L.M I—II. (c $\frac{1}{10}$)

from off the vase (Fig. 209). So also with the argonaut on a well-known vase in the British Museum, which was found in Egypt (Fig. 210). It is like looking through the glass of an aquarium.[1] Other animals occur, as the two ducks (at the very end of the period) on an amphora found at Argos (Fig. 211).

The L.M. I technique is dark varnish-paint on the fine buff surface of the vase. Only occasionally white spots or shading survive as the last relics of the Middle Minoan polychromy. New forms now arise : notably the slender one-handled "filler" in shape like a beer-warmer (Fig. 212), and the

[1] See *Aegean Archaeology*, p. 90 ff.

168

stirrup-vase (Fig. 287) or "Bügelkanne" (*vase à étrier*), which now develops out of an older form : an amphora with pinched-in mouth between two small handles, common in the M.M. III period. These vases had been "corked" in the usual way with clay over the stopper. It was always a trouble to remove this stopping. So it was commonly left, and the easier method adopted of boring a hole in the vase on the side lower down,

FIG. 212.—POTTERY FILLER : L.M. I : PALAIKASTRO. (*c.* ⅓)

into which was inserted a tube or siphon. Then somebody imitated the whole arrangement in a vase, and produced a pot with its proper mouth permanently stopped up and a tube-spout at the side, making the whole look rather like a kettle. The

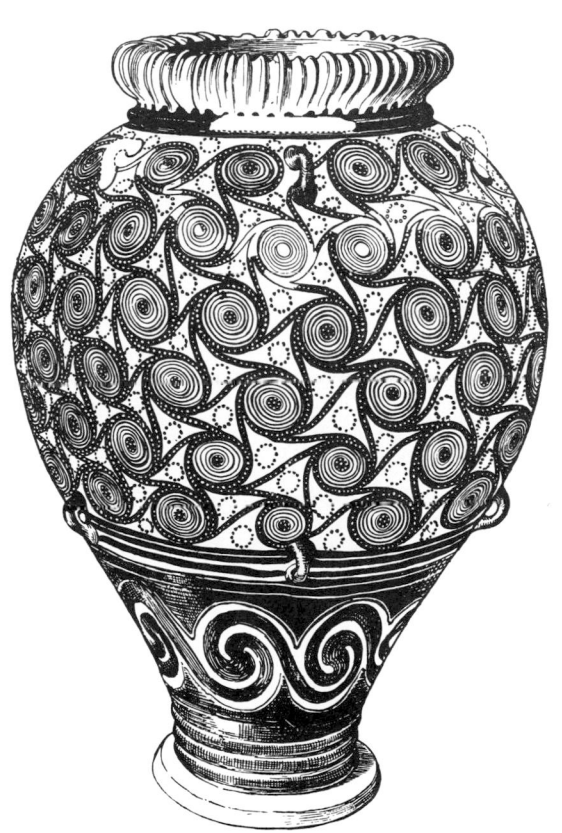

FIG. 213.—POTTERY PITHOS : L.M. I : PSEIRA. (⅛)

idea " caught on," and the stirrup-vase was henceforward one of the commonest types of Greek Bronze Age ceramic, and both it and the filler were imitated in Egypt, in both faience and alabaster (p. 222,

FIG. 214.—POTTERY PITHOS, WITH DESIGN OF DOUBLE-AXES, BULLS' HEADS, OLIVE-SPRAYS AND SPIRALS : L.M. I. PSEIRA

FIG. 215.—L.M. I MARINE DESIGN : KAKOVATOS (IMPORTED CRETAN VASE) $(\frac{1}{20})$

Figs. 288–290). The filler was undoubtedly derived from a metal original, and the finest specimen of it known is the "Gladiator Vase" from Hagia Triada (Fig. 196), already mentioned, which is a stone imitation of a gold original. Characteristic of L.M. I shapes are great pithoi and "amphorae" often with very fine designs, such as those found at Pseira, at Isopata, and at Kakovatos.

FIG. 216.—PITHOS WITH SUNFLOWER-DESIGN IN RELIEF : L.M. I–II. KNOSSOS $(\frac{1}{17})$

FIG. 217. — OCTOPUS-VASE : RELIEF CARVING, MYCENAE : L.M. I $(\frac{1}{5})$

One of very remarkable form, and another of very remarkable decoration, both from Pseira, are illustrated in Figs. 213, 214. A Kakovatos vase, imported from Crete (see p. 149), with marine designs, is shown in Fig. 215. A plant-design in relief (L.M. I–II) appears in Fig. 216.

FROM THE MIDDLE TO THE LATE BRONZE AGE

The naturalism of this period is exemplified in other arts besides that of the vase-painter. A steatite vase carved in relief, from one of the Mycenae shaft-graves, shews a fine octopus amid rocks (Fig. 217). The same design appears in relief on a great stone weight from Knossos and in gold *repoussé* on the splendid L.M. I–II " King's Vase " from the L.M. III tholos at Dendra (Mideia), found by the Swedes.[1] In the frescoes of the M.M. III–L.M. I period at Knossos, with their unconventional sketches of men and women, and in the " Harvesters Vase " from Hagia Triada, in the Oxford vase-fragment (Fig. 197), and on the Vapheio cups, we see representations of men freer and more natural than any we have hitherto met with. To L.M. I belongs the ivory and gold figure of a snake - goddess or priestess, at Boston[2] (Fig. 218), which is freer in style than the somewhat similar M.M. III faience figures (Figs. 151–2). We do not know where it was found, or the companion (?) figure of a boy (the young god), also of ivory, in a private collection, or the (doubtful) stone figure of a goddess holding her breasts, in the Fitzwilliam Museum, which " reproduces in

FIG. 218.—CHRYSELEPHANTINE FIGURE OF A SNAKE-GODDESS : BOSTON. ($\frac{1}{3}$)

[1] Wace, *Ill. Lond. News*, Sept. 18, 1926. [2] Caskey, *Boston Mus. Bull.*, 1914, p. 52 ff.

171

FIG. 219.—AN IVORY LEAPER : KNOSSOS : L.M. I. ($\frac{1}{2}$)

detail the costume " of the faience snake-goddesses from Knossos.[1] In a deposit of this period at Knossos, Sir Arthur Evans found the beautiful little ivory figures of the boy-leapers, with their twisted locks of bronze covered with gold, which are probably the finest Minoan works of art in the round (Fig. 219), as the " Harvesters Vase " is the finest in relief. The leapers are as Greek as is the Chieftain Vase.[2] And is not the bull on the

ivory pyxis-lid in the British Museum (Fig. 220) Greek in feeling and in line ?

A small bronze group in the round (Figs. 221–2) in the possession of Captain E. G. Spencer Churchill at Northwick,[3] may also be mentioned here, as it probably belongs to this period, though where it was found we do not know. It represents a youth

FIG. 220.—BULL : INCISED ON AN IVORY PYXIS-LID : BRITISH MUSEUM
(*natural size*)

[1] Forsdyke, *Encycl. Britt.*, xiiith ed., new vol. i. *s.v.* Archaeology ; Crete, p. 177. For the Cambridge figure see Wace, *A Cretan Statuette in the Fitzwilliam Museum* (Cambridge, 1927). Archaeologists are by no means agreed as to its genuineness.

[2] Evans, *B.S.A. Ann.*, viii, Figs. 37–39 ; Pll. ii, iii. See p. 158, above.

[3] Evans, *J.H.S.*, xli (1921), p. 247 ff.

FIG. 221.—
BRONZE GROUP
OF YOUTH
AND BULL:
NORTHWICK.
(*c.* $\frac{1}{3}$) FROM
A COMPLETED
CAST

turning his somersault over the back of a rushing bull, very like that of the "Harvesters Vase," but better proportioned. The figure of the boy forms a sort of handle to that of the bull, his feet touching the animal's rump, while his hair touches its head as he hurls himself through the air. This is quite possibly a weight.

The interesting series of naturalistic bronze figures of men and women with their hands raised, apparently in a gesture of prayer, may be mentioned here, as they are probably mostly of L.M. I date, though some may be older. The woman at Berlin (Fig. 223), in whose heavy coils of hair snakes have (somewhat doubtfully) been supposed to twist, shews well the

FIG. 222.—BRONZE GROUP OF YOUTH AND BULL: NORTHWICK: FRONT VIEW. (*c.* $\frac{1}{2}$)

FIG. 222

173

FIG. 223.—BRONZE WOMAN : BERLIN. $(\frac{1}{2})$

crinoline-like gear of the women.[1] From Palaikastro comes. the upper part of a youthful figure with similar hair, coiled and knotted and secured by clasps (Fig. 224), in which some may also perceive serpents.

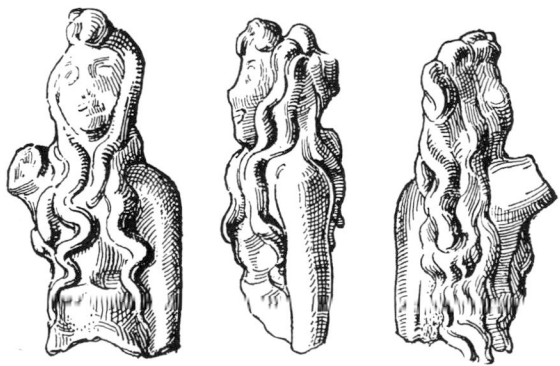

FIG. 224.—HEAD AND TORSO OF BRONZE FIGURE OF A YOUTH OR YOUNG GIRL : PALAIKASTRO. $(\frac{2}{3})$

[1] Often reproduced : see my *Aegean Archaeology*, pl. xix ; and Evans, *Palace*, Fig. 365, p. 507. Personally I am unable to see the snakes. (M.M. III ?)

174

Some of the men—*e.g.* one from Tylissos[1] (Fig. 225) and one in the British Museum [2] (Fig. 226)—are unusual, in that they have middle-aged and heavy figures : the Minoans usually preferred to reproduce the lines of youth. Another (Fig. 227), from the Dictaean Cave,[3] shews a younger figure, very naturalistic, without the

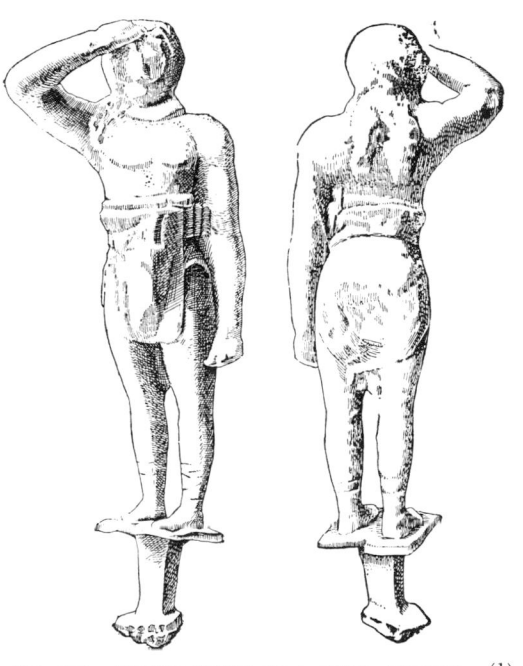

FIG. 225.—BRONZE FIGURE OF A MAN : TYLISSOS. ($\frac{1}{3}$)

FIG. 226.—BRONZE FIGURE OF A MAN : BRITISH MUSEUM. ($\frac{1}{2}$)

exaggeratedly narrow waist of the frescoes, and exactly like a modern Cretan in build. He wears an unusual type of long kilt. Another figure, however, at Leiden,[4] representing a youth in his 'teens, who has been supposed to be a flute-player, has a very narrow waist, and, most unusually, wears a regular *béret* or *petasos* of the well-known

[1] *Aegean Archaeology*, Fig. 14. (L.M. I.)   [2] Pryce, *J.H.S.*, xli (1921), p. 86 ff.
[3] Evans, *Palace*, Fig. 501, p. 682. (M.M. III.)   In the Ashmolean.
[4] Bossert, *Altkreta*, Figs. 143, 144. (Probably L.M.I.)   From Phaistos ?

175

Greek type on his head (Fig. 228). The appearance of the waist-cloth, with its projecting sheath or codpiece, is well shewn in this figure, which is probably of M.M. III date. Yet another figure of the kind from Tylissos, of a young man, with hair dressed in

FIG. 227.—BRONZE FIGURE OF A MAN : DICTAEAN CAVE : ASHMOLEAN
(*Enlarged*)

topknot and hanging tails, like the youths in Fig. 237, is shewn in Fig. 229. The casting of them is somewhat rough, and we may regard them as ordinary votive offerings of the people, of which thousands doubtless were made.

In the next lecture we pass into the fully developed culture of the

176

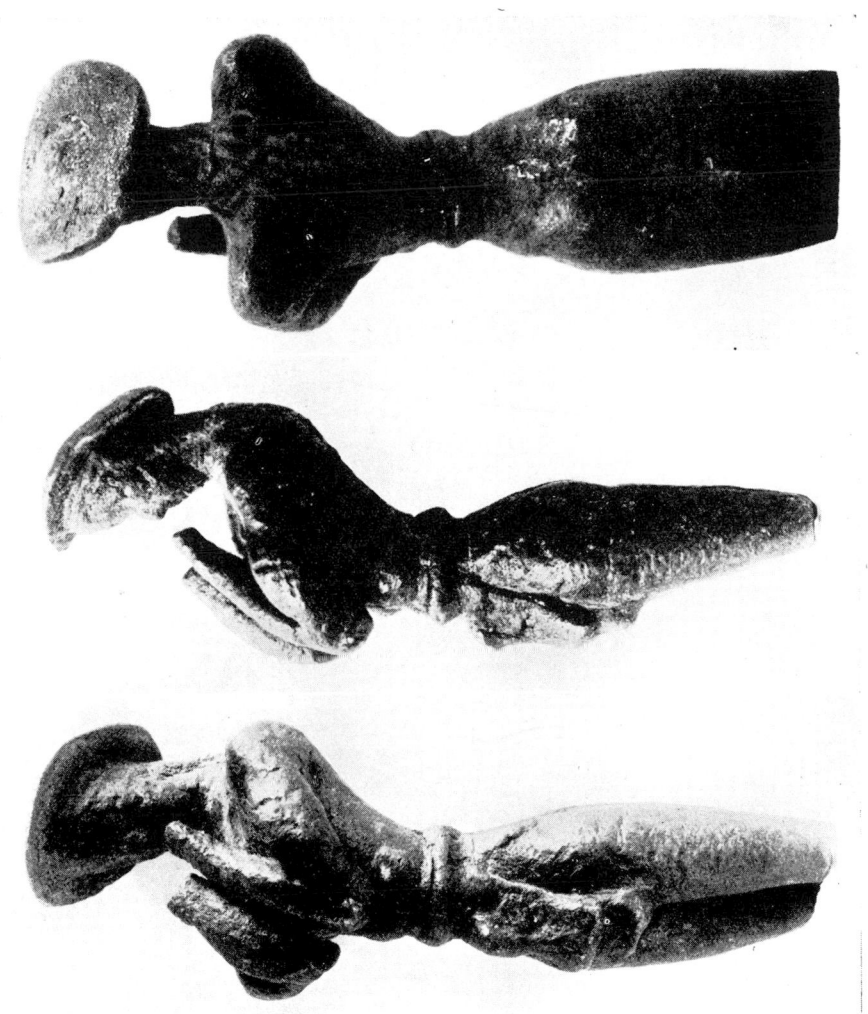

FIG. 228.—BRONZE FIGURE OF A YOUTH WEARING A PETASOS : LEIDEN $(\frac{3}{4})$

12

Late Bronze Age, the period of the ceramic style L.M. II, which was more purely Knossian than any other, so far as we can see. It was the

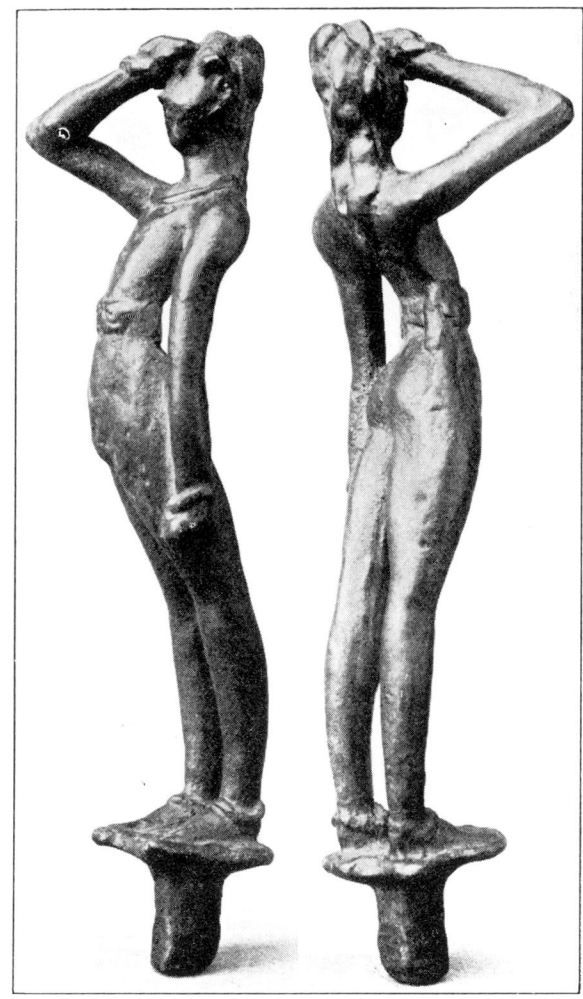

FIG. 229.—BRONZE FIGURE OF A YOUTH : TYLISSOS. ($\frac{3}{4}$). CANDIA MUSEUM

shortest of the Minoan style-periods of Evans, having lasted probably less than a century before its collapse, which seems to have taken place shortly before 1400 B.C.

178

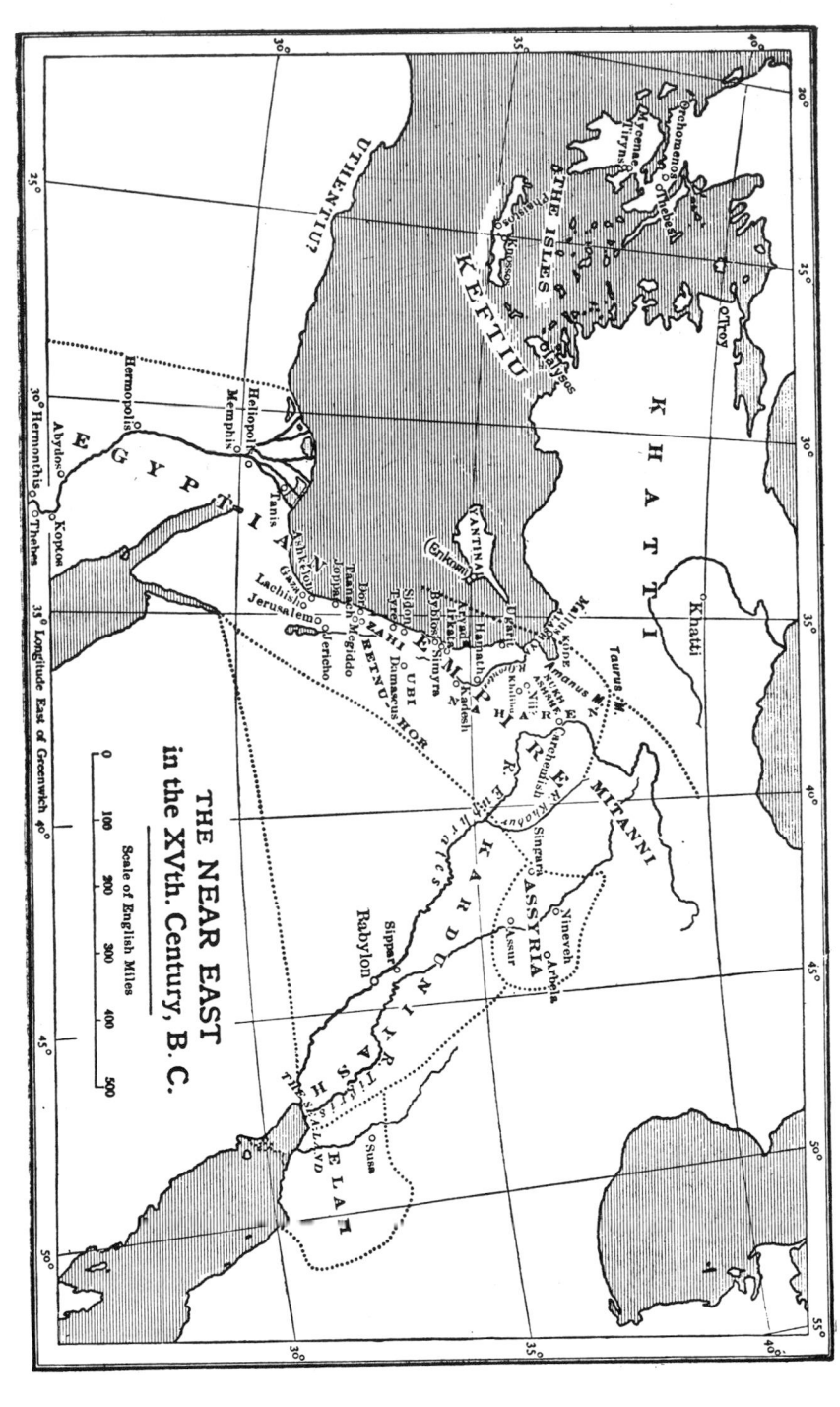

THE NEAR EAST in the XVth. Century, B. C.

Scale of English Miles

LECTURE V

THE LATE BRONZE AGE (CONTINUED)

(L.M. I–II–III, 1500–1200 B.C.)

L.M. II (*c.* 1450–1400 B.C.) at Knossos marks the apogee of Cretan culture in other than purely artistic matters. Architecture could hardly improve further in the circumstances of the time. L.M. II additions to the work of the preceding age are merely refinements. In other respects there is distinct ad-

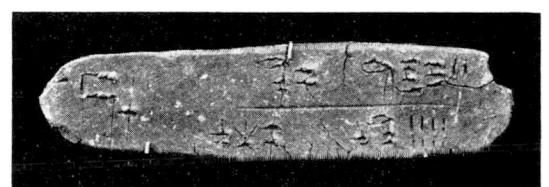

FIG. 230.—MINOAN INSCRIBED CLAY TABLETS : "CLASS B," KNOSSOS (BRIT. MUS.) ($\frac{1}{2}$)

vance, as in the matter of writing the script, at any rate at Knossos, assumes a new and modified form, described by Sir Arthur Evans as " Class B " (Figs. 230, 231). This " Class B " is not strictly speaking evolved out of " Class A " (pp. 93, 131),[1] but is rather a parallel,

[1] *Scripta Minoa*, p. 38.

179

closely-related system which seems peculiar to Knossos and the L.M. II period. It marks however an advance in the neater arrangement and better writing of the signs. The tablets are now usually larger and often narrower than before. They were generally unbaked ; their present baked condition being due to the fire in the palace in which they were consumed. They were found carefully arranged, probably in small cases or shelves, sometimes in the basement chambers, sometimes in upper rooms, of the palace. Their contents, judging from the object, would appear to relate to the domestic economy of the place : chariots, horses, cuirasses, bows, swords, titles or names (?) and other records, probably of a business nature. Graffiti now appear on the walls, "a truly Pompeian touch."

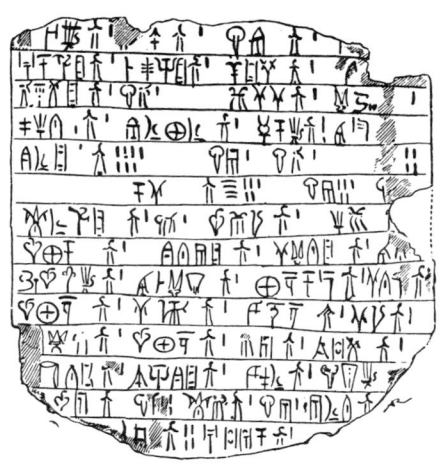

FIG. 231.—MINOAN INSCRIBED CLAY TABLET : " CLASS B," KNOSSOS

(*Reduced*)

The pure naturalism of L.M. I did not last long. The naturalistic designs on pottery became conventional and stylized : the last vestige of polychromy goes : the lilies and palms become stiff wallpaper plants (Fig. 232A) : the octopus and nautilus become stylized octopus and nautilus wall-paper designs (Fig. 232B) rather than real live animals as in Fig. 233, and a new style of design based upon architectural motives, the carved triglyphs of palace architraves, and so forth, or upon metal embossing (Fig. 234), comes into favour with a return to the older taste for spiral patterns supplemented by the wave or *kymation*. This stylized and rococo decoration of the "Great Palace Style" is often very splendid to look at : it is the characteristic of the later palace period, L.M. II, at Knossos, to which some of the finest relics of other arts besides vase-painting discovered at Knossos belong. And it does not appear elsewhere, except in local imitations, or of course, when

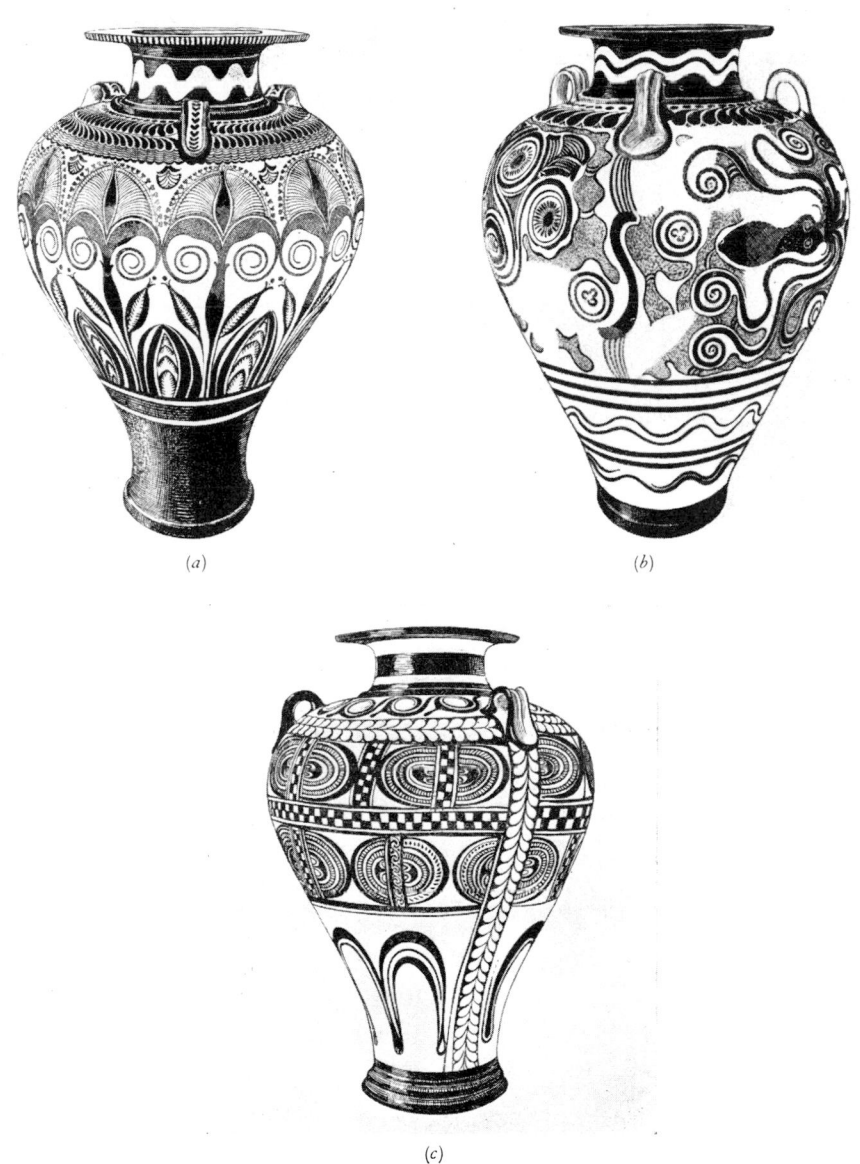

(a) (b)

(c)

FIG. 232.—L.M. II VASES (ISOPATA)

(a) Conventionalized Plant-designs ; (b) Conventional Spiral and Octopus ; (c) Imitation of Architectural and Glyptic Designs. ($\frac{1}{6}$ to $\frac{1}{10}$)

exported, as to Mycenae. At Pseira, for example, the L.M. III style is directly derived from L.M. I according to Mr. Seager.

At Knossos has been found fine metal-work of L.M. I; a bronze bowl (Fig. 234) with embossed handle and rim [1] (imitated

FIG. 233.—THE MARSEILLES VASE: L.M. 1b : MARINE DESIGNS

in pottery in Fig. 232c), and a vase (Fig. 235), almost a replica of one in silver and gold brought to Egypt by a Minoan envoy (wall-painting in the tomb of Sennemut at Thebes; Fig. 260). And the great silver vase that is held by the famous " Cup-bearer " at Knossos is one of the long conical "fillers" that also appear in the tomb of Rekhmire', at Thebes, in its painting of a procession of similar vase-bearers, Minoan ambassadors to Egypt (Fig. 236, see p. 200). For the " King's Vase " from Dendra,[2] which is perhaps, like the Cupbearer's Vase, earlier than L.M. II, see p. 171. The " Queen's Vase " is probably L.M. III, like the tholos itself (p. 233).

The Cup-bearer Fresco (Frontispiece),[3] which probably dates to the beginning of L.M. I, Sir Arthur Evans informs me, is one of the

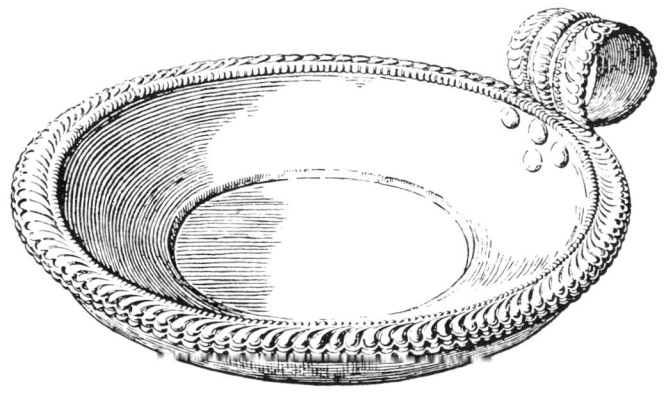

FIG. 234.—BRONZE EMBOSSED BOWL : KNOSSOS : L.M.I $(\frac{1}{4})$

[1] This embossed style is also found in bronze or copper platters at Mochlos, of L.M. I date. Cf. also the Mochlos gold ring (Fig. 356). [2] Wace, *Ill. Lond. News*, Sept. 18, 1926. [3] First published in *Monthly Review*, March, 1901, p. 124.

most striking, if not one of the best examples of Cretan painting, and is certainly the best known : we can all remember the sensation which it caused when discovered in 1901 and exhibited, reproduced in facsimile, on the walls of the Royal Academy in London. Similar processional figures carrying vases are seen, carved in relief, on a fragment of a steatite vase, found at Knossos, of the same type as those from Hagia Triada ; on it we see two pigtailed youths solemnly and pompously bearing their offerings towards a temple, the ascent to which seems to be indicated behind them [1] (Fig. 237).

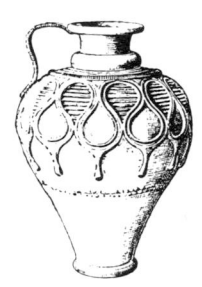

FIG. 235.—BRONZE EWER: KNOSSOS, L.M. I $(\frac{1}{10})$

Among L.M. II frescoes from Knossos are notably those of two girls,[2] and the hasty and crude sketch of a bull-leaping scene, in which

FIG. 236.—A MINOAN AMBASSADOR TO EGYPT: WALLPAINTING IN THE TOMB OF REKHMIRE', THEBES : c. 1450 B.C. $(\frac{1}{6})$

two girls as well as a boy contend with the bull, the girls being only distinguishable from the boy by their conventional white colour, as they wear a " sports costume," the male kilt only, and all three have the same hair flying to their waists (Fig. 238). In these frescoes we notice a decadence : they are more conventional and less interesting.

Costume, as shewn in the frescoes, etc., is much the same as in the preceding period, if a little more elaborate. The low-necked and flounced dresses of the women[3] were as characteristic as the kilts of the men, often now in the case of men of rank gaily decorated in colour and with a kind of complicated network hanging in front, first seen in L.M. Ia. This kilt, when donned for full-dress

[1] B.S.A. Ann., ix, p. 129, Fig. 85. [2] Ibid., vii, p. 57, Fig. 17 ; viii, p. 55, Fig. 28.
[3] On the women's costume see Wace, A Cretan Statuette, p. 15 ff.

occasions, was worn over the twisted waistcloth with sheath. Sometimes the effect is rather of bathing-drawers than a kilt, and this is probably

FIG. 237.—FRAGMENT OF STEATITE VASE WITH PROCESSION OF YOUTHS: KNOSSOS

(*Enlarged*)

merely a form of waistclout. More elaborate breeks were sometimes worn resembling " plus-fours " or the voluminous modern Cretan

184

βράκαις,[1] (Fig. 239), which are not impossibly derived from the ancient costume. The high boots or sandals with puttee-like straps coiled round the calf, which we well see on the two figures of the "Chieftain

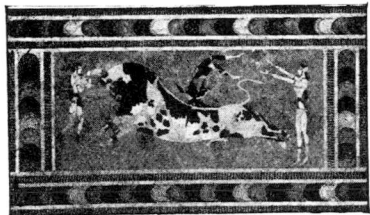

FIG. 238.—FRESCO OF BULL-LEAPING : KNOSSOS:
L.M. II. $(c. \frac{1}{30})$

FIG. 239.—MEN WEARING βράκαις: SEAL-
IMPRESSION
(Enlarged)

Vase," were necessary in stony and thorny Crete, as now, when long boots (characteristic of the island) are still worn of exactly the same length. In the full-dress of the L.M. I period, as we see from the Cupbearer fresco and the Egyptian wall-paintings, these boots or putteed sandals were as gaily decorated as the kilts. And a relief-fresco of a man at Knossos, of L.M.I., shews him, though wearing no kilt, but "bathing-drawers," adorned with a gorgeous headdress of nodding feathers (Fig. 240). Possibly however he is a divine, not a mortal figure. Relief-fresco, which we see first here in the M.M. IIIa period, was a combination of fresco and relief : the picture being modelled in stucco in relief and then painted. At Pseira was found part of a relief (L.M. I) of a seated lady, whose dress gives an idea of the elaborate patterns in vogue for women's clothes at that time (Fig. 241). Embroidered linen was no doubt in regular use as well as woollen clothing, and worked

FIG. 240.—RELIEF FRESCO OF A
KING OR GOD : KNOSSOS : L.M. I
$(\frac{1}{37})$

[1] Nilsson, *Minoan-Myc. Religion*, claims these "breeks," like the "capote," p. 156, as sacral garments. But I see no special reason for this conclusion in their case.

185

in gay patterns. The chief example of relief-fresco at Knossos is the great figure already mentioned of a divine genius, crowned with tall feathers. He is walking in a pleasaunce of flowers and probably originally was leading or tending a griffin, Sir Arthur Evans has supposed. The curious chamber in the palace, with frescoes of gryphons, in which the "throne of Minos," with its odd crocketed construction (evidently imitating woodwork) stands, is apparently of the

FIG. 241.—RELIEF FRESCO OF A WOMAN : PSEIRA, L.M. I

L.M. II period (Fig. 242). A bull's head, again in coloured gesso (shewn in Fig. 1), probably belongs to a great representation in coloured relief of the sport of bull-leaping, which, while common to the whole Minoan world (as we see from the fresco of the leaper and the bull from Tiryns), was probably most in vogue at Knossos, the home of the Minotaur An intaglio (Fig. 243), published by Sir Arthur Evans,[1] shews a scene interpreted by him as "a bull captured while

FIG. 242.—THE THRONE OF MINOS

[1] *Palace of Minos*, Fig. 274, p. 377.

186

drinking at a tank." To me the scene seems to be more probably a bull trying to escape from the arena by leaping the boundary-hurdles, while he tosses on one side one of the toreadors. The network design on the supposed "tank" seems to me probably to represent a hurdle of withies; we find it used as a wall-decoration in the palace (Fig. 244).

The great bull-fighting sports of the arena inspired Minoan artists in all materials,

FIG. 243.—A BULL TOSSES A MAN OVER THE HURDLES : INTAGLIO
(*Enlarged*)

from fresco-painting and bronze-modelling to gem-cutting, from the pictures of the court-ladies watching from the *loggie* of the palace to

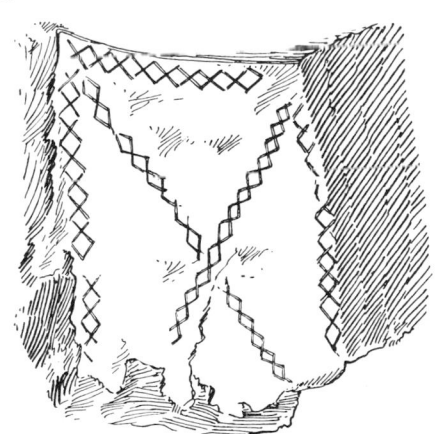

FIG. 244.—HURDLE-DESIGN : FRESCOED WALL, KNOSSOS

this gem, which probably depicts a scene that must often have occurred at Knossos, as it does in Spain.

All these representations of bulls and of bull-fighting, in the frescoes of Knossos and Tiryns, the Gladiator Vase, the Churchill bronze group, and numerous smaller examples of the theme on gems and rings, remind us again of the legend of the Minotaur, and of the rule of the bull-venerating princes of Knossos : so at least we read the Theseus-legend in the light of the discoveries at Knossos. And in the expedition of

187

Theseus of Athens himself and the slaying of the Minotaur may we not see a poetized adaptation of a revolt of prehistoric Athens against the tyranny of Knossos and even of the conquest of the tyrant-city by the mainlanders which reduced the labyrinth of the Minotaur to ruin ?

But before passing to the destruction of Knossos and the transference of power in the Aegean from Crete to the Greek mainland we must briefly consider the tombs as well as the palaces of the Minoans. We have already spoken of the shaft-graves and *tholoi* of the transplanted Cretans in Greece. Most " Helladic " graves before the advent of the Cretans (p. 140) were plain graves or cist-burials with very poor funeral offerings. The tombs of Crete were very different. On the hillside above Knossos on the east are chamber-tombs of the M.M. II–III period, used until L.M. III*b*, that were excavated in 1926–7 by Sir A. Evans and Mr. Forsdyke. Not far off is the necropolis of Zafer Papoura with its fine tombs of nobles, which, with the kingly sepulchre of Isopata, between Knossos and the sea, are among the finest discoveries of Sir Arthur Evans in the neighbourhood of the palace.

I have hitherto said little of Aegean funerary customs, because no particular method is so characteristic of any particular period as was the case in Egypt, and, with the exception of the primitive rock-shelters and caves in Crete and the stone cist-grave, which was characteristic of the early Cycladic period and was introduced into Crete from the Cyclades in E.M. III (to last but a short time), most types, *tholoi*, rock-chambers, pit- and shaft-tombs, and plain graves, seem to have been used together. Ossuaries, however, are generally early : up to M.M. I burial was usual in rock-shelters, rectangular chambers, or small *tholoi*.[1] Chamber-tombs in the Egyptian style, approached by a *dromos* cut straight in the side of a hill, first appear in M.M. II in Crete ; on the mainland, as at Asine [2] and the Argive Heræum,[3] they are much later, and no doubt of Cretan origin. We therefore judge the age of an Aegean tomb, except a cist-grave or an ossuary-tholos, by the nature of the objects found in it. This

---

[1] See Xanthoudides, *The Vaulted Tombs of Mesarà* (1924) ; Seager, *Mochlos*, pp. 13, 14.
[2] Persson, *K. Hum. Vet.* (Lund), *Årsberättelse*, 1922–3, p. 34 ; 1924–5, p. 40 ff., pll. xv ff.
[3] *Υ.W.*, 1926–7, p. 92.

fact of the diversity of Aegean tombs should warn against the idea that difference of burial in all cases necessarily means either difference of period or difference of race. In the M.M. I. and Middle Helladic periods (not before) occur pot-burials: they were most common in M.M. III (Fig. 245).

FIG. 245.—PAINTED POTTERY BURIAL-POT : L.M. I*a*. (*c.* ¼)

The bodies were placed in the contracted position in large pottery pithoi headforemost, and the pithoi were then buried bottom-upwards.[1] In E.M. III the pottery coffin or *larnax* makes its first appearance with no lid, four handles and rounded ends (Fig. 246) ;[2] in the Middle

[1] E. H. Hall, *Sphoungaràs* (Pennsylvania Univ. Mus. Anthrop. Publ., 1912).

[2] In a cave at Pyrgos, near Candia (Xanthoudides, *Ἀρχ. Δελτ.* 1918) ; also at Pachyammos, figured by Evans, *Palace*, Fig. 94, p. 125.

Minoan period it becomes general and in L.M. I–III looks very like a bath (Fig. 247): in fact pottery baths were often used instead

of *larnakes*, and the fact may account for the stories of great ones of the heroic period having been murdered in their baths, as for instance Agamemnon by Klytaimnestra.[1] The pot and larnax-burials are almost precisely paralleled in Babylonia, where even down to the Persian period bodies were buried in a

FIG. 246.—PAINTED POTTERY LARNAX : M.M. I. $(c. \frac{1}{6})$

contracted position in just similar *larnakes* and also in pots, often in two placed mouth to mouth, with vents to let out the fluids. Minoan *larnakes* had holes along the bottom edge for the same purpose.[2] We

FIG. 247.—PAINTED POTTERY LARNAX : L.M. III

can hardly refuse to see in the Aegean custom an introduction from the East parallel to that of the use of the clay tablet for writing. And

[1] Evans, *Prehist. Tombs of Knossos*, p. 170.   [2] Forsdyke, *Catalogue*, p. 127.

190

as in Babylonia sometimes the bodies were buried in the disgusting Asiatic fashion beneath the floors of the houses of the living, though this was usually the case only when children were concerned.[1] One difference is noticeable : the Minoan *larnax* (rare on the mainland) usually had a high-gabled lid (Fig. 248) : the Babylonian usually no lid at all. And the oldest Minoan *larnakes* often had no lids and had rounded corners. The Babylonian had rounded corners. The Middle Minoan were often oval ; the Late Minoan, when not of the bath form, were rectangular.[2] Both Babylonian and Minoan *larnakes* often had handles. I am inclined to credit the introduction of the pottery *larnax* to Babylonia, where it is exactly paralleled, rather than with Evans to find an origin for it in the Egyptian wooden coffin. It came from Babylonia like the clay tablet for writing, and roughly at the same period, when the potter's wheel also came from the East (p. 72). The idea that in the Mycenaean shaft-graves (M.M. III–L.M. I) the bodies lay in wooden coffins (which would argue Egyptian influence), decorated with gold appliqué ornaments, is possible.

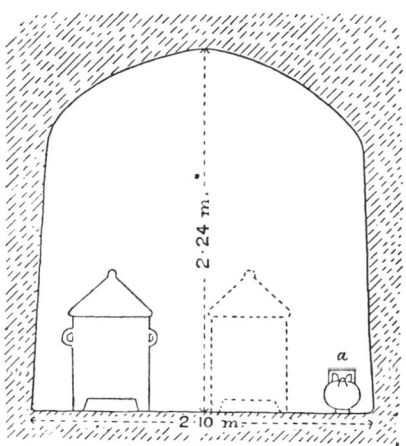

FIG. 248.—SECTION OF TOMB-CHAMBER WITH GABLED RECTANGULAR LARNAKES : L.M. III

The Cretan *tholos*-tombs were of course developments of the older *tholoi* or ossuaries, and these developed out of cave-burials. The *tholos* was an artificial cave, in Late Minoan days approached by a *dromos* or cutting leading to the entrance in the side of the mound or hillside in which the chamber was built, to be afterwards covered by the slope. The rectangular *tholoi* of the Late Minoan Age in Crete had gabled or vaulted roofs. When round, the roofs were domed, as in the case of the great circular *tholoi* of the mainland. Inside the chamber was the *larnax*

---

[1] As in the M.H. burials at Eutresis in Boeotia (*J.H.S.*, 1925, p. 212).
[2] On the Babylonian *larnax*-burials see Hall, *J.E.A.*, ix (1923), p. 187.

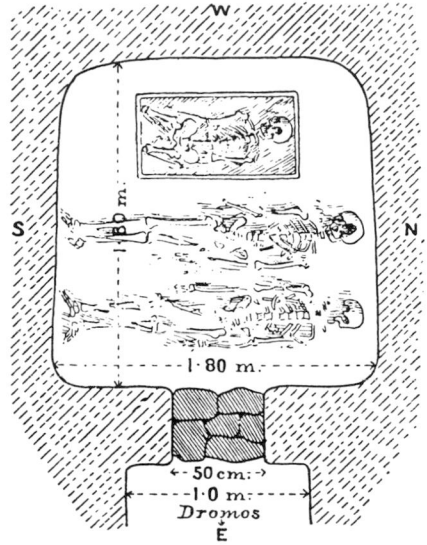

FIG. 249.—PLAN OF TOMB CHAMBER WITH FULL LENGTH AND CONTRACTED BURIALS : L.M. III

(usually decorated in the style of the ceramic paintings of the time), containing the body, often in a crouched position, sometimes on the back with the legs drawn up sufficiently for it to be introduced into the coffin. Other bodies may be laid on the floor in the extended position without a larnax (Fig. 249). At Isopata, near Knossos, is a great royal tomb, a rectangular *tholos* of the M.M. III–L.M. I period with descending *dromos* like the Mycenaean *tholoi*, but probably with a gabled roof [1] (Figs. 250, 251). Of the great circular *tholoi* of the mainland we have already spoken : their interiors were covered with bronze rosettes and they were closed with bronze doors : out of the Treasury of Atreus opens a small rectangular chamber which was no doubt the resting-place of the *larnax* (Figs. 252, 253). We have no exactly similar *tholoi* in Crete ; but the building of the Isopata tomb is better than that of the mainland *tholoi* with the exception of the two chief Mycenaean " treasuries," as they were called (see also p. 149). In a L.M. I–II tomb at Isopata we find in an outer chamber

FIG. 250.—THE ROYAL TOMB, ISOPATA : M.M. III–L.M. I

seats provided for the pious visitors, a provision which strongly recalls

[1] Evans, *Prehistoric Tombs of Knossos*, p. 136 ff.

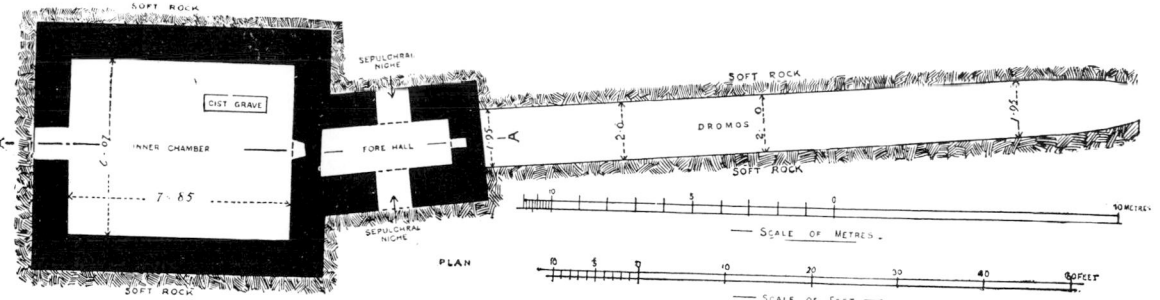

FIG. 251.—PLAN OF THE ROYAL TOMB, ISOPATA

Etruscan sepulchres. In the well-named "Tomb of the Double Axes," there is a grave-cist made in the form of the double axe. And in the same

FIG. 252.—INTERIOR OF THE "TREASURY OF ATREUS": MYCENAE

tomb were found several such axes, both for actual use and in the purely sacral form (Fig. 11). This tomb has therefore an unusually religious character, and it may be that it is the sepulchre of a high-priest or a

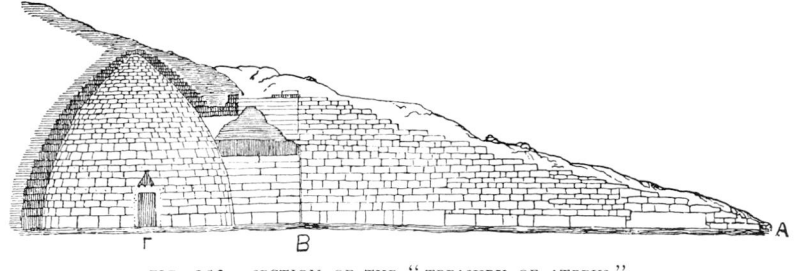

FIG. 253.—SECTION OF THE "TREASURY OF ATREUS"

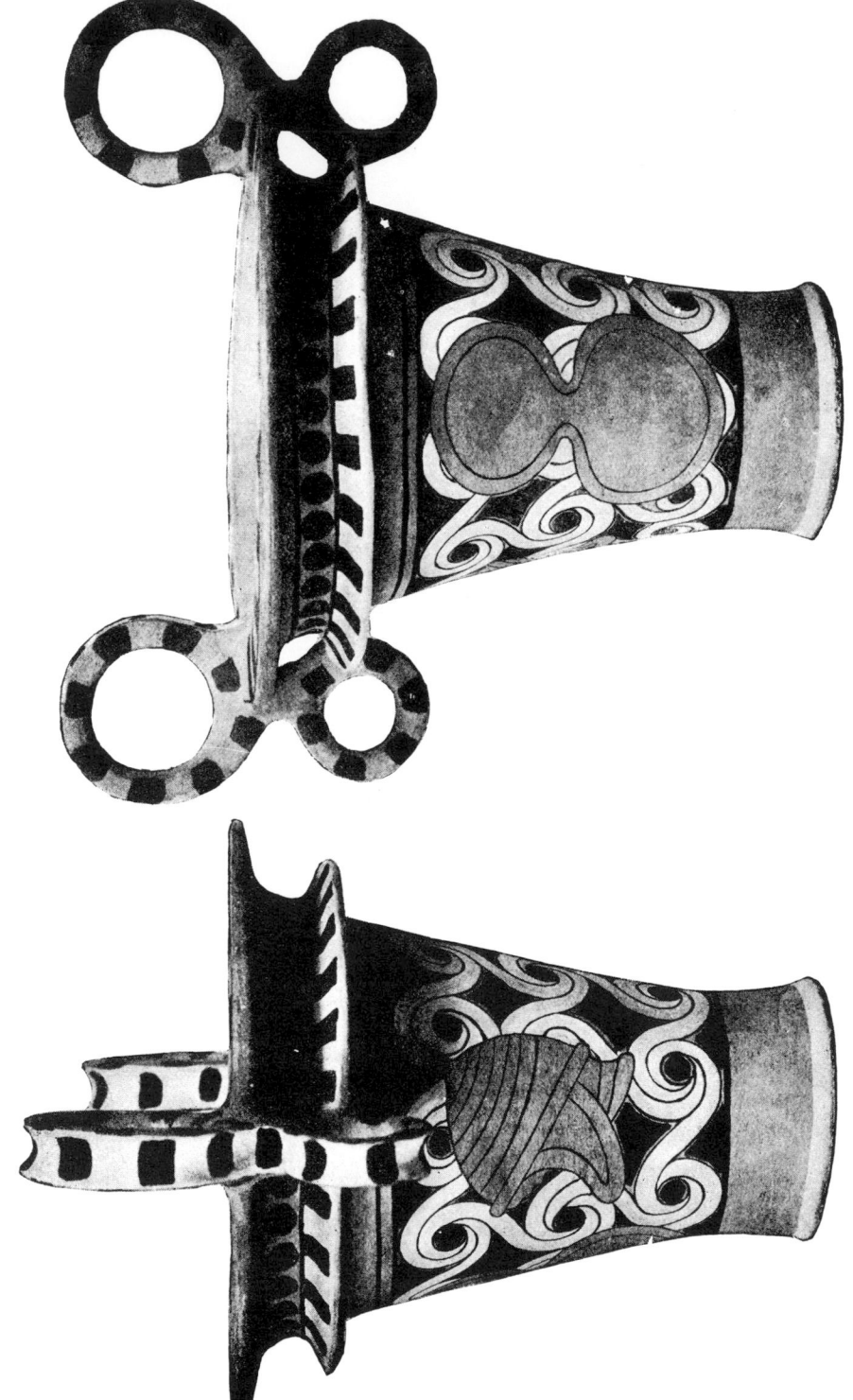

FIG. 254.—PAINTED POTTERY FUNERARY VASE WITH REPRESENTATION OF A HELMET AND SHIELD SUPERIMPOSED ON SPIRALS. TOMB OF THE POLYCHROME VASES

194

chief peculiarly devoted to the worship of the divinities of Knossos. In another tomb were found very interesting vases of a purely sepulchral character, painted in bright colours, a survival of Middle Minoan polychromy " in usu mortuorum." Two of these, with their remarkable design of helmet and shield superimposed above the ground design,

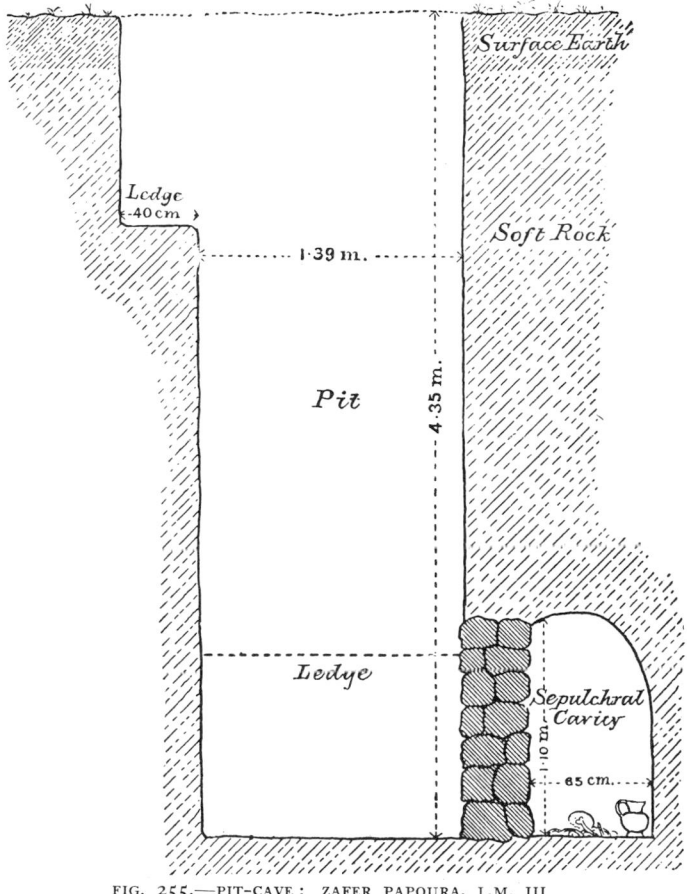

FIG. 255.—PIT-CAVE: ZAFER PAPOURA, L.M. III

are here illustrated (Fig. 254). A similar vase, from the Tomb of the Double Axes, has a small domed lid, missing in the case of the others. Among other objects connected with the ritual of the dead from these tombs pottery incense-burners are notable.

In some of the tombs of Zafer Papoura also is found a combination of shaft-grave and chamber-tomb, which Sir Arthur Evans

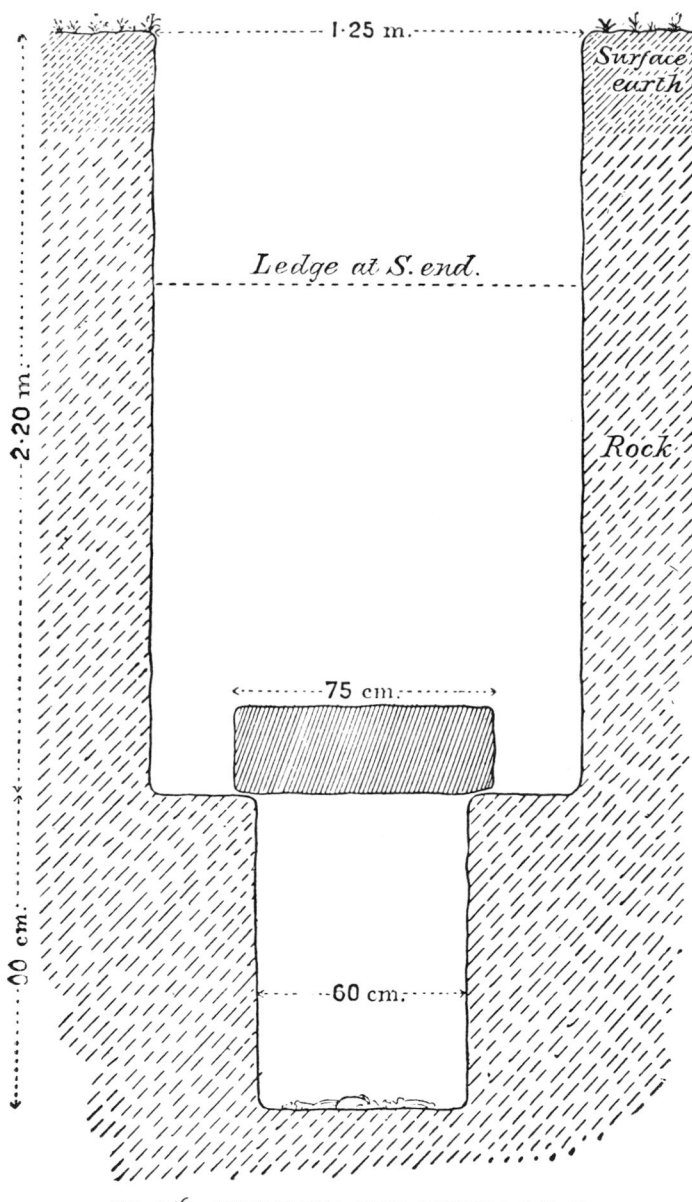

FIG. 256.—SHAFT-GRAVE : ZAFER PAPOURA : L.M. II

calls a " pit-cave," a grave of an Egyptian type with a small sepulchral cell at the bottom of a shaft (Fig. 255). The other tombs at Zafer Papoura are shaft-graves (Fig. 256) and more or less rectangular *tholoi* or chamber-tombs. Generally, the shaft-graves seem to be the older (L.M. II), and among them are several tombs, evidently royal (or at any rate those of important chiefs) that are of the highest interest. Just as the Mycenaean shaft-graves have yielded so rich a treasure of the funerary state, weapons, and adornments of the colonial princes on the mainland, so in the presumably royal tombs of Zafer Papoura were found some of the finest examples of Minoan bronze weapons, with hilts plated with gold and decorated with incised groups of lions and ibexes, and with pommels of ivory or of translucent banded agate.

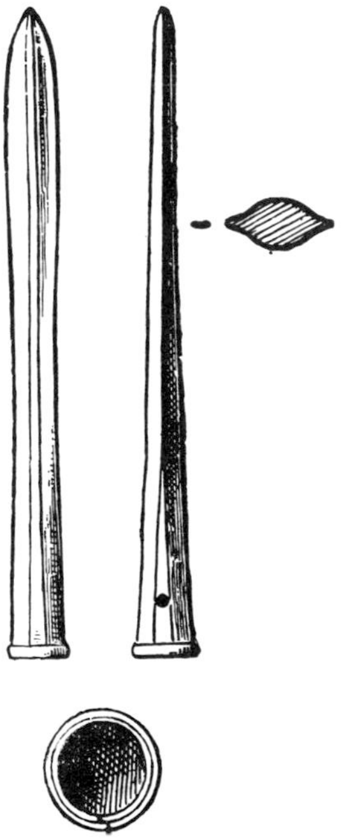

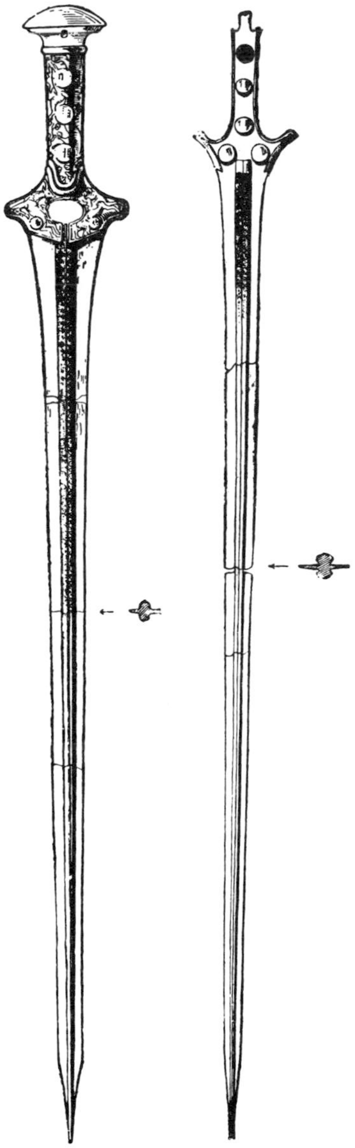

FIG. 257.—RAPIERS: L.M. II. $(\frac{1}{4}, \frac{1}{5})$

FIG. 258.—SPEARHEADS: L.M. II. (c. $\frac{1}{3}$)

The hilts have horned or cruciform grips of characteristic shape; the blades are of the rapier form into which the ancient copper and bronze daggers had now developed (Fig. 257). And spearheads of bronze were also found, of characteristically beautiful shape (Fig. 258), almost Japanese in their fineness of line and curve, very different from the ordinary leaf-shaped weapons elsewhere and of later days in Greece (see p. 257).

197

As at Mycenae, the dead were accompanied to the tomb by their personal decoration : Fig. 259 shews the mixture of glass-paste (kyanos) beads, lentoid gems or γαλόπετραις, and Egyptian faience scarabs of the latter part of the XVIIIth Dynasty with which the great ones of this time adorned themselves.[1]   Beads of Baltic amber were also used.[2]

So the chiefs of Knossos were buried with their funerary state around them.   The Isopata royal tomb is M.M.III–L.M. I ; the Zafer Papoura

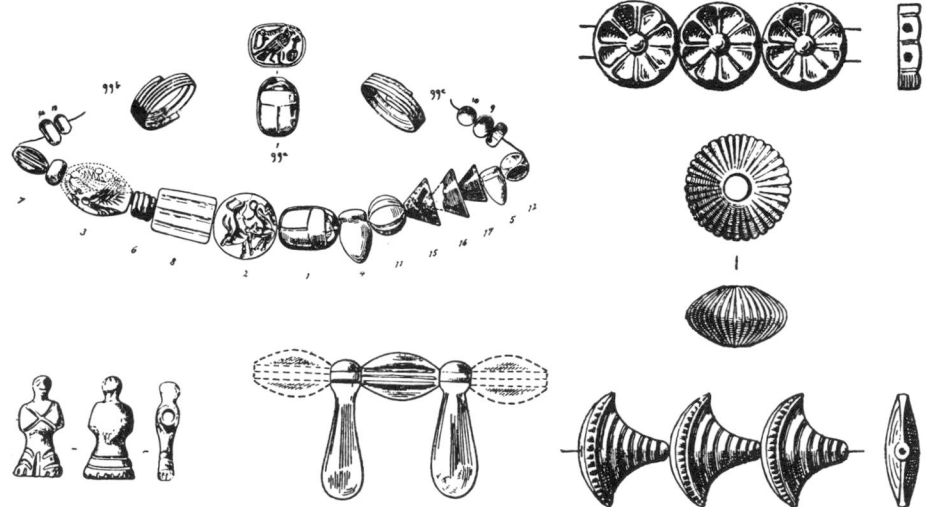

FIG. 259.—GLASS PASTE AND STONE BEADS : EGYPTIAN SCARABS OF THE LATE XVIIITH DYNASTY PERIOD : SEALSTONES, ETC.
(*Actual size and reduced*)

tombs are L.M. II–III, and some of them must precede the final catastrophe by but a short period of time.[3]

The L.M. II period ended with the catastrophic destruction of Knossos by a foreign enemy.   Possibly her thalassocracy was no more popular than that of the Athenians was to be, a thousand years later.   The fall of

---

[1] The glass-paste beads of Minoan type are peculiar to the Minoans and were not used in Egypt. A magnificent collection of them was found at Ialysos in Rhodes and is in the British Museum.

[2] Evans, *Tomb of the Double Axes*, p. 42 ff.

[3] While many of the Zafer Papoura tombs are no doubt L.M. III, belonging to the " period of partial reoccupation," the " Chieftain-Tomb " and others of the shaft-graves are perhaps older. (Evans, *Prehistoric Tombs of Knossos*, p. 133.)

198

Knossos took place between 1450 and 1400 B.C. This date is indicated by Egyptian evidence. Five tombs of the first half of the fifteenth century B.C. at Egyptian Thebes have pictures of Minoan Cretan envoys bearing splendid metal vases of Minoan work as gifts : those of Sennemut or Senmut (*c.* 1500 B.C., in the reign of Hatshepsut) ; of User, or Useramon, another vizier, not much later ; of Rekhmire', the vizier of Thutmosis III, who lived into the reign of Amenhotep II (*c.* 1440 B.C.) ; of Puimre', and of Menkheperre'senb, who was born in the reign of Thutmosis III.[1] Sennemut's Minoans (Fig. 260) carry a bronze vase of a well - known pithoid Minoan type with two rows of handles, which is paralleled to some extent, though without the lower handles, by a vase (possibly of foreign marble, though, judging by the form of the base, of Egyptian make) with the name of Hatshepsut in the

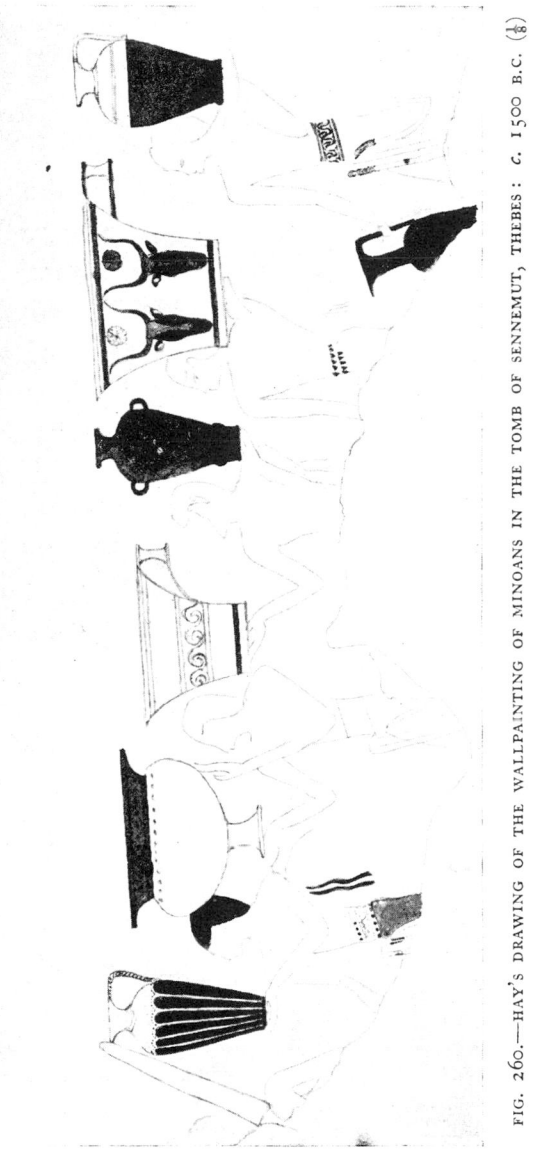

FIG. 260.—HAY'S DRAWING OF THE WALLPAINTING OF MINOANS IN THE TOMB OF SENNEMUT, THEBES : C. 1500 B.C. (⅛)

[1] For the tomb of Sennemut (No. 71), see Hall, *B.S.A. Ann.*, xvi, p. 254 ff. ; W. M. Müller, *Egyptological Researches*, i. p. 12 ff. His name was Sen-ne-Mut or Sen-en-Mut,

Cairo Museum (Fig. 261). Also they bear gigantic vases of Vapheio type, with decorations of gold bulls' heads on silver and with gold spiral ornamented rims, and other Minoan vases (Fig. 260). The vases are represented as gigantic only in order to exhibit their form and

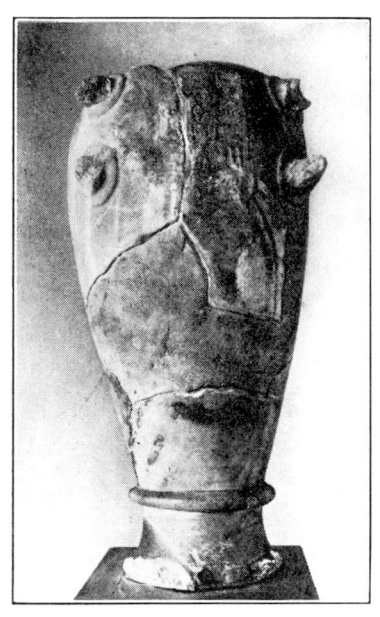

FIG. 261.—MARBLE VASE WITH NAME OF QUEEN HATSHEPSUT: *c.* 1480 B.C.: CAIRO MUSEUM. (*c.* $\frac{1}{12}$)

design more clearly; they were really of the usual size. Menkheperre'senb's men also have vases of similar type, not so well drawn, a great bull-rhyton, like those from Mycenae and Knossos (Fig. 262*a*), and a definitely Minoan figure of a bull (Fig. 263), as also do User's men (Fig. 264). Rekhmire's carry great " fillers " with shoulders, a variant type known in pottery, and Minoan jugs as well as ingots of copper (Figs. 265, 266). These Cretans are clearly recognizable by the details of their dress, especially the important detail of the hair, with its characteristic long locks to the waist and fantastic curls on the top of the head (Fig. 267; *cf.* Puimre') ; the high boots or putteed sandals, and the fringed waistcloth or kilt with its projecting sheath or codpiece (the latter especially in the tombs of Sennemut (Fig. 268) and User). In Fig. 262*a* the distinction between the Minoan (bearing the bull-rhyton) and the

also spelt Senmut. The pictures in the tombs of Rekhmire' (100) and Menkheperre'senb (86) have recently been copied accurately by Mrs. N. de G. Davies, and by the kindness of Dr. Alan Gardiner, to whom they belong, her copies are reproduced here, as no other non-photographic reproductions of the paintings are satisfactory. W. M. Müller's coloured drawings of Sennemut in his *Egyptological Researches*, i, pls. 5–7, are bad, the colour-reproduction being most crude. Nor are his coloured drawings of Menkheperre'senb in vol. ii, pls. 9–12, much better. Virey's (of Rekhmire') are very summary. Müller's identification of early XVIIIth Dynasty representations of Keftians in the tomb (17) of Nebamon (" Senye "), *M.V.O.G.* 9 (1904) was abandoned by him in *Egyptological Researches*, i, p. 18, n. 4. For Puimre' (39) see Davies, *Tomb of Puyemre*, p. 91, pls. i, xxxiii, xxxvi.

three Asiatics that precede him, in all characteristics of ethnic type and clothing, is most marked : in complexion too he is, as usual, a deep red, almost like an Egyptian, not yellow, like a Semite. These Minoans

A

B

FIG 262.—(a) ASIATICS AND A MINOAN : TOMB OF MENKHEPERRE'SENB $(c. \frac{1}{8})$; (b) MINOANS IN THE TOMB OF MENKHEPERRE'SENB

are described on Rekhmire's tomb as men of Keftiu or Kaphtor and " the Isles of the Sea," and from their appearance it is evident that Crete was included in the designation " Keftiu." It has been argued [1]

[1] Wainwright, *Liverp. Ann. Art and Arch.*, 1913, p. 24 ff.

that Keftiu and "the Isles" are two different things, "the Isles" being Crete and the Aegean, while Keftiu vas Cilicia, because Keftians are sometimes represented as bringing Syrian vases

FIG. 263.—MINOANS IN THE TOMB OF MENKHEPERRE'SENB, BEARING A MINOAN FILLER, A MINOAN "VAPHEIO" CUP, AND A MINOAN BULL. (½)

to Egypt. But we have no valid reason to dichotomize the expression "men of Keftiu and the Isles of the Sea" by which *all* the obvious Minoans of Rekhmire's paintings are described. Which of these are men of the Isles and which Keftians? All are

202

Minoans. To the Hebrews Kaphtor, which is undoubtedly Keftiu, meant primarily Crete, though since the Philistines, who were certainly not Cretans, are said to have come from " the isles (or coasts) of Kaphtor," the Hebrew term no doubt included S.W. Asia Minor as well,

FIG. 264.—MINOANS IN THE TOMB OF USER-AMON WITH MINOAN BULL-RHYTON, STANDING BULL, ETC.

and may just possibly have extended as far as Cilicia. But even if Kaphtor did include Cilicia, which is not certain, we have no proof that Rekhmire's Keftians were Cilician Keftians, because we have as yet no archaeological proof that Minoans ever lived in Cilicia. The fact that

FIG. 265.—MINOAN GIFTS FROM THE TOMBS OF USER-AMON AND REKHMIRE'

Syrian vases are sometimes shewn as brought to Egypt by Keftians does not necessarily prove that these Keftians lived in a country immediately bordering on Syria, as has been supposed. Keftian seafarers might well bring Syrian vases to Egypt (Keftian ships are mentioned as visiting Phoenicia), and, besides, the Egyptians were not too accurate in their

203

descriptions of foreigners, and Egyptian painters might well confuse the products of Syria with those of Keftiu or any other country of the North. In some of the representations of Keftians (not those in the tombs of Sennemut, User, and Rekhmire', who are very accurately costumed Minoans), they certainly look as if their appearance had been confused to some extent with that of Syrians or Anatolians. Still, since it is not impossible that Kaphtor-Keftiu did cover the whole of the southern coast of Asia Minor as far east as Cilicia there may in Cilicia bordering on Syria have lived " Syro-Keftians," so to speak, who brought " Syrizing "

FIG. 266.—" THE GREAT MEN OF KEFTIU AND THE ISLES ": TOMB OF REKHMIRE': c. 1440 B.C.

objects of art to Egypt, though as yet we have no direct proof of their existence, and I personally do not yet believe in their existence as real Minoans, though a mixed art of Syrian, Hittite, and Minoan affinities seems to have existed in or near the Cilician region at this time.[1] Rekhmire's " men of Keftiu and the Isles," however, are obviously not such hypothetical " Syro-Keftians " at all but genuine Minoans of Crete, as also are those of Sennemut's tomb, and of User's. Nobody could suppose that User's men, with their dress, and their figure of a running bull, are not Cretans ! And if Rekhmire's men are as much Keftians

[1] See my article in *Manchester J.O.S.*, 1913, on Alashiya.

204

as men of the Isles, User's must be Keftians as well as Men of the Isles, too. We know from archaeology that direct relations had existed between Crete and Egypt from the earliest times.[1] The name of Keftiu was familiar in Egypt long before the time of the XVIIIth Dynasty, as we see from the "Prophecies of Ipuwer," an Egyptian papyrus of the time between the VIth and XIIth Dynasties, in which it appears for the first time. And archaeology tells us that direct relations between Egypt and Crete still existed at this time, that of the XVIIIth Dynasty.

FIG. 267. — MINOAN IN THE TOMB OF REKHMIRE'. ($\frac{1}{9}$)

The Minoan or rather Mycenaean colony in Cyprus, to which we shall presently refer, perhaps was not founded till a few years later, though relations between Crete and Cyprus already existed. So probably enough these Keftians were actual envoys from Knossos bearing gifts to

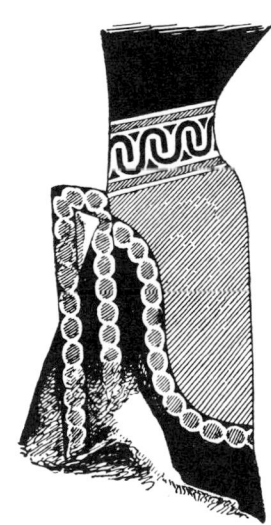

FIG. 268.—DETAIL OF MINOAN DRESS: TOMB OF SENNEMUT. ($\frac{1}{3}$)

Egypt, which was just now making such a noise in the world by her conquest of Syria in revenge for her oppression by the Syrian "Hyksos" kings, Khayan for example, of whom a relic in the shape of an inscribed alabastron-lid was found in M.M. III Knossos (p. 123). The Egyptian pharaoh Thutmase or Thutmosis III spoke of Keftiu and the Isles as being in fear of him, but we have no record that he ever carried war into Crete; he did not even reach Cyprus. Like the Cyprian king of Yantinai, the Minos of Knossos sent gifts, but acknowledged no overlordship thereby. The identity of these Keftians with "Mycenaeans," first pointed out by Steindorff in 1892,[2] sprang to the eye in 1901 when Sir Arthur Evans discovered at Knossos the famous fresco of the Cup-bearer (Frontispiece), which we can assign to L.M. I (p. 182). Here we had at once the Minoan

[1] See p. 25 ff. [2] *Archaeolog. Anzeiger (Jahrb. Arch.)*, 1892, p. 11 ff.

original of the ambassadors of Sennemut and Rekhmire', a Cretan youth carrying as a gift a great silver " filler " like the " Gladiator Vase," arrayed in kilt and wearing the long waving hair of his race just as the Egyptian artists depicted him and his fellows. Gifts of this royal kind could be brought by the ambassadors of Crete. Behind them we can see a whole apparatus of regular commercial relations, which had existed for centuries, at least since the time of the VIth Dynasty (E.M. II). To Egypt, Crete must have exported her staple, olive-oil, and such things as wine and honey, as well as a certain amount of pottery, while she no doubt acted as middleman for the silver of the Hellespontine region, for copper, and probably for bronze from the Pontic coast. To Crete, Egypt no doubt sent, first and foremost, gold, and then linen fabrics and corn, alabaster and other fine stones, worked and unworked,[1] and, apparently, also black soldiers ![2] If Egypt was wealthy, so also was Crete now. Her gifts were those of a great and rich power. Her palaces and their adornment testify to the wealth and even luxury of the dynasts of Knossos and Phaistos, and to the capacity and taste of their architects and artists. The stores of inscribed tablets of this period from Knossos with their linear script testify not only to the development of the writing since Middle Minoan times but also to a highly organized chancery and scribal system, with regular accounts, dockets, and lists for palace use and we doubt not, also, as in Babylonia, used for commercial purposes. Weights and scales did, but actual money of course did not exist in Crete, or anywhere else, yet.

Then suddenly the whole of this fabric passed away. At the end of

[1] Alabaster vases were commonly imported into Crete from Egypt under the XVIIIth Dynasty, as we see in the royal tomb at Isopata (p. 192 ; Evans, *Preh. Tombs*, p. 146 ff.). For a Minoan imitation (M.M. III) of an Egyptian form in which the vase has become one with the vase-stand, see Evans, *Palace*, i, Fig. 301.

[2] With the Sudanese blacks whose presence at Knossos as mercenaries, or more probably slave-guards of the palace, is attested by the fresco mentioned on pp. 119, 122, may be compared the black troops, who not so very much later we find upholding Egyptian authority at Jerusalem (Hall, *Anc. Hist. N.E.*, p. 348). But the Knossian blacks need not imply any Egyptian domination. They were no doubt exported by Pharaoh as a gift or recompense to " Minos," or were bought in Egypt by Cretan envoys. Still less do they indicate any kind of racial invasion from Africa at or before this time.

L.M. II Knossos was destroyed by an enemy, and for a time deserted. To Egypt no more envoys and no more products of Crete at this period came. With Knossos perished Keftiu. It is a most significant circumstance that the Keftians, the Minoans of the L.M. I and II period who brought Cretan gifts to Egypt under the XVIIIth Dynasty, cease to be mentioned by the Egyptians almost contemporarily with the fall of Knossos or not long after it. Under the XIXth and XXth Dynasties they are only mentioned once or twice, and there are no representations of them. Under the XXth Dynasty the word Keftiu only occurs once in a garbled form which shews that it is a mere corrupt copy of an older instance of the name. Already under the XIXth Dynasty the place of the Keftians is taken by the " Peoples of the Sea " when the Egyptians are referring to the Mediterraneans. We cannot doubt that the Keftians were indeed the old Minoan Cretans of the great days now gone.

But though Keftiu disappeared as a power, relations with the Greek lands continued uninterruptedly.

Archaeology shews us that the great age of Crete (L.M. I–II) was followed by the period L.M. III (= Myc. III), in which the centre of the Greek civilization was not Crete, but the mainland and the eastern islands of the Aegean, Rhodes and her neighbours. Now about 1380–1360 B.C. we find Greek pottery, not of the Cretan, but of the fully developed mainland Mycenaean (=L.M. IIIa) style (like that of Ialysos in Rhodes),[1] at el-Amarna in Egypt, in the ruins of the city built by the heretical king, Akhenaten, of whom we have heard so much lately, in connexion with the tomb of his son-in-law, Tutankhamen. His city, Akhetaten, was deserted soon after his death, and never reoccupied, so that this pottery must date to his time.[2] In connexion with

[1] Forsdyke, *Cat. Cases*, I, i, p. 183 ff. (A 990–9) : " This pottery can be definitely placed at the beginning of the Late Mycenaean style (L.M. III.) Its fabric is identical with that of the best Mycenaean ware from Rhodes and Cyprus." Mr. Forsdyke has definitely determined the style of the Amarna Mycenaean fragments, none of which can be later than about 1360 B.C. by the Egyptian evidence.

[2] Later objects may have been left there, of course, like a pot of the time of Seti I, found during the recent excavations of the Egypt Exploration Society, but there was no town there, and no regular reoccupation.

the Mycenaean pottery at Amarna, great interest attaches to certain casts from the faces of living subjects, made for a sculptor's use, that were found in his studio at Amarna and are now at Berlin. Most of these extraordinarily interesting portrait-masks are of Egyptians, including many of the royal family, but three illustrated here (Figs. 269, 270) are in my opinion non-Egyptian, and specifically European in type. Fig. 269a is of a young man or woman ; the sex is uncertain, as the ears were then bored in the case of both men and women, and the

FIG. 269.—*a*, *b*, CASTS FROM THE LIVING : PORTRAIT HEADS OF EUROPEANS (?). AMARNA : *c.* 1370 B.C.

hair proves nothing, except that the person was not Egyptian. The type is surely Nordic. Fig. 269b might be the rugged, brutal visage of one of the Shardina barbarian bodyguard (p. 254). And Fig. 270 is definitely that of a South European woman, a Greek, Italian, or Southern Frenchwoman. I see in these three portraits of Notherners : the lady may actually have been a Cretan. At about the same date, or a little earlier, we find pottery of the same kind (Fig. 276), with gold jewellery (Fig. 271) and Egyptian rings and scarabs with the names of King Amenhetep III and his wife Tiyi, the parents of Akhenaten, (*c.*

208

1412–1376 B.C.), and of Akhenaten himself (*c.* 1376–1360 B.C.), with Egyptian XVIIIth Dynasty faience[1] (Fig. 272), and imitations of it, at Enkomi in Cyprus, where the Minoan or Mycenaean culture now suddenly appears, without any preparation, as an intruder from without into the realm of the native Cyprian Bronze Age culture. Egyptian objects of the same reign have been found at Ialysos in Rhodes with L.M. III pottery of the same kind as that found at Amarna, and at Mycenae (Fig.

FIG. 270—PROFILE AND FULL-FACE VIEWS OF A PORTRAIT-CAST FROM THE LIVING OF A EUROPEAN (?) WOMAN : AMARNA : *c.* 1370 B.C.

273), with at least one object, a small figure of a monkey (Fig. 274), of an earlier reign, that of Amenhetep II (*c.* 1447–1421 B.C.).[2] Nothing of L.M. I or II is found with these things at Ialysos or Amarna, and very little at Enkomi or elsewhere in Cyprus, and we can

---

[1] Murray, Smith, and Walters, *Excavations in Cyprus*; Hall, *Brit. Mus. Cat. Scarabs*, i, Nos. 1915, 1944, 2660 (Amenhetep and Teie) ; No. 2678 (Akhenaten). On the general material see Fimmen, *Zeit u. Dauer der kret.-myk. Kultur*, p. 64 ff. ; *Die Kret.-myk. Kultur*, p. 174 ff. ; and cf. Hall, *Oldest Civilization of Greece*, p. 49 ff.

[2] Hall, *B.S.A. Ann*, viii, p. 188.

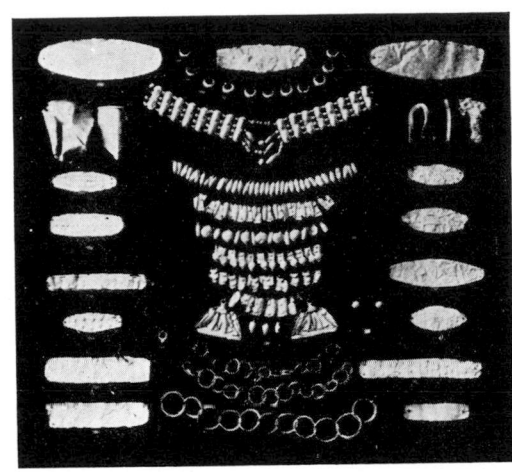

FIG. 271.—EGYPTIAN AND MYCENAEAN GOLD JEWELLERY : ENKOMI, CYPRUS, *c.* 1400 B.C. BRITISH MUSEUM. ($\frac{1}{10}$)

FIG. 272.—EGYPTIAN AND LOCAL IMITATION OF EGYPTIAN FAIENCE : ENKOMI, CYPRUS, *c.* 1400 B.C. ($\frac{1}{4}$)
(The central platter is probably a local imitation : the other two vases are XVIIIth Dynasty Egyptian.)

hardly avoid the conclusion that the destruction of Knossos which brought L.M. II to an end happened some time after 1450 B.C.

FIG. 273.—EGYPTIAN VASE WITH NAME OF AMENHETEP III : MYCENAE, *c.* 1400 B.C.

The Minoan or rather Mycenaean settlement in Cyprus at this time is of great interest in this connexion. I have hitherto said nothing of the old native culture of Cyprus, which lay outside the main stream of Greek development then as later.[1] Its pottery is connected primarily with that of Anatolia and North Syria, though it always possessed distinctive characteristics of its own, with its great dull-red bowls (the oldest of all), its fantastic horned vases and " milk-bowls " of white slip ware with geometrical decoration in dark paint, and its red or black shiny pots with deeply incised ornament (Fig. 275). Of other art we see nothing in Cyprus at this time. Nothing fine was developed, and the Minoan culture had so little influence on that of Cyprus, that it is most difficult to get any ceramic synchronism with Crete that would tell us the date of the early Cyprian wares.[2] L.M. I pottery was imported into the island occasionally, but that is the earliest

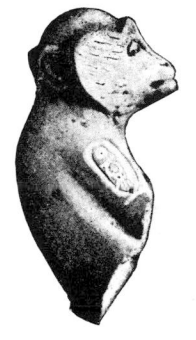

FIG. 274. — FAIENCE MONKEY WITH PRENOMEN OF AMENHETEP II : MYCENAE, *c.* 1430 B.C.

[1] On Cyprian culture, see Myres, *Cyprus Museum Catalogue* (1899), and *Catalogue of the Cesnola Collection*, New York.

[2] Mr. Einar Gjerstad has just published a detailed analysis of Cyprian Bronze Age ceramic, which should settle many questions, and will be most useful. (*Studies on Prehistoric Cyprus*, Uppsala, 1926.)

sign of Cretan influence. Then comes suddenly the appearance, obviously due to sudden transplantation from the west, of the L.M. III culture in the island, with its typical pottery. This has been thought to be due to a wholesale immigration from Crete after the fall of Knossos, but it is just as possible that the immigration came from the Greek mainland, and was part of a wave of expansion and conquest that radiated at this time from Greece, overthrew Knossos, and reached Cyprus. This would agree with the style of the L.M. III pottery of Cyprus, which is of the Ialysian and Mycenaean rather

FIG. 275.—NATIVE CYPRIAN BRONZE AGE POTTERY. ($\frac{1}{6}$)

than the Cretan type (Fig. 276), and would be more in accordance with Greek tradition, which, as we know, brought Arcadian colonists to Cyprus. But Greek-speaking Arcadians can hardly have come yet, or at any time before the Achaian movement of the thirteenth century (see p. 249). The Greeks will have come then. But there was a pre-Achaian movement, the Mycenaean immigration that founded the culture of Enkomi. We may with great plausibility regard the fall of Knossos as due to invasion from the mainland, and the replacement of the Minoan by Mycenaean hegemony in the Aegean, shortly before the reign of Amenhetep III (1412 B.C.). The Mycenaean immigration into

212

Cyprus was a result of this. The Minoan connexion with Sicily, of which we have unequivocal traces in the great island to the west, is more probably an older event,[1] possibly contemporary with the westward movement of Aegean culture of which we see evidence in the spiral relief decorations of the sepulchral " temple " of Hal Tarxien in Malta,[2] which on this evidence should be no older than about 2000 B.C., and may not be Neolithic. But at the same period as the undoubted Minoan

FIG. 276.—L.M. III (MYCENAEAN III), NATIVE CYPRIAN, AND IMPORTED SYRIAN POTTERY ; ENKOMI, CYPRUS, c. 1400 B.C. ($\frac{1}{10}$)

immigration into Cyprus we find at Cozzo Pantano and elsewhere in Sicily [3] L.M. III vases as well as weapons of undoubted Aegean inspiration which may point to something more than commercial connexion ; taken together with the legend of the expedition to Kamikos and Hyria "after the death of Minos " may they not be relics of a complementary

[1] Peet, *Stone and Bronze Ages in Italy*, pp. 135 ff., finds still earlier connexions on the Neolithic period (Stentinello and Molfetta pottery).

[2] Zammit, in *Archaeologia*, lxvii, lxviii.

[3] Peet, *l.c.*, p. 435 ff ; Mosso, *Dawn of Mediterranean Civilization*, p. 273 ff.

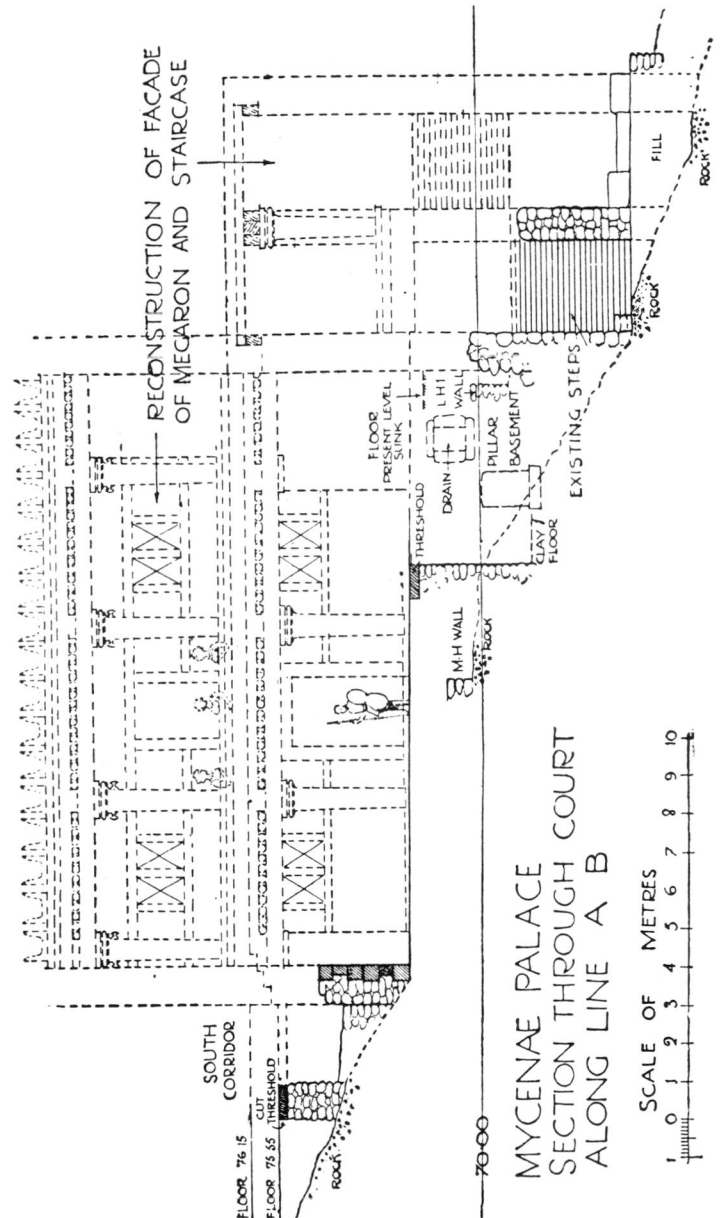

FIG. 277.— RECONSTRUCTION OF A SECTION OF THE LATE-MYCENAEAN (L.M. III) BUILDINGS, PALACE OF MYCENAE

westward movement after the fall of Knossos that brought actual Aegean immigrants to Sicily as to Cyprus ?[1]

For two centuries or more after the Cretan invasion of the mainland[2] the Minoan civilization in Greece proper, which we call Mycenaean, had developed, the great *tholoi* of Mycenae and Orchomenos had been built, the palace of Mycenae (Fig. 277),[3]—perhaps a not unworthy imitation of Knossos, *plus* certain northern elements, such as a great *megaron*—, with

L.M. I.II frescoes (Fig. 278), which was largely rebuilt in the succeeding period, perhaps the palace-fortress of Gla or Gha in Lake Kopais (Fig. 279) and that of Thebes with its frescoes (Fig. 280),[4] the older palace of Tiryns and its frescoes also (Fig. 281, see p. 153). We find its settlement in the southern Peloponnese at Amyklai (Vapheio), in the southwest at the two Pyloi; only in the north-west does it seem unrepresented : there, except possibly in the Islands, the native barbarism

FIG. 278.—L.M. I–II (MYC. I–II) FRESCO : A KNIGHT AND SQUIRE, PALACE OF MYCENAE. ($\frac{1}{3}$)
(Partly Restored)

still existed, unsubjected to Cretan domination. And north of Othrys Thessaly still maintained its cultural independence. With the culture

---

[1] Evans, *Preh. Tombs*, p. 108 ff. ; Childe, *Dawn of European Civilization*, pp. 97, 98.

[2] I cannot accept Nilsson's paradoxical idea (*Minoan-Myc. Religion*, p. 11 ff.) that though, as he rightly maintains, the mainland Mycenaean culture was Minoan, it was brought to the mainland by mainland conquerors of Crete (see p. 247).

[3] Probably begun in Myc. I (L.M. I) and completed in Myc. III (L.M. III). The fragmentary frescoes are L.M. I–II (*B.S.A.*, xxv, p. 147 ff.).

[4] Keramopoullos, '*Εφ. 'Αρχ.*, 1909, p. 90 ; '*Αρχ. Δελτ.*, iii, p. 339, Fig. 193.

of Crete came its art of writing. " The painted inscriptions found on

FIG. 279.—THE FORTRESS OF GHA

certain vases found at Thebes in Boeotia agree both in form and grouping

FIG. 280.—FRESCO : BŒOTIAN
THEBES (RESTORED). $(c. \frac{1}{32})$
(MYC. I)

with the script in use at Knossos in the latest Palace period (L.M. II) ", which argues identity of language [1] as well as of script with Crete.

The art of the mainland in the Early and Middle Mycenaean periods (Myc. I–II, the L.H. I–II of Wace,=L.M. I–II) is hardly distinguishable from the Cretan. Even in the pottery we see few differences yet. The style known as " Ephyraean " (Fig. 282) and claimed as distinctively " mainland " by Mr. Wace, may, Mr. Forsdyke thinks, though it is found in quantity on the mainland, prove to be not peculiar to it,[2] and

[1] Evans, quoted by Forsdyke, *Encycl. Britt.*, xiiith ed., new vol. i. *s.v.* Archaeology, Crete, p. 175.   [2] Forsdyke, *Catalogue*, pp. xxxix, 152.

be in fact of Cretan origin, like everything else in the way of good ceramic on the mainland. The old barbaric native " matt-painted " pottery has disappeared swiftly before the oncoming of a developed ceramic, and the civilized Minyan ware of the preceding age, already degenerate in M.M. III, now disappears also, but leaves behind it a partial legacy in the shape of the high-stemmed Late Mycenaean *kylix* (Fig. 283), which probably developed on the mainland as a combination of an old Cretan form (high-stemmed goblets were made in Crete in early Minoan times ; see p. 47) with the high-stemmed " Minyan " goblet, whose fluted or ribbed stem-decoration was imitated in bands of varnish-paint. It was therefore a

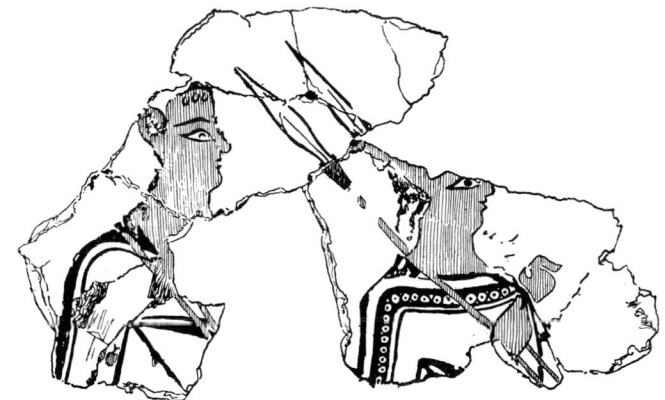

FIG. 281.—L.M. I–II (MYC. I–II) FRESCO FROM THE OLDER PALACE, TIRYNS. (½)

Minoan-Minyan form evolved on the mainland,[1] but presumably by the Minoan conquerors, not by the Helladic aborigines.

The Cyclades had preserved far more of their artistic independence. There we do not find, as on the mainland, a complete replacement of native by Minoan ceramic. Local ways persisted. The characteristic Cycladic local wares of L.C. I and II imitated the contemporary Cretan styles in a Cycladic medium using red paint on the porous native pottery to imitate the Cretan black varnish. This local style gave way but slowly to imported Cretan and Mycenaean ware, but eventually the

[1] An ultimate derivation on the mainland side through the Minyan *kylix* from the Hittite or Syrian " champagne-glass " standing cup is probable.

mainland L.M. III (Late Mycenaean) pottery took its place when the
κοίνη of Mycenaean culture had been established all over the Aegean.
In two centuries the colonial settlement of Minoans from Crete

FIG. 282.—MYC. II (EPHYRAEAN) WARE : KORAKOU. (*c.* $\frac{1}{6}$)

on the mainland had developed into a power capable of itself throwing
out a colonial effort that not only was able, it would seem probable,
to overthrow Knossos, but certainly succeeded in occupying Rhodes

FIG. 283.—MYCENAEAN III KYLIKES : IALYSOS. ($\frac{1}{3}$)

and even colonizing Cyprus, which the Minoans had never, so far as
we can see, attempted to do. And in Rhodes we find the pottery of
Ialysos, contemporary with that of Amarna, and Cyprus in the first half
of the fourteenth century, of the same mainland Mycenaean style,

218

which gradually varies from the Cretan, yet not so much as the Cycladic used to vary from the Cretan, and in no way as the Cretan formerly differed from the various pre-Minoan styles in Greece, Thessalian, Danubian, *Urfirnis*, Minyan, and *Mattmalerei*, whether we include all these under the term Helladic or confine it to the *Mattmalerei* style alone.[1] Late Mycenaean ware, properly so-called, is distinguishable from Cretan L.M. IIIa. Cretan culture did not disappear suddenly after the destruction of Knossos : an epoch of " partial reoccupation " of the palace followed, and we have remains of it in the fourteenth century. Some of the Zafer Papoura tombs may belong to this epoch at the beginning of L.M. III. And Cretan peculiarities in pottery are discernible to the end : even Cretan geometric pottery is quite characteristic. But notwithstanding this Cretan particularism the main features of the art of the Mycenaean period all over the Aegean area are the same, and we can now speak of an universal Mycenaean style and call it either " Late Mycenaean " (=" Myc. III ") or " L.M. III " in ceramics and in all other branches of art. We cannot call it " Helladic " because it is not Helladic, if all or any of the old individualistic pre-Minoan ceramic styles of mainland Greece are to be called Helladic. Its base is Minoan-Cretan. In fact at the end of the fourteenth century B.C. we find that the Cretan Minoan, the Cycladic, and the mainland " Mycenaean " cultures, with their artistic styles, have coalesced on the basis of the Minoan into one common culture and art of the Late Bronze Age in Greece. The dynamic force of the Cretan, Island and Mainland civilization has expended itself and come to rest in the static combination which we call generally the culture of the Late Mycenaean or Third Late Minoan period : a static culture that continued to exist, generally deteriorating during the second century of its existence, and in the third collapsing and falling to pieces under the onset of new dynamic forces from the

[1] Properly speaking the term " Helladic " should be applied to all mainland ceramic styles, and yet to apply a common term to them would be illogical, as they are all unconnected with each other. Equally the use of " Helladic " for the most characteristically " mainland " of pre-Minoan styles alone, the *Mattmalerei*, would be illogical. It is in fact difficult to apply the term to styles. To use it of periods is another matter.

North. From Palaikastro in Crete [1] and from Ialysos in Rhodes [2] we have great stores of L.M. III pottery, which will illustrate the style of the new age in ceramic.

FIG. 284.—L.M. III BIRD-VASE: PHAISTOS. ($\frac{1}{10}$)

FIG. 285.—L.M. III BIRD-VASE: PALAIKASTRO. ($\frac{1}{6}$)

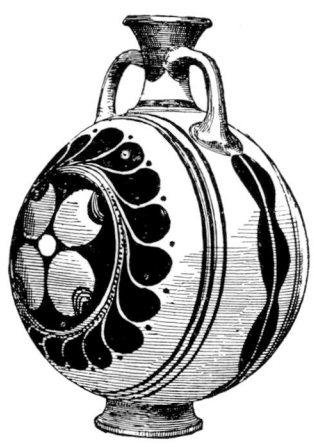

FIG. 286.—LATE MYCENAEAN VASE ENKOMI. ($\frac{1}{6}$)

Of the mainland or Rhodian type (Myc. III*a* = L.M. III*a*) are the fragments of Mycenaean pottery found at Amarna in Egypt, which have already been mentioned, and date to about 1380–1350 B.C.

The decoration of the new style is fundamentally a degenerate form of the L.M. I ornament. The naturalistic designs of the older period are stylized into a kind of shorthand. The octopus, triton-shell, and flowers progressively alter and deteriorate till they are hardly recognizable (Fig. 283). Bird-designs, derived partly from the L.M. I frescoes, partly from the decorative motives of Cycladic potters, with whom they had been very popular, appear, and gradually degenerate. The geese and ducks of the original tradition (Fig. 211) turn into birds looking like guinea-fowls and picking up food from the ground (Figs. 284, 285). In the period of Late Mycenaean *b* (Myc. III*b*= L.M. III*b*) they become very characteristic (see p. 246). Forms of vases, however, remain good, and the decoration, though stylized and summary, is generally well placed and designed (Fig. 286). This is especially the case in Crete, where character-

[1] Bosanquet, Dawkins, and others : *B.S.A. Ann. Suppl.* i (1923).
[2] The tombs of Ialysos in Rhodes were excavated in 1868–70 by the late Sir Alfred Biliotti. The vases are now in the British Museum (Forsdyke, *Cat. Vases*, i, pp. xxxviii, 139). The cost of the first year's work was borne by John Ruskin.

istic designs imitated from the L.M. II architectonic and toreutic motives,—the triglyph and imitation chasing and embossing,—(the

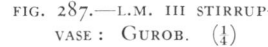

FIG. 287.—L.M. III STIRRUP-VASE : GUROB. (¼)

FIG. 288.—EGYPTIAN IMITATIONS OF STIRRUP-VASES IN FAIENCE AND ALABASTER (BRIT. MUS.) FROM THEBES : XVIIITH–XIXTH DYN.

latter typically Cretan), are not soon deteriorated. The deterioration in design is observable on the mainland and the islands earlier than in Crete, where the fine tradition still held sway for a time, and preserved the echo of its style till the end, even in geometric times (see p. 263).

FIG. 289.—ALABASTER STIRRUP-VASE : REA COLLECTION : XVIIITH DYN. (¾)

FIG. 290.—FAIENCE STIRRUP-VASE : LOCAL IMITATION OF EGYPTIAN WARE: ENKOMI, CYPRUS : c. 1400 B.C. (½)

But generally the simpler patterns of scales, chevrons, spirals, etc. all progressively, though very slowly, grow worse and worse.

Characteristic shapes generally are the new *skyphos* and *kylix*

221

(p. 217), and the great open-mouthed *krater* that succeeds the great Cretan so-called "amphorae" of L.M. I–II (Fig. 276). Of the older forms the most noticeable survival is the false-necked (stirrup) vase or *Bügelkanne* (Fig. 287). The latter and the *kylix* are the most universal and typical of all Late Mycenaean or L.M. III vase forms, and are found everywhere throughout the Greek world at this time. The stirrup-vase was in the fourteenth century exported in thou-

FIG. 291.—EGYPTIAN IMITATION OF MINOAN "FILLER" IN FAIENCE: THEBES: EARLY XVIIITH DYN. BRIT. MUS. NO. 22,731. (⅓)

FIG. 292.—FILLER OF EGYPTIAN ALABASTER: POSSIBLY MINOAN WORKMANSHIP. BRIT. MUS. (¼)

sands to Egypt, no doubt containing olive-oil (see p. 206). It is constantly found in Egyptian tombs of the late XVIIIth and XIXth Dynasties; it was, like the "filler," imitated in Egyptian blue faience of these periods (with Egyptian designs in black) and in alabaster (Figs. 288–292).[1] Oddly enough, the equally characteristic *kylix* was not so imitated in Egypt. We have great stores of *kylikes*, with their characteristic decoration of debased octopods or triton-shells (Fig. 283), from Enkomi in Cyprus, and from Ialysos, as well as from Crete and the mainland.

[1] Hall, *Oldest Civilization of Greece*, Figs. 52, 53, 56.

The pottery *larnakes* were decorated in the same way. Examples have been found at Gournià, at Palaikastro, and at Milatos (Fig. 247) in

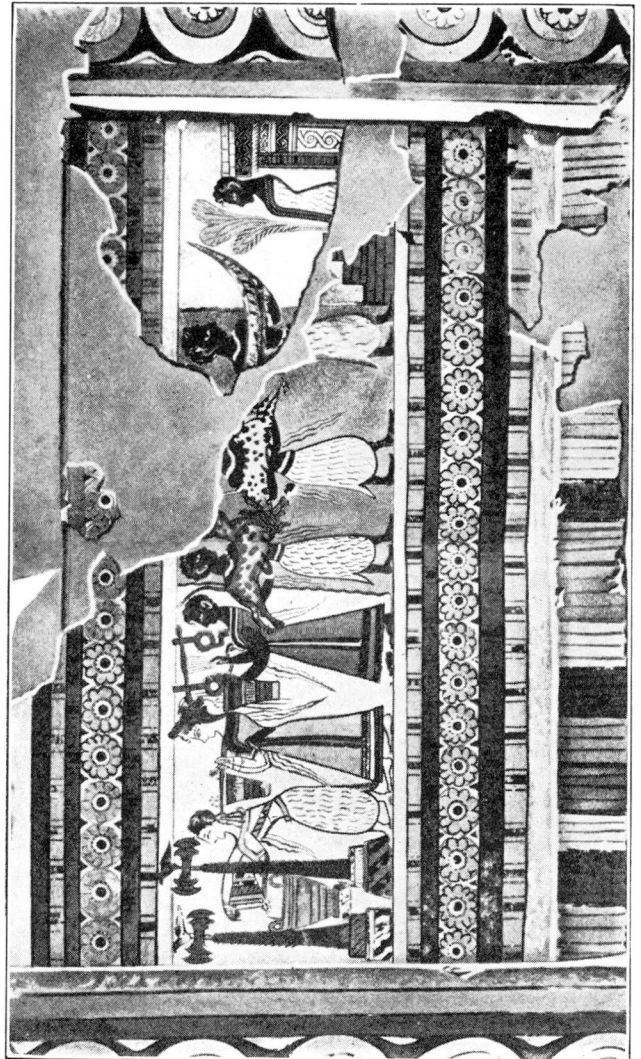

FIG. 293.—SIDE OF THE PAINTED POTTERY LARNAX FROM HAGIA TRIADA: L.M. III. (c. ⅛)

Crete with the typical debased ornament of the time, a pale ghost of the marine and floral designs of L.M. I, often imitating wooden chests with metal bands and rings, or even egyptianizing designs of spirals and papyrus-plants.[1] Egyptian influence is now often visible in the decoration of the *larnakes*.[2] A remarkable example of this is the magnificent painted *larnax* from Hagia Triada, which is of L.M. III date (Fig. 293).[3] On it we see offerings being brought to the dead man who stands in front of his tomb, a conception obviously inspired by the well-known Egyptian scene of the offerings being made to the mummy, placed upright before the tomb. The details are purely Minoan, but the inspiration is evidently Egyptian. Another (from Milatos) is very Minoan with its crude

FIG. 294.—CYPRIAN KRATER: ENKOMI. ($\frac{1}{8}$)

FIG. 295.—HORSE-HEAD CUP: MINOAN FAIENCE, ENKOMI, BRIT. MUS. ($\frac{1}{3}$)

picture of the young god Velchanos descending from the sky on to the sea, with his hair streaming up on either side of his head as he falls (Fig. 352),[4] and also very Greek (see p. 276, n.).

In Cyprus we have great amphorae or *kraters* which very soon shew much barbarism in ornament : very typical being the crude groups of persons driving chariots (Fig. 294).[5] The idea of depicting the human figure on vases, which is non-Cretan, must have come from the

[1] Evans, *Prehist. Tombs*, p. 90. On *larnakes* from Milatos see Xanthoudides, Παραρτ. ’Αρχ. Δελτ., 1920–1, p. 154 ff.

[2] Evans, "The Palace of Knossos in its Egyptian relations"; *Egypt Exploration Fund Archaeological Report*, 1899–1900 [published 1901], p. 62.

[3] Paribeni, *Rendiconti*, xiii, pp. 343–8.   [4] *Prehist. Tombs*, Fig. 107.

[5] Hall, *Aegean Archaeology*, p. 172 ; Forsdyke, *Cat.*, p. xxxviii.

224

Cyclades. But from Cyprus also we have very fine examples of good L.M. III*a* ware, and notable specimens of Minoan faience in the shape of the horse-head, ram-head and woman's head cups (one of the latter a Janus), besides smaller pottery from Enkomi

FIG. 296.—RAM-HEAD CUP AND JANUS-CUP: MINOAN FAIENCE, ENKOMI, BRIT. MUS. ($\frac{1}{4}$)

FIG. 297.—WOMAN'S HEAD CUPS: MINOAN FAIENCE, ENKOMI, BRIT. MUS. (*c.* $\frac{1}{5}$)

(Figs. 295–298), which are amongst the greatest treasures of the British Museum (making its collection to rank next after that of Athens in the matter of major examples of Minoan art) and are not unworthy to rank beside the older Knossian "Snake-goddesses" and their attendant vases[1] at Candia. Curiously enough at far-away Ashur in Assyria, Ḳalaʿat Sher-ḳat on the banks of the Tigris, Dr. Andrae has recently discovered

FIG. 298.—VASES OF MINOAN FAIENCE: ENKOMI, BRIT. MUS. (*c.* $\frac{1}{5}$)

[1] See above, Figs. 151–4.

FIG. 299.—UPPER PART OF A VASE OF MINOAN FAIENCE, KALA'AT SHERKAT (ASHUR), ASSYRIA, BRIT. MUS. ($\frac{3}{4}$)

exactly similar faience, identified by me, including the detachable top of a filler (?) vase of definitely Minoan type (Fig. 299) and a woman's head cup so absolutely identical with those from Enkomi, even in the smallest details, as to leave no doubt that it came from the same workshop, from the hands of the same potter as they. It also is in the British Museum with the other objects of the Sherkat find, and is figured here (Fig. 300). The find is to be published by the discoverer *in extenso*.[1] These things cannot be objects of Assyrian art imported into Cyprus. Their faience is characteristically Minoan, like that of the " Snake-goddesses," pale blue and haematite-brown. The Ashur cup was then imported from Cyprus into Assyria. Dr. Andrae would date the find not earlier than 1300, he tells me. And it is noticeable that the feminine *coiffure* of these heads from Enkomi and Ashur is different from

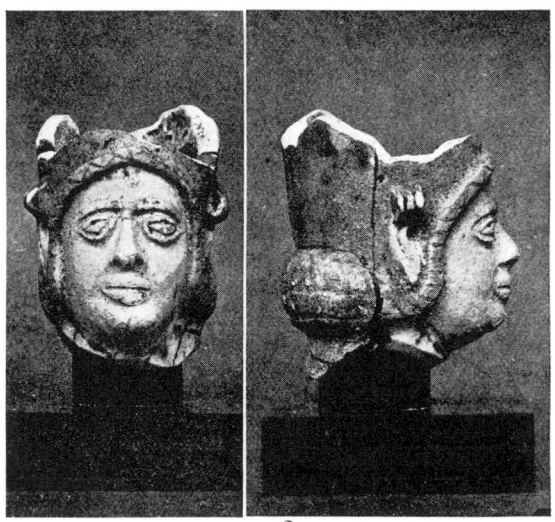

FIG. 300.—WOMAN'S HEAD CUP OF MINOAN FAIENCE : KALA'AT SHERKAT (ASHUR), ASSYRIA, BRIT. MUS. ($\frac{1}{2}$)

[1] Also an article on this Ashur faience and its connexion with Cyprus by myself will shortly appear in the *Journal of Hellenic Studies*.

that in vogue in Greece one or two centuries earlier than this : the loosely flowing or knotted curls of the older period are replaced by a stiff coil confined in a net. This may well point to a difference in date as well as locality.

The graves of Enkomi, like other chamber-tombs, were constantly reused in later times, so that the early Myc. III pottery of Cyprus is found in them mixed with that of later date.[1] The same is the case with the fine bronze, ivory, and other objects from Enkomi, which include a plain silver cup of Vapheio type and a beautiful bronze ewer (Fig. 301), both possibly of Cretan origin. But we can see that in Cyprus Minoan

FIG. 301.—BRONZE EWER AND VASE AND SILVER CUP : ENKOMI, BRIT. MUS. ($\frac{1}{5}$)

art lasted longer than in the Aegean ;[2] probably the convulsion that was brought about by the tribes who brought iron and cremation into Greece was little felt there ; and the old civilization and art melted gradually into the *Mischkunst* of Syro-Phoenician, Egyptian, and Greek elements which is characteristic of the island in the early classical period. Cyprus was always old-fashioned and conservative : still in the sixth century Cyprian princes went to war in chariots, which in Greece had

[1] See Evans, *Journ. R. Anthrop. Inst.*, 1900. Poulsen, *Zur Zeitbestimmung der Enkomi-funde* (*Jahrb. Arch. Inst.*, xxvi, p. 215 ff.), does not appear to realize that the confusion is not the fault of the excavators, who accurately recorded the contents of the tombs.

[2] Hall, *Oldest Civilization of Greece*, p. 63 (the footnote is of course now out of date).

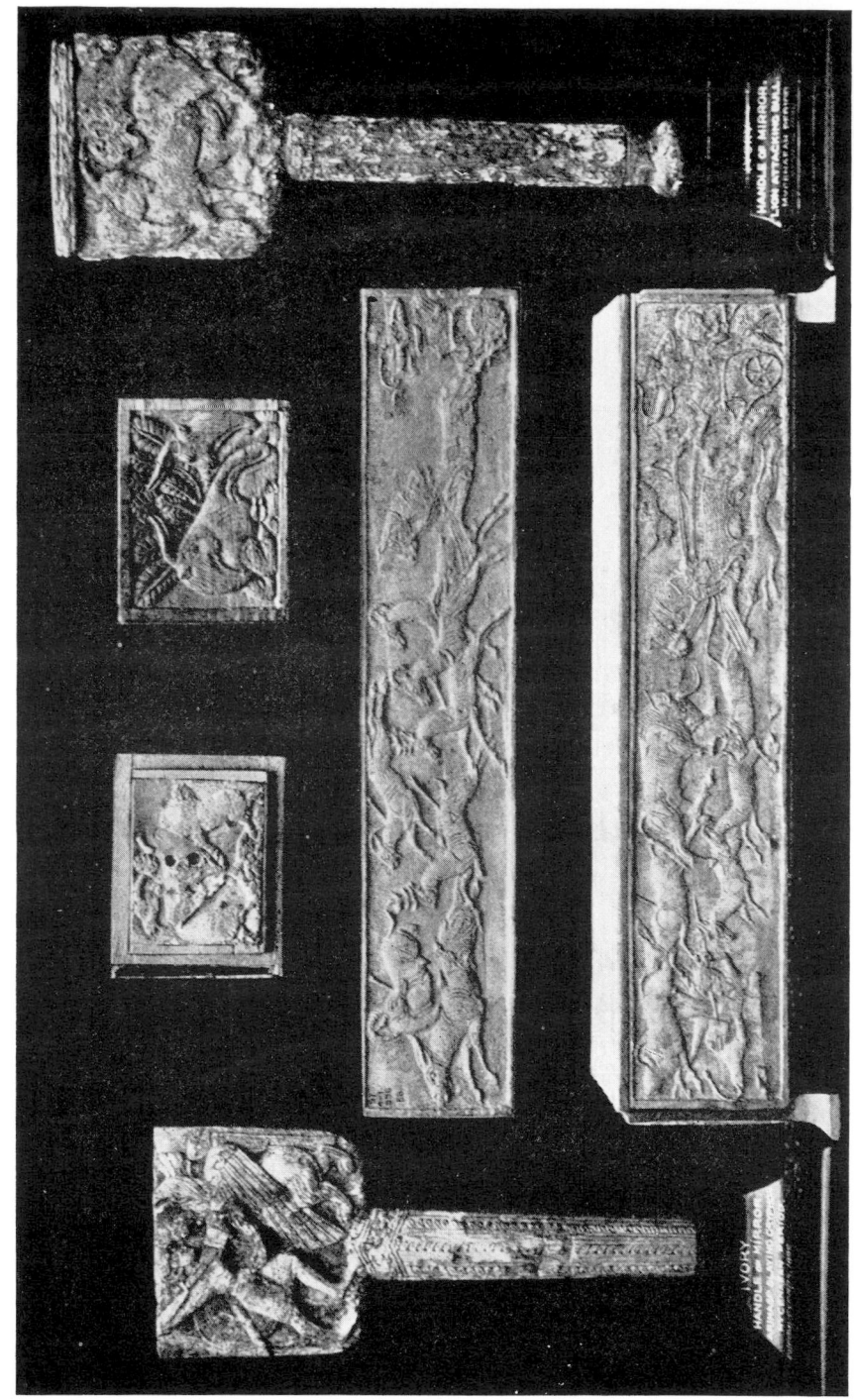

FIG. 302.—THE IVORY DRAUGHT-BOX AND TWO IVORY MIRROR-HANDLES: ENKOMI. (THE OTHER SIDE AND ENDS ARE SHEWN SEPARATELY.) (c. ⅔)

been relegated to the games two centuries before. Perhaps characteristic of the beginning of the mixed art is, if it is Cyprian at all, the ivory draught-board and box from Enkomi, with its hunting-scene, which shews bearded charioteers like Phoenicians, with a feather-crowned Philistine attendant on a box which might otherwise have been attributed to the best Minoan period (Fig. 302). One would think it could hardly date much earlier than 1200 B.C.,[1] but it may be considerably earlier. The famous ivory mirror-handles found with it (Fig. 302), carved, one with the group of an Arimaspian fighting a gryphon, the other with a fight between a bull and a lion, look older. The Arimaspian wears the characteristic dress of the Philistines or Shardina (see p. 244 n.1, below), the laminated cuirass, but a round helmet, without feathers. He wields the great Shardina sword (see p. 254). It is possible that all three objects are not Cyprian, but belong to a mixed art, owing its importance partly to Minoan, partly to Syro-Hittite models, with its (hypothetical) centre in Cilicia [1] in the fourteenth-thirteenth centuries B.C. They are not genuinely Mycenaean, though the mirrors are more so than the draught-box. To the same art perhaps belongs the small group of a lion and bull fighting, carved in the round in red jasper, found at el-Amarna with the famous cuneiform tablets, and so dating to about 1370 B.C., the British Museum, which was published by me as possibly Mycenaean in my *Oldest Civilization of Greece* in 1901 and again recently in the *Journal of Egyptian Archaeology* (xi, p. 159 ff.), though this seems to me now to be even less Minoan in feeling than the draught-box from Enkomi. It possibly really comes from further east, perhaps from Mitanni : it partakes of both Minoan and Babylonian art, and has its ancestors in the carved groups of bulls and lions fighting which we find on the stone vase from Warka, of the older Sumerian period, in the British Museum (*Brit. Mus. Quarterly*, ii. (1927), pl. v).

Characteristic of Cyprian conservatism was the retention into the classical period of the Cypriote syllabary for the writing of Greek : a syllabary which must have been merely a simplification of the older

[1] Hall, *Manchester Eg. Or. Journal*, 1913.

FIG. 303.—CYPRIAN MYCENAEAN INSCRIPTION : ENKOMI. ($\frac{2}{3}$)

FIG. 304.—FRESCO OF WOMAN HOLDING PYXIS : TIRYNS. ($\frac{1}{8}$)

230

Minoan ideographs on the tablets of Knossos and Hagia Triada, and the inscription on the pottery ball from Enkomi in Cyprus itself (Fig. 303). One would think that the easiest way to make out at any rate the sounds of Minoan-Cretan would be to identify the Cretan originals of the Cypriote syllabic signs.

We must now return to the Aegean. Of the middle of the Late Mycenaean period in Greece proper we have the later palace of Tiryns, with its remarkable frescoes, which cannot be dated any earlier than the latter part of the fourteenth century,[1] if indeed they are so early. On them we see a queen or princess (Fig. 304) holding an ivory *pyxis* (much resembling the Theban fresco, Fig. 280), maidens or young princes riding forth in chariots (Fig. 305), attendants leading dogs to the stag-hunt (Figs. 306-7),

[1] Rodenwaldt, *loc. cit.*

dogs chasing a boar across a field decorated with a flower-design which looks like a mediaeval tapestry-pattern (Fig. 308). The style and

FIG. 305.—CHARIOT-FRESCO, TIRYNS. (¼)

details are all Minoan; the dress and hair are Minoan in fashion with slight differences; but the men wear in addition to, or instead of, the

231

waistcloth, a short-sleeved chiton of the later Greek type, unknown in

FIG. 306.—HUNTSMAN-FRESCO, TIRYNS. ($\frac{4}{7}$)

Crete, which reminds us of the greater severity of the northern climate. And their hair is less elaborately dressed. The execution of the work is

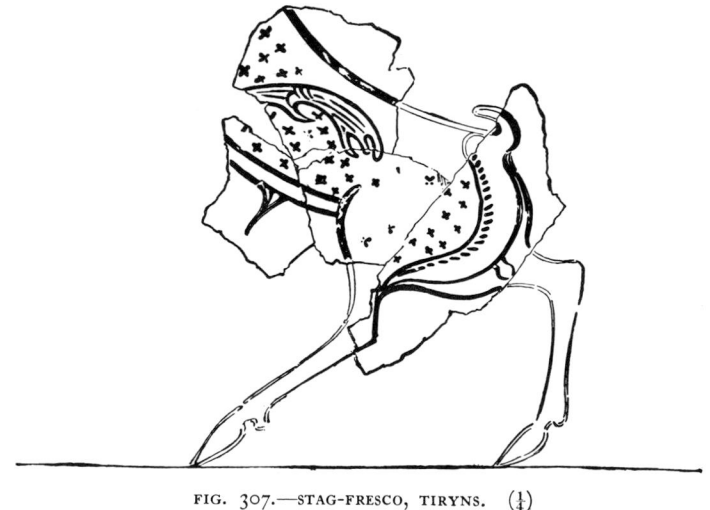

FIG. 307.—STAG-FRESCO, TIRYNS. ($\frac{1}{4}$)

much stylized, and the whole is of course inferior to the great Knossos

232

frescoes, but the interest of this swan-song of Minoan art is great.

Of the same period (1350–1250 B.C.) we have the town-remains of Mycenae, the Tirynthian later palace (Fig. 309), with its outer walls and casemates (Fig. 310), and numberless *tholoi* on the mainland, especially notable being those of Menidi [1] and Spata [2] in Attica, and above all that of Dendra (Mideia) with its splendid contents (pp. 171, 182), some of which are L.M. I–II.

FIG. 308.—FRESCO OF BOAR-HUNT, TIRYNS. ($\frac{1}{8}$)

In the pottery (Myc. III*b*) we see a growing degeneracy. The fine forms and well-placed designs of Myc. III*a*, the great period of Ialysos, of Enkomi, and of Amarna, give way to clumsy shapes and crowded, fussy,

[1] Conveniently published by Montelius, *La Grèce Préclassique*, i, p. 158 ff., from the original publication by Furtwaengler and others, *Das Kuppelgrab bei Menidi* (1880), Perrot-Chipiez, *Art de la Grèce primitive, etc.*

[2] *Ibid.* p. 165 ff., from Haussoullier, *Bull. Corr. Hell.* 1878, and Perrot-Chipiez.

and at the same time pompous decoration.   Not only are the forms and items of decoration degenerate ; they are put on the vase in a degenerate, vulgar and tasteless manner.   We see this best in the Late Mycenaean " close style "[1] as it is called from the " close " way in which everything possible in the way of pretentious ornament is got on to the vase (Fig.

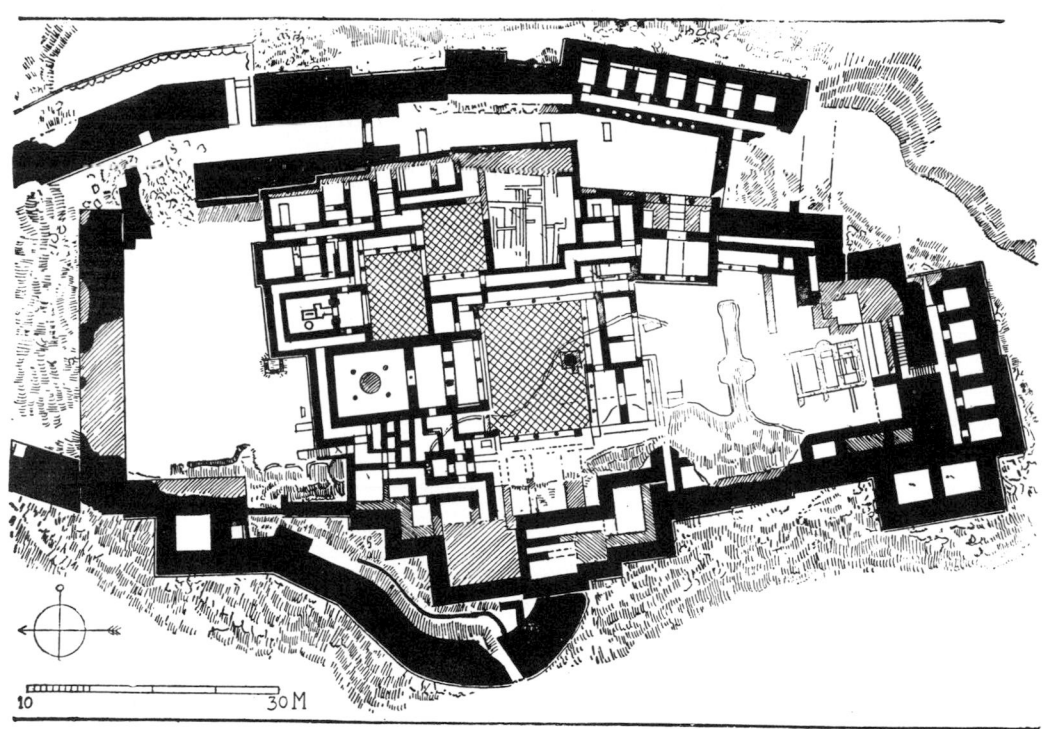

FIG. 309.—PLAN OF TIRYNS

311).   This style began in Crete early in the period in imitation of the full L.M. II designs, and then was not without taste.   But now it had degenerated wofully.   We see it also in the " panelled style," so-called from the typical division of the field of the design by straight lines into rectangular panels, in which appear birds or other objects [2] (Fig. 312).   Both styles are often combined.   The panelled style,

[1] Forsdyke, *Cat. Vases*, i, p. xxxviii.   [2] *Ibid.*, p. xlii.

234

FIG. 310.—A TIRYNTHIAN CASEMATE.

FIG. 311.—MYC. III*b* CLOSE STYLE OF DECORATION (BRIT. MUS. CATALOGUE)

235

which is probably of architectonic origin, is specially characteristic of
a series of handled bowls or *skyphoi*, which are generally regarded as

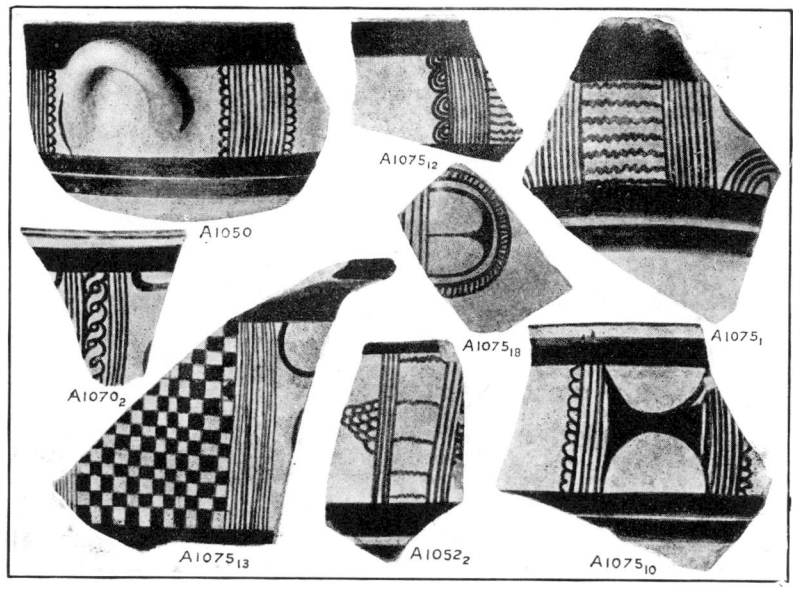

FIG. 312.—MYC. III*b* PANELLED STYLE (BRIT. MUS. CATALOGUE)

typical products of L.M. III*b* (Myc. III*b*) and the thirteenth century
(Figs. 313–314). There is no doubt whatever that they do come

FIG. 313.—MYCENAEAN III*b* (L.M. III*b*)
SKYPHOS: KALYMNOS (BRIT. MUS.). (¼)

FIG. 314.—LATE MYCENAEAN SKYPHOS: CLOSE
STYLE, KORAKOU

down late in the period, and they were the ceramic chiefly affected
and imitated by the Philistine invaders of Palestine at the beginning
of the twelfth century. Mr. Wace and Mr. Blegen however consider

236

that at the same time they and their characteristic panelled patterns occur at Mycenae very early, at the beginning of Myc. III in fact ;[1] and in that case the style, both in form and decoration, will be a native Mycenaean one that originated at Mycenae before the beginning of the fourteenth century and lasted until the twelfth, an unusually long period. In view of the obviously degenerate nature of the style it is permissible to ask for further proof of its antiquity than the finds at Mycenae, before this view is accepted. A mainland origin of the design can be conceded without making so degenerate a style early. To this later period belong the vases of the " Granary " class identified by Wace at Mycenae ; so-called from the place in which a large store of them was found (Fig. 315). In these occasionally good forms are noticeable, notwithstanding the degeneracy of the ornament.

FIG. 315.—VASE OF THE CLOSE STYLE, MYCENAE. ($\frac{1}{4}$)

In no form can we trace the progress of degeneration better than in the ubiquitous *Bügelkanne* or false-necked or " stirrup " vase. Those of this period are easily recognizable with their perked-up appearance, and the peculiarity of the false neck, sometimes absolutely flat, but often coned : those of the last period and the transition to

[1] *Korakou*, p. 61 ; *B.S.A. Ann.*, xxv, p. 26.

the geometric style are always coned in this way (Fig. 336). Isolated Mycenaean stirrup-vases found in Egypt may be dated as late as 1200 B.C. The XXth Dynasty gold stirrup-vases (Fig. 316) represented in the tomb of Rameses III (1196–1175 B.C.) [1] were probably Egyptian imitations. We have no later Mycenaean remains in Egypt.[2] The old connexion gradually ceased as barbarism increased in Greece

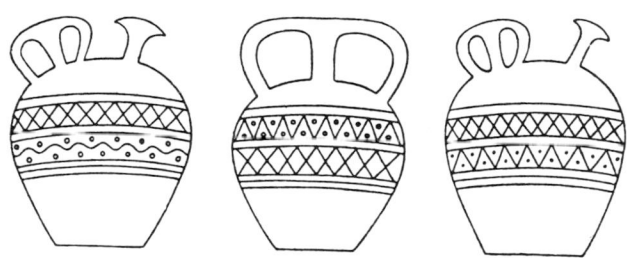

FIG. 316.—MYCENAEAN GOLDEN STIRRUP-VASES, FROM A WALL-PAINTING IN THE TOMB OF RAMESES III. *c.* 1180 B.C.

and piracy in the Mediterranean forbade intercourse. For the period to which we have now come is that of the " Peoples of the Sea," the wandering tribes of Asia Minor and Greece who in the thirteenth and twelfth centuries ranged the Mediterranean in quest of plunder and subsistence, " fighting to fill their bellies daily," as the Egyptian record pithily puts it. It was they who brought about the collapse of the Minoan culture in a welter of piracy, folk-wandering, and barbarism.

In the final lecture we shall consider the days of *Sturm und Drang* which now follow from the end of the thirteenth to the tenth century B.C., at the end of which in the fulness of time the new Greece of the Iron Age was brought to birth.

[1] Hall, *Oldest Civilization of Greece*, Fig. 27.

[2] The gold 'Vapheio' cup with bucrania represented in the XXth Dynasty tomb of Imesib or Imadua at Thebes (No. 65, see *B.S.A. Ann.*, viii, p. 172), which dates from the reign of Rameses IX (*c.* 1140 B.C.), is no evidence of connexion at this time or of the continued making of such vases, as it is in all probability a mere copy or renewal of a previous painting on the tomb, which originally belonged to an official of Hatshepsut's and contemporary of Senmut, named Nebamon, and was merely usurped by Imesib.

238

LECTURE VI

THE TRANSITION TO THE AGE OF IRON

(L.M. III*b* (Myc. III(*b*) : *c.* 1300–1000 B.C.)

RETROSPECT AND CONCLUSION

OUR knowledge of the " Peoples of the Sea " is derived solely from the Egyptian historical records of their raids and of the relations, hostile or friendly, that the Egyptians had with them.[1] They represent no art and no culture, but (in the case of the Philistines this is so at least) when they settled down anywhere their scanty remains, such as pottery, are of the latest and most debased L.M. III type. They first appear on the Syrian coast at the beginning of the fourteenth century : they attacked Egypt twice in the thirteenth, and last at the beginning of the twelfth century, after which the Philistine portion of them settled in Palestine. A short destructive dynamic period was then over, to be succeeded by a static period of barbarism which lasted till the revival of Greek culture in the new dynamic age of colonization which began in the eighth century : when a new Greece, formed of the old Minoan and the new invading Hellenic elements, had come into being, and, inspired by the civilized genius of the Minoan strain in its ancestry, strode quickly to the culture-hegemony of the world.

We have many Egyptian representatives of the Northern barbar-

[1] See Hall, " Keftiu and the Peoples of the Sea " (*B.S.A. Ann.*, viii, p. 157 ff.) ; "The Peoples of the Sea," *Recueil Champollion*, p. 297 ff. ; *Cambr. Anc. Hist.*, iii, p. 275 ff.

239

ians, labelled with their names. Among the names of the "Peoples of the Sea" which have been preserved to us by the Egyptian records we see several that figure in Greek legend and history. Danaans, Dardanians, and even once Achaians (Akaivasha) ; we see also Shardina (Figs. 317, 318, 324) and Tursha, who are apparently

FIG. 317.—SHARDINA MERCENARIES : 13TH CENT. B.C. (TEMPLE OF RAMESES II, ABYDOS)

not actually Sardinians and Tyrsenians (Etruscans of Italy) as they were formerly thought to be, but, possibly, ancestors of these peoples now in the course of their migrations from Asia Minor to Italy, which are attested by Herodotus and by certain historical indications and archaeological comparisons [1] ; and we see the Pelethites or Philistines (" *Pulesatha*," better vocalized as *Pulesti*)[2] and Cherethites, whom we identify as respectively Carians and Cretans, coming from Kaphtor

[1] Objections may be made to this view on other (Italian) archaeological grounds, but the theory of Asiatic origin seems the more probable to me.

[2] I am afraid I cannot give my suffrages to the old identification Pulesti = Πελασγοί, recently revised by Dr. Albright. It seems to me to be philologically quite impossible. If we may identify these two names, we may identify any name with any other however remotely resembling it.

and, after a great attack upon Egypt, in which they were defeated by King Rameses III, aided by his Shardina mercenaries, in a sea-fight (Fig. 318), settling down upon the coast of Palestine (Figs. 318–320). With them we hear of other tribes, Lukki (the Luka of the Amarna letters and Lugga of the Hittites), who are certainly the Lycians; Mysians probably; Ilians of Troy perhaps; Shakalesha doubtless from Sagalassos in Pisidia; Pidasa from

FIG. 318.—SHARDINA BOARDING A PHILISTINE SHIP; TEMP. RAMESES III (12TH CENT. B.C.): MEDINET HABU

FIG. 319.—A PHILISTINE CHIEF SEIZED BY THE FALCON SYMBOLIZING THE ROYAL NAME: MEDINET HABU

Pisidia or Caria; Uashasha possibly from Oaxos in Crete; and Zakkal or Zakaray (Fig. 322), who were early connected with the Pales-

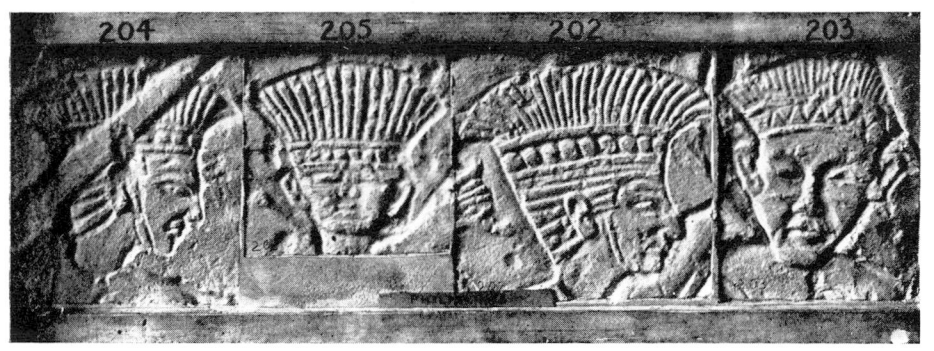

FIG. 320.—HEADS OF PHILISTINES: MEDINET HABU. $(\frac{1}{5})$

16

tinian coast and were considered by Petrie to have left their name at Zakro in Crete.[1] That all these peoples came from the Asia Minor coast and the Aegean is certain. There is nowhere else they can have come from : the cumulative evidence of their names is cogent ;

their dress as depicted by the Egyptians is of Carian style like that of the old people of the Phaistos Disk ; their faces are often definitely European in type (Figs. 322–324).

FIG. 321.—EGYPTIAN CARI-
CATURE DOLL OF FAIENCE,
REPRESENTING A PHILIS-
TINE. FOUND IN MALTA

FIG. 322.—ZAKARAY (AEGEANS ?) OF THE 12TH CENTURY B.C. :
(THEBES). ($\frac{1}{8}$)

The two lower heads in Fig. 324 are extremely Greek in type, the lowest reminding us remarkably of a well-known head of a youth of the early 5th century in the Acropolis Museum at Athens. The bearded types of

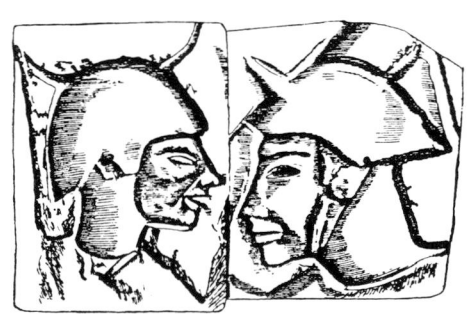

Zakaray (Fig. 322) are also very Greek-looking. A man of the same type is represented in a curious head of stag's horn in the British Museum,[2] found in Crete, in which we see a bearded face surmounted by the same feather headdress, repre-sented by a cunning use of the natural exfoliation of the horn

FIG. 323.—SHARDINA (SARDIANS ?) OF THE 12TH
CENTURY B.C. (THEBES). ($\frac{1}{4}$)

[1] I am now however very doubtful about this, since it is true that, as Mr. V. G. Childe points out (*The Aryans*, p. 74), they wear the feathered Pulesatha headdress (see below) and beards, neither of which are Cretan traits. [2] Forsdyke, *J.H.S.*, xl, pl. vi.

242

FIG. 324.— HEADS OF SHARDINA: THEBES. ($\frac{1}{5}$)

at its root (Fig. 325). A comparison with the famous gold bearded mask from Mycenae (Fig. 183) is also obvious.[1] Also these folk are exactly like the later people of the Asia Minor coast in

FIG. 325.—STAG'S-HORN HEAD OF A BEARDED MAN IN FEATHER HEADDRESS (BRIT. MUS.). ($c.$ $\frac{1}{2}$)

their dual rôle of pirates and mercenaries. In Ptolemaic days the Carians, Lycians, Pisidians, and Pamphylians were pirates and mercenaries

[1] Mr. Wace claims the gold mask, in connexion with the representations of the peoples of the sea (including the Achaians (Akaivasha) of whom we have no pictures), as evidence of the Achaian character of the men of the Mycenaean shaft-graves. But there are weightier reasons against that identification than this in favour of it, and the Mycenaeans may have communicated their fashion of wearing beards to the Achaians. We see it on the "Warrior Vase," which must be Achaian (p. 260; Fig. 338).

243

like their ancestors a thousand years before. The Shardina were not only the redoubtable foes of Egypt but also at the same time the Varangians of the Ramesside court.

None were Minoans of the old type, so far as we can see, or were regarded as Keftians.[1] It has been supposed that they ruled the Phoenician cities and that the Phoenicians derived their lore of the sea from them.[2] Of this there is no proof, nor is it likely. As we have seen, the Semites of the Syrian coast were seagoers long before the days of the Keftians and the Minoans. We cannot attribute Phoenician seamanship to the Minoans any more than to the Peoples of the Sea : of Keftian or Minoan settlement in Phoenicia we have no proof whatever. The sub-Mycenaean remains lately identified in the Beirut Museum by Mr. Woolley[3] are evidently relics of the Philistine migration. For that was a real folk-wandering both by land and sea, of peoples not merely engaged in casual piracy, but driven out of their own seats by necessity to find new homes. And some have seen this necessity in an invasion from Thrace, whether of the Phrygians or Bryges or not, that according to Meyer about 1200 B.C. crossed the Hellespont into Asia.[4] The dispossessed peoples broke eastward, overthrowing the Hittite kingdom,

[1] I cannot agree with Childe (*loc. cit.*, p. 76) that the Philistines were really Cretans (see below). Their faces it is true are European, but their feathered headdress, their laminated armour, their round shields, and their great " slashing " swords are all non-Cretan.

[2] Cf. Woolley, "Asia Minor, Syria, and the Aegean," *Liverpool Annals of Art and Archaeology*, ix (March 1922). [3] Woolley, " La Phénicie et les peuples égéens," *Syria* (1921).

[4] Meyer, *Sitzungsberichte* of the Berlin Academy, 1908, p. 18 ff. Chadwick however points out (*Heroic Age*, p. 189) that in the tale of Troy the Phrygians were already in Phrygia by 1150, the traditional date of the siege, " and no hint is given that their settlement there was believed to be in any sense recent." Cf. Childe, *The Aryans*, p. 63. So that Meyer's theory is at any rate doubtful. The identifications of Trojan tribes mentioned in Egyptian inscriptions, quoted by Childe, *ibid.*, and by Bury, *Cambridge Anc. Hist.* ii, p. 488, n., from Phythian-Adams, *Bull. Brit. Sch. Jerusalem*, i, had been made long ago by Egyptologists, *e.g.* de Rougé and Maspero. See my article " The Peoples of the Sea " in the *Recueil d'Études égyptologiques de dédiées à la mémoire de Jean-François Champollion* (*Receuil Champollion*), Paris, 1922, in which the history of all these identifications is given from the time of De Rougé and Chabas to the present. The well-known equation, for instance, of Ariunna or Iriunna with Ilion, which Prof. Bury (*loc. cit.*) seems to ascribe to Mr. Phythian-Adams (who, however, himself clearly implies that it was well-known), was made forty years ago by Maspero (see *Rec. Champ.*, p. 312).

and surged up against Egypt, to be defeated and thrown back by Rameses III (about 1196 B.C.) into Palestine, where they remained, a foreign intrusive element, for several centuries, until eventually they were absorbed into the Semitic population. We can see several traces of debased Minoan culture in the Hebrew accounts of the Philistines, notably their gladiatorial games.[1] For though they were themselves not Minoans nor Cretans, they were closely allied with Cretans (the Cherethites)[2], and since the days of the old independent culture of the Phaistos Disk

FIG. 326.—PHILISTINE POTTERY : GEZER

FIG. 327.—PHILISTINE STIRRUP-VASE OF L.M. IIIB STYLE : GEZER

(PALESTINE EXPL. FUND)

and of Caria they too had been absorbed into the general Aegean culture of late Minoan times, while retaining their old national costume. Their culture was sub-Mycenaean, their pottery was an imitation (often locally made) of the latest Mycenaean types (L.M. III*b*)[3] (Figs. 326-8). "At Gezer, Gath, Lachish, and elsewhere the pottery identified as Philistine contains some shapes and ornaments (particularly panelled bowls and spiral figures), which have definite affinities with the latest Mycen-

[1] Hall, *Anc. Hist. N.E.*, p. 418.   [2] For the Cretan traditions of Gaza see G. F. Hill, *Proc. Brit. Acad.*, 1912.   [3] Welch, *B.S.A. Ann.*, vi, p. 117 ff ; Thiersch, *Arch. Anz.*, 1908.

aean types."[1] Fragments of the same pottery have recently been found by Sir Flinders Petrie at Gerar. The bird-figures of late-Mycenaean pots are very characteristic of the Philistine pots (Figs. 327–8).[2] It might be maintained, of course, that the discovery of sub-Mycenaean pottery in Palestine proved merely that such pottery was

FIG. 328.—PHILISTINE KRATERS AND OTHER VASES (THE LOWEST DRAWING IS AN EXTENSION OF A DESIGN). ($\frac{1}{9}$) GEZER (P.E.F.)

imported there, and had nothing necessarily to do with the Philistines. It is true that Minoan pottery was imported into Palestine long before the Philistines ever came there, but if we find there about the time that the Philistines did come from the Aegean a notable increase in the amount of Aegean and pseudo-Aegean pottery, at places specially associated in history with the Philistines, and especially if we find this pottery actually made on the spot, as we do, that is ample justification for associating this pottery with the Philistines and calling it Philistine.

Both Pelethim and Cherethim were no doubt driven out by invaders of their lands. Contemporaneously with the Phrygian (?) invasion of Anatolia, probably owing to similar pressure from Thrace, the Achaian or Hellenic tribes of Thessaly, whom we have already seen raiding in the Mediterranean some thirty years earlier (in the reign of Merneptah, about 1230 B.C.) now, it would seem, moved south into central and southern Greece, and reached Crete, where on the ruins of the old Minoan palaces (at Hagia Triada, for example) we find they built their own buildings in the northern style.[3] They reached Cyprus, coming from Arcadia, as legend as well as dialectical peculiarities attest. And to the same migration is probably to be assigned the early Greek colonization of Mallos in Cilicia by Mopsos, which legend connects with the

[1] Forsdyke, *Brit. Mus. Cat. Vases*, I, i, p. xliii. [2] Macalister, *Excavations of Gezer*, pl. clxiii. [3] Mackenzie, *B.S.A. Ann.*, xiii, p. 424.

246

Philistine movement.[1] The old Thessalian neolithic culture had in the Middle Minoan Age first admitted the use of bronze, and in the later periods had gradually shed its stone-using character, and had partially adopted the common civilization of the Aegean world. *Tholoi* for instance were built at Iolkos (Volo), and the latest pottery is strongly influenced by the Third Late Minoan or Mycenaean style. The Achaians of Thessaly had been minoized to some extent.

Although I must admit that I was attracted by it at first sight, consideration of the evidence obliges me to say that I can hardly subscribe to the view of Mr. Wace [2] that while the Cretan Minoans were not Greeks, all the mainlanders, including the " Mycenaeans," may always have been Greek-speakers, even since neolithic days. The non-Greek element in place-names in Greece he would ascribe to the Cretan conquerors, but the Mycenaeans for him probably spoke Greek. That is to say, the Achaians did not come from Thessaly, but had always been in the Peloponnese ; they were conquered by non-Greek Cretans, whose culture they largely adopted, while retaining the use of their own language. This view seems to me to take a very great deal for granted, and to be unproveable. Prof. Nilsson,[3] as we have seen (p. 215, n. 2), takes a variant view, according to which the Greeks of the mainland conquered the Cretans but brought back Minoan culture with them. This view seems to me even less probable than that of Mr. Wace. There is no such obvious difference between the Mycenaean and the Minoan as would argue any racial distinction between them.[4] If the

---

[1] Hogarth, *Cambr. Anc. Hist.*, ii, p. 547, specially notes the appositeness of the legend of Moxos (Mopsos), " who according to a Greek legend about early Lydia, pushed into Syria and, reaching Askalon, threw its tutelary goddess into her own sacred lake ; a story that sounds curiously like an echo of the historic invasion of Palestine early in the twelfth century B.C. by peoples of Asia Minor."

[2] *Cambr. Anc. Hist.*, ii, p. 468 ; followed by Hogarth, *Twilight of History*, p. 10.

[3] *Minoan-Myc. Religion*, p. 11 ff.

[4] On the practical identity of the Mycenaean with the Minoan culture, see Childe, *The Aryans*, pp. 56, 57. Nilsson's argument (*loc. cit.*) that the use of the *megaron* at Mycenae and Tiryns argues the non-Minoan race of the princes of Mycenae, though the rest of their civilization was Minoan, seems to me unnecessary. If the *megaron* was northern, the Cretan invaders may well have adopted a northern modification of their architecture, as they adopted

Mycenaeans were Greek-speakers, so also were the Cretans, and to this view I can by no means agree.[1] If it is correct, what becomes of the apparent pre-Hellenic element in Greece, to which all tradition as well as archaeological evidence testifies ? Surely the true mainlanders, before the Minoan conquest in M.M. III, were the Pelasgi of legend, non-Hellenes. Herodotus thinks of two races in Greece, Pelasgi and Hellenes, of which the former were older than and preceded the latter, and were βάρβαροι : they did not speak Greek. The Achaians were Hellenes, and did speak Greek. It is natural to suppose that the Achaians were the first Indo-European Greeks in Greece, and that they came from the North, the last *étape* of their southward advance being in Thessaly (Achaia Phthiotis), where they had possibly lived since the (comparatively late) neolithic days of that part of the world. If we like to be precise, we may surmise that they may have been identical with the Dimini people (p. 64). Those neolithic invaders penetrated into the Peloponnese, but found no foothold there ; they probably retreated northward again before the Pelasgic inhabitants. But Achaian blood, if the Dimini-people were proto-Achaians, had no doubt come to stay in Central Greece, between Othrys and the Isthmus. So far perhaps the people that was conquered by the invading Cretans of M.M. III had Achaian blood. So much I can concede, but we have no warrant for supposing that they spoke Greek, and if it is improbable that they did so before the Cretan invasion, even more so is it after that event. The Mycenaeans were then according to my view minoized Pelasgi, Mediterraneans by race and culture, with probably a slight admixture of Achaian (Indo-European) blood, not true Achaians at all and so not, in all probability, Greek-speakers. Therefore I cannot subscribe either to Prof. Bury's assumption [2] that " there can be no reason-

---

the *chiton*, a northern modification of their clothing, which Prof. Nilsson takes to reinforce his argument. His remarks about the introduction of the horse and amber seem to me quite irrelevant. Why should the horse have come through the Greek mainland to Crete ? (see p. 85). And amber will merely have been more common in the North than in Crete.

[1] I do not understand Mr. J. W. Allen's view (*Homer*, p. 115) that the Achaians were originally Cretan Minoans. It seems to go against the archaeological evidence.

[2] *Ibid.*, p. 473.

able doubt the rulers of these states (those of ' Mycenaean Greece ' in the fourteenth and the thirteenth centuries B.C.) were of Greek stock or, at all events, spoke Greek." On the contrary, I think there is every reason to suppose that they did nothing of the kind in the fourteenth century, in the Peloponnese at any rate,[1] and that it was not until the thirteenth, the period of anarchy when Mycenaean culture declined, that the Greek-speaking Achaians, whose culture was now Mycenaean, or at any rate sub-Mycenaean, finally came into possession of Southern Greece, occupied Mycenae, and penetrated to Crete, as also, with Arcadian fellow-colonists, to Cyprus. If it be argued against this view that we already have Achaians on the Anatolian coast in the reign of the Hittite king Muršiliš, about 1330 B.C., according to a decipherment of some of the Boghaz Kyöi tablets, and so a century before I would bring them there, it must be pointed out that all these identifications of the land called Aḫḫiawa as "Achaia," of a king Tavagalavas as a Greek Eteokles and his father Antaravas as an Andreus (the Eteokles and Andreus who ruled the Boeotian Orchomenos according to Pausanias), rest entirely on the personal opinion of one scholar of enthusiastic views,[2] and until his results have been checked by other cuneiform scholars and also by archaeologists, they cannot be accepted as history. We must see the original texts first. Aḫḫiawa has been identified by another authority as not " Achaia " at all, but the classical Anchiale or Ingirá (as the Assyrians called it) in Cilicia.[3] So far are the doctors from agreement. It is a far cry from Boeotia to Cilicia ! But if the identification be eventually accepted as valid, we are confronted with a Greek-speaking dynast in Boeotia in the latter half of the fourteenth century. I do not deny that Greek-speakers may always have lived in Boeotia from neolithic times, though not further south, except for a moment (see p. 64); and confirmation of Prof. Forrer's view will merely mean that the Aryan element had already obtained the upper hand, probably reinforced by an Achaian movement southward from Thessaly in the fourteenth

---

[1] Boeotia is another matter ; see below. [2] Forrer, *Mitth. d. D. Or. Ges.*, 63 (1924).
[3] Mayer and Garstang, "Index of Hittite Names," *Br. Sch. Jerusalem Suppl. Papers*, i (1923).

century. And if the identifications are accepted, that of " Lazbas " with the island of Lesbos, which Tavagalavas attacked, will naturally present no difficulty. It will be the later Greek name of the island, though probably there were no Greeks there yet. But caution is advisable in the matter. I would point out that while " Antaravas " is a quite satisfactory transliteration of Andreus, which any Cypriote would have understood, the equivalence of Tavagalavas with $Ετεϝοκλεϝης$ is by no means so satisfactory. In the seventh century the name Eteandros was transliterated into cuneiform as Ituwandar [1] and so a correct transliteration of Eteokles would presumably be *Ituwakalawas*, not " Tavagalavas." Why should the initial syllable be omitted ? It was not, in the case of $Ετεϝανδρος$.

I am also inclined to caution in the matter of the same scholar's identification of a king Attarissiyas of Aḫḫiawa as Atreus, although the dates here fit in much better with what I conceive to be the probabilities. About 1225 B.C. is claimed as the date of Attarissiyas, who is said to have waged wars on the Pamphylian coast and in Cyprus : we know that Achaians (Akaivasha) and the other " peoples of the sea " were then active in the Eastern Mediterranean, though we have no Egyptian warrant for regarding them as subjects of a great and powerful king. The *Akaivasha* appear as merely a small and chance band of raiders, and only once. If Attarissiyas is really Atreus then Achaians were ruling in the last quarter of the thirteenth century at Mycenae, a conclusion I should, however, readily accept.[2] But there is a philological difficulty. The name Attarissiyas (if correctly so read) would be an attractive equivalent for Atreus, " the untrembling " (Atresyas), if it were at all certain (which it is not) that Atreus = " Atresyas " and means " the untrembling." There is, however, no certainty about the derivation at all.

Prof. Kretschmer, following the late Prof. Luckenbill, has discovered another Greek rather earlier (his date is *c.* 1400–1350 B.C.)

---

[1] Hall, *Oldest Civilization of Greece*, p. 262.

[2] But the name " Atreus " may have been usual among the Achaians and have been transferred in legend to a prince of the Minoan-Mycenaean time.

in a certain Alakshandu, chief of Uilusa, a place which Forrer identi-
fies with Elaioussa on the Cilician coast, and Prof. Garstang with Ialysos
in Rhodes.[1] So again the doctors disagree.[2] Prof. Kretschmer accepts
Uilusa as on the Cilician coast, but like Luckenbill makes Alakshandu
a Greek Alexandros, and no less an one than Paris of Troy himself :
the story was just shifted to Troy.[3] This seems mere fantasy ; but
the identification Alakshandu=Alexandros is accepted by Garstang, who
makes him an Achaian prince Alexandros of Ialysos. Against a Greek
identification it must again be pointed out that the philological equivalence of the two names is bad. We should expect to find Ἀλέξανδρος
transliterated in cuneiform by Alakshandar, not Alakshandu ; as Eteandros was by Ituwandar and as in fact the name of Alexander the Great
was transliterated (Alakshandara) in the fourth century B.C. The ϱ
was an indispensable element in the name, as we see from the cuneiform
and the Latin Alexander : it was not " Alexandos." And since Alakshandu is without ϱ we cannot admit that it = Alexandros at all.
Alakshandu is much more likely to be Asianic, and the name of some
Cilician prince (? a compound with the name of Sandon : compare
Sandakhshatra the Cimmerian and Šanduarri, a historical prince of the
seventh century B.C.). Uilusa may be in Cilicia or anywhere in
southern or western Anatolia : it may be the Hittite version of the
well-known territorial name Alashiya, as to which it is disputed
whether it is Cilicia or Cyprus : I think more probably part of
Cilicia (again, Elaioussa was in Cilicia). But whether it was Ialysos or not
(and since Alakshandu seems more probably an Anatolian, by his name,
I think it more probable that it was not),[4] and whether the land

---

[1] Garstang, *Liv. Annals of Art and Archaeology*, x (May, 1923).

[2] We have only to compare the work on Hittite place-identifications by Sayce, Forrer,
Garstang (*Hittite Names*), and Götze (*Kleinasier zur Hetiterzeit*, 1924) to see how far we are
yet from any real positive knowledge on the subject. But this is not to say that we shall not
attain such knowledge in the near future.

[3] Kretschmer, *Alexandros von Vilusa* ; *Glotta*, 1924, p. 205 ff.

[4] With regard to the identification of Ialysos, it must frankly be said that identifications
of this kind are nearly valueless : anything even remotely similar in sound to something else
is confidently identified with it, often with the result that the identifiers differ profoundly

Lazbas, mentioned in connexion with Antaravas and Tavagalavas, was the island of Lesbos or not, there is little doubt that it was not later than the thirteenth century that the Aegean became Greek-speaking; though relics of the older non-Aryan speech which, probably, the Minoans spoke, continued in Eastern Crete, the land of the Eteocretans, into classical days; we find it inscribed in Greek characters at Praisos.[1] Crete was probably one of the last Greek lands to speak Greek. Boeotia may have done so in the fourteenth century, but Boeotia is a long way from Crete, and we can hardly admit Greek-speakers in the southern islands and in Crete till the end of the thirteenth century at earliest. In the Greek language there survived a large number of words derived from the old tongue, for Greek, completely Indo-European though it is in structure and syntax, has a vocabulary containing elements for which no Aryan ancestry can be claimed.[2] These elements sometimes resemble forms which we know in Etruscan, though we still cannot read that language written though it is in Greek characters, any more than we can Eteocretan or the old Minoan hieroglyphs; it may be hoped however that we may shortly be able to do so.

It was not long after this period that the use of iron and the practice of cremation made their first appearance in Greece, about the twelfth century. Iron was already known as a rare metal as early as 2000 B.C. in Crete: one of Mr. E. J. Forsdyke's finds this year (1927) at Knossos was a cube or die of iron, found within a M.M. II grave deposit, in which

in their identifications, as we have seen in the identifications of Hittite place-names in Asia Minor by Prof. Garstang and Mr. Götze, already mentioned. It may be added that Prof. Forrer's identifications, though rather simplemindedly accepted without cavil at first in England and America, have had a "bad press" in Germany, where, at the "Orientalistentag" held at Hamburg in 1926 they were scouted vigorously (see *Z.D.M.G.*, 1927, p. 1, and *cf.* Friedrich, in *Kleinasiatische Forschungen* (1927), i. p. 87 ff.). Caution is advisable whether in accepting or rejecting views of this sort ,which depend upon the critical faculty of one man.

[1] Evans, *Pictographs*, pp. 354–67. Why we should want to torture the Praisos inscriptions into Greek in the face of the testimony of Herodotus (I, 173, and VII, 170–1) to the "barbarian" character of the pre-Hellenic inhabitants of Crete, who were represented in classical times by the Eteocretans of Praisos, it is hard to say. (See *J.H.S.*, 1925, p. 272 ff.).

[2] Kretschmer, *Einleitung in die Geschichte der griechischen Sprache*; Fick, *Vorgriechische Ortsnamen*; Glotz, *Civilisation égéenne*, p. 439 ff.

it had been placed as a precious object (see p. 86). This is presumably worked, and the most ancient known worked iron from the Aegean area. Mosso found a lump of iron of the Neolithic period at Phaestos, but this was merely a piece of unsmelted magnetite.[1] Iron finger-rings were made in the sixteenth century; one has been found in a *tholos* at Kakovatos (L.M. I) and another in the Vapheio tomb of the same date (*c.* 1550 B.C.).[2] Iron was well known to the Hittites in the thirteenth century, and no doubt long before, and the victories of this Anatolian people over the Egyptians may perhaps be partly attributable to their superior weapons. The Egyptians possessed iron weapons in the days of Tutankhamen [3] (*c.* 1360 B.C.), and possibly before,[4] but they depended largely on the Hittites for their provision of iron, and the Hittite king could withhold iron from Egypt when he willed, as he did on one occasion from Rameses II.[5] The Egyptians were still obliged to fight mainly with bronze weapons, and so also were the " Peoples of the Sea." One of the great bronze broadswords of the Shardina (very different from the Minoan rapiers of the fourteenth century, but very like a Hittite type on the monuments,[6] Fig. 329), found at Gaza, is in the British Museum.[7] The Egyptians always represent the Shar-

[1] *Palaces of Crete*, p. 26; *cf. Dawn of Medit. Civ.*, p. 71.

[2] Childe, *Dawn of European Civilization*, p. 83. These were " the earliest pieces of metallic iron in Europe " before Mr. Forsdyke's find.

[3] We know this from objects found in the young king's tomb at Thebes, notably the wonderful iron dagger with gold-worked and crystal hilt (Carter, *Tomb of Tutankhamen*, ii, p. 268, pl. lxxxviib.) I saw it in the tomb when first identified as iron by Mr. Lucas: it was as bright as steel, and I took it at first sight to be of speculum metal. Its crystal pommel is of the same type as those of the Minoan swords from Zafer Papoura (Fig. 257), and is obviously of foreign origin, but its ornament is not purely Minoan, consisting, like that of its fellow-dagger in gold, of zigzags and diamonds of granulated gold work.

[4] On the iron spearhead of the Hyksos period found in Nubia (Woolley and Maciver, *Buhen*, p. 193), see p. 86 n.

[5] Hogarth, *Cambr. Anc. Hist.*, ii, pp. 267, 272.

[6] On the slab representing a thunder-god from Zenjirli. Childe, *The Aryans*, pl. i, illustrates this, and comments on it, p. 28, but does not make the comparison with the Shardina sword. Nor does Cowley, *The Hittites*, p. 53, who also reproduces it.

[7] Hall, *Aeg. Arch.*, pp. 247, 252; *Proc. Soc. Ant.* For a Hittite parallel see the well-known relief of a warrior-god found at Babylon (Koldewey, *Excavations at Babylon*, Fig. 103).

dina, Philistines and their allies as wielding these great swords (Fig. 330), and using round shields.

Iron then came to Greece probably as much from Anatolia as from the Danubian region. North-eastern Anatolia, towards the Caucasus, was possibly the earliest centre of iron-working.[1] We cannot ascribe its introduction into the Aegean to the Achaians. In the Homeric poems, though iron was known, they ordinarily use bronze for weapons.[2] Iron is first found generally used for weapons in Greece in

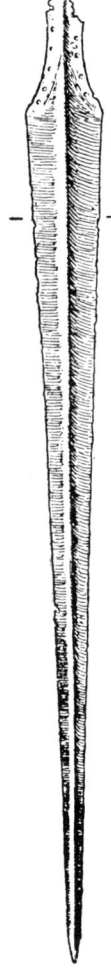

FIG. 330.—SHARDINA GUARDS, WITH BROADSWORDS

the Geometric period, which must for chronological reason be assigned to the time of the Dorian invasion and the period immediately succeeding it.

In the age between the Minoan-Mycenaean time (ending in the fourteenth–thirteenth centuries) and the beginning of the Iron Age that heralded the Dorian conquest (at earliest in the eleventh), a shorter broad-bladed bronze sword (Fig. 331d) appears in the Aegean (Naue's type II)[3], with the leaf-shaped sword (Fig. 332), which seems to have been contemporary with it

FIG. 329.—SHARDINA BRONZE BROAD-SWORD, FOUND AT GAZA (BRIT. MUS.). (c. $\frac{1}{6}$)

[1] Childe, *The Aryans*, p. 118.

[2] On mentions of iron in Homer, see Daremberg et Saglio, *Dict. Ant.*, p. 1602. The age of the heroes, the Achaian age, was for Hesiod one intermediate between the Ages of Bronze and Iron, in fact exactly the time at which we have arrived (Chadwick, *Heroic Age*, p. 178). [3] But with a cross-hilt.

(Naue's types IIa, IIb) and the transition-form to the Hallstatt type. These swords of Northern (that is to say Central-European) origin are very different from the rapier (Fig. 257) of the

a   *b*   *c*   *d*   *e*

FIG. 331.—GREEK BRONZE SWORDS WITH CROSS-HILTS: 14TH–12TH CENT. (BRIT. MUS.)

(a) Ialysos (Late Mycenaean)   (b, c) Ialysos (Late Mycenaean)
(d) Corfu (Achaian)   (e) Karpathos (Achaian)

Minoans (Naue's types Ia, Ib),[1] and the late-Mycenaean short sword (Naue's type IId, Fig. 331a–c). The broadswords of the Shardina

[1] For Naue's sword-types see his *Vorrömischen Schwerter*, pls. III–XII.

and Philistines (p. 253), also quite different again, are not found in Greece, and cannot be assigned to Greeks; but the short broadsword and the leaf-shaped sword were Greek.[1] A longer example

FIG. 332.—CRETAN BRONZE BROAD AND LEAF-SHAPED SWORDS, ROUND SHIELD-BOSSES, FIBULAE, ETC. EARLIER BURIALS: MOULIANÀ. (13TH–12TH CENT. B.C.) ($\frac{1}{6}$ TO $\frac{1}{8}$)

[1] On the broad-bladed Achaian type see Evans, *Preh. Tombs*, p. 113. One was found in the town of Mycenae (Daremberg et Saglio, *s.v. Gladius*, Fig. 3602), one in the late Mycenaean tomb-deposit of Moulianà in Crete (see p. 258); and its occurrence dates a find of bronzes in 1889 in the Athenian acropolis (Montelius, "Ett fynd från Athens akropolis," *Vitterhets Akademiens Månadsblad*, 1889, p. 49 ff.) as Achaian. A similar sword dates a *tholos*-tomb at Delphi (Perdrizet, *Fouilles de Delphes*, v (1908)) also as Achaian, unless it belongs to a later interment, which is unlikely. An example from the British Museum (Undset, *Die ältesten Schwertformen*, Fig. 20) figured above (Fig. 331) is said to have been found in Corfu. Of the leaf-shaped type a fine specimen has been found at Mycenae (Daremberg et Saglio, Fig. 3603), and others at Ialysos, Corinth, and Corfu (*Ibid.*, p. 1601); one in the British Museum from Enkomi in Cyprus (Murray, Smith, and Walters, *Brit. Mus. Excav. in Cyprus*, p. 16, Fig. 31). A very fine leaf-shaped example, hiltless, "from Beyrut," which probably came in reality from Cyprus, and possibly from Enkomi (formerly in the Pierpont Morgan Collection), one from Shkodra in Albania, evidently Greek (Undset, *loc. cit.*, Fig. 26), a dagger from Naxos (*Archaeologia*, viii, 6), and a small serrated leaf-shaped dagger with hilt in one piece with the blade, from Crete, are also in the British Museum. A similar (not serrated) dagger was found with geometrical remains at Spata (Philadelpheus, ʼΑρχ. Δελτ. παράρτ., 1920–21, p. 132, εἰκ. 1).

of type II, without cross-hilt, has been found in Egypt with the name of the Egyptian king Seti II (*c.* 1215–1205 B.C.) on it.[1] It is therefore contemporary within ten years or so with the historical attack of the Akaivasha on Egypt (p. 240), and may justly, with the leaf-shaped type, be assigned to the Achaians. There is no other people to whom they can be assigned. The Dorians used iron, and as the oldest Greek swords of iron, in Greece and Cyprus, are of two types whose shapes shew that they were copied directly from these two bronze types,[2] and as the Dorians succeeded the Achaians directly in Greece, the bronze types must belong to their immediate predecessors, the Achaians. And since these types are not Minoan at all, and not Mycenaean till the second half of the thirteenth century, they are definitely circumscribed to the Achaian period. "To Egypt the Minoans brought tribute or gifts; the Achaeans slashing swords."[3]

We can distinguish to some extent between the Minoan and the Achaian spear, since the finely formed spearheads of the Minoans with their beautiful lines (p. 197, Fig. 258) were no longer used by the Achaians, but had been entirely superseded by the broad-blade spearhead of the usual type (Fig. 333), known before, but not characteristic of a period, as was the Minoan spearhead.[4]

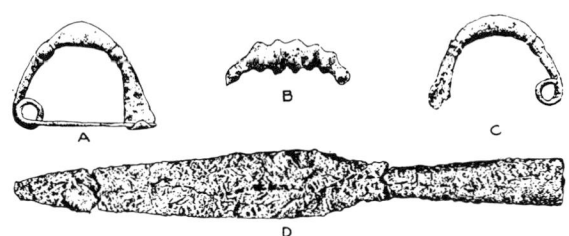

FIG. 333.—BRONZE SPEARHEAD AND FIBULAE : CRETE. ($\frac{1}{2}$)

The simple bronze fibula (Figs. 332–4) from the "fiddle-bow" to the "arch" type, belongs to the Achaians. It did not exist in Greece before

---

[1] Burchardt, *Äg. Zeits.*, 1912, p. 61 ff. ; Peet, *B.S.A. Ann.*, xviii (1912), p. 282 ff. For the type *cf.* Naue, *loc. cit.*, pl. vi, 3.

[2] Evans, *loc. cit.*, and Daremberg et Saglio, *loc. cit.*, Figs. 3604, 3605.

[3] Childe, *The Aryans*, p. 209. [4] Cf. Montelius, *La Grèce préclassique*, p. 179.

the thirteenth century at earliest, and formed no part of the old Minoan costume.[1] It occurs only at this time, in association with weapons of the kind we have described, and with the " sub-Mycenaean " pottery which, we shall see, is Achaian. The Dorians used fibulae, of course, but there were no Dorians and no geometrical pottery in Greece in the thirteenth century. The " spectacle " fibula is obviously Dorian at Sparta.

FIG. 334.—BRONZE FIBULA

If then the Achaians belonged primarily to the Bronze Age, and had nothing to do with the general introduction of iron for use in weapon-making, which must be assigned to the first appearance of the Dorians at the end of the twelfth century, notwithstanding the fact that its existence was known to the Achaians and it was prized by them, how is it with cremation ? In the poems the heroes burn their dead. The invaders of Asia Minor in the thirteenth century (p. 244) were certainly corpse-burners as well as apparently iron-users.[2] The Dorian invaders of Greece at the end of the next century were certainly both. The Achaians of Homer were bronze-users, although they burnt their dead. But the archaeological Achaians, the people of the bronze post-Minoan swords and sub-Mycenaean pottery, did not burn their dead.

At Moulianà in Crete we have a most interesting tomb in which a late Bronze Age (L.M. IIIb) burial containing uncremated bones and bronze swords with leaf-shaped blades and hilts like those of the short broadsword (Fig. 332), was found on one side, and on the other another burial containing iron weapons and cremated bones in a *krater* of the most debased sub-Mycenaean style, almost transitional to geometric, accom-

---

[1] I am unable to share Blinkenberg's belief that the fibula developed out of the long bronze Minoan pins with one end bent round (Evans, *Preh. Tombs*, Fig. 199), which are obviously hairpins : the short recurved end is eminently adapted to hold a hair-knot in position. The fact that a beautifully chased specimen has just been found by Forsdyke at Knossos seems to me no argument against this. The decoration would be hidden by clothes as much as by the hair.

[2] It is not long after 1200 B.C. and the overthrow of the Hittite kingdom in Anatolia that we find cremation-burials at Hittite Carchemish on the Euphrates.

258

panied by vases of sub-Mycenaean type(Fig. 335). "We may here have an instance of iron weapons succeeding bronze, and cremation succeeding burial, in the same race, and even in the same family."[1] We have, in fact, here a record, I think, of the actual change during the Achaian period from inhumation to cremation, and from bronze weapons to iron. The older of the two burials is obviously Achaian, and probably early twelfth century. Some of the vases of the cremation burial are not yet really geometric, even of the transition. The *krater* is however of the very latest pre-geometric type, and might perhaps be regarded as transitional. It may not be older than the coming of the Dorians, who reached Crete early, possibly by the beginning of the tenth century. If the Bronze Age burial dates not earlier than 1200–1150, judging by the type of the swords, there may have elapsed about a century and a half between the two burials, the later dating about 1000. The respect with which the older interment was treated is notable.

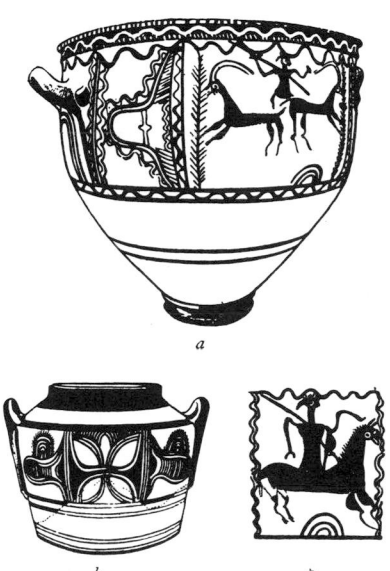

FIG. 335.—SUB-MYCENAEAN VASES FOUND WITH IRON WEAPONS. LATER BURIAL ; MOULIANÀ, CRETE. ($\frac{1}{10}$ TO $\frac{1}{15}$)

(*c*, inset from other side of larger vase.)

At "Thunder-hill," above Kavousi in Crete, we find another transitional burial, with iron weapons, vases transitional between Minoan and geometric, and uncremated skeletons.[2] This must be another late-Achaian burial, but an older one than the cremation-burial at Moulianà, to be dated to the eleventh century (1100–1050), after iron had come into general use, but, to judge from the pottery and the absence of cremation, before Crete was dorized. In Greece we have

[1] Evans, *Preh.Tombs*, pp. 112, 134 ; Xanthoudides, Ἐφημ.Ἀρχ., 1904, 22–37 ; Mackenzie, *B.S.A. Ann.*, xiii, p. 430 ff.

[2] Boyd, *Am. Jour. Arch.*, v (1901), Figs. 2, 3 ; pp. 128–137.

grave-deposits of probably a little later date, in the island of Salamis,[1] where as at Moulianà we find not only iron, but also cremation. The geometric pottery of the Dipylon, which is generally assigned to the Dorians with other pottery of the same style from other parts of Greece in spite of there being no literary evidence of Dorians in Attica, is associated with iron and cremation. It must belong to the Dorians ; to the Achaians it cannot, as they were bronze-users. If then the geometric style is not that of the Dorians, whose was it ? This appears to be an instance of archaeology proving something that literary evidence denies. Well can we imagine that the Athenians expunged all mention of Dorians from their early history !

Cremation then is chiefly associated with the Dorians rather than the Achaians, and probably did not reach Crete, at any rate, earlier than iron. We may therefore suppose that if it already existed in the Achaian period at all, it came in only at the end of the age, about the end of the eleventh century, after iron had become well known in Greece, but not before it came into general use. The general use of both belongs to the post-Achaian age, and the attribution of the custom of incineration to the Homeric heroes is probably an anachronism on the part of the poets if these heroes were the genuine archaeological Achaians, very certainly so if they were some of them originally Minoans.

So far as pottery is concerned, I should follow the views of Dr. Duncan Mackenzie,[2] and attribute to the Achaians the wares which we know as " L.M. IIIb " in Crete, the more debased types of which we may with examples from elsewhere call " Sub-Mycenaean " (Fig. 336), and the transition-types from Sub-Mycenaean to geometric all over Greece. The L.M. IIIb (not " sub-Mycenaean ") pottery from the chamber-tomb at Milatos in Crete [3] is probably pre-Achaian, and not later than 1300–1250 ; the older pottery from the tombs at Moulianà is definitely Achaian. The well-known " Warrior Vase " from Mycenae [4] is no doubt one of the best examples of Achaian

[1] Wide, *Ath. Mitth.*, xxxv.
[2] " Cretan Palaces, III " (*B.S.A. Ann.*, *loc. cit.*, p. 423 ff.).
[3] Evans, *loc. cit.*, p. 93 ff.
[4] Schuchhardt, *Schliemann*, Figs. 284, 285 ; Mackenzie, *loc. cit.*, p. 427.

ceramic (Fig. 338). The curious fragment with the men, dog, and horses (Fig. 339), also from Mycenae,[1] is one of the worst. It might be called transitional geometric. It may be said that the

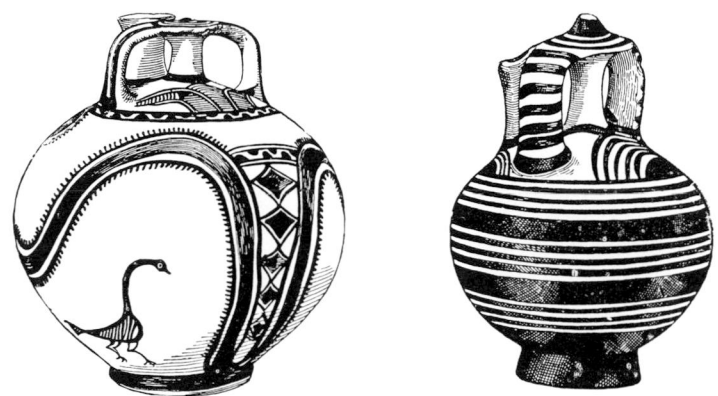

FIG. 336.—MYC. IIIB AND SUB-MYCENAEAN STIRRUP-VASES: IALYSOS AND ASSARLIK (BRIT. MUS CATALOGUE). ($c.$ $\frac{1}{4}$, $\frac{1}{3}$)

Achaians have not much "ceramic content," but the archaeological evidence is dead against their having possessed any more, or any good

FIG. 337.—GREEK VASE-DESIGN SHEWING MINOAN SURVIVALS: CRETE

ceramic at all, so far as decoration was concerned, while forms were clumsy in comparison with the old. The pottery of the Philistine

[1] Schuchhardt, *loc. cit.* Fig. 132.

261

settlers in Palestine at the beginning of the twelfth century is of the same L.M. III*b* and sub-Mycenaean type.[1]

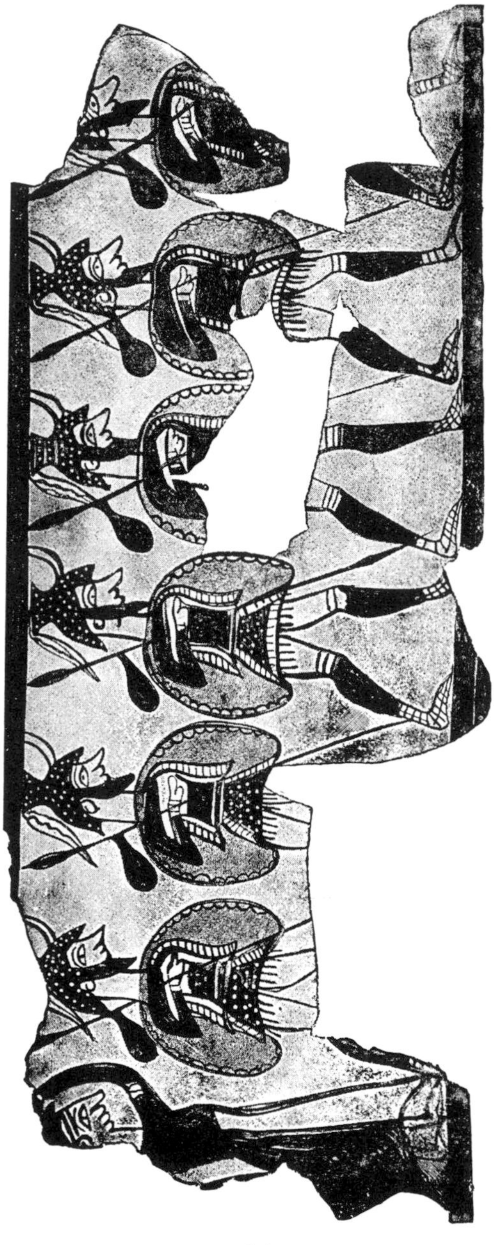

The transition from sub-Mycenaean to proto-geometric pottery was a gradual, not a catastrophic change. "It is hardly possible to separate (them). . . . Both types can be recognized at the same moment,

FIG. 339.—ACHAIAN VASE-FRAGMENT : MYCENAE. ($\frac{1}{9}$)

and often on the same vase. They are found together at the end of long series of burials in Mycenaean chamber-tombs," *e.g.* at Ialysos in Rhodes and Pothia in Kalymnos.[2] A probable example of the first signs of transition is the vase (Fig. 340) with friezes of running deer, in the

FIG. 338.—PROCESSION ON WARRIOR-VASE : MYCENAE. ($\frac{1}{4}$)

[1] See p. 245.
[2] Forsdyke, *loc. cit.*, p. xliv.

262

British Museum (A 1022), while two others (A 1023, A 1024) are good specimens of full transition to geometric.[1] At Vrokastro in Crete interesting transitional sub-Mycenaean to geometric ware

FIG. 340.—FRIEZE OF RUNNING DEER : ACHAIAN VASE (BRIT. MUS. CATALOGUE). ($\frac{1}{3}$)

(Fig. 341) also occurs with scarabs of XXIInd–XXVIth Dynasty date (Fig. 342). The ware from Assarlik in Caria (Fig. 336) is sub-

FIG. 341.—TRANSITIONAL WARE, VROKASTRO : CRETE. ($\frac{1}{5}$)

Mycenaean, and practically transitional.[2] Cretan transitional and geometric pottery is well illustrated by finds at Praisos (Fig. 343),[3] Kourtais (see p. 267), and Vrokastro [4] (Fig. 344).

[1] *Ibid.*, pp. 196, 197.
[2] Paton, *J.H.S.*, viii (1887), p. 64 ff.
[3] Droop, *B.S.A. Ann.*, xiv., p. 24 ff.
[4] *Vrokastro* : E. H. Hall, *Vrokastro* (Univ. Penna. Anthrop. publ. 1914). Cf. Forsdyke, *loc. cit.*, pp. xliv, 211 ff.

We then regard the Achaians as invaders from beyond Othrys, already minoized or mycenaeized in culture, who when they took over Southern Greece from probably effete " Mycenaean " rulers, appear merely as the inheritors of a debased Minoan art-tradition, which in their

FIG. 342.—EGYPTIAN SCARABS, VROKASTRO. ($\frac{3}{4}$)

semi-barbarous time became ever more and more debased. Their only good art was in their sword-making, apparently : a characteristic of a

FIG. 343.—TRANSITIONAL WARE, PRAISOS, CRETE. ($\frac{1}{2}$)

FIG. 344.—CRETAN EARLY GEOMETRIC VASE OF TYPE FOUND AT VROKASTRO. ($\frac{1}{8}$) (BRIT. MUS. CATALOGUE)

military era, as in mediaeval Japan. The same may be said of the Bronze Age culture of Central and Western Europe : beautiful weapons, but no other evidence of what we should call high civilization, such as existed in Crete. They belonged to the Bronze Age, though iron was known to them. Cremation may have been known to them at the end of their domination, but was not generally practised till the next age. The Dorians overthrew them largely with the help of iron weapons, no doubt.

264

THE TRANSITION TO THE AGE OF IRON

The Homeric panoply corresponds very well to that of the Warrior Vase and other indications at this period.[1] Greaves (Fig. 345) had supplanted the ancient Cretan boot or putteed sandal, and the breast-plate has finally been adopted. It was known to the Minoans, as we see from its occurrence in the Knossian list-tablets (Fig. 97), and is perhaps shewn on a Mycenaean fresco (Fig. 278). The Shardina are represented by the Egyptians as wearing laminated body-armour (Figs. 318, 330), and so is the Arimaspian (represented by a Cyprian or Cilician artist ?) fighting the griffin on the Enkomi mirror-handle (Fig. 302). We see a corselet on the Warrior Vase (Fig. 338). The round shield (Figs. 318, 330, 332, 339) has entirely sup-

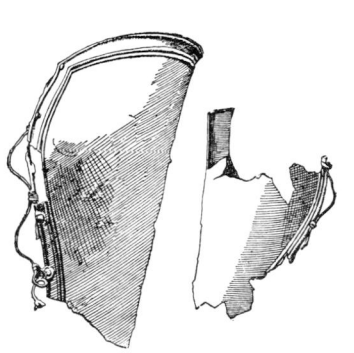

FIG. 345.—BRONZE GREAVES : ENKOMI. (BRIT. MUS.). ($\frac{1}{8}$)

planted the great Figure-of-Eight Minoan shield (Figs. 179, 254–6). The plumed helm has been inherited from the Minoans (p. 137).

We are now in a Dark Age. Mr. Hogarth would prefer to call it a Twilight Age; for him it was not dark.[2] We know however that the Aegean was fast being reduced to a state of barbarism. Piracy was un-checked, and the coast people fled to the hills to escape the pirates and slave-raiders, building their villages on almost inaccessible peaks, as on Thunder Hill above the Isthmus of Hierapetra in Crete, where was found the late-Achaian burial mentioned above. The Achaians are vested in Homer with the old Minoan Bronze Age glamour. It is difficult to distinguish what probably is really Achaian in Homeric legend from what should be assigned to the old Bronze Age days. Although Minos may be an Achaian in legend, how can we regard the epoch he repre-sents as Achaian ? Minos does not belong, any more than most of the other heroes, except perhaps those of evidently later date like Idomeneus in Crete, to the time of the Peoples of the Sea in which the actual

---

[1] R. S. Thompson, *Liv. A.A.A.*, v, p. 1 ff. Cf. Ridgeway, *Early Age of Greece*, p. 317. The pair of bronze greaves from Enkomi, illustrated above, are probably to be assigned to the Achaian period. [2] *The Twilight of History*, p. 13.

Achaians of Mycenae and of Crete lived. The Akaivasha of the Egyptians were hunters and hunted, pirates and freebooters, not upholders
of an ordered Minoan thalassocracy or even of the *pax achaica* which
the poets would assign to the days of the heroes. The figures of a Minos
and an Atreus (whether Atreus is a historical king Attarissiyas of the
thirteenth century or not), belong as conceived by the poets to the great
days of Crete and Mycenae, to the time between the twentieth and
the fourteenth centuries, not to sub-Mycenaean times and the transition
to the Age of Iron, to which we assign them if we insist on the literal
inspiration of the literary sources. But the wonders, the triumphs
of workmanship, come down from the older days. Are the political
arrangements of the poems too to be accepted as genuinely Achaian ?
Achaian dynasts ruled in the seats of the mighty at Mycenae and everywhere else : they " took over " from their predecessors. The Homeric
kingdoms may be correctly Achaian, and at the same time preserve the
old Mycenaean political divisions to a great extent. The Achaians
inherited the power and glory of the strong men who lived before
Agamemnon—if Agamemnon was originally an Achaian, any more
than Minos. Was the Trojan War, in the ultimately historical character of which we need not disbelieve, though it may not have lasted
ten years,[1] really an Achaian expedition or has it been transferred from
the Mycenaean times by Achaian poets ?

---

[1] Yet ancient sieges often did last a very long time. We have an instance in the siege of
Azotus in the sixth century mentioned by Herodotus (ii, 157) which according to him lasted
no less than twenty-nine years (!) : such sieges were no doubt really merely blockades, as was
that of Troy. When the besiegers had no siege-apparatus to speak of, sieges must often
have degenerated into blockades. Even Tyre resisted Nebuchadnezzar for thirteen years
though he possessed all the siege-artillery of Assyrian military science, which had always
proved irresistible, and with which Cyrus so soon reduced the fenced cities of Ionia. But
Tyre's insular position made her an exception, as she could not be attacked at close quarters.
We have no knowledge of any Minoan or Mycenaean siege-engines. There is a representation
of a siege (much older of course than the Siege of Troy) on the well-known fragment of a
repoussé silver cup found at Mycenae (Fig. 163) in which we see archers and slingers contending outside its walls : there is no hint of rams or " tortoises " like those of the Assyrians,
still less of great engines like the *ballistae* of the Hellenistic Greeks and the Romans. Probably nothing of the kind yet existed, and the fortified city could resist indefinitely till it fell
by famine or treachery.

THE TRANSITION TO THE AGE OF IRON

Its traditional date, at the beginning of the twelfth century, contemporary with the Philistine migration and not long after the attack of the Akaivasha on Egypt, fits in well with the date of the archaeological Achaians if we regard it as belonging to the later period of their domination in Greece. But its setting is that of the Mycenaean period of at least a century or more, probably two centuries before, and the expedition may really have happened then, and have been assigned to the Achaians by the poets.[1] In tradition the deeds and works and ways of all the men of all the foregoing centuries were naturally enough by Greeks concentrated in the period immediately preceding the return of the Heraklids, the age of the domination of the Achaian Greeks in Greece. Everything great and noble that had gone before was attributed to the Achaians, who can in reality have made but a sorry contribution in comparison.[2]

Yet probably more of the old culture survived in Crete than in Greece itself. The purely geometric (Iron Age) burials excavated by Mr. Hogarth near Knossos[3] are in ancient re-used *tholoi*. The stirrup-vase still survives in them in a debased form, as at Kourtais[4], with geometric decoration. If we suppose that the geometric pottery was first brought by the Dorians, these tombs should date at earliest as late as the tenth century on the current theory, as the Dorians are said

---

[1] On the other hand the coincidence of the traditional date with that of the Philistine migration is close enough to make it equally probable that the attack on Troy was really an Achaian, not a pre-Achaian Mycenaean expedition. By 1194 Mycenae would presumably be already Achaian. "In the general catastrophe of elder powers of Asia Minor under pressure from the north, whether from the Caucasian or the Thracian country or from both, men of the west seized an opportunity" (Hogarth, *Cambr. Anc. Hist.*, ii, p. 547). For the historical character of the story see Chadwick, *Heroic Age*, p. 294. On Atreus and Attarissiyas, see p. 250.

[2] This view of the Achaians may seem very different from that of Prof. Bury in the *Cambr. Anc. Hist.*, ii, ch. xvii, but it is one that is forced upon us by the archaeological evidence in accordance with which we must modify our appreciation of purely literary testimony. All statements on the subject of the Achaians and their precise place in the early story of Greece remain highly disputable. But views must be made and formulated, or we make no progress. And the view I have stated, which in the main agrees with that of Dr. Duncan Mackenzie, seems to me to reconcile the difficulties best.

[3] *B.S.A. Ann.*, vi, p. 70 ff.

[4] Mackenzie, *B.S.A.*, xiii, p. 442.

in one account to have reached Crete early in their migration.[1]   Usually
the beginning of the great Dorian or Thesprotian invasion of Greece
proper is dated about 1000 B.C.   It is undoubtedly a historical fact.
We find *étapes* of the southern advance of, presumably, the Dorians in
Bosnia and the Macedonians in the Vardar Valley.[2]

A bronze-using race left the Danube Valley " hardly later than
1500 B.C.," and settled, displacing or overlying a previous neolithic
population of the " painted pottery type," along the banks of the Vardar, where they left remains with which late Mycenaean pottery (imported) has been found by Mr. Casson.   Here they seem to have been
held up from further advance for some centuries by the peculiar chalcolithic culture of Thessaly, to which belonged the Dimini-folk, in whom
we have had some reason to recognize the ancestors of the Achaians.   If
the late Mycenaean pottery found by Mr. Casson dates to about 1300
B.C., as it must do, these people from the north cannot have been
Achaians, who were then already minoized and civilized, and perhaps
already lords of Northern Greece, if probably not yet of Mycenae
and the Peloponnese (see p. 249).   They must then be the second,
or Dorian-Macedonian, wave of Greek immigration : Dorians still in
the Bronze Age, not yet in the possession of iron.   If their culture was
closely related to that of the *terramare* folk of Italy, the eastern branch
of the movement of the *terramare* people out of the North was that of
the Dorians into Greece.   We might say " of the Macedonians," so
far as the Vardar movement is concerned, as the Dorians proper tradition-
ally moved through Illyria and Epirus.   Or perhaps we should say that
the " Dorians " (or " Wiros II," the Achaians having been the " Wiros
I ")[3] who were left behind in Macedonia when part of the race eventu-

---

[1] Wade-Geary, *Cambr. Anc. Hist.*, ii, p. 528.

[2] S. Casson, " The Bronze Age in Macedonia," *Archaeologia*, lxxiv, (1923–24), p. 73 ff.
(The excavations at Chauchitza : cf. *B.S.A.*, xxiv, p. 1 ff.)   Although no bronze was actually
found, Mr. Casson considers that there can be no doubt that these remains are of the
Bronze Age.

[3] The term "Wiro " is used by some philologists (*e.g.* by Dr. Peter Giles in the *Cambridge
Ancient History*, vol. iii) to signify the primitive Indo-European-speaker.   It = " Man "
(*vir, þhear*).

ally moved on southward through Thessaly [1] became the Macedonians. The final southward movement into Greece from Bosnia and Macedonia took place when the use of iron had been adopted, apparently *per saltum,* whereas " in Italy the terramare culture merged into the Iron Age by a process of transition." [2] This may have been due to a sudden reinforcement of people of the same race from the North, bringing iron, which carried the earlier people southward with it, overcoming all obstacles into Greece.

About 1100 B.C. then, or somewhat later, two hundred years after the Achaians had moved into southern Greece, the famous " Return of the Heraklids " (possibly enough under chiefs of Achaian origin, unless the whole of this part of the legend is a mere legitimation-fiction), began, the Dorians started to found their states in Greece, and the " Great Migration " to Asia took place. The chief Dorian states will have been fully constituted, and the Dorians have reached Crete, by 1000–950 B.C. [3]

To this period after the destruction of the Achaian power must be assigned the short period of Phoenician penetration in the Aegean, upon which we find ample authority in Homer as well as in several pieces of archaeological evidence, though we no longer can believe that Kadmos was really a Phoenician, or that Phoenicians ever settled inland in Greece as at Thebes. The legendary Phoenician origin of the Cadmeans of Thebes is probably to be attributed to a late confusion of the " red " Minoans from oversea with the Φοίνικες, analogous with the Ptolemaic confusion of Kefti with Phoenicia. But the worship of the Kabeiroi at Samothrace is Phoenician, and we can hardly doubt that Melikertes at Corinth is the Phoenician Melkarth, or that names

[1] Casson, *loc. cit.,* p. 88 : a genuine Dorian movement can be traced from Macedonia through Thessaly, where one excavation at Pherae had yielded several hundred spectacle-brooches, " together with lead figurines and ivory earrings of Spartan types."

[2] *Ibid.,* p. 85. The Macedonian early Hallstatt period (= Greek Geometric) is represented at Chauchitza by a geometric vase, which should date about 1000 B.C., after the migration (*ibid.,* p. 88). Mr. Casson dates it 1100–1000 B.C., which would surely be too late " in Southern Greece ? " Is it a southern import ?

[3] Chadwick, *Heroic Age,* p. 180.

like Karthaia, Samos, Adramyttion, and Atabyrion are Semitic.[1] So also perhaps Aradēn in Crete, which is close to the ancient twin port of Loutro, the " Phoinike " of St. Paul's journey. May not Loutro have been called " Arwadain " (" two Arvads," or double Arvad) by Phoenicians who occupied its havens, and the name have shifted a little since ? And we may find at Kameiros in Rhodes traces of Phoenician archaeology, though the imitations of blue Egyptian faience that are found there are more probably in reality of Naukratite origin, and to be dated to the seventh century.

The colonizing movements of the Greeks in the eighth century drove the Phoenicians from the Aegean.   During the time of their presence there, for nearly three centuries after the migration, the art (almost non-existent) of continental Greece is the barbarous geometrical pottery-decoration and crude metal-work of the Dipylon period, which spread early to Crete and later to Rhodes. The Ionians were of all the Greeks the tribe that had in it the most of the old Minoan or Pelasgic blood, and inherited probably much of the afterglow of Minoan culture,[2] a tradition which survived to inspire the new beginnings of Greek art in the eighth and seventh centuries. What remained of the old Minoan tradition was preserved only in Ionia, in Cyprus, and also in the islands and in Crete.   A strange survival of Cretan notions into classical days has been noted by Sir Arthur Evans in certain Cretan signets of the fourth century (Fig. 346),[3] which are almost literal transcripts of Minoan gems. Is there a conscious imitation in them ? And he points out the survival of Minoan tradition in numismatic types, especially in Crete.[4] We might see an earlier recrudescence or survival of Minoan art-tradition

---

[1] Hall, *Oldest Civilization of Greece*, p. 227 ff. While holding that these names are Phoenician, and considering that the evidence, such as it is, bears out the legendary presence of the " Sidonians " in the Aegean, I naturally no longer believe in some of the supposed Phoenician traces in Greece which seemed probable in 1901, and are mentioned *loc. cit.*

[2] Cf. Hogarth, *Ionia and the East*, p. 41. Mr. Hogarth has recently modified his view (*Twilight of History*, p. 13).   On the Great Migrations, see Hogarth, *Cambr. Anc. Hist.*, ii, p. 542 ff. Mr. Hogarth points out that the central portion of the east coast of Asia Minor had not previously been occupied by Greeks (Aegeans) probably on account of an extension of the Hittite or a connected power to the coast in Minoan days.

[3] *J.H.S.*, xxxii (1912), p. 296 (Figs. 5–7).   [4] *Ibid.*, p. 294.

in such a picture as Fig. 337 or in Fig. 347, a sixth-century vase-painting of a sailor struggling with a sea-monster. But at the same time we see here the characteristics of the new age : the hair is almost as long, but the pointed beard has arrived, and, above all, though there is a tight waistbelt, the figure is naked : the Minoans never represented the nude figure in detail. On the back of this vase is a picture of a youth riding a

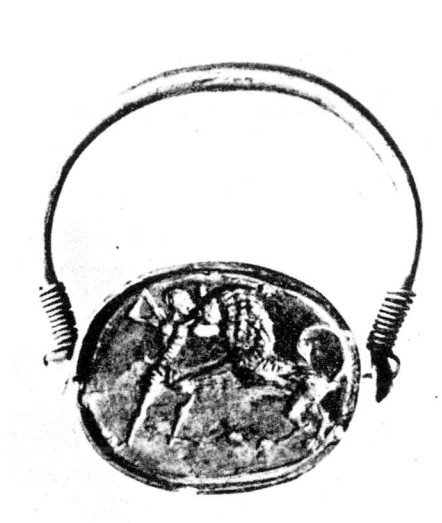 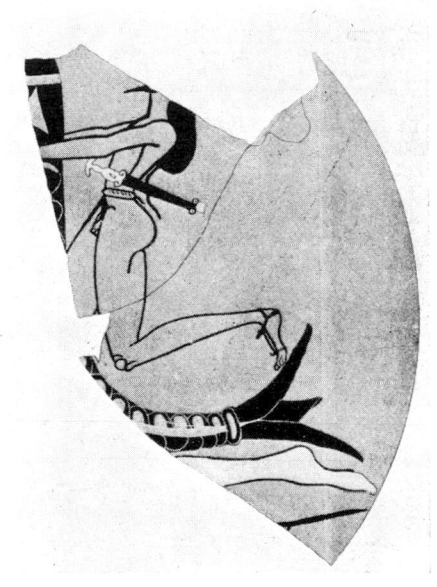

FIG. 346.—SURVIVAL OR REVIVAL OF MINOAN STYLE ON A GREEK SEAL OF THE FOURTH CENTURY (*Enlarged*)

FIG. 347.—MAN WRESTLING WITH A SEA-MONSTER : FROM A CRETAN BLACK-FIGURED PINAX : PRAISOS

horse in the peculiarly crude Cretan style of the sculptures of Priniàs, where we see one of the earliest of the renewed struggles of the Mediterranean art-spirit to revive in some temple-carvings that, rude as they are, still have something about them of the ancient heroic style.[1]

When Milchhöfer wrote his *Anfänge der Griechischen Kunst* in

---

[1] Pernier, *Ann. Sc. Arch. Atene*, i (1914), p. 48 ff. I confess however that I cannot see, as some have done, in one of the very archaic reliefs in the Candia Museum a representation of a cowed Cretan aborigine, a descendant of the Minoans and Achaians, doing homage to his gigantic Dorian conqueror. The figure of the "suppliant" seems to me to be that of a woman, probably the Dorian's wife.

271

the Mycenaean shaft-grave tombstones (M.M. III ??) are childish : the lion group at Mycenae is crude. The rigid formalism of the Egyptian sculptors, with their canons of proportion, was foreign to him, and he could not produce what they produced with its aid. Their genius for portraiture (the finest achievement of Egyptian art) he did not possess or had not cultivated. Their uniformity of excellence was not his ideal ; when he essayed to imitate them, he adapted in his own free way (p. 122). The Egyptian was different : except at recognized periods of decadence his art was always at a dead level of excellence within the limits of the convention : he was the supreme art-craftsman : the Minoan was the truer artist. Herein the Minoan is the more modern.

The apparent modernity of Minoan society has often been remarked. It is hardly possible to doubt from the evidence of the frescoes, etc., that women were on a par with men in many ways. Though their participation in the brutal sport of bull-leaping may not have been entirely voluntary on their part, they certainly took part in the chase with men. Here we are reminded of the Cretan huntress-goddess Britomartis

FIG. 350.—THE HUNTRESS-GOD-
DESS WITH HER LION
(*Enlarged*)

or Diktynna (Fig. 350), who became the Artemis of all Greece. And with the legend of the Amazons in our minds, we cannot say that we should be surprised if it were to appear that the Minoan women also went to war. Evidently the later Greeks conceived of the women of early days in Anatolia and Crete as huntresses and even sometimes as warriors.

This feminism, if we may call it so, was probably a development of strong matriarchal ideas as opposed to the predominantly patriarchal ideas of the Aryan Greeks as were the similar matriarchal ideas of the Dasyus or Dravidians of India to the patriarchal ideas of the invading Aryans.[1] In Egypt too the woman was important : far more

[1] Barnett, *Antiquities of India*, p. 4.

so than in the Semitic East or in later Greece, though probably not so much so as in Minoan Crete. In Egypt descent was traced through the mother. But in Egypt the gods were on the whole more important than the goddesses, while in Crete there is little doubt that the reverse was the case : the goddess was more important than the god.

This leads us to some general considerations with regard to Minoan religion, on which hitherto I have touched but incidentally. Prof. Martin Nilsson has recently (1927) published a work on *The Minoan-Mycenaean Religion*, to which I have already more than once referred. It covers the whole ground, so far as we know it, in some detail, and devotes special attention to the matter of Minoan survivals in Hellenic religion, which of course he accepts without question. He sees old Minoan gods in the Laconian Hyakinthos and in Rhadamanthys, both of which have the non-Greek–νθ– termination in their names. The remarkable gold rings said to come from Thisbe in Boeotia, and published by Sir Arthur Evans (*J.H.S.*, 1925, p. 1 ff.), are, if their authenticity is certain, conclusive proof of such survival of legendary stories, and after all it is only to be expected that the religion and folk-tales of the Bronze Age people of Greece should have come down to their successors and partial descendants in the Age of Iron. On these rings we find older versions of such tales as that of Oedipus or that of Persephone (*ibid.*, Figs. 36, 16 ; see p. 280 n., below).

As Prof Nilsson says, " the standard work on Minoan religion is still, after twenty-five years, the treatise of Sir Arthur Evans on ' The Mycenaean Tree and Pillar Cult.' " As in Anatolia, the highest Minoan deity seems to have been a Mother-goddess, the Rhea of later Greece (Fig. 351). And with her was associated a god, it is true, but not as the Aryan Zeus was associated with his inferior consort the lady Hera : this Cretan god, Velchanos, was a double of the Anatolian Atys : a youthful god, who adores his mother, as her inferior. We see this in numberless representations, chiefly on gems ; as we have as yet no fresco representation of the two. We see him not seldom descending armed from the sky to place himself at the mother's side, or else he swoops down, with hair flying, upon the sea

(Fig. 352).[1]   The god seems to be the inferior being.   And the Cretans made their gods in their own image as surely as the later aryanized Greeks made theirs in theirs, with their Aryan Zeus and his inferior wife.   Then Velchanos was identified with Zeus ; but Zeus Kretagenes was always somewhat different from the Olympian who had conquered him and had absorbed him.   In old days, even as early as E.M. II, the *labrys* or double-axe (Figs. 11, 353) springing from the horns of the altar, or between the horns of a bull (Figs. 22, 354), was his emblem, and perhaps belonged to the goddess also.   The pillar (Figs. 355, 360). was an emblem of divinity, as in Syria and Palestine.   So also was the

FIG. 351.—THE MOTHER GOD-
DESS, ATTENDED BY PRIEST-
ESSES : THE GOD DESCENDS
ARMED FROM THE SKY, ON
THE LEFT.   GOLD RING :
MYCENAE
(*Actual size*)

FIG. 352.—POTTERY LARNAX
WITH REPRESENTATION OF
THE YOUNG GOD, HOLDING
A SHIELD, DESCENDING FROM
THE SKY UPON THE SEA. ($\frac{1}{16}$)

FIG. 353.—THE CLASHING OF
THE DOUBLE-AXES : FROM A
SEAL IMPRESSION
(*Enlarged*)

tree.   One of the most curious representations is that of a goddess in a fantastic boat, beneath a tree, on the gold ring from Mochlos (Fig. 355).   Snakes, perhaps regarded as chthonic animals, were venerated in connexion with the goddess as we see from the representations of the snake-priestesses or goddesses (Figs. 151–2).   Birds were associated with the sacred tree-pillar (Hagia Triada Sarcophagus, Fig. 283), —just as we see the Egyptian Horus-hawk perched on the sacred tree-pillar (the *Ded*) of Osiris (Fig. 19),—and also with the horned altar as well (Fig. 355).   Caves and clefts in the mountains, such as those of

[1] The upflying hair and the fish below indicate this in true Greek vase-painter's fashion.

276

Kavousi and of Arvi in Crete, the latter the seat of Zeus Arbios, were abodes of divinity (Fig. 357). Demons of the mountains, of wood and spring and sea (Fig. 358), Naiads, Nereids, and Hamadryads were

FIG. 354.—GODDESS HOLDING THE DOUBLE AXE AND RITUAL GARMENT (SEAL-IMPRESSION) (*Enlarged*)

FIG. 355.—GOLDEN REPRESENTATION OF A SHRINE, WITH PILLARS BETWEEN THE HORNS OF CONSECRATION, AND DOVES : MYCENAE (*Actual size*)

feared; sometimes water-demons, holding vases in their hands, were depicted in a form obviously borrowed from that of the Egyptian hippopotamus-goddess, Thoueris (Fig. 359). This is probably not a

FIG. 356.—THE GODDESS IN A BOAT, BENEATH A TREE. GOLD RING : MOCHLOS. L.M. I (*Enlarged*)

primeval borrowing, but a comparatively late one of Middle Minoan times. The hawk-headed gryphon, borrowed from Egypt at the same

277

time, accompanies the deities at a sedate walk, draws their cars (*Aeg. Arch.*, pl. xxix*a*), or guards sejant the throne of the Knossian priest-

FIG. 357.—THE GORGE OF KAVOUSI

king (Fig. 242), or the sacred pillar (Fig. 360). He is often, like the lion (also a sacred animal), represented at the " flying gallop (Fig. 361), as in

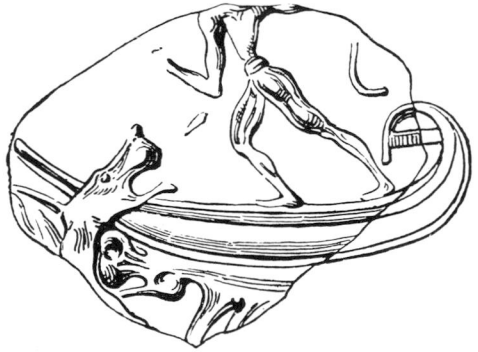

FIG. 358.—BOATMAN ATTACKED BY A SEA-
DEMON (SEAL-IMPRESSION)
(*Enlarged*)

FIG. 359.—WATER-DEMONS WITH TREE AND
ALTAR (SEAL-IMPRESSION)
(*Enlarged*)

Egypt, where the lively motion would seem to be of Minoan origin : such Egyptian representations first appear shortly before the XVIIIth

278

Dynasty (=M.M. III).[1] The huntress-goddess, who, like a similar divine hunter,[2] is accompanied by lions (Fig. 350), has already been mentioned. The Zakro sealings (Fig. 160), and Melian pots (Fig. 172), shew us what queer elves (some no doubt of semi-religious character), the Aegean artists could imagine. The seated winged sphinx of Thebes

FIG. 361.—GRYPHON AT THE FLYING GALLOP. GOLD:
MYCENAE
(*Actual size*)

FIG. 360.—PILLAR GUARDED BY
GRYPHONS (SEAL IMPRESSION)
(*Enlarged*)

FIG. 362.—THE BEZEL OF THE GOLD "RING OF NESTOR"
(*Magnified three times*)

[1] Evans, *Palace*, i., p. 713 ff. ; Fig. 534 ff. This "flying gallop," which certainly looks much more Minoan than Egyptian, became very popular under the XVIIIth Dynasty, and the Egyptian artists were fond of using it to represent the gambolling of calves, often on carved wooden toilet boxes.

[2] Nilsson, *Minoan-Myc. Religion*, p. 328 ff.

was already known (Fig. 369).[1]   Very curious representations, undoubtedly of a religious nature, occur on the wonderful gold ring from the *tholos* " of Nestor " at Kakovatos, published by Sir Arthur Evans (Fig.

362) ; but whether they refer to the after-death, as Sir Arthur thinks,[2] or not, seems susceptible of argument.   The gryphon-headed women who on it appear to take charge of a human pair are certainly of the other world as weirdly imagined by the Minoans.[3]

A curious object of religious import was the " sacral knot," a sort of fringed towel or napkin tied in a knot, which is so often represented in religious scenes [4] (Fig. 363).   Trumpets (Fig. 364) and shawms were used in religion, and the conch was as sacred as in India (Fig. 365). Great rhytons or filler-vases, sometimes in the form of bulls' heads (Fig. 366, see pp. 144, 200),[5] were used in the service of both gods and men.   As to places of worship, it is difficult to find among the buildings of Bronze Age Greece any temples on the vast scale of

FIG. 363.—THE "SACRAL KNOT" :
FAIENCE : MYCENAE
(*Actual size*)

[1] This should be remembered, and we should not be too startled if we find Persephone or Oedipus and the sphinx (in an altered form) on a Minoan gold ring, or any other Greek legend, in fact.   Anything is possible (see Evans, *J.H.S.* xxv, pp. 15, 27).

[2] Evans, *J.H.S.*, 1925, p. 53 ff.   The illustration here is enlarged three diameters.   The curious drops or blobs surrounding the bodies of the men and women shewn on it represent their hair (a convention usual on the gold rings).

[3] The eagle-headed and winged figures of the Assyrians were probably priests dressed to play parts, but they represented beings of the world of the gods and demons.

[4] For a somewhat similar Egyptian object, of funerary import, *cf*. Brit. Mus. No. 708 (Hall, *Hierogl. Texts*, v, p. 10, pl. 32 ; *Journ. Eg. Arch.* xiv (1928).

[5] This magnificent object is made of black steatite, its nostrils were inlaid with white shell, its eyes painted behind crystal inlay, and its horns of gilt wood.   It was found in the " Little palace " of Knossos (Evans, *Tomb of the Double Axes*, 79 ff.).

those of Egypt and Mesopotamia. The gods seem to have been worshipped in certain rooms of a palace, and in all kinds of sacred spots in the open air or in caves. Lustral ceremonies seem to have been performed in tank-like spaces in the palaces, approached by descending steps, which used to be taken for baths (Fig. 367). Great vats for libations were placed between pillars, as we see in the "Little Palace," and between the two trees on the Hagia Triada sarcophagus, where a priestess officiates. Images for household use were often of the crudest description (Fig. 368). The act of worship seems to have been accompanied by the use of a sort of salute (Fig. 225 ff.), standing up. Votive objects, such as model axes, etc., were dedicated in thou-

FIG. 365.—PRIESTESS BLOWING A CONCH BEFORE THE ALTAR, WITH SACRED PINE-TREES AND HORNS OF CONSECRATION (SEAL IMPRESSION) (*Enlarged*)

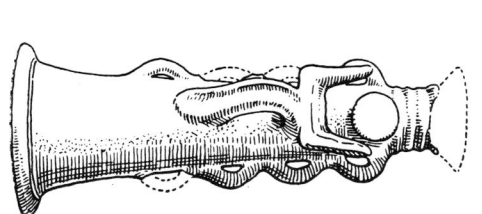

FIG. 364.—POTTERY MODEL RITUAL TRUMPET (?): GOURNIÀ

sands to reinforce the prayers of the devotees. Of the priesthood we know nothing, but can see that priestesses were of equal importance with, or perhaps greater importance than, priests.

The Hagia Triada sarcophagus (Fig. 293) gives us suggestions as to the rites of funerary religion, and we see that chants were sung at the grave to the sound of barbiton or lyre : in this religious ceremony some of the men wear female dress. In such ceremonies priestesses probably led the rites, and if a man took a subordinate part, he apparently had sometimes to be dressed as a woman, like the Lydian priests.[1] The men have their hair shorn, in token of grief (?). There

[1] Ramsay, *Asianic Elements in Greek Civilization*, p. 174.

281

were religious dances, in which a string of women were led by a leaping and pirouetting man, exactly as in the modern χορός, which has

FIG. 366.—BULL-RHYTON : LITTLE PALACE, KNOSSOS. ($\frac{1}{5}$)

descended unaltered from Minoan days. The dances of the warrior Kouretes, whose name seems to refer to their maiden-like appearance (χλιδῶν τε πλόκαμος ὥστε παρθένοις ἁβραῖς·, ὅθεν καλεῖν Κουρῆτα λαὸν ἤνεσαν),[1] were famous in later Greece. Funerary games no doubt were celebrated, and then there is the oft-mentioned bull-leaping, which was certainly of a sacred character.

FIG. 367.—LUSTRAL AREA : KNOSSOS

It gives us an impression of cruelty underlying this brilliant civilization, which is confirmed by the dread legend of the Minotaur. There was a Roman or Spanish touch about these Cretans that was not prominent in the classical Greeks. There was an atmosphere of eerie mystery about the Labyrinth, the Minotaur, and Minos himself in the minds of the later Greeks. The Cretans seem sometimes, in some ways, to have resembled those dark and inscrutable Etruscans, who may have been their relatives, whether they came from Anatolia or not.[2] The Etruscan characteristics of Rome are those which remind us of Labyrinth and Minotaur. Yet cruel though it may have been, the Minoan culture was not gloomy as that of the Etruscans is supposed to have been ; perhaps wrongly, just as that of Egypt has been similarly misjudged. Like the Egyptians, the Minoans seem to us rather a joyous than a gloomy

FIG. 368.—CRUDE HOUSEHOLD IMAGE OF A GODDESS : L.M. III, KNOSSOS. ($\frac{1}{3}$)

[1] Aesch. Fragm. 322 (310 Paley) ; Athenaeus, xii, 37 (528 c) ; quoted by Evans, *J.H.S*, 1925, p. 14, n. 33.   [2] See p. 240, *antea*.

people. The Egyptians were much preoccupied with the state of the dead in the underworld ; but that made them all the more inclined to enjoy life while they had it. And we do not see that the Minoans were so interested in the dead as the Egyptians or worshipped quite such weird and gloomy infernal deities as the Etruscans. Their life as revealed to us in their art was singularly free, joyous, and artistic, full of love of beautiful things, almost too aesthetic. The court of Knossos resembles the court of good king René, with his troubadours (unless we ought to compare it rather with that of a mediaeval Italian prince, like Borso d'Este). It was to their Minoan not to their Indo-European ancestors that the later Greeks owed their own aesthetic characteristics and their supreme love of beauty. Probably they did not owe their political ideas to the Minoans : this side of the Greek genius must be due to the Aryan blood which gave them their language. Of the political ideas of the Minoans we know nothing. In all probability they were ruled by despotic monarchs of the Egyptian type, and it may be that these also had a priestly character, so that " Minos " was high-priest as well as king. The legendary Minos was a law-giver, but we know nothing of his laws. Nor do we know anything of other traits of a highly civilized state, such as a current means of exchange, though commerce certainly existed, as in Egypt, with, of course, fixed weights, but without any currency, and account-lists were certainly kept, as we see from Knossian inscribed tablets. The general state of civilization in such matters was possibly analogous to that of Egypt. Towns were many ; the population large.

I may perhaps be allowed to quote at length, (although I do not altogether agree with it, as will be seen from my omissions and comments), an appreciation of the Bronze Age civilization of Greece from the pen of Prof. V. Gordon Childe.[1]

"We have seen that Minoan civilization was deeply indebted both to Mesopotamia and Egypt. Now I must insist that it was no mere copy of either, but an original and creative force. As such Crete stands out as essentially modern in outlook. The Minoan spirit was thoroughly European and in no sense Oriental. A comparison with Egypt and Meso-

---

[1] *Dawn of European Civilization*, p. 29.

potamia will make the contrast plain. . . . The Cretan artist was not limited to perpetua-
ting the cruel deeds of a selfish despot nor doomed to formalism by the innate conservatism
of priestly superstition. Hence the modern naturalism, the truly occidental feeling for life
and nature that distinguish Minoan vase paintings, frescoes, and intaglios . . . I do not of
course mean that the Minoans were either democrats or atheists. Chiefs and kings there
were, but a study of the plans of a Minoan city such as Gournià, Palaikastro, or Vasiliki, will
betray no extreme disparity among the houses . . . Traces of an overgrown and complicated
priesthood such as exercised a fatal sway in Egypt and Babylon there were none. Besides the
palaces themselves the only places of worship were rustic mountain shrines and sacred caves."

Personally I consider that the debt to Egypt was much greater than
that to Babylonia, but Prof. Childe is the first to insist in some detail on
the undoubted fact that there did exist a debt to Babylonia. To the
truth of his remarks on the occidental character of Minoan art those
who really know ancient Egypt and Babylonia can bear their testimony.
It is only to those who have but the most superficial acquaintance with
the ancient East that Minoan civilization appears Oriental. Prof. Childe
himself, however, has something to learn with regard to the Easterns.
To say, as he does later, that " we find in Crete none of those stupendous
palaces that betoken the aristocratic power of the oriental despot " is
surely rendered impossible by the mere facts of Knossos and Phaistos,
which are more " stupendous " than any Assyrian royal palace, and in
comparison with which Egyptian royal palaces were but collections of
glorified mud huts, beautifully decorated but still made of mud brick :
stone was only used for the dwellings of the gods. " Gigantic temples "
did not exist, it is true, in Crete unless the palaces were also temples,
as Sir Arthur Evans implies, and to quote the absence of pyramids as
revealing " an excessive preoccupation with ghostly things " in comparison with Cretan tombs is hardly fair, as the Pyramids were an exception in Egypt. Prof. Childe adds: " Even at Knossos, in the days of its
hegemony, frescoes were not restricted to the royal residence." Nor
were they in Egypt.

We must too remember that the Egyptians also depicted " charming
scenes of games and processions, animals and fishes, flowers and trees,"
not so freely, or with " so European an atmosphere " as the Minoans,
it is true, but with equal charm in their own way. And we must remember also that the Minoans owed their first inspiration to depict these

things properly to the Egyptians, though they did it in their own way. To appreciate Crete we need not unduly depreciate Egypt. Prof. Childe's remarks that follow about industry and the attachment of industrial workshops, etc., to palaces and temples, as foreshadowing " the most distinctive feature of European civilization," I do not follow, as precisely the same thing existed in Egypt and Babylonia.

What the last half-century has revealed to us of the Greek culture of the Bronze Age I have endeavoured to sketch in these lectures. It is a new age that has been revealed to us, that saw the origins of, at any rate, Greek art and of most of that that makes Greek things of the classical age gracious and sympathetic to us; further, it is therefore the age that ultimately was the original of most of that that is gracious and sympathetic in our own modern life, of amenity and of φιλοκαλία, though perhaps not so much of φιλοσοφία. But this we do not know: the philosophic debt of the later Greeks to the earlier is less easy to appraise than the philocalic. Still, in the realm of art and amenity and aesthetic the Minoan was our culture-ancestor, through the classic Greek, and so the Aryan world of " Wiros " owes its artistic inspiration to the Mediterranean non-Aryans in the beginning as it always has during the succeeding centuries when Greeks and Italians, like Bengalis, have spoken Aryan tongues without being themselves of aught but much mixed Aryan blood. We may instance various minor characteristics of the classical Greeks that with more or less reason we may be inclined to trace to their Minoan rather than to their Indo-European ancestors; but we may say that while on the whole they no doubt owed their political ideas and genius to their Aryan ancestry, their love of beauty and all μουσική they derived from the Minoans, as the Northerner always has derived it from the Mediterranean. In the Greek love of symmetry and proportion, of ordered beauty, we see the union of both characteristics, a ἱερὸς γάμος of the two racial minds that existed in the Greek brain.

FIG. 369.—THE (Actual  MYCENAEAN SPHINX size)

286

APPENDIX

ON THE RACIAL AFFINITIES OF THE IN-HABITANTS OF GREECE IN THE BRONZE AGE

I HAVE in these lectures distinguished between the Minoan and the Indo-European ancestors of the classical Greeks. To some classical students the idea that the Greeks may have had any but an Indo-European origin still seems to be a hard saying. We still have attempts to interpret Knossian hiero-glyphs by means of Aryan Greek. The view that the Minoan Cretans were prob-ably not Aryans seems difficult for some to credit, and historians of Greece [1] seem disinclined to admit any but an Aryan ancestry for the Greeks, although they may grudgingly admit that the "Pelasgi" may have been pre-Aryan. No doubt they were, and they were the non-Aryan predecessors and part-ancestors of the Greeks, from whom the poets transferred the great deeds of the heroic age to the Aryan Achaians (see above, p. 267). Let us drop the somewhat abused terms "Aryan" and "Indo-European," and speak of the "Wiros," as Dr. Peter Giles does.[2] In my belief, which is shared I think by most others, the Minoans were not "Wiros" or "Nordic," or even "Alpine" in origin, nor did they speak Greek. No one will deny that they were not "Nordics." Their representations, whether by their own or by Egyptian artists, depict them as a brunet race, black-haired, very like the modern Italians. Few Italian *savants* would, I think, claim their fellow-country-men as "Nordics" in race, south of the Apennines, though north of it they may, if they regard "Alpines" as "Nordics," and recognize any of the true Nordic blood of the Lombards as still existing. They would agree, I think, that the great majority of the Italian race is Mediterranean, a brunet race distinct from the Cen-tral and Northern Europeans. It was an Italian, Sergi, who clearly differentiated the Mediterranean race, which is that to which the majority of the neolithic peoples of south and west Europe, even as far as Britain, belonged. In Crete the develop-ment of the Bronze Age civilization directly, without a break, from the neolithic, is clear. The neolithic Cretans were probably akin to the Asian tribes of Anatolia,

[1] *e.g.* Prof. Bury, *in Cambr. Anc. Hist.*, ii.
[2] *Cambr. Anc. Hist.*, ii, p. 23 ff.; and *Cambr. Hist. India*, i, p. 66 ff.

with a strong intrusive element from Libya and the Egyptian Delta, who can hardly have been Aryans ! We have only at the end of the Early Minoan period trace of an invasion of broad-heads, probably from Anatolia, which we may perhaps connect with the arrival of the Minyan pottery in Greece itself. The broad-heads brought, however, no Minyan pottery to Crete, if it was theirs, and we see no trace of any foreign influence which they can have exerted on the development of Cretan culture, which continued on its own way undisturbed by them. They caused no radical change like that of the dark age succeeding the Minoan-Mycenaean power, when the Achaian Wiros ruled. They must have been comparatively few in number and soon absorbed. In any case they are likely to have been of native Anatolian (Asianic) blood and speech, not " Wiros," but if they were, they had no influence on Crete. As has been said, the appearance of the Minoans, of the First Late Minoan period, is Mediterranean ; and there is in them no trace of fair hair or complexion ; perhaps these broad-heads were not conspicuously fair, that is to say there was nothing particularly " Nordic " about them. Now the Achaians, the Homeric Greeks, were fair in comparison with the Mediterraneans. They were brown or auburn-haired (ξανθοί) and evidently the fairer they were the more beautiful they were considered, and Apollo was χρυσοχαίτης, perhaps red-gold haired, rather than yellow-haired : the Homeric Greeks were never of Teutonic complexion. The Tanagra figures and Athenian funerary lekythoi give us cop-pery-red or brown hair side by side with dark-brown or black, and generally fair complexions, resembling a certain Irish Celtic type.[1] This ruddy complexion and rufous or fair-brown hair must be in Greece the contribution of people from the North, obviously, since there are no other claimants, the Aryan Greeks, the " Wiros " who invaded Greece and brought the Greek language thither. They were not in Crete in Minoan days, or probably in the Aegean at all. Is it likely that the Medi-terraneans who were in Crete and the Aegean then talked the language of " Wiros " ? They were not Wiros : they had been there since neolithic days. And we have the tradition of the non-Greek-speaking Pelasgi (representing, as Prof. Myres pointed out,[2] " pre-Hellenic " in much the same way as " British " is popularly used in England for " pre-Roman "), and the apparently non-Aryan Eteocretan inscriptions, besides the wealth in Greek of non-Aryan and the numberless place-names that are insusceptible of interpretation in any tongue of " Wiros." Like Sanskrit,[3] Greek, with all its entirely Indo-European syntax and grammar, has a vast non-Indo-European vocabulary. The reason was the

[1] *Pace* the poets, of course the Irish Celts were never dark : the " black " people in Ireland and Wales are pre-Celtic, in fact Mediterraneans.
[2] " A History of the Pelasgian Theory," *J.H.S.*, 1907, p. 170 ff. ; esp. p. 221.
[3] Berriedale Keith, *Cambr. Hist. India*, i, p. 110.

288

APPENDIX

same in both cases. In both lands the invading Wiros found a previously-existing non-Aryan race with which they mingled, the Hindus with the Dravidians, the Greeks with the Minoans, and in both cases while the language of the conqueror prevailed, that of the conquered supplied innumerable names and words to its vocabulary. In both countries the conquered race continued to exist side by side with the conquerors, the dark Dasyus with the fair Aryans, the dark Minoans with the fairer Hellenes. Their blood mingled, and in classic days in Greece fair and dark Greeks existed side by side, the fairer being regarded as the nobler and more beautiful, as in India the fair *varna* (colour) of the Aryans continued among the Brahmans and Kshatriyas, and was the foundation of the caste-distinction between them (with the Vaisyas) and the Sudras.[1] Now, in both countries, the fair *varna* has practically disappeared, as it has also in Italy and Spain, in spite of reinforcement by Gauls, Lombards, and Visigoths, though, to judge from the pictures, it still existed there among the nobles as late as the sixteenth century A.D. In Greece one can only meet with an occasional ruddy-fair type in Crete or the islands. The dark people have conquered in the end, but they speak the speech of their ancient conquerors, as the Bengali, who has hardly an ounce of Aryan blood in his veins, talks an Aryan language. What his Mongol-Dravidian ancestors talked we do not know; I suppose something akin to Tamil or Telugu, or something Mongoloid. Nor do we know what the Minoans talked, but it was probably something akin to Etruscan or to the Asianic dialects of Anatolia, to which Etruscan may have been allied, or it may have been like Libyan or Egyptian, or have elements of both Asianic and north-African speech. The believer in Minoan Hellenism may point to the fact that in Anatolia the Hittites spoke an Indo-European tongue, apparently more akin to Latin than to Greek, as early as 1400 B.C.[2] That is true. The Aryan Hittite speech was apparently the tongue of a ruling tribe, of the king and his aristocracy, and was used for the purposes of the royal chancery and archives (the Boghaz Kyöi tablets); but seven other languages seem also to have been spoken and some of them written in the Anatolian realm of the Hittites, most of which were distinctly un-Aryan, including the "Protohattic" which was probably the tongue of the people whom the aristocracy of "Wiros" ruled.[3] In fact Anatolia had already been conquered by one tribe of "Wiros" just as Greece was shortly going to be by another, coming from the Central-European plain which, as Dr. Peter Giles has acutely suggested, rather than South Russia, is to be regarded as the *Aryânem vaêjô*, the original home of the Wiros and the Indo-European

---

[1] *Ibid.*, p. 92; P. Giles, *ibid.*, p. 54.

[2] Discovered by Hrozný; reff. in Hall, *Anc. Hist. N.E.*, 7th edition (1927), p. 329.

[3] Forrer, *Mitth. Deutsch-Orient Gesellschaft*, 61, p. 23 ff. Cf. Hall, in *Anatolian Studies*, p. 168 ff.

tongues. The fact that an Aryan tongue was spoken in Hittite-land, when Minoans still ruled in Crete, in no way makes it probable that those Minoans spoke an Aryan tongue yet. Still, in all probability, the language of the "Wiros" was already spoken in Northern Continental Greece at that time by the ancestors of the Achaians. It is in fact not impossible that it had been spoken already for many centuries north of the isthmus of Corinth, and possibly even some way at some time into the Peloponnese, where neolithic pottery of the Dimini type is known, which I personally am inclined to identify hypothetically as the pottery of the first "Wiros," in Greece, coming from Transylvania (see pp. 22, 62). Here they were swamped by the native Pelasgic element and overlaid by others from Crete and the Cyclades. The Mycenaeans then possibly had some "Wiro" blood in them. Then at the end of the Mycenaean Age, the Achaians, genuine "Wiros," moved southward from Thessaly, and brought with them the Greek language, to be followed two centuries later by the Dorians. The Ionians are the example of the mixed race half Achaian, half Pelasgic, produced by the first invasion. If the "Dimini" Thessalians were the ancestors of the Achaians, and were "Wiros," we should have to place the first arrival of "Wiros" in Thessaly about 2500 B.C., which is not impossibly early. The royal Hittites in Asia Minor will represent a somewhat later migration from Europe, while that of the Indians, of whom we find an *étape* left behind in Mitanni about 1400 B.C.,[1] may have been roughly contemporary in its starting with the movement that brought the ancestors of the Aryan Greeks as far as the Isthmus of Corinth, not far south of which they were stopped, probably by the impossibility of penetrating further the mass of the Mediterranean population, and were thrown back to Othrys, just as the Indian Aryas were stopped by the mass of the snub-nosed *Anāsah* ("the noseless ones") on the line of the Narbadá and the Vindhya hills.

We should then deprecate any attempt to discover "Wiros" and "Greeks" in Crete or the southern islands before about 1250 B.C., at earliest, though of course, if the cogency of Prof. Forrer's identification of the names Antaravas and Tavagalavas with Andreus and Etewoklewes of Orchomenos as early as about 1330 is admitted (and as I have stated I prefer to suspend judgment on the subject at present, for several reasons; see p. 250), we have Greeks in Boeotia and warring in Lesbos (Lazbas) in the latter half of the fourteenth century. But Boeotia and Lesbos are not Crete and the southern islands, and, as I have said, it is not probable that "Wiros" came there and to Cyprus before the days of the Akaivasha and Attarissiyas (?), *c.* 1225 B.C. I do not accept the identification of Alakshandu of Vilusa as an "Alexandros of Ialysos" at all (p. 251), since the equivalence of the names is impossible, quite apart from the difficulty of his early date (1400–1350),

[1] See p. 85, n.1.

APPENDIX

when, therefore, I see no reason to suppose Greeks so far south as Rhodes. It seems to me that we cannot talk of Achaian Greeks, and so of Wiros, in Rhodes, or Crete, or Cyprus, till at least a hundred years later.

The parallel of the conquest of Greece by the Achaians to that of the conquest of Northern India by the Aryas appears apposite. The difference between the two perhaps lies in the comparative degrees of culture attained by conquerors and conquered in the respective countries. In Greece we know that a highly cultured luxuriously civilized race that had degenerated was overthrown by a comparatively barbarous people. In India we are less instructed. How much of Vedic civilization was really due to the conquered Dravidians we do not know. On the face of it, it would seem probable that here the two contestants were more on an equality of culture. But we may yet discover that Northern India in pre-Aryan days was an ancient home of civilization, as we have found out in the last half-century that Greece was. And the recent discoveries of prehistoric Indian culture, closely related to that of the Sumerians and dating from the third millennium B.C., at Harappā in the Punjab and at Mohenjo Daro in Sind,[1] are extremely significant.

[1] See *Encycl. Britt.*, 13th ed., new vol. i, *s.v.* Archæology (W. Asia), for references.

ADDITIONAL NOTES

1. The very interesting fragment of stone relief in the British Museum, illustrated in my *Aegean Archæology*, Pl. xxxi, 2, shewing the head and shoulders of a leaping bull, with olive trees in the background, should have been mentioned and re-illustrated here *à propos* of the bull-leaping and its representations. It is a very important piece of Minoan sculpture, and has interested many writers, notably Prof. Lethaby (*J.H.S.*, 1917, p. 1 ; *The Builder*, Feb. 6, 1914, p. 154). For an illustration of it I refer readers to *Aegean Archæology*, *loc. cit.*, where the photograph admirably reproduces it, or to Bossert, *Altkreta*, 2, Pl. 237, 1. Its Minoan character is strikingly evident. An interesting point is the representation of the coloured patches on the bull's hide in the conventional quatrefoil form commonly seen on Mycenaean representations of bulls, and closely paralleled in Egypt (see p. 25, n. 1). This point alone would be quite enough to determine the Minoan-Mycenaean character of the relief, even if this were not already sufficiently evident from the treatment of the bull's head and the tree. It belongs to the Elgin collection, but its provenance is unknown, though it may be considered with some probability to have come from Mycenae. M. Perrot, who published a rather poor illustration of it placed on one side, and described it as a lion, in his *Histoire de l'Art*, vi, p. 646, thinks that it and another slab shewing the lower part of the legs of a bull " ont appartenu à des tombes-à-coupole " at Mycenae. The fact that it is a bull, not a lion, that is represented, was pointed out by Hauser in *Jhb. Arch. Inst.*, 1894, p. 54 ff. (I owe this reference to Mr. F. N. Pryce, of the Department of Greek and Roman Antiquities). I do not believe in Perrot's idea that the leaves of the olive or laurel (?) bush were inlaid in metal : for me the raised portions of the relief depicting the tree represent the foliage, the sunk portions, which Perrot thinks were inlaid, " . . . le creux des feuilles parait avoir été recouvert par une feuille de bronze . . ." being simply the interstices between the leaves.

2. A point of great importance has been raised by Prof. A. A. Zakhárov, of Moscow, in an article entitled *Kavkaz, Malaya Aziya i Egeiskii Mir* (" Caucasus, Asia Minor, and the Aegean World ") in *Inst. Arch. Aesth. Mosc. Tr. Arch. ; Sect. II.* (1928), pp. 33–45, in which he compares both the slashing swords (see above, p. 253, Figs. 329, 330) and daggers (Fig. 317) of the Shardina and Pulesatha with extraordinarily similar swords and daggers of copper and bronze from the Caucasus in the Russian museums, and the ball-and-crescent helmet of the Shardina with the crescent-horned helmets of copper figurines of the same origin. The resemblance is striking, as is also the likeness of the Caucasian figurines to those of Sardinian warriors of the Bronze Age (cf. Perrot-Chipiez, *Hist. de l'Art*, iv. pp. 53–56), which have often been compared with the Egyptian representation of the Shardina, and with justice (*ibid.*, p. 14 ff. ; Figs. 4–6). The conclusion will be that the Shardina, who did colonize Sardinia and gave it its name, came, with other peoples of the sea, as both Brugsch and Petrie have surmised, ultimately from the Caucasus. But it is probable that they came all the way round by sea from the ends of the Euxine, rather than across country, to Syria, where we find the Shardina on the coast of Phoenicia as early as the fifteenth century B.C., and the Danuna and Shaka-

292

lasha as well. Leaving these out of account, since we have no reason to suppose them to be Caucasians or aught but Aegeans and West Anatolians (Sagalassians), the Shardina must certainly be supposed to have reached Syria by sea from the Caucasus in the fifteenth century, and eventually passed on to Sardinia in the age of confusion that began in the thirteenth. The bearing of Prof. Zakhárov's find on the question of the origins of the Pulesatha (Philistines) who were certainly, as their weapons show, nearly related to the Shardina, is very important. Ultimately they also must have been of Caucasian origin. (The big sword, seen, as Prof. Zakhárov points out, in the tombs of Menkheperre'senb and Senmut, borne by Keftian Minoans, may either be a Minoan borrowing from this Caucasian weapon-centre or an independent Minoan broad type of which we have no actual representatives except the much older (M.M. I.) sword from Mallia, Fig. 102, above.)

3. In *Man*, March, 1928, 33, p. 49, Mr. H. Frankfort refers to "the extraordinary importance" in connexion with the discussion as to the geographical extension of the term *Keftiu* (see above, p. 203 ff.) of the supposed figures of men of Anatolian type wearing the Minoan girdle on two silver *pinakes* found "in a cave in Cilicia" with "the most miscellaneous objects of Hittite, Greek, and Roman age," and now at Berlin, published by Valentin Müller, *Ath. Mitth.* 50 (1925), p. 63, pl. vi, 2, 3. I should say that I am not personally much impressed with the supposed Minoan appearance of these figures : belts and kilts, after all, were worn in Asia Minor as in Crete : the characteristic Minoan waist is absent from these figures, and there is no kilt or waistclout that can be seen. I do not therefore admit that this find supplies us with the needed archaeological proof that Minoans ever lived in Cilicia. The Hittite cylinder-seal, with two long-haired and belted figures fighting with daggers while a judge (?) of the same appearance stands by, published by V. Müller, *Jhb. Arch. Inst.*, 1927, p. 25, Fig. 12, seems to me to afford no Anatolian parallel to Minoan art at all, but shews a deliberate borrowing from it by a Hittite *Mischkunst*. *These* figures are Minoan, obviously ; but the scene is an imitation or adaptation of a Minoan motive, as the *ankh* sign between the two contending figures is an imitation of an Egyptian motive, by the *Mischkünstler*.

4. Sir Arthur Evans has in the recently published second volume of his *Palace of Minos* (ii, p. 211 ff.) described and illustrated the M.M. II. polychrome pottery found by Mr. R. Engelbach in XIIth Dynasty graves at Harāgeh, near Lahun, in Egypt. This was described but not illustrated by Engelbach in his book *Harageh* (with the exception of a single pot with crinkly rim, pl. x, 8, which looks to me of Kamárais style, so far as can be judged from the photograph). It is important as evidence confirming the XIIth Dynasty date of the Middle Minoan period, if any is needed.

5. *A propos* of Minoan building-methods (p. 100) it should be noted that in the new second volume of *The Palace of Minos* Sir Arthur Evans records in the Little Palace at Knossos (L.M.I.) "remains of upper stories showing sun-dried brick construction, the bricks being about 45 cm. square and 12 cm. high. . . . . Good examples of similar brick structures occurred in the S. E. Magazines of the Great Palace" (p. 519). Brick was rarely used in Crete. The square form of the bricks points to a Babylonian rather than an Egyptian origin for Minoan bricks. In a stony country like Greece brick is not a native invention.

CHRONOLOGICAL TABLE

APPROX. DATE B.C.	EGYPT	CRETE	AEGEAN	SOUTHERN GREECE	NORTHERN GREECE	ASIATIC COAST	CYPRUS	PALESTINE AND SYRIA	ANATOLIA	MESOPOTAMIA
4500	*Late Neolithic* (*Predynastic*)									*Neolithic ?*
4000						*Neolithic*			*Neolithic*	
3500	EARLY BRONZE AGE *Chalcolithic* (*Predynastic*)	*Neolithic* Knossos (Egyptian influx ?) Magasa				?	*Neolithic*			BRONZE AGE (*Chalcolithic*) al-ʿUbaid ; Shahrain
3200	1st IInd } Dyns. IIIrd }	EARLY BRONZE AGE *Sub-Neolithic Chalcolithic* E.M.I.	EARLY BRONZE AGE (*Chalcolithic*) E.C.I.	*Neolithic* Gonia	*Neolithic* Thessaly I Phokis Lianokladi	Troy I	*Neolithic ?* Kalavaso ?		BRONZE AGE ?	1st Dyn. of Ur (A-anni-padda) al-ʿUbaid
2800	IIIrd–IVth (Pyramid-kings)	Knossos H. Onouphrios Miamu E.M. II	Cyclades	EARLY BRONZE AGE (*Chalcolithic*) E.H.		EARLY BRONZE AGE		BRONZE AGE ?		Patesis of Lagash (Ur-Ninâ)
2500	VIth Dyn. (Pepi I) VIIth–Xth Dyns.	Mochlos Vasiliki E.M. III Knossos	E.C. II Phylakopi (Bronze) E.C. III	(Dimini invasion ?) Korakou	EARLY BRONZE AGE Thessaly II Dimini (invasion) Thessaly III	(Bronze) Troy II	EARLY BRONZE AGE (Copper)		(Semitic influx into Argaeus region)	Dyn. of Akkad (Sargon ; Naramsin) Lagash (Gudea)
2300 or 2100	MIDDLE BRONZE AGE (*Bronze*) XIth Dyn.	MIDDLE BRONZE AGE (*Bronze*) M.M. I {a b}	MIDDLE BRONZE AGE M.C. I	MIDDLE BRONZE AGE (*Bronze*) M.H.	Lianokladi Thessaly IV	Troy {III IV V}	MIDDLE BRONZE AGE (*Bronze*)	(Syrian expansion E. and S.)	(Oldest Hittite kingdom ?)	IIIrd Dyn. of Ur (Ur-Nammu ; Shulgi) (*Bronze*) 1st Dyn. of Babylon.
2100 or 1900	XIIth Dyn. (Senusret II) Lahun	Knossos Mallia M.M. II {a b}	Phylakopi M.C. II	*Minyan*	and *Minyan*	Troy VI *Minyan*				(Hammurabi) *Syrians*
2000 or 1800	Harâgeh (Amenemhet III)	Kamarais Phaistos	*Minyan*	Orchomenos Korakou						

	Egypt	Crete	Cyclades / C. Greece	Mycenae / Mainland		Crete-Mainland	Syria	Egypt-Palestine	Hittites / Anatolia	Assyria / Babylonia
?1800	XIIIth Dyn. & HYKSOS PERIOD	M.M. III Knossos {a / b	M.C. III	M.M. III Mycenae				(Hyksos invasion of Egypt)		(Early Assyrian kings)
1700	LATER BRONZE AGE	LATER BRONZE AGE	LATER BRONZE AGE	LATER BRONZE AGE			(Hyksos pottery)			
	HYKSOS PERIOD and XVIIth Dyn.		L.C. I	Mycenae Kakovatos L.M. I =				(Expulsion of Hyksos from Egypt)	(Early Hittite kings)	
1600		Hag. Triada L.M. I. a (*Keftiu*)		= (L.H. I) = = Myc. I Vapheio						
	XVIIIth Dyn. (Thutmosis III) Gurob	L.M.I. b. Knossos					LATER BRONZE AGE (Syrian pottery)	(Egyptian Conquest)		(Mitannian Kingdom)
1500		L.M. II (Fall of Knossos)	L.C. II	(L.H. II) = = Myc. II						KASSITE PERIOD
1400	(Amenhetep III) (Akhenaten) el-Amarna (*Iron*)	(Reoccupation period) L.M. III	a = (L.C. III) Ialysos	(L.H. III) = Myc. III	= Late Mycenaean a.			(Revolt supported by Hittites) (*Iron*)	(Shubbiluliu)	
1300	XIXth Dyn. (Rameses II Meneptah)	Milatos	(Peoples of the Sea) b = Myc. III b.					(Wars between Egypt and the Hittites)	(Mutallu and Mursilis; Khattusilis) (Philistine invasion. Fall of Khatti)	
	IRON AGE XXth Dyn. (Rameses III)		ACHAIAN PERIOD	Mycenae				(Philistine Conquest) Bethshemesh, Gezer	IRON AGE	IRON AGE
1200		Mouliana (*Sub-Mycenaean*)	Sub-*Mycenaean*					IRON AGE	(Phrygian domination)	(Rise of Assyria)
1100	XXIst Dyn.	Kavousi	IRON AGE (Dorian Invasion)		IRON AGE	*Sub-Mycenaean*		(Philistine Domination) (David: Solomon)		(Tiglath-pileser I)
1000	XXIInd Dyn.	*Geometric*		Dipylon			Cypro-Phoenician styles	(Israel and Judah)	(Shishak)	

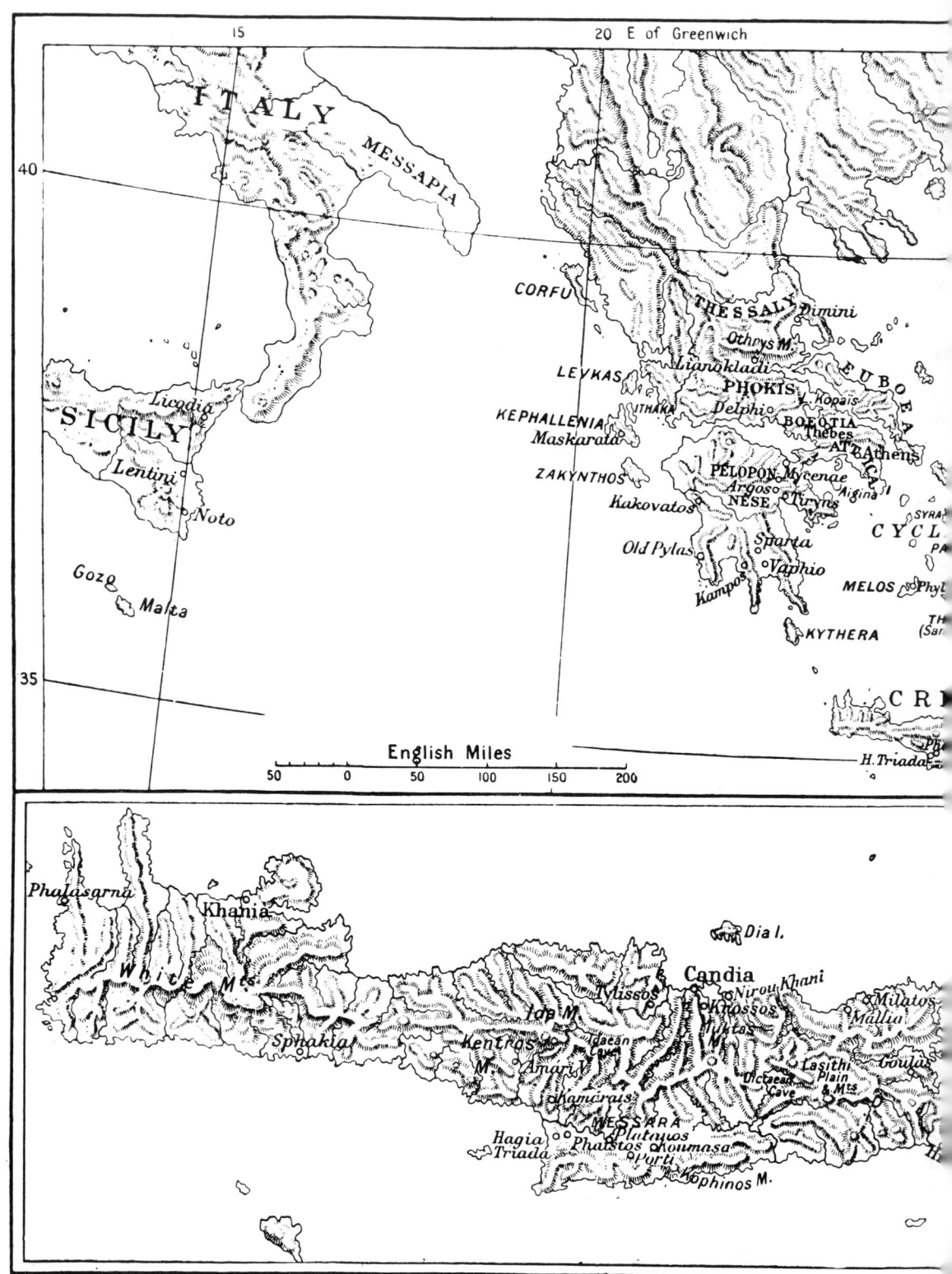

GREECE WITH INSETS OF

CENTRAL GREECE

EUBOEA

Delphi Orchomenos Gla
Chaironeia L. Kopais

BOEOTIA
Thebes

G. OF CORINTH

ATTICA

Menidi

Athens Spata

ARGOLIS

Korakou

Mycenae

Salamis
SARONIC GULF

Thorikos

Argos Tiryns
Phlamidi

Aigina

G. OF
NAUPLIA

English Miles
5 0 10 20

Hissarlik
(Troy)

(MASA?)

KALAKISHA

KODE

ESBOS

PIDASA

HIOS

SAMOS

CARIA

(ALAŠIYA)

AMURRU

ndriani
NAXOS KALYMNOS
AMORGOS KOS

LYCIA
LUKKI

Ialysos

Enkomi

RHODES

KARPATHOS
KASOS

KEFTIU
(KAPHTOR)

Hala Sultan Tekke

Byblos
(Gebal)

CANAAN

CYPRUS
(YANTINAI)?

Amathus

Palaikastro
Zakro
Ournià

Sidon

Tyre

Dor

CRETE

Jerusalem

English Miles
5 0 10 20

Gaza

Tell es Safi
Tell el-Hesy

Dionysiades
Is

Palaikastro

eiral
Mochlos Praisos
Kavousi
urna T E Zakro

Tanis

ra

EGYPT

Memphis

CENTRAL GREECE AND CRETE

INDEX

Abydos, M.M. pottery from, 74
Achaians, 18, 240 ff., 246 ff.; pottery, 261; armour, 265; Prof. Bury on, 248, 267; Dr. D. Mackenzie on, 260; Allen, Mr. J. W., on, 248; Hogarth, Dr., on, 247
Aestheticism, 272
Ahhiawa, n.l., 249
"Aigisthos, tomb of," 149
Akaivasha, tr.n., 240, 250
Akhenaten, k., 207
Akhetaten, n.l., 207
Alaskshandu, k., 251
Amarna, Tell el-, 207; Myc. pottery from, 220; jasper group from, 229; date of, 207
Amazons, 274
Amenhetep, II, k., 199, 211
Amenhetep, III, k., 208
Amorgos, 58
Amyklai (see Vapheio)
Anatolian influences on pottery, 49; religion, 275; invasion, 81, 111
Andrae, Dr., 226
Animistic worship, 277
Antaravas, k., 249
Antithetical groups, 146
Ape, on Minoan seals, 69; Knossian fresco, 118; Egyptian, from Mycenae, 211
Aradēn, n.l., 270
Architecture, 46, 95, 109 ff., 147 ff., 214
Architectural motives in art, 180
Argive Heraeum, 188; Minyan ware, 82
Arimaspian fighting gryphon, 229
Arkalokhori, n.l., 47, 56
Armour, 265
Art, characteristics of Minoan, 274; artistic legacy to the Greeks, 284
Artemis, 274
Aryans, 287; invasion of, 290
Ashmolean Museum, 4
Ashur, n.l., 225
Asinè, n.l., 188
Assarlik, n.l., 60, 263
Athens Museum, 3
Atreus, 250; "treasury of," 147, 151

Attarissiyas, n pr., 250, 290
Attica, Dorians in, 260
Atys, 275

Babylonian seal from Platanos, 107; influences in Minoan art and culture, 93, 123, 160, 191, 285
Barbiton, 281
Barbotine ware, 75, 129
Beak-vases, 48
Beards, 145; bearded head of a man in stags' horn, 242
Beads, 198
Birds in religious representations, 26, 276; ceramic decoration, 168, 220, 246; frescoes, 118
"Black Earth" region, 60, 64
Black soldiers in Crete, fresco, 119, 206
Blegen, Dr., 19, et passim
"Blue Boy" fresco, Knossos, 102
Boar-hunt fresco, Tiryns, 231
Boar's-tusk helmets, 136
Boats, 34
Boeotia, early culture of, 22, 61
Boots, 185
Boston Museum, figure at, 41, 171
Boyd-Hawes, Mrs., 164, et passim
Brick buildings, 293
British Museum, 3
Britomartis, 274
Bronze, 87; weapons (q.v.); praying figures, 173 ff.; bull-leaping group, 172
Bügelkanne (see stirrup-vase)
Building (see Architecture)
Bulls, 15, 26, 276; fighting, 187; leaping (taurokathapsia), 172, 183, 219; bronze group, 172; fresco, 185; bull's head rhytons, 26, 280; head in coloured gesso, Knossos, 186; legends, 15
Burial-customs, 188 ff.
Bury, Prof., 18, 248, 267
Butmir, n.l., 63

Candia Museum, 3, 8
"Caravansarai," the, at Knossos, 117
Carians, 60, 138

Casson, Mr. S., 268
" Cat and Pheasant " fresco, Hagia Triada, 118
Caucasus, 292
Cauldrons, copper, 164
Caves, burial, 23, 40, 107 ; in religion, 276
Celts, 29
Ceramic (see Pottery)
Cesnola collection, 4
Chaironeia, 61
Chamber-tombs, 188
Chariots, 84 ff., 224, 230
Chauchitza, n.l., 268
Cherethites, 245
" Chieftain " vase, 156
Childe, Prof. V. G., 83, 284, et passim
Chronology of Minoan periods, 17 ff. ; Egyptian, 108
Chryselephantine figures, 171
Chthonic deities, 276
Cilicia, 202, 293
Cist-graves, 188 ; Cycladic, 58 ; Minyan, 82
" Close style," Myc. vase-decoration, 234
Commerce, 206
Conch, 280
Convention, in art, 180
Copper, 31, 40 ff., 87 ff.
Costume, 27, 105, 121 ff., 125, 174 ff., 183
Cozzo Pantano, n.l., 213
Cranial types, 111
Cremation, 252, 258
Crest, the Lycian, 135 ff.
Crete, 5 ff., et passim ; characteristics of culture, 272 ; survivals, 267 ; copper-working, 31
Crocodile, on Minoan seals, 69
Cucuteni, n.l., 60, 64, 82
Culture, characteristics of Minoan, 7, 272
" Cupbearer " fresco, Knossos, 119 182, 205
Cyclades, 56, 217 ; cist-graves, 58 ; marble idols, 58 ; Cycladic pottery, 56, 78, 138-9 ; influence on Crete, 84 ; art absorbed by Minoan, 139
Cyprus, 21, 205 ; metal-working, 33 ; copper blades, 87 ; pottery, 211 ; in Myc. period, 211, 227 ; faience, 225

Dagger-blades, M.M., 88 ; inlaid, Myc., 143
Dances, religious, 282
Danubian pottery, 64
Degeneration, in artistic design, 234
Delos, 60
Delta-cults, Egypt, 25
Demons, 277
Dendra (Mideia), n.l., 182, 233
Diadems, gold, 145
Dictaean Cave, 107, 175
Diktynna, g., 274

Dimini, n.l., 22 ; ware, 62 ; people, 248
Disk, Phaistos, 5, 133 ff.
Dorians, 257 ff. ; invasion, 268
Double-axe, 15, 26, 276 ; " Double-Axes," tomb of the, 193
Doves, sacred, 277
Drachmani, n.l., 61
Drains, 101
Draught-boards, 125, 229
" Duck "-vases, 57

Early Minoan period, 41 ff.
Earthquakes, 109, 163
" Egg-shell " ware, 75
Egypt, stone age in, 30 ; predynastic boats, 37 ; early connexion of Crete with, 25 ; Egyptian predynastic and archaic stone vases in Crete, 42 ; imitated in Crete, 42, 51 ; Egyptian imitation of Aegean designs, 68 ; of Kamarais ware, 73 ; Egyptian influences in Minoan art and culture, 122, 206, 222, 224, 285 ; Egyptian objects in Crete, 107, 123 ; chronology, 108 ; synchronisms, 17
Emery, 31
Embossing, metal, 182
Enkomi, tombs, 209, 212, 225, 227
Epano-Phournos tholos, Mycenae, 149
" Ephyraean " ware, 216
Erösd, n.l., 60
Eteocretans, 252, 288
Etruscans, 240, 252
Euboea, 56, 81
Europeans, at Amarna, 208
Evans, Sir Arthur, 6, 18, 19, et passim ; on Minoan religion, 275
Evidence, archaeological and literary, 260

Faience, 125, 225
Fantasy in art, 133, 272
Female costume, hairdressing (see Costume, Hairdressing)
Feminism, 274
Fibula, 257
Figure-of-eight shield, 26
Figurines, Cretan and Egyptian, 30 ; Koumása, 44 ; Cycladic, 59 ; steatopygous, 29 ; praying, 173 ff. ; pottery, 105
" Filler "-vase, 168 ; imitated in Egypt, 222
Fimmen, Dr., 20, 209
Fitzwilliam Museum, 4, 172
" Flower-stands," M.C., 79
Flying-fish, in faience, 127 ; fresco (Phylakopi), 119, 138
" Flying gallop," 279
Forrer, Prof., 249
Forsdyke, Mr. E. J., 83, 252, et passim
Fortifications, 97

INDEX

Frankfort, Mr. H., 22, 83, *et passim*
Frescoes, 102, 117 ff., 183, 215, 285; influence on ceramic decoration, 130
Funerary rites, 224, 281; vases, 195

Games, religious, 283
Gaming-board (Knossos), 125; box (Enkomi), 229
Gardner, Prof. P., 153
Garstang, Prof., 251
Gath, n.l., 245
Gavdos, n.l., 31
Gems, lentoid, 273
" Genius "-fresco, Knossos, 186
Geometric ware, early, of Lianokladhi III, 82; Cretan, 219, 263; Attic, 260
Gerar, n.l., 246
Gesso, coloured, 186
Gezer, n.l., 245
Gha, (Gla or Goulás), n.l., 215
Giles, Dr., 289
Gjerstad, Mr. E., 21, 33, 211
" Gladiator " vase, 156
Glass, 104; glass-paste, 198
Glaze, 70
Gold, 51, 66, 133, 143 ff., 210; tinted, 143; in Babylonia, 37
Gonia, n.l., 22
Gournais, n.l., 68
Gournià, n.l., 40, 75, 164
Graffiiti, 131, 180
" Granary " style, Myc., 237
Gravestones, Mycenae, 140
Greaves, 265
Gryphons, 229, 277

Hagia Marina, n.l., 65
Hagia Triada, 12; palace, 160; agora, 114; frescoes, 118; vases, 156; sarcophagus, 224, 281
Hairdressing, 105 ff., 121 ff., 145, 173 ff.
Hal Tarxien, n.l., 213
Halbert-blades, 87
Halbherr, Prof., 44, *et passim*
Hall, Miss E. H. (Mrs. Dohan), 263
Hand-turned pottery, 48
Harāgeh, 293
Harappà, n.l., 291
" Harvesters " vase, 123, 156
Hatshepsut, q., 9, 199
Hatzidakis, Dr., 32, 164, *et passim*
Helladic periods and styles, 1, 20, 61, 219
Hellenes, 247
Hellespontine region, connexion with, 81
Helmets, 136
Hera, g., 275
Heraeum, Argive, 188
Heroic traditions, 6, 266

Hieroglyphs, 131
Hill, Mr. G. F., 245
Hissarlik (*see* Troy)
Hittites, 253; language, 289; influence of, 124
Hoeck, on Crete, 272
Hogarth, Dr. D. G., 107, 247, 265, 270, *et passim*
Homeric legends, 265, armour, *ibid*.
Horse, introduction of the, 84 ff.
Houses, 44, 95, 97, 103, 165; house-mosaic, Knossos, 103
Household gods, 281
Human representation on pottery, 79, 139
Hunting-deities, 274
Hyakinthos, g., 275
Hyksos, tr.n., 88, 123
Hypogaeum, at Knossos, 96
Hyria, n.l., 213

Ialysos, n.l., 209, 251
Idols, 281
Imps, 139
India, prehistoric culture of, 291; Indian racial analogies, 289; gods, 85
Indo-European Greeks, 288; *see* Aryans
Ink, 131
Inlay, metal, 143; stone, ivory, etc., 125
Inscriptions on walls, 131
Ionians, 270
Ipuwer, n.pr., 205
Iron, 86, 252, 253
" Isles of the Sea," 201
Isopata, royal tomb, 188, 192
Italy, connexion with, 49, 213
Iuktas, m., 14, 107
Ivory, 70, 171, 229

Jewellery, 51

" Kahun," 17, 73
Kakovatos, tholoi, 149, 253; vases, 170
Kala 'Sherḳat, n.l., 225
Kalopsida, n.l., 21
Kamárais cave, 17, 74, 107; ware, 73 ff.
Kamikos, n.l., 213
Kaphtor, 203
Keftiu, 201, 207, 244, 293
Kephala (Knossos), 12, 14, 24
Khamaëzi, n.l., 97
Khayan, k., 123
Kilt, Minoan, 183
" King's Vase " (Dendra), 182
" Klytaimnestra, treasury of," 147
Knossos, 4, 12 ff.; neolithic, 22; keep, 95; M.M., 95 ff.; west façade, 97; north gate, 97; earthquake and rebuilding, 109; S. portico, viaduct and " caravansarai," 96, 116,

plan, 109; Domestic Quarter, 112; theatral area, 163; destruction, 198, 207; partial re-occupation, 219
Komò, n.l., 96
Korakou, n.l., 19
Koumása, n.l., 44
Kouretes, 282
Kourtais, n.l., 263
Krater, 222, 224
Kretschmer, Prof., 250
Kylix, 44, 217

Labrys, 15, 276
Labyrinth, the, 14
Lachish, 245
" Ladies in Blue " fresco, Knossos, 118
Lahun, n.l. 17, 73
Language, 247 ff.
Larnax, 94, 189, 223
Late Minoan periods, 115; L.M. I., 160; II., 180; III, 207
Latrines, 101
Laws, 284
Lazbas, n.l., 250
Leaper-figures, ivory, 172
Legends, 6, 265
Leiden Museum, 175
Leleges, 60
Lianokladhi, n.l., 61, 82
Libation-vases, 281
Light-wells, 101, 112
Lily-petal design, 58; lily-spiral, 59, 68
Lion Gate, Mycenae, 146
Liparite, 49, 75
Literary *v.* Archaeological evidence, 260
Luckenbill, Prof., 250
Lukki, (Lugga = Lycians), 241
Lustral areas, 102, 281
Lycians, 61, 134, 137, 241
Lyre, 281

Macalister, Prof. R. F., 246
Macedonia, early, 64; Dorians in, 268
Macehead, 29
Mackenzie, Dr. D., 8; on Achaians, 260
Maeander designs, 69
Magasà, n.l., 22
Magazines, Phaestian, 99; Knossian, 124
Mainland, Aegean, influence-invasions of, 61, 140; later culture, 154
Male costume, hairdressing, etc. (*see* Costume, Hairdressing)
Mallia, palace, 88, 95
Mallos, n.l., 246
Malta, 213
Marine designs, 167
" Marseilles Vase," 180

Masks of the dead, gold, 145
Masts, 36
Matriarchy, 274
Mattmalerei, 80
Megaron, 215
Mediterranean race, 27, 287
Melos, 23, 119, 138
Menkheperre'senb, tomb of (paintings), 199
Mesarà, n.l., 44
Metal-work, imitated in pottery, 75
Miamú, n.l., 40
Mideia, n.l., 182, 233
Middle Cycladic period, 78
Middle Minoan period, 67 ff., 99, 109, 128
Migrations, Great, 269
Milatos, n.l., 260
Milchhöfer, on Crete, 271
Milk-bowls, M.C., 79
Miniature frescoes, 119
Minos, 18, 284; death of, 213
Minoan periods, 18, 19; survivals, 270
Minotaur-legend, 14, 187
Minyan ware, 80 ff.
Minyas, " treasury of," 147
Mirror-handles, ivory, 229
Mochlos, n.l., 44, 50
Mohenjo Daro, n.l., 291
Monkey and papyrus fresco, Knossos, 118
Molfetta, 213
Mopsos, n.pr., 246
Mosaic, Knossos, 103
Mosso, Dr., 253
Mother-goddess, 275
Mouliandà, n.l., 258
Müller, W. M., on Eg. wall-paintings, 200
Muršiliš, k., 249
Museums, 3 ff.
Musical instruments, 281
Mycenae, 4, 8 ff.; grave-area, 140; shaft-graves, 143; palace, 215; frescoes, 153; town, 233; culture, 215; race, 248; periods, 20, 207; Myc. III (= L.M. III), ware, 220
Myres, Prof. J. L., 17, 73, 105

Naqada, n.l., 44
Naturalism in decoration, 167, 171
Naxos, n.l., 31
Negroes, 122
Neith, g., 25
Neolithic period, Crete, 16, 25, 28; mainland Greece, 21, 61
Newberry, Prof. P. E., 26, 36
New York Metropolitan Museum, 4
Nikosia Museum, 3
Nilsson, Prof., 247, 275
Nirou Khani, n.l., 287

INDEX

North Greece, early culture, 22
Northwick collection, 172
Numerals, Minoan, 94

Obsidian, 22, 31
Octopus-designs, 168
Oedipus legend, 275, 280
Offering-table, Dictaean, 132
Orchomenos, n.l., 61, 82, 147
Ossuary-tholoi, 40, 44, 188
Oval house, 97

Painting, mural, 44 (see Frescoes)
Palaces, 285; Mallia, 95; Knossos, 95 ff., 109 ff.; Phaistos, 95, 114, 160; Hagia Triada, 114, 160; Tylissos, 164; Mycenae, 215; Tiryns, 215
Palaikastro, n.l., 22, 220
"Panelled style," ceramic decoration, 234
Panoply, Homeric, 265
Pelasgi, 248
Pelopids, 82
"Peoples of the Sea," 239 ff.
Persephone, g., 275
Petasos, 175
Petrie, Prof., Sir W. M. F., 108, 242, 246
Petsofà figurines, 105
Phaistos, palace, 12, 95, 99, 114, 160; plan, 115; frescoes, 118; disk, 5, 133 ff.
Philistines, 137, 240 ff. (see Pulesatha); pottery, 245
Phoenicians, 38, in Aegean, 269
Phokis, early culture of, 22, 61
Phrygians, 244
Phylakopi, n.l., 58
Pidasa, tr.n., 241
Pillar-bases, 101
Pit-tombs, 195
Pithoi, Phaestian (M.M. II), 99; Knossian (M.M. II–III), 124
Plant-motives, in ceramic decoration, 129, 167
Platanos, n.l., 44, 107
Political ideas, 284
Polychrome ware, M.M. I–II, 74, 77
Population, 284
Portico, stepped, Knossos, 96
Pot-burials, 189
Potter's wheel, 47
Pottery, Cretan neolithic, 28; E.M., 41 ff.; M.M., 72 ff., 128, 130; L.M. I, 167 ff.; L.M. II, 180 ff.; L.M. III *a*, 220 ff.; L.M. III *b*, 234 ff.; mainland neolithic, 23, 60; Helladic pre-Myc., 60, 143; Mycenaean, 143, 207, 218, 220; domestic, 164; sub-Mycenaean, 260; transitional, 262; geometric, 263; Philistine, 245
Praisos, n.l., 263; inscriptions, 252
Priniàs, n.l., 271

Pseira, n.l., 164; relief-fresco, 185
Puimre', tomb of, 199
Pulesatha (Philistines), 240
Pylos, Triphylian (Kakovatos), 149, 215; Messenian, 149

"Queen's Vase" (Dendra), 182

Racial affinities, 288
Rapiers, 197
Rekhmire', tomb of, 182, 199 ff.
Relief-frescoes, 185; sculpture, 51, 153, 156 ff., 292
Religion, 107, 275 ff.; funerary, 283
Reoccupation, partial, at Knossos, 219
Repositories, Knossos, 124
Rhadamanthys, g., 275
Rhea, g., 275
Rhodes, n.l., 209, 251
Rhodian Myc. ware, 207, 218
Rhytons, 135, 281
Ridgeway, Prof. Sir W., 18
"Ring of Nestor," 280
Roads, 96
Rock-shelters, 23, 40

Sacral knot, 280
Saffron-gatherer ("Blue Boy"), fresco, 102
Salamis, tombs at, 260
Sanitation, 101
Sardinia, 292
Scarabs, 68, 92, 208
Schnabelkanne, 48
Scimitar (*khepesh*), 89
Script, Cretan, Class A, 93; Class B, 179
Sculpture, 51; in the round, 273; relief (*q.v.*)
Seafaring, 34
Seager, Mr. R. B., 44, 164
Seal-designs, 132
Sennemut (Senmut), tomb of, 182, 199
Senusret I, k., 68; II, 74
Sergi, Prof., 287
Sesklo, n.l., 61
Seti II, k., sword of, 257
Shaft-graves, Mycenae, 153
Shakalasha, tr.n., 241, 293
Shardina, tr.n., 240, 292; swords, 253, 256, 293
Shields, figure-of-eight, 26, 159; round, 265
Sicily, relations with, 213
Signet-rings, 133, 143
Silver, 52, 75, 81, 135
Sistrum, 156
Skulls, Cretan, 111
Skyphos, 221, 236
Sled, in Egypt, 84
Slow wheel, potter's, 47, 71
Snakes, 173; snake-goddesses or priestesses, 125, 171, 276

Society, 274
Son-god, 275
Spearheads, 197, 257
Sphinx, 124, 275
Spiral design, origin of, 56, 59; in Egypt, 59; in decoration, 67; on scarabs, 68
Spouted vases, 48
Stag-hunt frescoes, Tiryns, 232
Stairways, Knossos, 113; Phaistos, 114
Steatite, 70, 156
Steatopygous figures, 29, 30
Steindorff, Prof., 205
Stentinello ware, 213
Stirrup-vases (*Bügelkannen*), 169, 222, 237; imitated in Egypt, 222, 238
Stone vases, E.M. II, 51
Stylized designs, 180
Sub-Mycenaean ware, 261
Sub-Neolithic period, 40
Sumerian art, 229
Sword, M.M. (Mallia), 88; L.M., 197; Shardina, 253, 256, 293; Achaian, 254
Syllabary, Cyprian, 229
" Syro-Keftians," 204

Tablets, clay, 93, 131, 179
Taurokathapsia, 15, 172, 183, 219
Teie, q., 208
Tell el-Amarna, n.l., 207
Temples, 281, 285
Terramare-culture, in Italy, 269
Tête-bêche designs, 69
Textiles, 29
Thalassocracy, Carian, 60, 138; Minoan, 60
Theatral area, Knossian, 163; Phaestian, 114
Thebes, Boeotian, frescoes, 153; Egyptian, tombs, 199 ff.
Thera, 109; earthquake, 163
Theseus, 15, 16
Thessaly, early culture, 22, 61
Thisbe rings, 275
Tholos-tombs, 44, 146 ff., 149, 191
Thoueris, g., 277
" Throne of Minos," Knossos, 186
Thunder Hill, 259, 265
Thutmosis III, k., 199
Tin, 87
Tiryns, 11, 103, 146, 152; frescoes, 153, 230
Tombs, 188 ff.
Tournette, 47, 71
Towns, 114, 164, 284
Transitional geometric ware, 262
" Treasuries," 147 ff., 192

Trees in religious representations, 276, 281
" Trickle " ware, M.M. III, 128
Troy, 8, 52 ff.
Trojan War, 266
Trumpets, 280
Tsani, n.l., 61
Tsangli, n.l., 61
Tursha, (Tyrrhenians?) 240
Tut'ankhamen, k., 207, 253
Tylissos, n.l., 119, 163

Uashasha, tr.n., 241
Uilusa, n.l., 250
Ur, spirals at, 59; gold daggers, 37
Urfirnis, 61, 65, 80
Useramon, tomb of, 199
Utensils, household, 164

Vapheio, tholos, 149, 215, 253; cups, 154
Varnish-painting, 41
Vasiliki ware, 44
Velchanos, g., 175, 224
Viaduct, at Knossos, 96; rebuilt, 116
Vitreous paste, 71
Volo, *tholoi*, 247
Votive offerings, 86, 281; figurines, 105, 107
Vrokastro, n.l., 263

Wace, Mr. A. J. B., 10, 19, 247; on Mycenae, 146 ff.
Waist, Minoan, 106; -clout, 27
"Warrior "-vase, 260
Wealth, 206
Weapons, E.M., 54; M.M., 87 ff.; Myc., 143; L.M., 197; Achaian, 254
Wheel, potter's, 72, 80; cart-, 84, 85 ff.
" Wiros," 268, 287
Women, position of, 272
Wood and water spirits, 277
Woolley, Mr. C. L., 37, 244
Writing, Minoan, 5, 92, 131, 179, 206; Cyprian, 229

Xanthoudides, Dr. St., 32, 44, *et passim*

Yantinai (Cyprus), 205
Yellow Minyan ware, 82
Yortan pottery, 56, 81

Zafer Papoura, tombs, 188, 197, 218
Zakkal (Zakaray), tr.n., 241
Zakro seals, 133
Zerelia, n.l., 61
Zeus, 276

NOTE.—g., = god, goddess; k., = king; q., = queen; m., mountain; n.l., place-name; n.pr., proper name; tr.n., tribal name. (Not inserted in all cases.)